"Every bit as good . . .
volume of Father Coples
has been worth waiting f
readability. Every impor
time of the Fathers-Apol
treated."

The Catholic Review Service

"Only one thoroughly conversant with the vast and complex field of patristic and medieval thought, who is besides a
competent philosopher and theologian in his own right, could
display such good judgement in the selection, ordering, and
evaluation of his material and in the emphasis that he gives
to certain dominant themes and doctrinal developments
without detracting in any way from the comprehensiveness
of the work as a whole."

JAMES J. CONWAY, S.J.
Theological Studies

"Father Copleston has the ability to express profound and
subtle points of doctrine with remarkable clarity. In the present work he offers accurate and sufficiently complete syntheses of the thought of the great masters of the Middle
Ages. His selection of material and his emphases reveal a rich
understanding of the period."

The Catholic Booklist

"Father Copleston's first volume (*Greece and Rome*) has
already established a reputation for its author which this second volume will reaffirm. There is nothing comparable in
English for either the specialist or the general student."

The Priest

A History of Philosophy

VOLUME II

Mediaeval Philosophy

PART I

Augustine to Bonaventure

by Frederick Copleston, S.J.

IMAGE BOOKS
A Division of Doubleday & Company, Inc.
Garden City, New York

Image Books edition 1962
by special arrangement with The Newman Press

PRINTING HISTORY
The Newman Press edition published July, 1950
1st printing   June, 1950
2nd printing   November, 1952
3rd printing   February, 1955
4th printing   July, 1959
5th printing   December, 1959
Image Books edition published September, 1962

CONTENTS

PART II

THE CAROLINGIAN RENAISSANCE

Part III

THE TENTH, ELEVENTH AND TWELFTH CENTURIES

Part IV

ISLAMIC AND JEWISH PHILOSOPHY: TRANSLATIONS

A HISTORY OF PHILOSOPHY

VOLUME II PART I

MEDIAEVAL PHILOSOPHY

Chapter One

INTRODUCTION

1. In this second volume of my history of philosophy I had originally hoped to give an account of the development of philosophy throughout the whole period of the Middle Ages, understanding by mediaeval philosophy the philosophic thought and systems which were elaborated between the Carolingian renaissance in the last part of the eighth century A.D. (John Scotus Eriugena, the first outstanding mediaeval philosopher was born about 810) and the end of the fourteenth century. Reflection has convinced me, however, of the advisability of devoting two volumes to mediaeval philosophy. As my first volume[1] ended with an account of neo-Platonism and contained no treatment of the philosophic ideas to be found in the early Christian writers, I considered it desirable to say something of these ideas in the present volume. It is true that men like St. Gregory of Nyssa and St. Augustine belonged to the period of the Roman Empire, that their philosophic affiliations were with Platonism, understood in the widest sense, and that they cannot be termed mediaevals; but the fact remains that they were Christian thinkers and exercised a great influence on the Middle Ages. One could hardly understand St. Anselm or St. Bonaventure without knowing something of St. Augustine, nor could one understand the thought of John Scotus Eriugena without knowing something of the thought of St. Gregory of Nyssa and of the Pseudo-Dionysius. There is scarcely any need, then, to apologise for beginning a history of mediaeval philosophy with a

consideration of thinkers who belong, so far as chronology is concerned, to the period of the Roman Empire.

The present volume, then, begins with the early Christian period and carries the history of mediaeval philosophy up to the end of the thirteenth century, including Duns Scotus (about 1265–1308). In my third volume I propose to treat of the philosophy of the fourteenth century, laying special emphasis on Ockhamism. In that volume I shall also include a treatment of the philosophies of the Renaissance, of the fifteenth and sixteenth centuries, and of the 'Silver Age' of Scholastic thought, even though Francis Suarez did not die until the year 1617, twenty-one years after the birth of Descartes. This arrangement may appear to be an arbitrary one, and to some extent it is. But it is extremely doubtful if it is possible to make any hard and fast dividing line between mediaeval and modern philosophy, and a good case could be made out for including Descartes with the later Scholastics, contrary to tradition as this would be. I do not propose, however, to adopt this course, and if I include in the next volume, the third, some philosophers who might seem to belong properly to the 'modern period', my reason is largely one of convenience, to clear the decks, so that in the fourth volume I may develop in a systematic manner the interconnection between the leading philosophical systems from Francis Bacon in England and Descartes in France up to and including Kant. Nevertheless, whatever method of division be adopted, one has to remember that the compartments into which one divides the history of philosophic thought are not watertight, that transitions are gradual, not abrupt, that there is overlapping and interconnection, that succeeding systems are not cut off from one another with a hatchet.

2. There was a time when mediaeval philosophy was considered as unworthy of serious study, when it was taken for granted that the philosophy of the Middle Ages was so subservient to theology that it was practically indistinguishable therefrom and that, in so far as it was distinguishable, it amounted to little more than a barren logic-chopping and word-play. In other words, it was taken for granted that European philosophy contained two main periods, the ancient period, which to all intents and purposes meant the philosophies of Plato and Aristotle, and the modern period, when the speculative reason once more began to enjoy freedom after the dark night of the Middle Ages when ecclesiastical

authority reigned supreme and the human reason, chained by heavy fetters, was compelled to confine itself to the useless and fanciful study of theology, until a thinker like Descartes at length broke the chains and gave reason its freedom. In the ancient period and the modern period philosophy may be considered a free man, whereas in the mediaeval period it was a slave.

Apart from the fact that mediaeval philosophy naturally shared in the disesteem with which the Middle Ages in general were commonly regarded, one factor which was partly responsible for the attitude adopted towards mediaeval thinkers was doubtless the language used concerning Scholasticism by men like Francis Bacon and René Descartes. Just as Aristotelians are prone to evaluate Platonism in terms of Aristotle's criticism, so admirers of the movement apparently initiated by Bacon and Descartes were prone to look on mediaeval philosophy through their eyes, unaware of the fact that much of what Francis Bacon, for instance, has to say against the Scholastics could not legitimately be applied to the great figures of mediaeval thought, however applicable it may have been to later and 'decadent' Scholastics, who worshipped the letter at the expense of the spirit. Looking on mediaeval philosophy from the very start in this light historians could perhaps scarcely be expected to seek a closer and first-hand acquaintance with it: they condemned it unseen and unheard, without knowledge either of the rich variety of mediaeval thought or of its profundity: to them it was all of a piece, an arid playing with words and a slavish dependence on theologians. Moreover, insufficiently critical, they failed to realise the fact that, if mediaeval philosophers were influenced by an external factor, theology, modern philosophers were also influenced by external factors, even if by other external factors than theology. It would have seemed to most of these historians a nonsensical proposition were one to suggest to them that Duns Scotus, for example, had a claim to be considered as a great British philosopher, at least as great as John Locke, while in their praise of the acumen of David Hume they were unaware that certain thinkers of the late Middle Ages had already anticipated a great deal of the criticism which used to be considered the peculiar contribution to philosophy of the eminent Scotsman.

I shall cite one example, the treatment accorded to mediaeval philosophy and philosophers by a man who was himself a great philosopher, Georg Wilhelm Friedrich Hegel. It is an interesting example, since Hegel's dialectical idea of the history of philosophy obviously demanded that mediaeval philosophy should be portrayed as making an essential contribution to the development of philosophic thought, while Hegel personally was no mere vulgar antagonist of mediaeval philosophy. Now, Hegel does indeed admit that mediaeval philosophy performed one useful function, that of expressing in philosophic terms the 'absolute content' of Christianity, but he insists that it is only formalistic repetition of the content of faith, in which God is represented as something 'external', and if one remembers that for Hegel faith is the mode of religious consciousness and is definitely inferior to the philosophic or speculative standpoint, the standpoint of pure reason, it is clear that in his eyes mediaeval philosophy can be philosophy only in name. Accordingly he declares that Scholastic philosophy is really theology. By this Hegel does not mean that God is not the object of philosophy as well as of theology: he means that mediaeval philosophy considered the same object as is considered by philosophy proper but that it treated that object according to the categories of theology instead of substituting for the external connections of theology (for example, the relation of the world to God as external effect to free creative Cause) the systematic, scientific, rational and necessary categories and connections of philosophy. Mediaeval philosophy was thus philosophy according to content, but theology according to form, and in Hegel's eyes the history of mediaeval philosophy is a monotonous one, in which men have tried in vain to discern any distinct stages of real progress and development of thought.

In so far as Hegel's view of mediaeval philosophy is dependent on his own particular system, on his view of the relation of religion to philosophy, of faith to reason, of immediacy to mediacy, I cannot discuss it in this volume; but I wish to point out how Hegel's treatment of mediaeval philosophy is accompanied by a very real ignorance of the course of its history. It would be possible no doubt for an Hegelian to have a real knowledge of the development of mediaeval philosophy and yet to adopt, precisely because he was an Hegelian, Hegel's general standpoint in regard to it; but there can be no shadow of doubt, even allowing for the fact that the philosopher did not himself edit and publish his lectures on the history of philosophy, that Hegel did not possess the real knowledge in question. How could one, for instance, attribute a real knowledge of mediaeval philosophy to a writer who includes Roger Bacon under the heading 'Mystics' and simply remarks 'Roger Bacon treated more especially of physics, but remained without influence. He invented gunpowder, mirrors, telescopes, and died in 1297'? The fact of the matter is that Hegel relied on authors like Tennemann and Brucker for his information concerning mediaeval philosophy, whereas the first valuable studies on mediaeval philosophy do not antedate the middle of the nineteenth century.

In adducing the instance of Hegel I am not, of course, concerned to blame the philosopher: I am rather trying to throw into relief the great change that has taken place in our knowledge of mediaeval philosophy through the work of modern scholars since about 1880. Whereas one can easily understand and pardon the misrepresentations of which a man like Hegel was unconsciously guilty, one would have little patience with similar misrepresentations to-day, after the work of scholars like Baeumker, Ehrle, Grabmann, De Wulf, Pelster, Geyer, Mandonnet, Pelzer, etc. After the light that has been thrown on mediaeval philosophy by the publication of texts and the critical editing of already published works, after the splendid volumes brought out by the Franciscan Fathers of Quaracchi, after the publications of so many numbers of the *Beiträge* series, after the production of histories like that of Maurice De Wulf, after the lucid studies of Étienne Gilson, after the patient work done by the Mediaeval Academy of America, it should no longer be possible to think that mediaeval philosophers were 'all of a piece', that mediaeval philosophy lacked richness and variety, that mediaeval thinkers were uniformly men of low stature and of mean attainments. Moreover, writers like Gilson have helped us to realise the continuity between mediaeval and modern philosophy. Gilson has shown how Cartesianism was more dependent on mediaeval thought than was formerly supposed. A good deal still remains to be done in the way of edition and interpretation of texts (one needs only to mention William of Ockham's Commentary on the *Sentences*), but it has now became possible to see the currents and development, the pattern and texture, the high lights and low lights of mediaeval philosophy with a synoptic eye.

3. But even if mediaeval philosophy was in fact richer and

more varied than has been sometimes supposed, is it not true
to say that it stood in such a close relation to theology that it
is practically indistinguishable therefrom? Is it not, for example, a fact that the great majority of mediaeval philosophers were priests and theologians, pursuing philosophic
studies in the spirit of a theologian or even an apologist?

In the first place it is necessary to point out that the relation of theology to philosophy was itself an important theme
of mediaeval thought and that different thinkers adopted different attitudes in regard to this question. Starting with the
endeavour to understand the data of revelation, so far as this
is possible to human reason, early mediaevals, in accordance
with the maxim *Credo, ut intelligam*, applied rational dialectic to the mysteries of faith in an attempt to understand
them. In this way they laid the foundations of Scholastic
theology, since the application of reason to theological data,
in the sense of the data of revelation, is and remains theology: it does not become philosophy. Some thinkers indeed,
in their enthusiastic desire to penetrate mysteries by reason
to the utmost degree possible, appear at first sight to be ra-
tionalists, to be what one might call Hegelians before Hegel.
Yet it is really an anachronism to regard such men as 'ra-
tionalists' in the modern sense, since when St. Anselm, for
example, or Richard of St. Victor, attempted to prove the
mystery of the Blessed Trinity by 'necessary reasons' they had
no intention of acquiescing in any reduction of the dogma or
of impairing the integrity of divine revelation. (To this subject I shall return in the course of the work.) So far they
were certainly acting as theologians, but such men, who did
not make, it is true, any very clear delimitation of the spheres
of philosophy and theology, certainly pursued philosophical
themes and developed philosophical arguments. For instance,
even if St. Anselm is primarily important as one of the founders of Scholastic theology, he also contributed to the growth
of Scholastic philosophy, for example, by his rational proofs
of God's existence. It would be inadequate to dub Abelard a
philosopher and St. Anselm a theologian without qualification. In any case in the thirteenth century we find a clear
distinction made by St. Thomas Aquinas between theology,
which takes as its premisses the data of revelation, and philosophy (including, of course, what we call 'natural theology'), which is the work of the human reason unaided positively by revelation. It is true that in the same century St

Bonaventure was a conscious and determined upholder of what one might call the integralist, Augustinian view; but, though the Franciscan Doctor may have believed that a purely philosophical knowledge of God is vitiated by its very incompleteness, he was perfectly well aware that there are philosophical truths which are ascertainable by reason alone. The difference between him and St. Thomas has been stated thus.[2] St. Thomas held that it would be possible, *in principle*, to excogitate a satisfactory philosophical system, which, in respect of knowledge of God for instance, would be incomplete but not false, whereas St. Bonaventure maintained that this very incompleteness or inadequacy has the character of a falsification, so that, though a true natural philosophy would be possible without the light of faith, a true metaphysic would not be possible. If a philosopher, thought St. Bonaventure, proves by reason and maintains the unity of God, without at the same time knowing that God is Three Persons in One Nature, he is attributing to God a unity which is not the divine Unity.

In the second place, St. Thomas was perfectly serious when he gave philosophy its 'charter'. To a superficial observer it might appear that when St. Thomas asserted a clear distinction between dogmatic theology and philosophy, he was merely asserting a formalistic distinction, which had no influence on his thought and which he did not take seriously in practice; but such a view would be far from the truth, as can be seen by one example. St. Thomas believed that revelation teaches the creation of the world in time, the world's non-eternity; but he maintained and argued stoutly that the philosopher as such can prove neither that the world was created from eternity nor that it was created in time, although he can show that it depends on God as Creator. In holding to this point of view he was at variance with, for example, St. Bonaventure, and the fact that he maintained the point of view in question shows clearly that he seriously accepted in practice his theoretical delimitation of the provinces of philosophy and dogmatic theology.

In the third place, if it were really true to say that mediaeval philosophy was no more than theology, we should expect to find that thinkers who accepted the same faith would accept the same philosophy or that the differences between them would be confined to differences in the way in which they applied dialectic to the data of revelation. In point of

fact, however, this is very far from being the case. St. Bonaventure, St. Thomas Aquinas, and Duns Scotus, Giles of
Rome, and, one may pretty safely say, William of Ockham
accepted the same faith, but their philosophical ideas were
by no means the same on all points. Whether or not their
philosophies were equally compatible with the exigencies of
theology is, of course, another question (William of Ockham's philosophy could scarcely be considered as altogether
compatible with these exigencies); but that question is ir-
relevant to the point at issue, since, whether they were all
compatible with orthodox theology or not, these philosophies
existed and were not the same. The historian can trace the
lines of development and divergence in mediaeval philosophy, and, if he can do this, there must clearly be such a thing
as mediaeval philosophy: without existence it could not have
a history.

We shall have to consider different views on the relation
between philosophy and theology in the course of this work,
and I do not want to dwell any more on the matter at present; but it may be as well to admit from the very start that,
owing to the common background of the Christian faith, the
world presented itself for interpretation to the mediaeval
thinker more or less in a common light. Whether a thinker
held or denied a clear distinction between the provinces of
theology and philosophy, in either case he looked on the
world as a Christian and could hardly avoid doing so. In his
philosophic arguments he might prescind from Christian revelation, but the Christian outlook and faith were none the less
there at the back of his mind. Yet that does not mean that
his philosophic arguments were not philosophic arguments
or that his rational proofs were not rational proofs: one would
have to take each argument or proof on its own merits or
demerits and not dismiss them as concealed theology on the
ground that the writer was a Christian.

4. Having argued that there really was such a thing as
mediaeval philosophy or at any rate that there could be such
a thing, even if the great majority of mediaeval philosophers
were Christians and most of them theologians into the bar-
gain, I want finally to say something about the aim of this
book (and of the succeeding volume) and the way in which
it treats its subject.

I certainly do not intend to attempt the task of narrating
all the known opinions of all known mediaeval philosophers.

In other words, the second and third volumes of my history are not designed to constitute an encyclopaedia of mediaeval philosophy. On the other hand, it is not my intention to give simply a sketch or series of impressions of mediaeval philosophy. I have endeavoured to give an intelligible and coherent account of the development of mediaeval philosophy and of the phases through which it passed, omitting many names altogether and choosing out for consideration those thinkers who are of special importance and interest for the content of their thought or who represent and illustrate some particular type of philosophy or stage of development. To certain of these thinkers I have devoted a considerable amount of space, discussing their opinions at some length. This fact may possibly tend to obscure the general lines of connection and development, but, as I have said, it was not my intention to provide simply a sketch of mediaeval philosophy, and it is probably only through a somewhat detailed treatment of the leading philosophical systems that one can bring out the rich variety of mediaeval thought. To place in clear relief the main lines of connection and development and at the same time to develop at some length the ideas of selected philosophers is certainly not an easy task, and it would be foolish to suppose that my inclusions and omissions or proportional allotment of space will be acceptable to everybody: to miss the trees for the wood or the wood for the trees is easy enough, but to see both clearly at the same time is not so easy. However, I consider it a task worth attempting, and while I have not hesitated to consider at some length the philosophies of St. Bonaventure, St. Thomas, Duns Scotus and Ockham, I have tried to make intelligible the general development of mediaeval philosophy from its early struggles, through its splendid maturity, to its eventual decline.

If one speaks of a 'decline', it may be objected that one is speaking as philosopher and not as historian. True enough, but if one is to discern an intelligible pattern in mediaeval philosophy, one must have a principle of selection and to that extent at least one must be a philosopher. The word 'decline' has indeed a valuational colouring and flavour, so that to use such a word may seem to constitute an overstepping of the legitimate territory of the historian. Possibly it is, in a sense; but what historian of philosophy was or is *merely* an historian in the narrowest meaning of the term? No Hegelian, no Marxist, no Positivist, no Kantian writes his-

tory without a philosophic viewpoint, and is the Thomist
alone to be condemned for a practice which is really necessary, unless the history of philosophy is to be rendered unintelligible by being made a mere string of opinions?

By 'decline', then, I mean decline, since I frankly regard
mediaeval philosophy as falling into three main phases. First
comes the preparatory phase, up to and including the twelfth
century, then comes the period of constructive synthesis, the
thirteenth century, and finally, in the fourteenth century, the
period of destructive criticism, undermining and decline. Yet
from another point of view I should not hesitate to admit
that the last phase was an inevitable phase and, in the long
run, may be of benefit, as stimulating Scholastic philosophers
to develop and establish their principles more firmly in face
of criticism and, moreover, to utilise all that subsequent philosophy may have to offer of positive value. From one point
of view the Sophistic phase in ancient philosophy (using the
term 'Sophist' in more or less the Platonic sense) constituted
a decline, since it was characterised by, among other things,
a flagging of constructive thought; but it was none the less
an inevitable phase in Greek philosophy, and, in the long
run, may be regarded as having produced results of positive
value. No one at least who values the thought of Plato and
Aristotle can regard the activity and criticism of the Sophists
as an unmitigated disaster for philosophy.

The general plan of this volume and of its successor is thus
the exhibition of the main phases and lines of development
in mediaeval philosophy. First of all I treat briefly of the
Patristic period, going on to speak of those Christian thinkers
who had a real influence on the Middle Ages: Boethius, the
Pseudo-Dionysius and, above all, St. Augustine of Hippo.
After this more or less introductory part of the volume I proceed to the preparatory phase of mediaeval thought proper,
the Carolingian renaissance, the establishment of the Schools,
the controversy concerning universal concepts and the growing use of dialectic, the positive work of St. Anselm in the
eleventh century, the schools of the twelfth century, particularly those of Chartres and St. Victor. It is then necessary to
say something of Arabian and Jewish philosophy, not so
much for its own sake, since I am primarily concerned with
the philosophy of mediaeval Christendom, as for the fact that
the Arabs and Jews constituted an important channel whereby
the Aristotelian system in its fullness became known to the

Christian West. The second phase is that of the great syntheses of the thirteenth century, the philosophies of St. Bonaventure, St. Thomas Aquinas and Duns Scotus in particular. The succeeding phase, that of the fourteenth century, contains the new directions and the destructive criticism of the Ockhamist School in a wide sense. Finally, I have given a treatment of the thought which belongs to the period of transition between mediaeval and modern philosophy. The way will then be clear to start a consideration of what is generally called 'modern philosophy' in the fourth volume of this history.

In conclusion it may be as well to mention two points. The first is that I do not conceive it to be the task of the historian of philosophy to substitute his own ideas or those of recent or contemporary philosophers for the ideas of past thinkers, as though the thinkers in question did not know what they meant. When Plato stated the doctrine of reminiscence, he was not asserting neo-Kantianism, and though St. Augustine anticipated Descartes by saying *Si fallor, sum*, it would be a great mistake to try to force his philosophy into the Cartesian mould. On the other hand, some problems which have been raised by modern philosophers were also raised in the Middle Ages, even if in a different setting, and it is legitimate to draw attention to similarity of question or answer. Again, it is not illegitimate to ask if a given mediaeval philosopher could, out of the resources of his own system, meet this or that difficulty which a later philosopher has raised. Therefore, although I have tried to avoid the multiplication of references to modern philosophy, I have on occasion permitted myself to make comparisons with later philosophies and to discuss the ability of a mediaeval system of philosophy to meet a difficulty which is likely to occur to a student of modern thought. But I have strictly rationed my indulgence in such comparisons and discussions, not only out of considerations of space but also out of regard for historical propriety.

The second point to be mentioned is this. Largely owing to the influence of Marxism there is a certain demand that an historian of philosophy should draw attention to the social and political background of his period and throw light on the influence of social and political factors on philosophic development and thought. But apart from the fact that to keep one's history within a reasonable compass one must concentrate on philosophy itself and not on social and political events and developments, it is ridiculous to suppose that all philosophies or all parts of any given philosophy are equally influenced by the social and political *milieu*. To understand a philosopher's political thought it is obviously desirable to have some knowledge of the actual political background, but in order to discuss St. Thomas's doctrine on the relation of essence to existence or Scotus's theory of the univocal character of the concept of being, there is no need at all to introduce references to the political or economic background. Moreover, philosophy is influenced by other factors as well as politics and economics. Plato was influenced by the advance of Greek mathematics; mediaeval philosophy, though distinguishable from theology, was certainly influenced by it; consideration of the development of physics is relevant to Descartes's view of the material world; biology was not without influence on Bergson, and so on. I regard it, therefore, as a great mistake to dwell so exclusively on economics and political development, and to explain the advance of other sciences ultimately by economic history, that one implies the truth of the Marxist theory of philosophy. Apart, then, from the fact that considerations of space have not permitted me to say much of the political, social and economic background of mediaeval philosophy, I have deliberately disregarded the unjustifiable demand that one should interpret the 'ideological superstructure' in terms of the economic situation. This book is a history of a certain period of mediaeval philosophy: it is not a political history nor a history of mediaeval economics.

Part One

PRE-MEDIAEVAL INFLUENCES

Chapter Two

THE PATRISTIC PERIOD

Christianity and Greek philosophy—Greek Apologists (Aristides, St. Justin Martyr, Tatian, Athenagoras, Theophilus)—Gnosticism and writers against Gnosticism (St. Irenaeus, Hippolytus)—Latin Apologists (Minucius Felix, Tertullian, Arnobius, Lactantius)—Catechetical School of Alexandria (Clement, Origen)—Greek Fathers (St. Basil, Eusebius, St. Gregory of Nyssa)—Latin Fathers (St. Ambrose)—St. John Damascene—Summary.

1. Christianity came into the world as a revealed religion: it was given to the world by Christ as a doctrine of redemption and salvation and love, not as an abstract and theoretical system, and He sent His Apostles to preach, not to occupy professors' chairs. Christianity was 'the Way', a road to God to be trodden in practice, not one more philosophical system added to the systems and schools of antiquity. The Apostles and their successors were bent on converting the world, not on excogitating a philosophical system. Moreover, so far as their message was directed to the Jews, the Apostles had to meet theological rather than philosophical attacks, while, in regard to the non-Jews, we are not told, apart from the account of St. Paul's famous sermon at Athens, of their being confronted with, or of their approaching, Greek philosophers in the academic sense.

However, as Christianity made fast its roots and grew, it aroused the suspicion and hostility, not merely of the Jews and the political authorities, but also of pagan intellectuals and writers. Some of the attacks levelled against Christianity were due simply to ignorance, credulous suspicion, fear of what was unknown, misrepresentation; but other attacks were delivered on the theoretical plane, on philosophical grounds, and these attacks had to be met. This meant that philosophical as well as theological arguments had to be used. There are, then, philosophical elements in the writings of early Christian apologists and Fathers; but it would obviously be idle to look for a philosophical system, since the interest of these writers was primarily theological, to defend the Faith. Yet, as Christianity became more firmly established and better known and as it became possible for Christian scholars to develop thought and learning, the philosophical element tended to become more strongly marked, especially when there was question of meeting the attacks of pagan professional philosophers.

The influence of apologetic on the growth of Christian philosophy was clearly due primarily to a cause external to Christianity, namely hostile attack; but there was also another reason for this growth which was internal, independent of attacks from outside. The more intellectual Christians naturally felt the desire to penetrate, as far as it was open to them to do so, the data of revelation and also to form a comprehensive view of the world and human life in the light of faith. This last reason operated in a systematic way perhaps later than the first and, so far as the Fathers are concerned, reached the zenith of its influence in the thought of St. Augustine; but the first reason, the desire to penetrate the dogmas of the Faith (an anticipation of the *Credo, ut intelligam* attitude), was operative in some way from the beginning. Partly through a simple desire to understand and appreciate, partly through the need of further clearer definition of dogma in face of heresy, the original data of revelation were rendered more explicit, 'developed', in the sense of the implicit being made explicit. From the beginning, for instance, Christians accepted the fact that Christ was both God and Man, but it was only in the course of time that the implications of this fact were made clear and were enshrined in theological definitions, for example, that the perfect human Nature of Christ implied His possession of a human will. Now, these definitions were of course theological, and the advance from the implicit to the explicit was an advance in theological science; but in the process of argument and definition concepts and categories were employed which were borrowed from philosophy. Moreover, as the Christians had no philosophy of their own to start with (i.e. in the academic sense of philosophy), they very naturally turned to the prevailing philosophy, which was derived from Platonism but was strongly impregnated with other elements. As a rough generalisation, therefore, one may say that the philosophic ideas of the early Christian writers were Platonic or neo-Platonic in character (with an admixture of Stoicism) and that the Platonic tradition continued for long to dominate Christian thought from the philosophic viewpoint. In saying this, however, one must remember that the Christian writers did not make any clear distinction between theology and philosophy: they aimed rather at presenting the Christian wisdom or 'philosophy' in a very wide sense, which was primarily theological, though it contained philosophical elements in the strict sense. The task of the historian of philosophy is to isolate these philosophic elements: he cannot reasonably be expected to present an adequate picture of early Christian thought, for the very good reason that he is not, *ex hypothesi*, an historian of dogmatic theology or of exegesis.

Since on the one hand pagan philosophers were inclined to attack the Church and her doctrine, while on the other hand Christian apologists and theologians were inclined to borrow the weapons of their adversaries when they thought that these weapons could serve their purpose, it is only to be expected that the Christian writers should show a divergence of attitude in regard to ancient philosophy, according as they chose to regard it as a foe and rival of Christianity or as a useful arsenal and store-house or even as a providential preparation for Christianity. Thus while in Tertullian's eyes pagan philosophy was little more than the foolishness of this world, Clement of Alexandria regarded philosophy as a gift of God, a means of educating the pagan world for Christ, as the Jews' means of education had been the Law. He thought indeed, as Justin thought before him, that Plato had borrowed his wisdom from Moses and the Prophets (a Philonic contention); but just as Philo had tried to reconcile Greek philosophy with the Old Testament, so Clement tried to reconcile Greek philosophy with the Christian religion. In the end, of course, it was the attitude of Clement, not that of Tertullian, which triumphed, since St. Augustine made abundant use of neo-Platonic ideas when presenting the Christian *Weltanschauung*.

2. As the first group of those Christian writers whose works

contain philosophic elements one can count the early apologists who were particularly concerned to defend the Christian faith against pagan attack (or rather to show to the Imperial authorities that Christianity had a right to exist), men like Aristides, Justin, Melito, Tatian, Athenagoras and Theophilus of Antioch. In a brief sketch of Patristic philosophy, a sketch which is admittedly only included by way of preparation for the main theme of the book, one can treat neither of all the apologists nor of any one of them fully: my intention is rather to indicate the sort of philosophical elements which their works contain.

(i) *Marcianus Aristides*, styled a 'philosopher of Athens', wrote an Apology, which is to be dated about A.D. 140 and is addressed to the Emperor Antoninus Pius.[1] A good deal of this work is devoted to an attack on the pagan deities of Greece and Egypt, with some animadversions on the morals of the Greeks; but at the beginning Aristides declares that 'amazed at the arrangement of the world', and understanding that 'the world and all that is therein are moved by the impulse of another', and seeing that 'that which moveth is more powerful than that which is moved', he concludes that the Mover of the world 'is God of all, who made all for the sake of man'. Aristides thus gives in a very compendious form arguments drawn from the design and order in the world and from the fact of motion, and identifies the designer and mover with the Christian God, of whom he proceeds to predicate the attributes of eternity, perfection, incomprehensibility, wisdom, goodness. We have here, then, a very rudimentary natural theology presented, not for purely philosophic reasons, but in defence of the Christian religion.

(ii) A much more explicit attitude towards philosophy is to be found in the writings of *Flavius Justinus* (St. Justin Martyr), who was born at Neapolis (Nablus) of pagan parents about A.D. 100, became a Christian, and was martyred at Rome about 164. In his Dialogue with Trypho he declares that philosophy is a most precious gift of God, designed to lead man to God, though its true nature and its unity have not been recognised by most people, as is clear from the existence of so many philosophical schools.[2] As to himself, he went first for instruction to a Stoic, but, finding the Stoic doctrine of God unsatisfactory, betook himself to a Peripatetic, whose company he soon forsook, as he turned out to be a grasping fellow.[3] From the Peripatetic he went, with zeal still unabated, to a Pythagorean of repute, but his own lack of acquaintance with music, geometry and astronomy unfitted him for philosophy in his prospective teacher's eyes, and as he did not wish to spend a lot of time in acquiring knowledge of these sciences, he turned to the Platonists and was so delighted with the doctrine of the immaterial Ideas that he began to expect a clear vision of God, which, says Justin, is the aim of Plato's philosophy.[4] Shortly afterwards, however, he fell in with a Christian, who showed him the insufficiency of pagan philosophy, even of that of Plato.[5] Justin is thus an example of the cultured convert from paganism, who, feeling his conversion as the term of a process, could not adopt a merely negative and hostile attitude to Greek philosophy.

Justin's words concerning Platonism in the *Dialogue* show clearly enough the esteem in which he held the Platonic philosophy. He prized its doctrine of the immaterial world and of the being beyond essence, which he identified with God, though he became convinced that the sure and safe and certain knowledge of God, the true 'philosophy', is to be attained only through the acceptance of revelation. In his two *Apologies* he makes frequent use of Platonic terms, as when he speaks of God as the 'Demiurge'.[6] I am not suggesting that when Justin makes use of Platonic or neo-Platonic words and phrases he is understanding the words in precisely the Platonic sense: the use of them is rather the effect of his philosophic training and of the sympathy which he retained for Platonism. Thus he does not hesitate on occasion to point out analogies between Christian and Platonic doctrine, in regard, for example, to reward and punishment after death,[7] and his admiration for Socrates is evident. When Socrates, in the power of *logos*, or as its instrument, tried to lead men away from falsehood into truth, evil men put him to death as an impious atheist: so Christians, who follow and obey the incarnate Logos itself and who denounce the false gods, are termed atheists.[8] In other words, just as the work of Socrates, which was a service of truth, was a preparation for the complete work of Christ, so the condemnation of Socrates was, as it were, a rehearsal or anticipation of the condemnation of Christ and His followers. Again, the actions of men are not determined, as the Stoics thought, but they act rightly or wrongly according to their free choice, while it is owing to the activity of the evil demons that Socrates and those like

him are persecuted, while Epicurus and those like him are
held in honour.[9]

Justin thus made no clear distinction between theology
and philosophy in the strict sense: there is one wisdom, one
'philosophy', which is revealed fully in and through Christ,
but for which the best elements in pagan philosophy, especially Platonism, were a preparation. In so far as the pagan
philosophers divined the truth, they did so only in the power
of *logos*: Christ, however, is the Logos itself, incarnate. This
view of Greek philosophy and of its relation to Christianity
was of considerable influence on later writers.

(iii) According to Irenaeus,[10] *Tatian* was a pupil of Justin.
He was of Syrian nationality, was educated in Greek literature
and philosophy, and became a Christian. There is no real
reason for doubting the truth of the statement that Tatian
was in some sense a pupil of Justin Martyr, but it is quite
clear from his *Address to the Greeks* that he did not share
Justin's sympathy for Greek philosophy in its more spiritual
aspects. Tatian declares that we know God from His works; he
has a doctrine of the Logos, distinguishes soul (ψυχή) from
spirit (πνεῦμα), teaches creation in time and insists on free-
will; but all these points he could have got from the Scriptures and Christian teaching: he had little use for Greek
learning and Greek thought, though he can hardly have
escaped its influence altogether. He was in fact inclined to
excessive rigorism, and we learn from St. Irenaeus and St.
Jerome[11] that after Justin's martyrdom Tatian fell away from
the Church into Valentinian Gnosticism, subsequently founding the sect of the Encratites, denouncing not only the
drinking of wine and the use of ornaments by women but
even marriage as such, which he said was defilement and
fornication.[12]

Tatian certainly recognised the human mind's ability to
prove God's existence from creatures and he made use of
philosophical notions and categories in the development of
theology, as when he maintains that the Word, proceeding
from the simple essence of God, does not 'fall into the void',
as human words do, but remains in its subsistence and is the
divine instrument of creation. He thus uses the analogy of the
formation of human thought and speech to illustrate the procession of the Word, and, while holding to the doctrine of
creation, he uses language reminiscent of the *Timaeus* in respect of the Demiurge. But, if he made use of terms and

ideas taken from pagan philosophy, he did not do so in any spirit of sympathy, but rather with the notion that the Greek philosophers had taken from the Scriptures whatever truth they possessed and that whatever they added thereto was nothing but falsity and perversion. The Stoics, for instance, perverted the doctrine of providence by the diabolic theory of fatalistic determinism. It is indeed something of an historical irony that a writer who betrayed so pronounced an hostility towards Greek thought and who drew so sharp a distinction between pagan 'sophistry' and Christian wisdom should himself end in heresy.

(iv) A more tactful approach to the Greeks, and one in harmony with that of Justin Martyr, was the approach of *Athenagoras*, who addressed to the Emperors Marcus Aurelius and Commodus, 'conquerors of Armenia and Sarmatia, and above all philosophers', a *Plea for the Christians* (πρεσβεία περὶ χριστιανῶν) about the year A.D. 177. In this book the author is concerned to defend the Christians against the three accusations of atheism, cannibalistic feasts and incest, and in answering the first accusation he gives a reasoned defence of the Christian belief in one eternal and spiritual God. First of all he cites various Greek philosophers themselves, for instance Philolaus, Plato, Aristotle and the Stoics. He quotes Plato in the *Timaeus* to the effect that it is difficult to find the Maker and Father of the universe and impossible, even when He is found, to declare Him to all, and asks why Christians, believing in one God, should be called atheists, when Plato is not so called because of his doctrine of the Demiurge. The poets and philosophers, moved by a divine impulse, have striven to find God and men pay heed to their conclusions: how foolish it would be, then, to refuse to listen to the very Spirit of God, speaking through the mouths of the Prophets.

Athenagoras then goes on to show that there cannot be a multitude of material gods, that God, who forms matter, must transcend matter (though he scarcely succeeds in conceiving God without relation to space), that the Cause of perishable things must be imperishable and spiritual, and he appeals especially to the testimony of Plato. He thus adopts the same attitude as that of Justin Martyr. There is one true 'philosophy' or wisdom, which is attained adequately only through the Christian revelation, though Greek philosophers divined something of the truth. In other words, their very respect for the Greek thinkers and poets should lead thoughtful men like Marcus Aurelius to appreciate and esteem, even if not to embrace, Christianity. His primary purpose is theological and apologetic, but he utilises philosophic arguments and themes in his pursuit of that purpose. For instance, in his attempt to prove the reasonable character of the doctrine of the resurrection of the body, he makes clear his conviction, as against the Platonic view, that the body belongs to the integral man, that man is not simply a soul using a body.[13]

(v) A similar appeal to the intelligent pagan was made by *Theophilus of Antioch* in his *Ad Autolycum*, written about A.D. 180. After emphasising the fact that moral purity is necessary for anyone who would know God, he proceeds to speak of the divine attributes, God's incomprehensibility, power, wisdom, eternity, immutability. As the soul of man, itself invisible, is perceived through the movements of the body, so God, Himself invisible, is known through His providence and works. He is not always accurate in his account of the opinions of Greek philosophers, but he clearly had some esteem for Plato, whom he considered 'the most respectable philosopher among them',[14] though Plato erred in not teaching creation out of nothing (which Theophilus clearly affirms) and in his doctrine concerning marriage (which Theophilus does not give correctly).

3. The foregoing Apologists, who wrote in Greek, were mainly concerned with answering pagan attacks on Christianity. We can now consider briefly the great opponent of Gnosticism, St. Irenaeus, to whom we add, for the sake of convenience, Hippolytus. Both men wrote in Greek and both combated the Gnosticism which flourished in the second century A.D., though Hippolytus's work has a wider interest, containing, as it does, many references to Greek philosophy and philosophers.

Of Gnosticism suffice it to say here that, in general, it was a monstrous conflation of Scriptural and Christian, Greek and Oriental elements, which, professing to substitute knowledge (*gnosis*) for faith, offered a doctrine of God, creation, the origin of evil, salvation, to those who liked to look upon themselves as superior persons in comparison with the ordinary run of Christians. There was a Jewish Gnosticism before the 'Christian' form, and the latter itself can be looked on as a Christian heresy only in so far as the Gnostics borrowed certain specifically Christian themes: the Oriental and Hellenic elements are far too conspicuous for it to be possible to call Gnosticism a Christian heresy in the ordinary sense, although it was a real danger in the second century and seduced those Christians who were attracted by the bizarre theosophical speculations which the Gnostics offered as 'knowledge'. As a matter of fact, there were a number of Gnostic systems, such as those of Cerinthus, Marcion, the Ophites, Basilides, Valentinus. We know that Marcion was a Christian who suffered excommunication; but the Ophites were probably of Jewish-Alexandrian origin, while in regard to famous Gnostics like Basilides and Valentinus (second century) we do not know that they were ever Christians.

Characteristic of Gnosticism in general was a dualism between God and matter, which, though not absolute, approached that of the later Manichaean system. The resulting gulf between God and matter was filled up by the Gnostics with a series of emanations or intermediary beings in which Christ found a place. The complement of the process of emanation was the return to God by way of salvation.

In the system of Marcion, as one would expect, the Christian element was to the fore. The God of the Old Testament, the Demiurge, is inferior to the God of the New Testament, who remained unknown until He revealed Himself in Jesus Christ. In the systems of Basilides and Valentinus, however, the Christian element is less important: Christ is depicted as an inferior being (an Eon) in a fantastic hierarchy of divine and semi-divine emanations, and His mission is simply that of transmitting to man the salvific knowledge or *gnosis*. As matter is evil, it cannot be the work of the Supreme God, but it is due to the 'great Archon', who was worshipped by the Jews and who gave himself out as the one Supreme God. The Gnostic systems were thus not dualistic in the full Manichaean sense, since the Demiurge, identified with the God of the Old Testament, was not made an independent and original principle of evil (the neo-Platonic element was too prominent to admit of absolute dualism), and their main common characteristic was not so much the tendency to dualism as the insistence on *gnosis* as the means of salvation. The adoption of Christian elements was largely due to the desire to absorb Christianity, to substitute *gnosis* for faith. To enter further upon the differentiating features of the various Gnostic systems and to detail the series of emanations would be a tiresome and profitless task: it is enough to point out that the general framework was a mixture of Oriental and Greek (e.g. neo-Pythagorean and neo-Platonic) themes, with a varying dosage of Christian elements, taken both from Christianity proper and from apocryphal and spurious documents. To us to-day it is difficult to understand how Gnosticism could ever have been a danger to the Church or an attraction to any sane mind; but we have to remember that it arose at a time when a welter of philosophical schools and mystery-religions was seeking to cater for the spiritual needs of men. Moreover, esoteric and theosophical systems, surrounded with the pseudo-glamour of 'eastern wisdom', have not entirely lost their attraction for some minds even in much more recent times.

(i) *St. Irenaeus* (born about A.D. 137 or 140), writing against the Gnostics in his *Adversus Haereses*, affirms that there is one God, who made all things, Creator of heaven and earth. He appeals, for example, to the argument from design and to that from universal consent, observing that the very heathen have learnt from creation itself, by the use of reason, the existence of God as Creator.[15] God created the world freely, and not by necessity.[16] Moreover, He created the world out of nothing and not out of previously existing matter, as the Gnostics pretend relying on 'Anaxagoras, Empedocles and Plato'.[17] But, though the human mind can come to know God through reason and revelation, it cannot comprehend God, whose essence transcends the human intelligence: to pretend to know the ineffable mysteries of God and to go beyond humble faith and love, as the Gnostics do, is mere conceit and pride. The doctrine of reincarnation is false, while the revealed moral law does not abrogate, but fulfils and extends, the natural law. In fine, 'the teaching of the Apostles is the true *gnosis*'.[18]

According to Irenaeus the Gnostics borrowed most of their notions from Greek philosophers. Thus he accuses them of borrowing their morals from Epicurus and the Cynics, their doctrine of reincarnation from Plato. In this tendency to attach Gnostic theories to Greek philosophies Irenaeus was closely followed by

(ii) *Hippolytus* (died probably about A.D. 236), who was a disciple of Irenaeus, according to Photius,[19] and certainly utilised his teaching and writing. In the *Proemium* to his *Philosophumena* (now generally attributed to Hippolytus) he declares his intention, only imperfectly fulfilled, of exposing the plagiarism of the Gnostics by showing how their various opinions were taken from Greek philosophers, though they were made worse by the Gnostics, and, in order to do this more easily, he first recounts the opinions of the philosophers, relying for his information mainly, if not entirely, on the doxography of Theophrastus. The information, however, is not always accurate. His main accusation against the Greeks is that they glorified the parts of the creation with dainty phrases, but were ignorant of the Creator of all things, who made them freely out of nothing according to His wisdom and foreknowledge.

4. The foregoing authors wrote in Greek; but there was also a group of Latin Apologists, Minucius Felix, Tertullian, Arnobius and Lactantius, of whom the most important is Tertullian.

(i) It is uncertain whether *Minucius Felix* wrote before or after Tertullian, but in any case his attitude towards Greek philosophy, as shown in his *Octavius*, was more favourable than Tertullian's. Arguing that God's existence can be known with certainty from the order of nature and the design involved in the organism, particularly in the human body, and that the unity of God can be inferred from the unity of the cosmic order, he affirmed that Greek philosophers, too, recognised these truths. Thus Aristotle recognised one Godhead and the Stoics had a doctrine of divine providence, while Plato speaks in almost Christian terms when he talks in the *Timaeus* of the Maker and Father of the universe.

(ii) *Tertullian*, however, speaks in a rather different way of Greek philosophy. Born about A.D. 160 of pagan parents and educated as a jurist (he practised in Rome), he became a Christian, only to fall into the Montanist heresy, a form of rigorous and excessive Puritanism. He was the first outstanding Christian Latin writer, and in his works his contempt for paganism and pagan learning is made clear and explicit. What have the philosopher and the Christian in common, the disciple of Greece, the friend of error, and the pupil of heaven, the foe of error and friend of truth?[20] Even Socrates' wisdom did not amount to much, since no one can really know God apart from Christ, nor Christ apart from the Holy Spirit. Moreover, Socrates was, self-confessedly, guided by a demon![21] As to Plato, he said that it was hard to find the Maker and Father of the universe, whereas the simplest Christian has already found Him.[22] Moreover, the Greek philosophers are the patriarchs of the heretics,[23] inasmuch as Valentinus borrowed from the Platonists, Marcion from the Stoics, while the philosophers themselves borrowed ideas from the Old Testament and then distorted them and claimed them as their own.[24]

However, in spite of the antithesis he makes between Christian wisdom and Greek philosophy, Tertullian himself developed philosophical themes and was influenced by the Stoics. He affirms that the existence of God is known with certainty from His works,[25] and also that from the uncreatedness of God we can argue to His perfection (*Imperfectum non potest esse, nisi quod factum est*);[26] but he makes the astounding statement that everything, including God, is corporeal, bodily. 'Everything which exists is a bodily existence *sui generis*. Nothing lacks bodily existence but that which is non-existent':[27] 'for who will deny that God is a body, although "God is a Spirit"? For Spirit has a bodily substance of its own kind, in its own form.'[28] Many writers have concluded from these statements that Tertullian maintained a materialistic doctrine and held God to be really a material being, just as the Stoics considered God to be material: some, however, have suggested that by 'body' Tertullian often meant simply substance and that when he attributes materiality to God, he is really simply attributing substantiality to God. On this explanation, when Tertullian says that God is a *corpus sui generis*, that He is *corpus* and yet *spiritus*, he would mean that God is a spiritual substance: his language would be at fault, while his thought would be acceptable. One is certainly not entitled to exclude this explanation as impossible, but it is true that Tertullian, speaking of the human soul, says that it must be a bodily substance since it can suffer.[29] However, he speaks ambiguously even on the nature of the soul, and in his *Apology*[30] he gives as a reason for the resurrection of the bodies of the wicked that 'the soul is not capable of suffering without the solid substance, that is, the flesh'. It is probably best to say, then, that, while Tertullian's language often implies materialism of a rather crass sort, his meaning *may* not have been that which his language would often imply. When he teaches that the soul of the infant is derived from the father's seed like a kind of sprout (*surculus, tradux*),[31] he would seem to be teaching a clearly materialistic doctrine; but this 'traducianism' was adopted partly for a theological reason, to explain the trans-

mission of original sin, and some later writers who inclined
to the same view, did so for the same theological reason, without apparently realising the materialistic implications of the
doctrine. This does not show, of course, that Tertullian was
not a materialist; but it should at least lead one to hesitate
before forming the conviction that his general meaning always coincided with the words he used. His assertion of the
freedom of the will and of the natural immortality of the soul
will scarcely fit in, from the logical viewpoint, with sheer
materialism; but that again would not justify one in flatly
denying that he was a materialist, since he may have held a
materialistic theory without realising the fact that some of
the attributes he ascribed to the soul were incompatible with
a fully materialist position.

One of the great services rendered by Tertullian to Christian thought was his development of theological and, to some
extent, of philosophical terminology in the Latin language.
Thus the technical use of the word *persona* is found for the
first time in his writings: the divine Persons are distinct as
Personae, but they are not different, divided, *substantiae*.[32]
In his doctrine of the Word[33] he appeals explicitly to the
Stoics, to Zeno and Cleanthes.[34] However, of Tertullian's
theological developments and of his orthodoxy or unorthodoxy
it is not our concern to speak.

(iii) In his *Adversus Gentes* (about 303) *Arnobius* makes
some curious observations concerning the soul. Thus, although
he affirms creationism, as against the Platonic doctrine of
pre-existence, he makes the creating agent a being inferior to
God, and he also asserts the *gratuitous* character of the soul's
immortality, denying a natural immortality. One motive was
evidently that of using the gratuitous character of immortality as an argument for becoming a Christian and leading
a moral life. Again, while combating the Platonic theory of
reminiscence, he asserts the experiential origin of all our ideas
with one exception, the idea of God. He depicts a child
brought up in solitude, silence and ignorance throughout his
youth and declares that, as a result, he would know nothing:
he would certainly not have any knowledge by 'reminiscence'.
Plato's proof for his doctrine in the *Meno* is not cogent.[35]

(iv) The origin of the soul by God's direct creation, in
opposition to any form of traducianism, was clearly affirmed
by *Lactantius* (about 250 to about 325) in his *De opificio
Dei*.[36]

5. Gnosticism, as combated by St. Irenaeus and Hippolytus, was, so far as it can reasonably be connected with Christianity, an heretical speculative system, or, more accurately, set of systems, which, in addition to Oriental and Christian elements, incorporated elements of Hellenic thought. One of its effects, therefore, was to arouse a determined opposition to Hellenic philosophy on the part of those Christian writers who exaggerated the connections between Gnosticism and Greek philosophy, which they considered to be the seed-ground of heresy; but another effect was to contribute to the effort to construct a non-heretical 'gnosis', a Christian theologico-philosophical system. This effort was characteristic of the Catechetical School at Alexandria, of which the two most famous names are Clement and Origen.

(i) *Titus Flavius Clemens* (*Clement of Alexandria*) was born about 150, perhaps at Athens, came to Alexandria in 202 or 203 and died there about 219. Animated by the attitude which was later summed up in the formula, *Credo, ut intelligam*, he sought to develop the systematic presentation of the Christian wisdom in a true, as opposed to a false *gnosis*. In the process he followed the spirit of Justin Martyr's treatment of the Greek philosophers, looking on their work rather as a preparation for Christianity, an education of the Hellenic world for the revealed religion, than as a folly and delusion. The divine Logos has always illumined souls; but whereas the Jews were enlightened by Moses and the Prophets, the Greeks had their wise men, their philosophers, so that philosophy was to the Greeks what the Law was to the Hebrews.[37] It is true that Clement thought, following Justin again, that the Greeks borrowed from the Old Testament and distorted, from vainglorious motives, what they borrowed; but he was also firmly convinced that the light of the Logos enabled the Greek philosophers to attain many truths, and that philosophy is in reality simply that body of truths which are not the prerogative of any one Greek School but are found, in different measure and degree, in different Schools, though Plato was indeed the greatest of all the philosophers.[38]

But not only was philosophy a preparation for Christianity: it is also an aid in understanding Christianity. Indeed, the person who merely believes and makes no effort to understand is like a child in comparison with a man: blind faith, passive acceptance, is not the ideal, though science, speculation, reasoning, cannot be true if they do not harmonise with

synthetic thinker of Christianity, but although he attached them to Scriptural passages freely interpreted, his enthusiasm for Greek thought led him sometimes into heterodoxy.

6. The Greek Fathers of the fourth and fifth centuries were occupied mainly with theological questions. Thus *St. Athanasius*, who died in 373, was the great foe of Arianism; *St. Gregory Nazianzen*, who died in 390 and was known as the Theologian, is particularly remarkable for his work on Trinitarian and Christological theology; *St. John Chrysostom* (died 406) is celebrated as one of the greatest orators of the Church and for his work on the Scriptures. In treating of dogmas like those of the Blessed Trinity and the Hypostatic Union the Fathers naturally made use of philosophical terms and expressions; but their application of reasoning in theology does not make them philosophers in the strict sense and we must pass them over here. One may point out, however, that *St. Basil* (died 379) studied in the University of Athens, together with St. Gregory Nazianzen, and that in his *Ad Adolescentes* he recommends a study of the Greek poets, orators, historians and philosophers, though a selection should be made from their writings which would exclude immoral passages: Greek literature and learning are a potent instrument of education, but moral education is more important than literary and philosophic formation. (St. Basil himself in his descriptions of animals apparently depended almost entirely on the relevant works of Aristotle.)

But, though we cannot consider here the theological speculations of the Greek Fathers, something must be said of two eminent figures of the period, the historian Eusebius and St. Gregory of Nyssa.

(i) *Eusebius of Caesarea* was born in Palestine about 265, became Bishop of Caesarea, his birthplace, in 313, and died there in 339 or 340. Best known as a great Church historian, he is also of importance for his Christian apologetic, and under this heading comes his attitude towards Greek philosophy, since, in general, he regarded Greek philosophy, especially Platonism, as a preparation of the heathen world for Christianity, though he was fully alive to the errors of Greek philosophers and to the contradictions between the many philosophical Schools. Yet, though he speaks sharply on occasion, his general attitude is sympathetic and appreciative, an attitude which comes out most clearly in his *Praeparatio evangelica* in fifteen books. It is greatly to be regretted that we

have not got the twenty-five books of the work which Eusebius
wrote in answer to Porphyry's attack on Christianity, as his
reply to the eminent neo-Platonist and pupil of Plotinus
would doubtless throw much light on his philosophical ideas;
but the *Praeparatio evangelica* is sufficient to show, not only
that Eusebius shared the general outlook of Justin Martyr,
Clement of Alexandria and Origen, but also that he had read
widely in the literature of the Greeks. He was in fact an extremely learned man, and his work is one of the sources for
our knowledge of the philosophy of those thinkers whose
works have perished.

One would probably only expect, given the attitude of his
predecessors, to find Eusebius especially appreciative of
Plato: in fact he devotes to Platonism three books (11–13)
of the *Praeparatio*. Clement had spoken of Plato as Moses
writing in Greek, and Eusebius, agreeing with Clement, considered that Plato and Moses were in agreement,[49] that
Plato may be called a prophet of the economy of salvation.[50]
Like Clement and Origen, and like Philo also, Eusebius
thought that Plato had borrowed the truths he exposes from
the Old Testament;[51] but at the same time he is willing to
admit the possibility of Plato having discovered the truth for
himself or of his having been enlightened by God.[52] In any
case, not only does Plato agree with the sacred literature of
the Hebrews in his idea of God, but he also suggests, in his
Letters, the idea of the Blessed Trinity. On this point Eusebius is, of course, interpreting Plato in a neo-Platonic sense
and is referring to the three principles of the One or Good,
the *Nous* or Mind, and the World-Soul.[53] The Ideas are the
ideas of God, of the Logos, the exemplar patterns of creation,
and the picture of creation in the *Timaeus* is similar to that
contained in Genesis.[54] Again, Plato agrees with the Scriptures in his doctrine of immortality,[55] while the moral teaching of the *Phaedrus* reminds Eusebius of St. Paul.[56] Even
Plato's political ideal found its realisation in the Jewish
theocracy.[57]

Nevertheless, it remains true that Plato did not affirm these
truths without an admixture of error.[58] His doctrine of God
and of creation is contaminated by his doctrine of emanation
and by his acceptance of the eternity of matter, his doctrine
of the soul and of immortality by his theory of pre-existence
and of reincarnation, and so on. Thus Plato, even if he was a
'prophet', was no more than a prophet: he did not himself

enter into the promised land of truth, though he approached near to it: it is Christianity alone which is the true philosophy. Moreover, Plato's philosophy was highly intellectualist, caviar for the multitude, whereas Christianity is for all, so that men and women, rich and poor, learned and unlearned, can be 'philosophers'.

To discuss Eusebius's interpretation of Plato would be out of place here: it is sufficient to note that he, in common with most other Christian Greek writers, gives the palm to Plato among Hellenic thinkers, and that, in common with all the early Christian writers, he makes no real distinction between theology in a strict sense and philosophy in a strict sense. There is one wisdom, which is found adequately and completely only in Christianity: Greek thinkers attained to true philosophy or wisdom in so far as they anticipated Christianity. Among those who anticipated the true philosophy Plato is the most outstanding; but even he stood only on the threshold of truth. Naturally the notion that Plato and other Hellenic thinkers borrowed from the Old Testament, although itself partly a consequence of their understanding of 'philosophy', helped also to confirm Christian writers like Eusebius in their very wide interpretation of 'philosophy', as including not only the result of human speculation but also the data of revelation. In fact, in spite of his very favourable judgement on Plato, the logical conclusion from Eusebius's and others' conviction that the Greek philosophers borrowed from the Old Testament would inevitably be that human speculation unaided by direct illumination from God is not of any great avail in the attainment of truth. For what are the errors with which even Plato contaminated the truth but the result of human speculation? If you say that the truth contained in Greek philosophy came from the Old Testament, that is to say, from revelation, you can hardly avoid the conclusion that the errors in Greek philosophy came from human speculation, with a consequently unfavourable judgement as to the power of that speculation. This attitude was very common among the Fathers and, in the Middle Ages, it was to be clearly expressed by St. Bonaventure in the thirteenth century, though it was not to be the view that ultimately prevailed in Scholasticism, the view of St. Thomas Aquinas and of Duns Scotus.

(ii) One of the most learned of the Greek Fathers and one of the most interesting from the philosophic standpoint was the brother of St. Basil, *St. Gregory of Nyssa*, who was born in Caesarea (in Cappadocia, not Palestine) about A.D. 335 and, after having been a teacher of rhetoric, became Bishop of Nyssa, dying about the year 395.

Gregory of Nyssa realised clearly that the data of revelation are accepted on faith and are not the result of a logical process of reasoning, that the mysteries of faith are not philosophical and scientific conclusions: if they were, then supernatural faith, as exercised by Christians, and Hellenic philosophising would be indistinguishable. On the other hand, the Faith has a rational basis, in that, logically speaking, the acceptance of mysteries on authority presupposes the ascertainability by natural reasoning of certain preliminary truths, especially the existence of God, which are capable of philosophic demonstration. Accordingly, though the superiority of faith must be maintained, it is only right to invoke the aid of philosophy. Ethics, natural philosophy, logic, mathematics, are not only ornaments in the temple of truth but may also contribute to the life of wisdom and virtue: they are, therefore, not to be despised or rejected,[59] though divine revelation must be accepted as a touchstone and criterion of truth since human reasoning must be judged by the word of God, not the word of God by human reasoning.[60] Again, it is right to employ human speculation and human reasoning in regard to dogma; but the conclusions will not be valid unless they agree with the Scriptures.[61]

The cosmic order proves the existence of God, and from the necessary perfection of God we can argue to His unity, that there is one God. Gregory went on to attempt to give reasons for the Trinity of Persons in the one Godhead.[62] For instance, God must have a Logos, a word, a reason. He cannot be less than man, who also has a reason, a word. But the divine Logos cannot be something of fleeting duration: it must be eternal, just as it must be living. The internal word in man is a fleeting accident, but in God there can be no such thing: the Logos is one in Nature with the Father, for there is but one God, the distinction between the Logos and the Father, the Word and the Speaker, being a distinction of relation. To enter into Gregory's Trinitarian doctrine as such is not our concern here; but the fact that he tries, in some sense, to 'prove' the doctrine is of interest, since it afforded a precedent for the later attempts of St. Anselm and Richard of St. Victor to deduce the Trinity, to prove it *rationibus necessariis.*

Obviously, however, St. Gregory's intention, like that of St. Anselm, was to render the mystery more intelligible by the application of dialectic, not to 'rationalise' the mystery in the sense of departing from dogmatic orthodoxy. Similarly, his theory that the word 'man' is primarily applicable to the universal and only secondarily to the individual man was an attempt to render the mystery more intelligible, the application of the illustration being this, that the word 'God' refers primarily to the divine essence, which is one, and only secondarily to the divine Persons, who are Three, so that the Christian cannot be rightly accused of tritheism. But, though the illustration was introduced to defeat the charge of tritheism and make the mystery more intelligible, it was an unfortunate illustration, since it implied a hyperrealist view of universals.

St. Gregory's 'Platonism' in regard to universals comes out clearly in his *De hominis opificio,* where he distinguishes the heavenly man, the ideal man, the universal, from the earthly man, the object of experience. The former, the ideal man or rather ideal human being, exists only in the divine idea and is without sexual determination, being neither male nor female: the latter, the human being of experience, is an expression of the ideal and is sexually determined, the ideal being, as it were, 'splintered' or partially expressed in many single individuals. Thus, according to Gregory, individual creatures proceed by creation, not by emanation, from the ideal in the divine Logos. This theory clearly goes back to neo-Platonism and to Philonism, and it was adopted by the first outstanding philosopher of the Middle Ages, John Scotus Eriugena, who was much influenced by the writings of St. Gregory of Nyssa. It must be remembered, however, that Gregory never meant to imply that there was ever an historic ideal man, sexually undetermined; God's idea of man will be realised only eschatologically, when (according to St. Paul's words as interpreted by Gregory) there will be neither male nor female, since in heaven there will be no marriage.

God created the world out of an abundance of goodness and love, in order that there might be creatures who could participate in the divine goodness; but though God is goodness and created the world out of goodness, He did not create the world from necessity, but freely. A share in this freedom

God has given to man, and God respects this freedom, permitting man to choose evil if he so wills. Evil is the result of man's free choice, God is not responsible. It is true that God foresaw evil and that He permits it, but in spite of this foreknowledge He created man, for He knew also that He would in the end bring all men to Himself. Gregory thus accepted the Origenist theory of the 'restoration of all things': every human being, even Satan and the fallen angels, will at length turn to God, at least through the purifying sufferings of the hereafter. In a sense, then, every human being will at length return to the Ideal and be therein contained, though Gregory certainly accepted individual immortality. This notion of the return of all things to God, to the Principle from whom they sprang, and of the attainment of a state in which God is 'all in all', was also borrowed by John Scotus Eriugena from St. Gregory, and in interpreting the somewhat ambiguous language of John Scotus one should at least bear in mind the thought of St. Gregory, even while admitting the possibility of John Scotus having attached a different meaning to similar words.

But, though St. Gregory of Nyssa shared Origen's theory of the restoration of all things, he did not share Origen's acceptance of the Platonic notion of pre-existence, and in the *De hominis opificio*[63] he says that the author of the *De Principiis* was led astray by Hellenic theories. The soul, which is not confined to any one portion of the body, is 'a created essence (οὐσία γεννητή), a living essence, intellectual, with an organic and sensitive body, an essence that has the power of giving life and perceiving sensible objects, so long as the bodily instruments endure'.[64] As simple and uncompounded (ἁπλῆν καὶ ἀσύνθετον), the soul has the power of surviving the body,[65] with which, however, it will in the end be reunited. The soul is thus spiritual and incorporeal; but how is it different from body, for body, i.e. a concrete material object, is composed, according to Gregory, of qualities which in themselves are incorporeal? In the *De hominis opificio*[66] he says that the union of qualities like colour, solidity, quantity, weight, results in body, whereas their dissolution spells the perishing of the body. In the preceding chapter he has proposed a dilemma: either material things proceed from God, in which case God, as their Source, would contain matter in Himself, would be material, or, if God is not material, then material things do not proceed from Him and matter is eternal. Gregory, however, rejects both the materiality of God and dualism, and the natural conclusion of this would be that the qualities of which bodily things are composed are not material. It is true that, while asserting creation *ex nihilo*, Gregory asserts that we cannot comprehend how God creates the qualities out of nothing; but it is reasonable to suppose that in his eyes the qualities which form body are not themselves bodies: in fact they could not be, since there is no concrete body at all except in and through their *union*. Presumably he was influenced by Plato's doctrine of the qualities in the *Timaeus*. How, then, are they not spiritual? And, if they are spiritual, how does soul differ essentially from body? The reply would doubtless be that, though the qualities unite to *form* body and cannot, considered in abstraction, be called 'bodies', yet they have an essential relation to matter, since it is their function to form matter. An analogous difficulty recurs in regard to the Aristotelian-Thomistic doctrine of matter and form. Prime matter is not in itself body, but it is one of the principles of body: how, then, considered in *itself*, does it differ from the immaterial and spiritual? Thomistic philosophers answer that prime matter never *exists* by itself alone and that it has an exigency for quantity, an essential ordination to concrete body, and presumably Gregory of Nyssa would have to say something of the same sort in regard to his primary qualities. In passing, one may note that similar difficulties might be raised in regard to certain modern theories concerning the constitution of matter. Plato, one might reasonably suppose, would welcome these theories, were he alive to-day, and it is not improbable that St. Gregory of Nyssa would follow suit.

From what has been said it is clear that Gregory of Nyssa was much influenced by Platonism, neo-Platonism, and the writings of Philo (he speaks, for example, of the ὁμοίωσις Θεῷ as being the purpose of man, of the 'flight of the alone to the Alone', of justice-in-itself, of *eros* and the ascent to the ideal Beauty); but it must be emphasised that, although Gregory undeniably employed Plotinian themes and expressions, as also to a less extent those of Philo, he did not by any means always understand them in a Plotinian or Philonic sense. On the contrary, he utilised expressions of Plotinus or Plato to expose and state Christian doctrines. For example, the 'likeness to God' is the work of grace, a development under the activity of God, with man's free co-operation, of the image or εἰκών of God implanted in the soul at baptism. Again, justice-in-itself is not an abstract virtue nor even an idea in *Nous*; it is the Logos indwelling in the soul, the effect of this inhabitation being the participated virtue. This Logos, moreover, is not the *Nous* of Plotinus, nor is it the Logos of Philo: it is the Second Person of the Blessed Trinity, and between God and creatures there is no intermediary procession of subordinate hypostases.

Finally, it is noteworthy that St. Gregory of Nyssa was the first real founder of systematic mystical theology. Here again he utilised Plotinian and Philonic themes, but he employed them in a Christian sense and within a Christocentric framework of thought. Naturally speaking man's mind is fitted to know sensible objects, and contemplating these objects the mind can come to know something of God and His attributes (symbolic theology, which is partly equivalent to natural theology in the modern sense). On the other hand, though man by nature has as his proper object of knowledge sensible things, these things are not fully real, they are mirage and illusion except as symbols or manifestations of immaterial reality, that reality towards which man is spiritually drawn. The consequent tension in the soul leads to a state of ἀνελπιστία or 'despair', which is the birth of mysticism, since the soul, drawn by God, leaves its natural object of knowledge, without, however, being able to see the God to whom it is drawn by love: it enters into the darkness, what the mediaeval treatise calls the Cloud of Unknowing. (To this stage corresponds the negative theology, which so influenced the Pseudo-Dionysius.) In the soul's advance there are, as it were, two movements, that of the indwelling of the Triune God and that of the soul's reaching out beyond itself, culminating in 'ecstasy'. Origen had interpreted the Philonic ecstasy intellectually, as any other form of 'ecstasy' was then suspect, owing to Montanist extravagances; but Gregory set ecstasy at the summit of the soul's endeavour, interpreting it first and foremost as ecstatic *love*.

The 'darkness' which envelops God is due primarily to the utter transcendence of the divine essence, and Gregory drew the conclusion that even in heaven the soul is always pressing forward, drawn by love, to penetrate further into God. A static condition would mean either satiety or death: spiritual life demands constant progress and the nature of the divine transcendence involves the same progress, since the human mind can never comprehend God. In a sense, then, the 'divine darkness' *always* persists, and it is true to say that Gregory gave to this knowledge in darkness a priority over intellectual knowledge, not because he despised the human intellect but because he realised the transcendence of God.

St. Gregory's scheme of the soul's ascent certainly bears some resemblance to that of Plotinus; but at the same time it is thoroughly Christocentric. The advance of the soul is the work of the Divine Logos, Christ. Moreover, his ideal is not that of a solitary union with God, but rather of a realisation of the *Pleroma* of Christ: the advance of one soul brings grace and blessing to others and the indwelling of God in the individual affects the whole Body. His mysticism is also thoroughly sacramental in character: the εἰκών is restored by Baptism, union with God is fostered by the Eucharist. In fine, the writings of St. Gregory of Nyssa are the source from which not only the Pseudo-Dionysius and mystics down to St. John of the Cross drew, directly or indirectly, much of their inspiration; but they are also the fountain-head of those Christian philosophical systems which trace out the soul's advance through different stages of knowledge and love up to the mystical life and the Beatific Vision. If a purely spiritual writer like St. John of the Cross stands in the line that goes back to Gregory, so does the mystical philosopher St. Bonaventure.

7. Of the Latin Fathers the greatest, without a shadow of doubt, is St. Augustine of Hippo; but, because of the importance of his thought for the Middle Ages, I shall consider his philosophy separately and rather more at length. In this section it is sufficient to mention very briefly St. Ambrose (about 333 to 397), Bishop of Milan.

St. Ambrose shared the typically Roman attitude towards philosophy, i.e. an interest in practical and ethical matters, coupled with little facility or taste for metaphysical speculation. In his dogmatic and Scriptural work he depended mainly on the Greek Fathers; but in ethics he was influenced by Cicero, and in his *De officiis ministrorum*, composed about 391 and addressed to the clergy of Milan, he provided a Christian counterpart to the *De officiis* of the great Roman orator. In his book the Saint follows Cicero closely in his divisions and treatment of the virtues, but the whole treatment is naturally infused with the Christian ethos, and the Stoic ideal of happiness, found in the possession of virtue, is complemented by the final ideal of eternal happiness in God. It is not that St. Ambrose makes any particularly new contributions to Christian ethic: the importance of his work lies rather in its influence on succeeding thought, in the use made of it by later writers on ethics.

8. The Greek Fathers, as has been seen, were mainly influenced by the Platonic tradition; but one of the factors which helped to prepare the way for the favourable reception eventually accorded to Aristotelianism in the Latin West was the work of the last of the Greek Fathers, St. John Damascene.

St. John Damascene, who died probably at the end of the year A.D. 749, was not only a resolute opponent of the 'Iconoclasts' but also a great systematiser in the field of theology, so that he can be looked on as the Scholastic of the Orient. He explicitly says that he does not intend to give new and personal opinions, but to preserve and hand on the thoughts of holy and learned men, so that it would be useless to seek in his writings for novelty of content; yet in his systematic and ordered presentation of the ideas of his predecessors a certain originality may be ascribed to him. His chief work is the *Fount of Wisdom*, in the first part of which he gives a sketch of the Aristotelian logic and ontology, though he draws on other writers besides Aristotle, e.g. Porphyry. In this first part, the *Dialectica*, he makes clear his opinion that philosophy and profane science are the instruments or handmaids of theology, adopting the view of Clement of Alexandria and the two Gregories, a view which goes back to Philo the Alexandrian Jew and was often repeated in the Middle Ages.[67] In the second part of his great work he gives a history of heresies, using material supplied by former writers, and in the third part, the *De Fide Orthodoxa*, he gives, in four books, an orderly treatment of orthodox Patristic theology. This third part was translated into Latin by Burgundius of Pisa in 1151 and was used by, among others, Peter Lombard, St. Albert the Great and St. Thomas Aquinas. In the East, St. John Damascene enjoys almost as much esteem as St. Thomas Aquinas in the West.

9. From even the brief survey given above it is evident that one would look in vain for a systematic philosophical synthesis in the works of any of the Greek Fathers or indeed in any of the Latin Fathers save Augustine. The Greek Fathers, making no very clear distinction between the provinces of philoso-

phy and theology, regarded Christianity as the one true wisdom or 'philosophy'. Hellenic philosophy they tended to regard as a propaedeutic to Christianity, so that their main interest in treating of it was to point out the anticipation of Christian truth which they saw therein contained and the aberrations from truth which were also clear to them. The former they frequently attributed to borrowing from the Old Testament, the latter to the weakness of human speculation and to the perverse desire of originality, the vainglory, of the philosophers themselves. When they adopted ideas from Hellenic philosophy they generally accepted them because they thought that they would help in the exposition and presentation of the Christian wisdom, not in order to incorporate them in a philosophic system in the strict sense.

Nevertheless, there are, as we have seen, philosophic elements in the writings of the Fathers. For instance, they make use of rational arguments for God's existence, particularly the argument from order and design; they speculate about the origin and nature of the soul; St. Gregory of Nyssa even had some ideas which fall under the heading of philosophy of nature or cosmology. Still, since their arguments, the arguments for God's existence, for example, are not really worked out in any developed, systematic and strict manner, it may appear out of place to have considered them at all. I think, however, that this would be a mistake, as even a brief treatment of Patristic thought is sufficient to bring out one point which may tend to be forgotten by those who know little of Christian philosophic thought. Owing to the fact that St. Thomas Aquinas, who has in recent times been accorded a peculiar status among Catholic philosophers, adopted a great deal of the Aristotelian system, and owing to the fact that early thinkers of the 'modern era', e.g. Descartes and Francis Bacon, fulminate against Scholastic Aristotelianism, it is sometimes taken for granted that Christian philosophy, or at least Catholic philosophy, means Aristotelianism and nothing else. Yet, leaving out of account for the present later centuries, a survey of Patristic thought is sufficient to show that Plato, and not Aristotle, was the Greek thinker who won the greatest esteem from the Fathers of the Church. This may have been due in great part to the fact that neo-Platonism was the dominant and vigorous contemporary philosophy and to the fact that the Fathers not only saw Plato more or less in the light of neo-Platonic interpretation and development but also knew comparatively little about Aristotle, in most cases at least; but it also remains true that, whatever may have been the cause or causes, the Fathers tended to see in Plato a forerunner of Christianity and that the philosophic elements they adopted were adopted, for the most part, from the Platonic tradition. If one adds to this the further consideration that Patristic thought, especially that of Augustine, profoundly influenced, not only the early Middle Ages, not only such eminent thinkers as St. Anselm and St. Bonaventure, but even St. Thomas Aquinas himself, it will be seen that, from the historical viewpoint at least, some knowledge of Patristic thought is both desirable and valuable.

Chapter Three

ST. AUGUSTINE–I

Life and writings—St. Augustine and Philosophy.

1. In Latin Christendom the name of Augustine stands out as that of the greatest of the Fathers both from a literary and from a theological standpoint, a name that dominated Western thought until the thirteenth century and which can never lose its lustre, notwithstanding the Aristotelianism of St. Thomas Aquinas and his School, especially as this Aristotelianism was very far from disregarding and still further from belittling the great African Doctor. Indeed, in order to understand the currents of thought in the Middle Ages, a knowledge of Augustinianism is essential. In the present work the thought of Augustine cannot be treated with the fullness which it merits, but treated it must be, even if summarily.

Born at Tagaste in the Province of Numidia on November 13th, A.D. 354, Augustine came of a pagan father, Patricius, and a Christian mother, St. Monica. His mother brought up her child as a Christian, but Augustine's baptism was deferred, in accordance with a common, if undesirable, custom of the time.[1] The child learnt the rudiments of Latin and arithmetic from a schoolmaster of Tagaste, but play, at which he wished always to be the winner, was more attractive to him than study, and Greek, which he began after a time, he hated, though he was attracted by the Homeric poems considered as a story. That Augustine knew practically no Greek is untrue; but he never learned to read the language with ease.

In about A.D. 365 Augustine went to the town of Madaura, where he laid the foundation of his knowledge of Latin literature and grammar. Madaura was still largely a pagan place, and the effect of the general atmosphere and of his study of the Latin classics was evidently to detach the boy from the faith of his mother, a detachment which his year of idleness at Tagaste (369–70) did nothing to mitigate. In 370, the year in which his father died after having become a Catholic, Augustine began the study of rhetoric at Carthage, the largest city he had yet seen. The licentious ways of the great port and centre of government, the sight of the obscene rites connected with cults imported from the East, combined with the fact that Augustine, the southerner, was already a man, with passions alive and vehement, led to his practical break with the moral ideals of Christianity and before long he took a mistress, with whom he lived for over ten years and by whom he had a son in his second year at Carthage. In spite, however, of his irregular life Augustine was a very successful student of rhetoric and by no means neglected his studies.

It was soon after reading the *Hortensius* of Cicero, which turned the youth's mind to the search for truth, that Augustine accepted the teaching of the Manichaeans,[2] which seemed to offer him a rational presentation of truth, in distinction from the barbaric ideas and illogical doctrines of Christianity. Thus Christians maintained that God created the whole world and that God is good: how, then, could they explain the existence of evil and suffering? The Manichaeans, however, maintained a dualistic theory, according to which there are two ultimate principles, a good principle, that of light, God or Ormuzd, and an evil principle, that of darkness, Ahriman. These principles are both eternal and their strife is eternal, a strife reflected in the world which is the production of the two principles in mutual conflict. In man the soul, composed of light, is the work of the good principle, while the body, composed of grosser matter, is the work of the evil principle. This system commended itself in Augustine's eyes because it seemed to explain the problem of evil and because of its fundamental materialism, for he could not yet conceive how there could be an immaterial reality, imperceptible to the senses. Conscious of his own passions and sensual desires, he felt that he could now attribute them to an evil cause outside himself. Moreover, although the Manichaeans condemned sexual intercourse and the eating of flesh-meat and prescribed ascetic practices such as fasting, these practices obliged only the elect, not the 'hearers', to which level Augustine belonged.

Augustine, now detached from Christianity both morally and intellectually, returned to Tagaste in 374 and there taught grammar and Latin literature for a year, after which he opened a school of rhetoric at Carthage in the autumn of 374. He lived with his mistress and their child, Adeodatus, and it was during this period that he won a prize for poetry (a dramatic piece, not now extant) and published his first prose work, *De pulchro et apto*. The sojourn at Carthage lasted until 383 and it was shortly before Augustine's departure for Rome that an event of some importance occurred. Augustine had been troubled by difficulties and problems which the Manichaeans could not answer; for example, the problem of the source of certitude in human thought, the reason why the two principles were in eternal conflict, etc. It happened that a noted Manichaean bishop, Faustus by name, came to Carthage, and Augustine resolved to seek from him a satisfactory solution of his difficulties; but, though he found Faustus agreeable and friendly, he did not find in his words the intellectual satisfaction which he sought. It was, therefore, with his faith in Manichaeanism already somewhat shaken that he set out for Rome. He made the journey partly because the students at Carthage were ill-mannered and difficult to control, whereas he had heard good reports of the students' behaviour at Rome, partly because he hoped for greater success in his career in the imperial metropolis. Arrived at Rome, Augustine opened a school in rhetoric, but, though the students were well behaved in class, they had the inconvenient habit of changing their school just before the payment of fees was due. He accordingly sought for and obtained a position at Milan as municipal professor of rhetoric in 384; but he did not leave Rome without having lost most of his belief in Manichaeanism and having been consequently attracted towards Academic scepticism, though he retained a nominal adherence to Manichaeanism and still accepted some of the Manichaean positions, for example their materialism.

At Milan, Augustine came to think a little better of Christianity owing to the sermons on the Scriptures delivered by St. Ambrose, Bishop of Milan; but though he was ready to become a catechumen again, he was not yet convinced of the truth of Christianity. Moreover, his passions were still too strong for him. His mother wished him to marry a certain girl, hoping that marriage would help to reform his life; but, being unable to wait the necessary time for the girl in question, he took another mistress in place of the mother of Adeodatus, from whom he had parted in sorrow in view of the proposed marriage. At this time Augustine read certain 'Platonic' treatises in the Latin translation of Victorinus, these treatises being most probably the *Enneads* of Plotinus. The effect of neo-Platonism was to free him from the shackles of materialism and to facilitate his acceptance of the idea of immaterial reality. In addition, the Plotinian conception of evil as privation rather than as something positive showed him how the problem of evil could be met without having to have recourse to the dualism of the Manichaeans. In other words, the function of neo-Platonism at this period was to render it possible for Augustine to see the reasonableness of Christianity, and he began to read the New Testament again, particularly the writings of St. Paul. If neo-Platonism suggested to him the idea of the contemplation of spiritual things, of wisdom in the intellectual sense, the New Testament showed him that it was also necessary to lead a life in accordance with wisdom.

These impressions were confirmed by his meeting with two men, Simplicianus and Pontitianus. The former, an old priest, gave Augustine an account of the conversion of Victorinus, the neo-Platonist, to Christianity, with the result that the young man 'burned with the desire to do likewise',[3] while the latter spoke of the life of St. Anthony of Egypt, which made Augustine disgusted with his own moral state.[4] There followed that intense moral struggle, which culminated in the famous scene enacted in the garden of his house, when Augustine hearing a child's voice over a wall crying repeatedly the refrain *Tolle lege! Tolle lege!* opened the New Testament at random and lighted on the words of St. Paul in the Epistle to the Romans,[5] which sealed his moral conversion.[6] It is perfectly clear that the conversion which then took place was a moral conversion, a conversion of will, a conversion which followed the intellectual conversion. His reading of neo-Platonic works was an instrument in the intellectual conversion of Augustine, while his moral conversion, from the human viewpoint, was prepared by the sermons of Ambrose and the words of Simplicianus and Pontitianus, and confirmed and sealed by the New Testament. The agony of his second or moral conversion was intensified by the fact that he already knew what he ought to do, though on the other hand he felt himself without the power to accomplish it: to the words of St. Paul, however, which he read in the garden, he gave, under the impulse of grace, a 'real assent' and his life was changed. This conversion occurred in the summer of 386.

A lung ailment from which he was suffering gave Augustine the excuse he wanted to retire from his professorship and at Cassiciacum, through reading and reflection and discussions with friends, he endeavoured to obtain a better understanding of the Christian religion, using as an instrument concepts and themes taken from neo-Platonic philosophy, his idea of Christianity being still very incomplete and tinctured, more than it was to be later, by neo-Platonism. From this period of retirement date his works *Contra Academicos, De Beata Vita* and *De Ordine.* Returning to Milan Augustine wrote the *De Immortalitate Animae* (the *Soliloquia* were also written about this time) and began the *De Musica.* On Holy Saturday of 387 Augustine was baptised by St. Ambrose, soon after which event he set out to return to Africa. His mother, who had come over to Italy, died at Ostia, while they were waiting for a boat. (It was at Ostia that there occurred the celebrated scene described in the *Confessions.*[7]) Augustine delayed his return to Africa and while residing at Rome wrote the *De libero arbitrio,* the *De Quantitate Animae* and the *De moribus ecclesiae Catholicae et de moribus Manichaeorum.* In the autumn of 388 he set sail for Africa.

Back at Tagaste, Augustine established a small monastic community. From this period (388–91) date his *De Genesi contra Manichaeos, De Magistro* and *De Vera Religione,* while he completed the *De Musica.* It is probable that he also polished up or completed the *De moribus,* mentioned above. At Cassiciacum Augustine had resolved never to marry, but he did not apparently intend to seek ordination, for it was contrary to his own wishes that the Bishop of Hippo ordained him priest in 391, when he was on a visit to that seaport town, about a hundred and fifty miles due west of Carthage. The bishop desired Augustine's help, and the latter settled down at Hippo and established a monastery. Engaged in controversy with the Manichaeans he composed the *De utilitate credendi,* the *De duabus animabus,* the *Disputatio contra Fortunatum,* the *De Fide et Symbolo,* a lecture on the Creed delivered before a synod of African bishops, and, against the Donatists, the *Psalmus contra partem Donati*. He started a literal commentary on *Genesis*, but, as its name implies (*De Genesi ad litteram liber imperfectus*), left it unfinished. The *De diversis quaestionibus* (389–96), the *Contra Adimantum Manichaeum*, *De sermone Domini in monte*, the *De Mendacio* and *De Continentia*, as well as various Commentaries (on *Romans* and *Galatians*) also date from the early period of Augustine's priestly life.

In the year 395–6 Augustine was consecrated auxiliary Bishop of Hippo, setting up another monastic establishment within his residence very shortly after his consecration. When Valerius, Bishop of Hippo, died in 396, within a year of Augustine's consecration, he became ruling Bishop of Hippo in Valerius's place, and remained in that post until his death. This meant that he had to face the task of governing a diocese in which the Donatist schism was well entrenched instead of being able to devote himself to a life of quiet prayer and study. However, whatever his personal inclinations, Augustine threw himself into the anti-Donatist struggle with ardour, preaching, disputing, publishing anti-Donatist controversy. Nevertheless, in spite of this activity, he found time for composing such works as the *De diversis quaestionibus ad Simplicianum* (397), part of the *De Doctrina Christiana* (the fourth book being added in 426), part of the *Confessions* (the whole work being published by 400), and the *Annotationes in Job*. Augustine also exchanged controversial letters with the great scholar St. Jerome, on Scriptural matters.

In the year 400 St. Augustine started on one of his greatest treatises, the fifteen books *De Trinitate*, which were completed in 417, and in 401 began the twelve books of the *De Genesi ad litteram*, completed in 415. In the same year (400) appeared the *De catechizandis rudibus*, the *De Consensu Evangelistarum*, the *De Opera Monachorum*, the *Contra Faustum Manichaeum* (thirty-three books), the first book of the *Contra litteras Petiliani* (Donatist Bishop of Cirta), the second book dating from 401–2 and the third from 402–3. These were followed by other anti-Donatist works, such as the *Contra Cresconium grammaticum partis Donati* (402), though various publications have not been preserved, and several writings against the Manichaeans. In addition to this controversial activity Augustine was constantly preaching and writing letters: thus the letter to Dioscorus,[8] in which, in answer to certain questions about Cicero, Augustine develops his views on pagan philosophy, still showing a strong predilection for neo-Platonism, dates from 410.

Imperial edicts were issued in the course of time against the Donatists, and about the year 411, after the conference that then took place, Augustine was able to turn his attention to another set of opponents, the Pelagians. Pelagius, who exaggerated the rôle of human volition in man's salvation and minimised that of grace, denying original sin, visited Carthage in 410 accompanied by Coelestius. In 411, after Pelagius had left for the East, Coelestius was excommunicated by a Council at Carthage. Pelagius had tried to use texts from Augustine's *De libero arbitrio* in support of his own heresy, but the bishop made his position quite clear in his *De peccatorum meritis et remissione, et de baptismo parvulorum, ad Marcellinum*, following it up in the same year (412) by the *De spiritu et littera*, and later by the *De fide et operibus* (413), the *De natura et gratia contra Pelagium* (415) and the *De perfectione iustitiae hominis* (415). However, not content with his anti-Pelagian polemic, Augustine began, in 413, the twenty-two books of the *De Civitate Dei* (completed in 426), one of his greatest and most famous works, written against the background of the barbarian invasion of the Empire, and prepared many of his *Enarrationes in Psalmos*. In addition he published (415) the *Ad Orosium, contra Priscillianistas et Origenistas*, a book against the heresy started by the Spanish bishop, Priscillian, and in the course of further anti-Pelagian polemic the *De Gestis Pelagii* (417) and the *De Gratia Christi et peccato originali* (418). As if all this were not enough, Augustine finished the *De Trinitate*, and wrote his *In Joannis Evangelium* (416–7) and *In Epistolas Joannis ad Parthos* (416), not to speak of numerous letters and sermons.

In 418 Pelagianism was condemned, first by a Council of African bishops, then by the Emperor Honorius, and finally by Pope Zosimus, but the controversy was not yet over, and when Augustine was accused by Julian, heretical Bishop of Eclanum, of having invented the concept of original sin, the Saint replied in the work *De nuptiis et concupiscentia* (419–20), while in 420 he addressed two books, *Contra duas epistolas Pelagianorum ad Bonifatium Papam*, to the Pope, and followed them up by his *Contra Iulianum haeresis Pelagianae defensorem* (six books) in 421. The *De anima et eius origine* (419), the *Contra mendacium ad Consentium* (420), the *Contra adversarium Legis et Prophetarum* (420), the *Enchiridion ad Laurentium, De fide, spe, caritate* (421), the *De cura pro mortuis gerenda, ad Paulinum Nolanum* (420–1), also date from this period.

In 426 Augustine, feeling that he would not live very much longer, provided for the future of his diocese by nominating his successor, the priest Eraclius, the nomination being acclaimed by the people; but the Saint's literary activity was by no means over, and in 426–7 he published the *De gratia et libero arbitrio ad Valentinum*, the *De correptione et gratia* and the two books of *Retractationes*, which contain a critical survey of his works and are of great value for establishing their chronology. All this time the situation of the Empire was going from bad to worse, and in 429 Genseric led the Vandals from Spain into Africa; but Augustine continued writing. In 427 he published the *Speculum de Scriptura Sacra*, a selection of texts from the Bible, and in 428 his *De haeresibus ad Quodvultdeum*, followed by the *De praedestinatione sanctorum ad Prosperum* and the *De dono perseverantiae ad Prosperum* in 428–9. In addition, Augustine began the *Opus imperfectum contra Julianum* in 429, a refutation of an anti-Augustinian treatise by the Pelagian Julian which had been written some time previously but had come into the Saint's hands only in 428; but he did not live to finish the work (hence its name). Augustine also came into contact with Arianism, and in 428 appeared his *Collatio cum Maximino Arianorum episcopo* and his *Contra Maximinum haereticum*.

In the late spring or early summer of 430 the Vandals laid siege to Hippo, and it was during the siege that Augustine died on August 28th, 430, as he was reciting the Penitential Psalms. Possidius remarks that he left no will, since, as one of God's paupers, he had nothing to leave. The Vandals subsequently burnt the city, though the cathedral and the library of Augustine were left intact. Possidius wrote the Life of Augustine, which is to be found in the Latin Patrology. 'Those who read what he (Augustine) has written on divine things can profit much; but I think that they would profit more were they able to hear and see him preaching in the church, and especially those who were privileged to enjoy intimate conversation with him.'[9]

2. It may perhaps seem strange that I have spoken of St.

Augustine's theological controversies and listed a large number of theological treatises; but a sketch of his life and activity will suffice to make it plain that, with a few exceptions, Augustine did not compose purely philosophical works in our sense. In a book like this, one does not, of course, intend to treat of Augustine's purely theological doctrine, but, in order to elicit his philosophical teaching one has to have frequent recourse to what are primarily theological treatises. Thus, in order to obtain light on Augustine's theory of knowledge, it is necessary to consult the relevant texts of the *De Trinitate*, while the *De Genesi ad litteram* expounds the theory of *rationes seminales* and the *Confessions* contain a treatment of time. This mingling of theological and philosophical themes may appear odd and unmethodical to us to-day, used as we are to a clear distinction between the provinces of dogmatic theology and philosophy; but one must remember that Augustine, in common with other Fathers and early Christian writers, made no such clear distinction. It is not that Augustine failed to recognise, still less that he denied, the intellect's power of attaining truth without revelation; it is rather that he regarded the Christian wisdom as one whole, that he tried to penetrate by his understanding the Christian faith and to see the world and human life in the light of the Christian wisdom. He knew quite well that rational arguments can be adduced for God's existence, for example, but it was not so much the mere intellectual assent to God's existence that interested him as the real assent, the positive adhesion of the will to God, and he knew that in the concrete such an adhesion to God requires divine grace. In short, Augustine did not play two parts, the part of the theologian and the part of the philosopher who considers the 'natural man'; he thought rather of man as he is in the concrete, fallen and redeemed mankind, man who is able indeed to attain truth but who is constantly solicited by God's grace and who requires grace in order to appropriate the truth that saves. If there was question of convincing someone that God exists, Augustine would see the proof as a stage or as an instrument in the total process of the man's conversion and salvation: he would recognise the proof as *in itself* rational, but he would be acutely conscious, not only of the moral preparation necessary to give a real and living assent to the proof, but also of the fact that, according to God's intention for man in the concrete, recognition of God's existence is not enough, but should lead on, under the impulse of grace, to supernatural faith in God's revelation and to a life in accordance with Christ's teaching. Reason has its part to play in bringing a man to faith, and, once a man has the faith, reason has its part to play in penetrating the data of faith; but it is the total relation of the soul to God which primarily interests Augustine. Reason, as we have seen, had its part to play in the intellectual stage of his own conversion and reason had its part to play after his conversion: generalising his own experience, then, he would consider the fullness of wisdom to consist in a penetration of what is believed, though in the approach to wisdom reason helps to prepare a man for faith. 'The medicine for the soul, which is effected by the divine providence and ineffable beneficence, is perfectly beautiful in degree and distinction. For it is divided between Authority and Reason. Authority demands of us faith, and prepares man for reason. Reason leads to perception and cognition, although authority also does not leave reason wholly out of sight, when the question of who may be believed is being considered.'[10]

This attitude was characteristic of the Augustinian tradition. St. Anselm's aim is expressed in his words *Credo, ut intelligam*, while St. Bonaventure, in the thirteenth century, explicitly rejected the sharp delimitation of the spheres of theology and philosophy. The Thomist distinction between the sciences of dogmatic theology and philosophy, with the accompanying distinction of the modes of procedure to be employed in the two sciences, no doubt evolved inevitably out of the earlier attitude, though, quite apart from that consideration, it obviously enjoys this very great advantage that it corresponds to an actual and real distinction between revelation and the data of the 'unaided' reason, between the supernatural and natural spheres. It is at once a safeguard of the doctrine of the supernatural and also of the powers of man in the natural order. Yet the Augustinian attitude on the other hand enjoys this advantage, that it contemplates always man *as he is*, man in the concrete, for *de facto* man has only one final end, a supernatural end, and, as far as actual existence is concerned, there is but man fallen and redeemed: there never has been, is not, and never will be a purely 'natural man' without a supernatural vocation and end. If Thomism, without of course neglecting the fact that man in the concrete has but a supernatural end, places emphasis on the distinction between the supernatural and the natural, between faith and reason, Augustinianism, without in the least neglecting the gratuitous character of supernatural faith and grace, always envisages man in the concrete and is primarily interested in his actual relation to God.

This being so, it is only natural that we should have to unravel Augustine's 'purely philosophical' ideas from the total fabric of his thought. To do this is, of course, to survey Augustinianism more or less from a Thomist viewpoint, but that does not mean that it is an illegitimate approach: it means that one is asking what ideas of Augustine are philosophical in the academic understanding of the term. It does indeed mean tearing his ideas from their full context, but in a history of philosophy, which presupposes a certain idea of what philosophy is, one can do nothing else. It must, however, be admitted that a concentration of this sort on Augustine's philosophical ideas, using the word in the Thomist sense, tends to give a rather poor idea of the Saint's intellectual achievement, at least to one who is trained in the academic and objective atmosphere of Thomism, since he never elaborated a philosophical system as such, nor did he develop, define and substantiate his philosophical ideas in the manner to which a Thomist is accustomed. The result is that it is not infrequently difficult to say precisely what Augustine meant by this or that idea or statement, how precisely he understood it: there is often an aura of vagueness, allusion, lack of definition about his ideas which leaves one dissatisfied, perplexed and curious. The rigid type of Thomist would, I suppose, maintain that Augustine's philosophy contains nothing of value which was not much better said by St. Thomas, more clearly delineated and defined; but the fact remains that the Augustinian tradition is not dead even to-day, and it may be that the very incompleteness and lack of systematisation in Augustine's thought, its very 'suggestiveness', is a positive help towards the longevity of his tradition, for the 'Augustinian' is not faced by a complete system to be accepted, rejected or mutilated: he is faced by an approach, an inspiration, certain basic ideas which are capable of considerable development, so that he can remain perfectly faithful to the Augustinian spirit even though he departs from what the historic Augustine actually said.

Chapter Four

ST. AUGUSTINE—II: KNOWLEDGE

Knowledge with a view to beatitude—Against scepticism—
Experiential knowledge—Nature of sensation—Divine ideas—
Illumination and Abstraction.

1. To start with the 'epistemology' of St. Augustine is perhaps to give the impression that Augustine was concerned
with elaborating a theory of knowledge for its own sake or
as a methodological propaedeutic to metaphysics. This would
be a wrong impression, however, since Augustine never sat
down, as it were, to develop a theory of knowledge and then,
on the basis of a realist theory of knowledge, to construct a
systematic metaphysic. If Spinoza, according to his own
words,[1] aimed at developing the philosophy of God or Substance because it is only contemplation of an infinite and
eternal Object which can fully satisfy mind and heart and
bring happiness to the soul, far more could an analogous
statement be made of Augustine, who emphasised the fact
that knowledge of the truth is to be sought, not for purely
academic purposes, but as bringing true happiness, true beatitude. Man feels his insufficiency, he reaches out to an object
greater than himself, an object which can bring peace and
happiness, and knowledge of that object is an essential condition of its attainment; but he sees knowledge in function
of an end, beatitude. Only the wise man can be happy and
wisdom postulates knowledge of the truth; but there is no
question in Augustine's thought of speculation as an end in
itself. When the young man Licentius, in the *Contra Academicos*, maintains that wisdom consists in seeking for the
truth and declares, like Lessing, that happiness is to be found

rather in the pursuit of truth than in the actual attainment and possession of truth, Augustine retorts that it is absurd to predicate wisdom of a man who has no knowledge of truth. In the *De Beata Vita*[2] he says that no one is happy who does not possess what he strives to possess, so that the man who is seeking for truth but has not yet found it, cannot be said to be truly happy. Augustine himself sought for truth because he felt a need for it, and looking back on his development in the light of attainment, he interpreted this as a search for Christ and Christian wisdom, as the attraction of the divine beauty, and this experience he universalised. This universalisation of his own experience, however, does not mean that his ideas were purely subjective: his psychological introspection enabled him to lay bare the dynamism of the human soul.

Yet to say that Augustine was not an 'intellectualist' in an academic sense and that his philosophy is eudaemonistic is not to say that he was not acutely conscious of the problem of certitude. It would, however, be a mistake to think that Augustine was preoccupied with the question, '*Can* we attain certainty?' As we shall see shortly, he did answer this question, but the question that occupied his attention in the mature period of his thought was rather this, '*How* is it that we can attain certainty?' That we do attain certainty being assumed as a datum, the problem remains: 'How does the finite, changing human mind attain certain knowledge of eternal truths, truths which rule and govern the mind and so transcend it?' After the breakdown of his faith in Manichaeanism, Augustine was tempted to relapse into Academic scepticism: his victory over this temptation he expressed in the *Contra Academicos*, where he shows that we indubitably do attain certainty of some facts at least. This granted, his reading of 'Platonic works' suggested to him the problem, how it is that we are able not only to know with certainty eternal and necessary truths, but also to know them as eternal and necessary truths. Plato explained this fact by the theory of reminiscence; how was Augustine to explain it? The discussion of the problem no doubt interested him in itself, for its own sake; but he also saw in what he considered to be the right answer a clear proof of God's existence and operation. The knowledge of eternal truth should thus bring the soul, by reflection on that knowledge, to knowledge of God Himself and God's activity.

2. As I have already said, in the *Contra Academicos* Augustine is primarily concerned to show that wisdom pertains to happiness, and knowledge of truth to wisdom; but he also makes it clear that even the Sceptics are certain of some truths, for example, that of two disjunctive propositions one is true and the other false. 'I am certain that there is either one world or more than one world, and, if more than one, then that there is either a finite or an infinite number of worlds.' Similarly I know that the world either has no beginning or end or has a beginning but no end or had no beginning but will have an end or has both a beginning and an end. In other words, I am at least certain of the principle of contradiction.[3] Again, even if I am sometimes deceived in thinking that appearance and reality always correspond, I am at least certain of my subjective impression. 'I have no complaint to make of the senses, for it is unjust to demand of them more than they can give: whatever the eyes can see they see truly. Then is that true which they see in the case of the oar in the water? Quite true. For, granted the cause why it appears in that way (i.e. bent), if the oar, when plunged into the water, appeared straight, I should rather accuse my eyes of playing me false. For they would not see what, granted the circumstances, they ought to see. . . . But I am deceived, if I give my assent, someone will say. Then don't give assent to more than the fact of appearance, and you won't be deceived. For I do not see how the sceptic can refute the man who says, "I know that this object seems white to me, I know that this sound gives me pleasure, I know this smell is pleasant to me, I know that this tastes sweet to me, I know that this feels cold to my touch."'[4] St. Augustine refers in the above passage to the Epicureans and it is clear that what he means is that the senses as such never lie or deceive us, even if we may deceive ourselves in judging that things exist objectively in the same way that they appear. The mere appearance of the bent oar is not deception, for there would be something wrong with my eyes were it to appear straight. If I go on to judge that the oar is really bent in itself, I am wrong, but as long as I simply say, 'It appears to me bent', I am speaking the truth and I know that I am speaking the truth. Similarly, if I come out of a hot room and put my hand in tepid water, it may seem to me cold, but as long as I merely say, 'This water *seems* cold to me', I am saying

something the truth of which I am certain of, and no sceptic can refute me.

Again, everyone who doubts knows that he is doubting, so that he is certain of this truth at least, namely the fact that he doubts. Thus everyone who doubts whether there is such a thing as truth, knows at least one truth, so that his very capacity to doubt should convince him that there is such a thing as truth.[5] We are certain, too, of mathematical truths. When anyone says that seven and three make ten, he does not say that they ought to make ten, but knows that they do make ten.[6]

3. But what of real existences? Are we certain of the existence of any real object or are we confined to certain knowledge of abstract principles and mathematical truths? Augustine answers that a man is at least certain of his existence. Even supposing that he doubts of the existence of other created objects or of God, the very fact of his doubt shows that he exists, for he could not doubt, did he not exist. Nor is it of any use to suggest that one might be deceived into thinking that one exists, for 'if you did not exist, you could not be deceived in anything.'[7] In this way St. Augustine anticipates Descartes: Si fallor, sum.

With existence Augustine couples life and understanding. In the De libero arbitrio[8] he points out that it is clear to a man that he exists, and that this fact would not and could not be clear, unless he were alive. Moreover, it is clear to him that he understands both the fact of his existence and the fact that he is living. Accordingly he is certain of three things, that he exists, that he lives and that he understands. Similarly, in the De Trinitate,[9] he observes that it is useless for the sceptic to insinuate that the man is asleep and sees these things in his dreams, for the man is affirming not that he is awake but that he lives: 'whether he be asleep or awake he lives.' Even if he were mad, he would still be alive. Again, a man is certainly conscious of what he wills. If someone says that he wills to be happy, it is mere impudence to suggest to him that he is deceived. Sceptical philosophers may babble about the bodily senses and the way in which they deceive us, but they cannot invalidate that certain knowledge which the mind has by itself, without the intervention of the sense.[10] 'We exist and we know that we exist and we love that fact and our knowledge of it; in these three things which I have enumerated no fear of deception disturbs us; for we do not attain them by any bodily sense, as we do external objects.'[11]

Augustine thus claims certainty for what we know by inner experience, by self-consciousness: what does he think of our knowledge of external objects, the things we know by the senses? Have we certainty in their regard? That we can deceive ourselves in our judgements concerning the objects of the senses Augustine was well aware, and some of his remarks show that he was conscious of the relativity of sense-impressions, in the sense that a judgement as to hot or cold, for example, depends to a certain extent on the condition of the sense-organs: moreover, he did not consider that the objects apprehensible by the senses constitute the proper object of the human intellect. Being chiefly interested in the soul's orientation to God, corporeal objects appeared to him as a starting-point in the mind's ascent to God, though even in this respect the soul itself is a more adequate starting-point: we should return within ourselves, where truth abides, and use the soul, the image of God, as a stepping-stone to Him.[12] Nevertheless, even if corporeal things, the objects of the senses, are essentially mutable and are far less adequate manifestations of God than is the soul, even if it is through concentration on the things of sense that the most harmful errors arise, we are dependent on the senses for a great deal of our knowledge and Augustine had no intention of maintaining a purely sceptical attitude in regard to the objects of the senses. It is one thing to admit the possibility of error in sense-knowledge and quite another to refuse any credence at all to the senses. Thus, after saying that philosophers may speak against the senses but cannot refute the consciousness of self-existence, Augustine goes on at once to say, 'far be it from us to doubt the truth of what we have learned by the bodily senses; since by them we have learned to know the heaven and the earth.' We learn much on the testimony of others, and the fact that we are sometimes deceived is no warrant for disbelieving all testimony: so the fact that we are sometimes deceived in regard to the objects of our senses is no warrant for complete scepticism. 'We must acknowledge that not only our own senses, but those of other persons too, have added very much to our knowledge.'[13] For practical life it is necessary to give credence to the senses,[14] and the man who thinks that we should never believe the senses falls into a worse error than any error he may fall into through believing them. Augustine thus says that we 'believe' the senses, that we give credence to them, as we give credence to the testimony of others, but he often uses the word 'believe' in opposition to direct inner knowledge, without meaning to imply that such 'belief' is void of adequate motive. Thus when someone tells me a fact about his own mental state, for example, that he understands or wishes this or that, I 'believe': when he says something that is true of the human mind itself, not simply of his own mind in particular, 'I recognise and give my assent, for I know by self-consciousness and introspection that what he says is true.'[15] In fine, Augustine may have anticipated Descartes by his '*Si fallor, sum*', but he was not occupied with the question whether the external world really exists or not. That it exists, he felt no doubt, though he saw clearly enough that we sometimes make erroneous judgements about it and that testimony is not always reliable, whether it be testimony of our own senses or of other people. As he was especially interested in the knowledge of eternal truths and in the relation of that knowledge to God, it would hardly occur to him to devote very much time to a consideration of our knowledge of the mutable things of sense. The fact of the matter is that his 'Platonism', coupled with his spiritual interest and outlook, led him to look on corporeal objects as not being the proper object of knowledge, owing to their mutability and to the fact that our knowledge of them is dependent on bodily organs of sense which are no more always in the same state than the objects themselves. If we have not got 'true knowledge' of sense-objects, that is due, not merely to any deficiency in the subject but also to a radical deficiency in the object. In other words, Augustine's attitude to sense-knowledge is much more Platonic than Cartesian.[16]

4. The lowest level of knowledge is, therefore, that of sense-knowledge, dependent on sensation, sensation being regarded by Augustine, in accordance with his Platonic psychology, as an act of the soul using the organs of sense as its instruments. *Sentire non est corporis sed animae per corpus.* The soul animates the whole body, but when it increases or intensifies its activity in a particular part, i.e. in a particular sense-organ, it exercises the power of sensation.[17] From this theory it would seem to follow that any deficiency in sense-knowledge must proceed from the mutability both of the instrument of sensation, the sense-organ, and of the object of

sensation, and this is indeed what Augustine thought. The rational soul of man exercises true knowledge and attains true certainty when it contemplates eternal truths in and through itself: when it turns towards the material world and uses corporeal instruments it cannot attain true knowledge. Augustine assumed, with Plato, that the objects of true knowledge are unchanging, from which it necessarily follows that knowledge of changing objects is not true knowledge. It is a type of knowledge or grade of knowledge which is indispensable for practical life; but the man who concentrates on the sphere of the mutable thereby neglects the sphere of the immutable, which is the correlative object of the human soul in regard to knowledge in the full sense.

Sensation in the strict sense is common, of course, to men and brutes; but men can have and do have a rational knowledge of corporeal things. In the *De Trinitate*[18] St. Augustine points out that the beasts are able to sense corporeal things and remember them and to seek after what is helpful, avoiding what is harmful, but that they cannot commit things to memory deliberately nor recall them at will nor perform any other operation which involves the use of reason; so that, in regard to knowledge of sense-objects, human knowledge is essentially superior to that of the brute. Moreover, man is able to make rational judgements concerning corporeal things and to perceive them as approximations to eternal standards. For instance, if a man judges that one object is more beautiful than another, his comparative judgement (granted the objective character of the beautiful) implies a reference to an eternal standard of beauty, while a judgement that this or that line is more or less straight, that this figure is a well-drawn circle, implies a reference to ideal straightness and the perfect geometrical circle. In other words, such comparative judgements involve a reference to 'ideas' (not to be understood as purely subjective). 'It is the part of the higher reason to judge of these corporeal things according to incorporeal and eternal considerations, which, if they were not above the human mind, would certainly not be immutable. And yet, unless something of our own were subjoined to them, we should not be able to employ them as standards by which to judge of corporeal things. . . . But that faculty of our own which is thus concerned with the treatment of corporeal and temporal things, is indeed rational, in that it is not common to us and the beasts, but is drawn, as it were, out of the rational substance of our mind, by which we depend upon and adhere to the intelligible and immutable truth and which is deputed to handle and direct the inferior things.'[19]

What St. Augustine means is this. The lowest level of knowledge, so far as it can be called knowledge, is sensation, which is common to men and brutes; and the highest level of knowledge, peculiar to man, is the contemplation of eternal things (wisdom) by the mind alone, without the intervention of sensation; but between these two levels is a kind of half-way house, in which mind judges of corporeal objects according to eternal and incorporeal standards. This level of knowledge is a rational level, so that it is peculiar to man and is not shared by brutes; but it involves the use of the senses and concerns sensible objects, so that it is a lower level than that of direct contemplation of eternal and incorporeal objects. Moreover, this lower use of reason is directed towards action, whereas wisdom is contemplative not practical. 'The action by which we make good use of temporal things differs from the contemplation of eternal things, and the former is classed as knowledge, the latter as wisdom. . . . In this distinction it must be understood that wisdom pertains to contemplation, knowledge to action.'[20] The ideal is that contemplative wisdom should increase, but at the same time our reason has to be partly directed to the good use of mutable and corporeal things, 'without which this life does not go on', provided that in our attention to temporal things we make it subserve the attainment of eternal things, 'passing lightly over the former, but cleaving to the latter'.[21]

This outlook is markedly Platonic in character. There is the same depreciation of sense-objects in comparison with eternal and immaterial realities, the same almost grudging admission of practical knowledge as a necessity of life, the same insistence on 'theoretic' contemplation, the same insistence on increasing purification of soul and liberation from the slavery of the senses to accompany the epistemological ascent. Yet it would be a mistake to see in Augustine's attitude a mere adoption of Platonism and nothing more. Platonic and neo-Platonic themes are certainly utilised, but Augustine's interest is always first and foremost that of the attainment of man's supernatural end, beatitude, in the possession and vision of God, and in spite of the intellectualist way of speaking which he sometimes uses and which he adopted from the Platonic tradition, in the total scheme of his thought the primacy is always given to love: *Pondus meum, amor meus*.[22] It is true that even this has its analogy in Platonism, but it must be remembered that for Augustine the goal is the attainment, not of an impersonal Good but of a personal God. The truth of the matter is that he found in Platonism doctrines which he considered admirably adapted for the exposition of a fundamentally Christian philosophy of life.

5. The objects of sense, corporeal things, are inferior to the human intellect, which judges of them in relation to a standard in reference to which they fall short; but there are other objects of knowledge which are above the human mind, in the sense that they are discovered by the mind, which necessarily assents to them and does not think of amending them or judging that they should be otherwise than they are. For example, I see some work of art and I judge it to be more or less beautiful, a judgement which implies not only the existence of a standard of beauty, an objective standard, but also my knowledge of the standard, for how could I judge that this arch or that picture is imperfect, deficient in beauty, unless I had some knowledge of the standard of beauty, of beauty itself, the idea of beauty? How could my supposedly objective judgement be justified unless there were an objective standard, not mutable and imperfect, like beautiful *things*, but immutable, constant, perfect and eternal?[23] Again, the geometer considers perfect circles and lines, and judges of the approximate circles and lines according to that perfect standard. Circular things are temporal and pass away, but the nature of circularity in itself, the idea of the circle, its essence, does not change. Again, we may add seven apples and three apples and make ten apples, and the apples which we count are sensible and mutable objects, are temporal and pass away; but the numbers seven and three considered in themselves and apart from things are discerned by the arithmetician to make ten by addition, a truth which he discovers to be necessary and eternal, not dependent on the sensible world or on the human mind.[24] These eternal truths are common to all. Whereas sensations are private, in the sense that, e.g., what seems cold to one man does not necessarily seem cold to another, mathematical truths are common to all and the individual mind has to accept them and recognise their possession of an absolute truth and validity which is independent of its own reactions.

Augustine's attitude in this matter is obviously Platonic. The standards of goodness and beauty, for example, correspond to Plato's first principles or ἀρχαί the exemplary ideas, while the ideal geometrical figures correspond to Plato's mathematical objects, τὰ μαθηματικά the objects of διάνοια. The same question which could be raised in regard to the Platonic theory recurs again, therefore, in regard to the Augustinian theory, namely, 'Where are these ideas?' (Of course, one must remember, in regard to both thinkers, that the 'ideas' in question are not subjective ideas but objective essences, and that the query 'where?' does not refer to locality, since the 'ideas' are *ex hypothesi* immaterial, but rather to what one might call ontological situation or status.) Neo-Platonists, seeing the difficulty in accepting a sphere of impersonal immaterial essences, i.e. the condition *apparently* at least assigned to the essences in Plato's published works, interpreted the Platonic ideas as thoughts of God and 'placed' them in *Nous*, the divine mind, which emanates from the One as the first proceeding hypostasis. (Compare Philo's theory of the ideas as contained within the Logos.) We may say that Augustine accepted this position, if we allow for the fact that he did not accept the emanation theory of neo-Platonism. The exemplar ideas and eternal truths are in God. 'The ideas are certain archetypal forms or stable and immutable essences of things, which have not themselves been formed but, existing eternally and without change, are contained in the divine intelligence.'[25] This theory must be accepted if one wishes to avoid having to say that God created the world unintelligently.[26]

6. A difficulty, however, immediately arises. If the human mind beholds the exemplar ideas and eternal truths, and if these ideas and truths are in the mind of God, does it not follow that the human mind beholds the essence of God, since the divine mind, with all that it contains, is ontologically identical with the divine essence? Some writers have believed that Augustine actually meant this. Among philosophers, Malebranche claimed the support of Augustine for his theory that the mind beholds the eternal ideas in God, and he tried to escape from the seemingly logical conclusion that in this case the human mind beholds the essence of God, by saying that the mind sees, not the divine essence as it is in itself (the supernatural vision of the blessed) but the divine essence as participable *ad extra*, as exemplar of creation. The

ontologists too claim the support of Augustine for their theory of the soul's immediate intuition of God.

Now, it is impossible to deny that some texts of Augustine taken by themselves favour such an interpretation. But, granting that Augustine seems on occasion to teach ontologism, it seems clear to me that, if one takes into account the totality of his thought, such an interpretation is inadmissible. I should certainly not be so bold as to suggest that Augustine was never inconsistent, but what I do believe is that the ontologistic interpretation of Augustine fits in so badly with his spiritual doctrine that, if there are other texts which favour a non-ontologistic interpretation (and there are such texts), one should attribute a secondary position and a subordinate value to the apparently ontologistic texts. Augustine was perfectly well aware that a man may discern eternal and necessary truths, mathematical principles, for example, without being a good man at all: such a man may not see these truths in their ultimate Ground, but he undoubtedly discerns the truths. Now, how can Augustine possibly have supposed that such a man beholds the essence of God, when in his spiritual doctrine he insists so much on the need of moral purification in order to draw near to God and is well aware that the vision of God is reserved to the saved in the next life? Again, a man who is spiritually and morally far from God can quite well appreciate the fact that Canterbury Cathedral is more beautiful than a Nissen hut, just as St. Augustine himself could discern degrees of sensible beauty before his conversion. In a famous passage of the *Confessions* he exclaims: 'Too late am I come to love Thee, O thou Beauty, so ancient and withal so new; too late am I come to love Thee . . . in a deformed manner I cast myself upon the things of Thy creation, which yet Thou hadst made fair.'[27] Similarly, in the *De quantitate animae*[28] he clearly affirms that the contemplation of Beauty comes at the end of the soul's ascent. In view of this teaching, then, it seems to me inconceivable that Augustine thought that the soul, in apprehending eternal and necessary truths, actually apprehends the very content of the divine mind. The passages which appear to show that he did so think can be explained as due to his adoption of Platonic or neo-Platonic expressions which do not, literally taken, fit in with the general direction of his thought. It does not seem possible to state exactly how Augustine conceived of the status of the eternal truths as apprehended by the human mind (the ontological side of the question he probably never worked out); but, rather than accept a purely neo-Platonic or an ontologistic interpretation, it seems to me preferable to suppose that the eternal truths and ideas, as they are in God, perform an ideogenetic function; that it is rather that the 'light' which comes from God to the human mind enables the mind to see the characteristics of changelessness and necessity in the eternal truths.

One may add, however, a further consideration against an ontologistic interpretation of Augustine. The Saint utilised the apprehension of eternal and necessary truths as a proof for the existence of God, arguing that these truths require an immutable and eternal Ground. Without going any further into this argument at the moment it is worth pointing out that, if the argument is to have any sense, it clearly presupposes the possibility of the mind's perceiving these truths without at the same time perceiving God, perhaps while doubting or even denying God's existence. If Augustine is prepared to say to a man, 'You doubt or deny God's existence, but you must admit that you recognise absolute truths, and I shall prove to you that the recognition of such truths implies God's existence,' he can scarcely have supposed that the doubter or atheist had any vision of God or of the actual contents of the divine mind. This consideration seems to me to rule out the ontologistic interpretation. But before pursuing this subject any further it is necessary to say something of Augustine's theory of illumination, as this may make it easier to understand his position, though it must be admitted that the interpretation of this theory is itself somewhat uncertain.

7. We cannot, says Augustine, perceive the immutable truth of things unless they are illuminated as by a sun.[29] This divine light, which illumines the mind, comes from God, who is the 'intelligible light', in whom and by whom and through whom all those things which are luminous to the intellect become luminous.[30] In this doctrine of light, common to the Augustinian School, Augustine makes use of a neo-Platonic theme which goes back to Plato's comparison of the Idea of the Good with the sun,[31] the Idea of the Good irradiating the subordinate intelligible objects or Ideas. For Plotinus the One or God is the sun, the transcendent light. The use of the light-metaphor, however, does not by itself tell us very clearly what Augustine meant. Happily we

have to help us such texts as the passage of the *De Trini-tate*[32] where the Saint says that the nature of the mind is such that, 'when directed to intelligible things in the natural order, according to the disposition of the Creator, it sees them in a certain incorporeal light which is *sui generis,* just as the corporeal eye sees adjacent objects in the corporeal light'. These words seem to show that the illumination in question is a spiritual illumination which performs the same func-tion for the objects of the mind as the sun's light per-forms for the objects of the eye: in other words, as the sun-light makes corporeal things visible to the eye, so the divine illumination makes the eternal truths visible to the mind. From this it would appear to follow that it is not the illumi-nation itself which is seen by the mind, nor the intelligible Sun, God, but that the characteristics of necessity and eter-nity in the necessary and eternal truths are made visible to the mind by the activity of God. This is certainly not an ontologistic theory.

But why did St. Augustine postulate such an illumination; why did he think it necessary? Because the human mind is changeable and temporal, so that what is unchangeable and eternal transcends it and seems to be beyond its capacity. 'When the human mind knows and loves itself, it does not know and love anything immutable,'[33] and if truth 'were equal to our minds, it also would be mutable', for our minds see the truth, now more now less, and by this very fact show themselves to be mutable. In fact, truth is neither inferior nor equal to our minds, but 'superior and more excellent'.[34] We need, therefore, a divine illumination, in order to enable us to apprehend what transcends our minds, 'for no crea-ture, howsoever rational and intellectual, is lighted of itself, but is lighted by participation of eternal Truth'.[35] 'God hath created man's mind rational and intellectual, whereby he may take in His light . . . and He so enlighteneth it of Him-self, that not only those things which are displayed by the truth, but even truth itself may be perceived by the mind's eye.'[36] This light shines upon the truths and renders visible to the mutable and temporal human mind their characteris-tics of changelessness and eternity.

That the divine illumination is something imparted and *sui generis* is explicitly stated by St. Augustine, as we have seen. It hardly seems possible, therefore, to reduce the illu-mination-theory to nothing more than a statement of the truth that God conserves and creates the human intellect and that the natural light of the intellect is a participated light. Thomists, who wish to show St. Augustine the same reverence that St. Thomas showed him, are naturally reluctant to admit a radical difference of opinion between the two great theologians and philosophers and are inclined to interpret St. Augustine in a way that would attenuate the difference between his thought and that of St. Thomas; but St. Augustine most emphatically did not mean by 'light' the intellect itself or its activity, even with the ordinary concurrence of God, since it is precisely because of the deficiencies of the human intellect that he postulated the existence and activity of the divine illumination. To say that St. Augustine was wrong in postulating a special divine illumination and that St. Thomas was right in denying the necessity of such an illumination is an understandable attitude; but it seems to be carrying conciliation too far, if one attempts to maintain that both thinkers were saying the same thing, even if one affirms that St. Thomas was saying clearly and unambiguously what St. Augustine had said obscurely and with the aid of metaphor.

I have already indicated that I accept the interpretation of Augustine's thought, according to which the function of the divine illumination is to render visible to the mind the element of necessity in the eternal truths, and that I reject the ontologistic interpretation in any form. This rejection obviously involves the rejection of the view that according to Augustine the mind beholds directly the idea of beauty, for example, as it is in God; but I am also unwilling to accept the view that according to Augustine God actually infuses the idea of beauty or any other normative idea (i.e. in reference to which we make comparative judgements of degree, such as that this object is more beautiful than that, this action juster than that, etc.) ready-made into the mind. This extreme ideogenetic view would make the function of divine illumination that of a kind of separate active intellect: in fact, God would Himself be an ontologically separate active intellect which infuses ideas into the human mind without any part being played by the human sensibility or intellect other than the mind's purely passive rôle. (This reference to an active intellect is not, of course, meant to imply that Augustine thought or spoke in terms of the Aristotelian psychology.) It does not seem to me that such an interpretation, although doubtless much can be said for it,[37] is altogether satisfactory. According to St. Augustine, the activity of the divine illumination in regard to the mind is analogous to the function of the sun's light in regard to vision, and though the sunlight renders corporeal objects visible, Augustine certainly did not think of it as creating images of the objects in the human subject. Again, although the divine illumination takes the place in Augustine's thought of reminiscence in the Platonic philosophy, so that the illumination would seem to fulfil some ideogenetic function, it must be remembered that Augustine's problem is one concerning *certitude*, not one concerning the content of our concepts or ideas: it concerns far more the form of the certain judgement and the form of the normative idea than the actual content of the judgement or the idea. In the *De Trinitate*[38] Augustine remarks that the mind 'gathers the knowledge of corporeal things through the senses of the body', and, so far as he deals at all with the formation of the concept, he would seem to consider that the human mind discerns the intelligible in the sensible, performing what is in some way at least equivalent to abstraction. But when it comes to discerning that a corporeal thing is, for example, more or less beautiful, to judging the object according to a changeless standard, the mind judges under the light of the regulative action of the eternal Idea, which is not itself visible to the mind. Beauty itself illuminates the mind's activity in such a way that it can discern the greater or less approximation of the object to the standard, though the mind does not behold Beauty itself directly. It is in this sense that the illumination of Augustine supplies the function of Plato's reminiscence. Again, though Augustine does not clearly indicate *how we obtain* the notions of seven and three and ten, the function of illumination is not to infuse the notions of these numbers but so to illuminate the judgement that seven and three make ten that we discern the necessity and eternity of the judgement. From a passage already referred to,[39] as from other passages,[40] it seems to follow that, while we obtain the concept of corporeal objects, a horse, for example, in dependence on the senses, and of an immaterial object like the soul through self-consciousness and interpretation, our certain judgements concerning these objects are made in the light of 'illumination' under the regulative action of the eternal Ideas. If the illumination has an ideogenetic function, as I believe it to have in Augustine's view, then this function has reference not to the content of the concept, as if it infused that content, but to the quality of our judgement concerning the concept or to our discernment of a character in the object, its relation to the norm or standard, which is not contained in the bare notion of the thing. If this is so, then the difference between St. Augustine and St. Thomas does not so much consist in their respective attitudes towards abstraction (since, whether Augustine explicitly says so or not, his view, as interpreted above, would at least *demand* abstraction in some form) as in the fact that Augustine thought it necessary to postulate a special illuminative action of God, beyond His creative and conserving activity, in the mind's realisation of eternal and necessary truths, whereas St. Thomas did not.

On this view of illumination one can understand how it was that St. Augustine regarded the qualities of necessity and unchangeability in the eternal truths as constituting a proof of God's existence, whereas it would be inexplicable on the ontologistic interpretation, since, if the mind perceives God or the divine ideas directly, it can need no proof of God's existence. That Augustine did not explain in detail how the content of the concept is formed, may be regrettable, but it is none the less understandable, since, though interested in psychological observation, he was interested therein, not from an academic motive, but rather from spiritual and religious motives: it was the soul's relation to God which concerned him primarily and, while the necessity and unchangeability of the eternal truths (as contrasted with the contingency and changeability of the human mind) and the doctrine of illumination helped to set this relation in a clear light and to stimulate the soul in its Godward direction, an investigation concerning the formation of the concept as such would not have had such a clear relation to the *Noverim me, noverim Te.*

To sum up. St. Augustine asks himself the question, How is it that we attain knowledge of truths which are necessary, immutable and eternal? That we do attain such knowledge is clear to him from experience. We cannot gain such knowledge simply from sense-experience, since corporeal objects are contingent, changeable and temporal. Nor can we produce the truths from our minds, which are also contingent and changeable. Moreover, such truths rule and dominate our minds, impose themselves upon our minds, and they would not do this if they depended on us. It follows that we are enabled to perceive such truths under the action of the Being who alone is necessary, changeless and eternal, God. God is like a sun which illumines our minds or a master who teaches us. At this point the difficulty in interpretation begins. The present writer inclines to the interpretation that, while the content of our concepts of corporeal objects is derived from sense-experience and reflection thereon, the regulative influence of the divine ideas (which means the influence of God) enables man to see the relation of created things to eternal supersensible realities, of which there is no direct vision in this life, and that God's light enables the mind to discern the elements of necessity, immutability and eternity in that relation between concepts which is expressed in the necessary judgement. Owing, however, to St. Augustine's use of metaphor and to the fact that he was not primarily interested in giving a systematic and carefully defined 'scholastic' account of the process of knowledge, it does not seem possible to obtain a definitive interpretation of his thought which would adequately explain all the statements he made.

Chapter Five

ST. AUGUSTINE—III: GOD

Proof of God from eternal truths—Proofs from creatures and from universal consent—The various proofs as stages in one process—Attributes of God—Exemplarism.

1. It is probably true to say that the central and favourite proof of God's existence given by St. Augustine is that from thought, i.e. a proof from within. The starting-point of this proof is the mind's apprehension of necessary and changeless truths, of a truth 'which thou canst not call thine, or mine, or any man's, but which is present to all and gives itself to all alike.'[1] This truth is superior to the mind, inasmuch as the mind has to bow before it and accept it: the mind did not constitute it, nor can it amend it: the mind recognises that this truth transcends it and rules its thought rather than the other way round. If it were inferior to the mind, the mind could change it or amend it, while if it were equal to the mind, of the same character, it would itself be changeable, as the mind is changeable. The mind varies in its apprehension of truth, apprehending it now more clearly now less clearly, whereas truth remains ever the same. 'Hence if truth is neither inferior nor equal to our minds, nothing remains but that it should be superior and more excellent.'[2]

But the eternal truths must be founded on being, reflecting the Ground of all truth. Just as human imaginations reflect the imperfection and changeable character of the human mind in which they are grounded, and as the impressions of sense reflect the corporeal objects in which they are grounded, so the eternal truths reveal their Ground, Truth itself, reflecting the necessity and immutability of God. This refers to all essential standards. If we judge of an action that it is more or less just, for example, we judge of it according to an essential and invariable standard, essence or 'idea': human actions in the concrete may vary, but the standard remains the same. It is in the light of the eternal and perfect standard that we judge of concrete acts, and this standard must be grounded in the eternal and all-perfect Being. If there is an intelligible sphere of absolute truths, this cannot be conceived without a Ground of truth, 'the Truth, in whom, and by whom, and through whom those things are true which are true in every respect'.[3]

This argument to God as the Ground of eternal and necessary truth was not only accepted by the 'Augustinian School', but reappears in the thought of several eminent philosophers, like Leibniz.

2. St. Augustine does indeed prove the existence of God from the external, corporeal world; but his words on the subject are rather of the nature of hints or reminders or summary statements than developed proofs in the academic sense: he was not so much concerned to prove to the atheist that God exists as to show how all creation proclaims the God whom the soul can experience in itself, the living God. It was the dynamic attitude of the soul towards God which interested him, not the construction of dialectical arguments with a purely theoretical conclusion. To acknowledge with a purely intellectual assent that a supreme Being exists is one thing; to bring that truth home to oneself is something more. The soul seeks happiness and many are inclined to seek it outside themselves: St. Augustine tries to show that creation cannot give the soul the perfect happiness it seeks, but points upwards to the living God who must be sought within. This basically religious and spiritual attitude must be borne in mind, if one is to avoid first looking on Augustine's proofs as dialectical proofs in a theoretic sense and then belittling them as inadequate and trifling statements of what St. Thomas was to express much better. The purposes of the two men were not precisely the same.

Thus when Augustine, commenting on Psalm 73, remarks, 'How do I know that thou art alive, whose soul I see not? How do I know? Thou wilt answer, Because I speak, because I walk, because I work. Fool! by the operations of the body I know thee to be living, canst thou not by the works of creation know the Creator?' he is indeed stating the proof of

God's existence from His effects; but he is not setting out to develop the proof for its own sake, as it were: he brings it in by way of commentary in the course of his Scriptural exegesis. Similarly, when he asserts in the *De Civitate Dei*[4] that 'the very order, disposition, beauty, change and motion of the world and of all visible things silently proclaim that it could only have been made by God, the ineffably and invisibly great and the ineffably and invisibly beautiful', he is rather reminding Christians of a fact than attempting to give a systematic proof of God's existence. Again, when Augustine, commenting on Genesis,[5] states that 'the power of the Creator and His omnipotent and all-swaying strength is for each and every creature the cause of its continued existence, and if this strength were at any time to cease from directing the things which have been created, at one and the same time both their species would cease to be and their whole nature would perish . . . ', he is stating the fact and necessity of divine conservation, reminding his readers of an acknowledged fact, rather than proving it philosophically.

Augustine gives, again in very brief form, what is known as the argument from universal consent. 'Such', he says, 'is the power of true Godhead that it cannot be altogether and utterly hidden from the rational creature, once it makes use of its reason. For, with the exception of a few in whom nature is excessively depraved, the whole human race confesses God to be the author of the world.'[6] Even if a man thinks that a plurality of gods exists, he still attempts to conceive 'the one God of gods' as 'something than which nothing more excellent or more sublime exists. . . . All concur in believing God to be that which excels in dignity all other objects.'[7] No doubt St. Anselm was influenced by these words of Augustine when he took as the universal idea of God in the 'ontological argument' 'that than which no greater can be conceived'.

3. Professor Gilson, in his *Introduction à l'étude de Saint Augustin*,[8] remarks that in the thought of St. Augustine there is really one long proof of God's existence, a proof which consists of various stages.[9] Thus from the stage of initial doubt and its refutation through the *Si fallor, sum*, which is a kind of methodical preliminary to the search for truth, assuring the mind of the attainability of truth, the soul proceeds to consider the world of sense. In this world, however, it does not discover the truth which it seeks and so

it turns inwards, where, after considering its own fallibility
and changeableness, it discovers immutable truth which
transcends the soul and does not depend on the soul. It is
thus led to the apprehension of God as the Ground of all
truth.

The picture of Augustine's total proof of the existence of
God given by M. Gilson is doubtless representative of the
Saint's mind and it has the great advantage not only of bringing into prominence the proof from thought, from the eternal
truths, but also of linking up the 'proof' with the soul's search
for God as the source of happiness, as objective beatitude, in
such a way that the proof does not remain a mere academic
and theoretic string or chain of syllogisms. This picture is
confirmed by a passage such as that contained in Augustine's
two hundred and forty-first sermon,[10] where the Saint depicts the human soul questioning the things of sense and
hearing them confess that the beauty of the visible world, of
mutable things, is the creation and reflection of immutable
Beauty, after which the soul proceeds inwards, discovers itself and realises the superiority of soul to body. 'Men saw
these two things, pondered them, investigated both of them,
and found that each is mutable in man.' The mind, therefore, finding both body and soul to be mutable goes in search
of what is immutable. 'And thus they arrived at a knowledge
of God the Creator by means of the things which He created.' St. Augustine, then, in no way denies what we call a
'natural' or 'rational' knowledge of God; but this rational
knowledge of God is viewed in close connection with the
soul's search for beatifying Truth and is seen as itself a kind
of self-revelation of God to the soul, a revelation which is
completed in the full revelation through Christ and confirmed in the Christian life of prayer. Augustine would thus
make no sharp dichotomy between the spheres of natural and
revealed theology, not because he failed to see the distinction
between reason and faith, but rather because he viewed the
soul's cognition of God in close connection with its spiritual
search for God as the one Object and Source of beatitude.
When Harnack reproaches Augustine with not having made
clear the relation of faith to science,[11] he fails to realise that
the Saint is primarily concerned with the spiritual experience
of God and that in his eyes faith and reason each have their
part to play in an experience which is an organic unity.

4. Augustine insists that the world of creatures reflects

and manifests God, even if it does so in a very inadequate
manner, and that 'if any thing worthy of praise is noticed in
the nature of things, whether it be judged worthy of slight
praise or of great, it must be applied to the most excellent
and ineffable praise of the Creator.' Creatures tend indeed
to not-being, but as long as they are, they possess some form,
and this is a reflection of the Form which can neither decline
nor pass away.[12] Thus the order and unity of Nature proclaims the unity of the Creator,[13] just as the goodness of
creatures, their positive reality, reveals the goodness of
God[14] and the order and stability of the universe manifest
the wisdom of God.[15] On the other hand, God, as the self-
existent, eternal and immutable Being, is infinite, and, as infinite, incomprehensible. God is His own Perfection, is 'simple', so that His wisdom and knowledge, His goodness and
power, are His own essence, which is without accidents.[16]
God, therefore, transcends space in virtue of His spirituality
and infinity and simplicity, as He transcends time in virtue
of His eternity: 'God is Himself in no interval nor extension
of place, but in His immutable and pre-eminent might is
both interior to everything because all things are in Him and
exterior to everything because He is above all things. So too
He is in no interval nor extension of time, but in His immutable eternity is older than all things because He is before
all things and younger than all things because the same He
is after all things.'[17]

5. From all eternity God knew all things which He was
to make: He does not know them because He has made
them, but rather the other way round: God first knew the
things of creation though they came into being only in time.
The species of created things have their ideas or *rationes* in
God, and God from all eternity saw in Himself, as possible
reflections of Himself, the things which He could create and
would create. He knew them before creation as they are in
Him, as Exemplar, but He made them as they exist, i.e. as
external and finite reflections of His divine essence.[18] God
did nothing without knowledge, He foresaw all that He
would make, but His knowledge is not distinct acts of knowledge, but 'one eternal, immutable and ineffable vision'.[19] It
is in virtue of this eternal act of knowledge, of vision, to
which nothing is past or future, that God sees, 'foresees',
even the free acts of men, knowing 'beforehand', for example,
'what we should ask of Him and when, and to whom He

would listen or not listen, and on what subjects'.[20] An adequate discussion of this last point, which would necessitate consideration of the Augustinian theory of grace, cannot be attempted here.

Contemplating His own essence from eternity God sees in Himself all possible limited essences, the finite reflections of His infinite perfection, so that the essences or *rationes* of things are present in the divine mind from all eternity as the divine ideas, though, in view of Augustine's teaching on the divine simplicity previously mentioned, this should not be taken to mean that there are 'accidents' in God, ideas which are ontologically distinct from His essence. In the *Confessions*[21] the Saint exclaims that the eternal 'reasons' of created things remain unchangeably in God, and in the *De Ideis*[22] he explains that the divine ideas are 'certain archetypal forms or stable and unchangeable reasons of things, which were not themselves formed but are contained in the divine mind eternally and are always the same. They neither arise nor pass away, but whatever arises and passes away is formed according to them.' The corollary of this is that creatures have ontological truth in so far as they embody or exemplify the model in the divine mind, and that God Himself is the standard of truth. This exemplarist doctrine was, of course, influenced by neo-Platonic theory, according to which the Platonic exemplary ideas are contained in *Nous*, though for Augustine the ideas are contained in the Word, who is not a subordinate hypostasis, like the neo-Platonic *Nous*, but the second Person of the Blessed Trinity, consubstantial with the Father.[23] From Augustine the doctrine of exemplarism passed to the Middle Ages. It may be thought of as characteristic of the Augustinian School; but it must be remembered that St. Thomas Aquinas did not deny it, though he was careful to state it in such a way as not to imply that there are ontologically separate ideas in God, a doctrine which would impair the divine simplicity, for in God there is no real distinction save that between the three divine Persons.[24] Still, though Aquinas was in this respect a follower of Augustine, it was St. Bonaventure who most insisted in the thirteenth century on the doctrine of exemplarism and on the presence of the divine Ideas in the Word of God, an insistence which contributed to his hostile attitude to Aristotle the metaphysician, who threw overboard the ideas of Plato.

Chapter Six

ST. AUGUSTINE–IV: THE WORLD

Free creation out of nothing–Matter–Rationes seminales–
Numbers–Soul and body–Immortality–Origin of soul.

One would hardly expect, once given the general attitude
and complexion of Augustine's thought, to find the Saint
showing very much interest in the material world for its own
sake: his thought centred round the soul's relation to God;
but his general philosophy involved a theory of the corporeal
world, a theory consisting of elements taken from former
thinkers and set in a Christian framework. It would be a
mistake, however, to think that Augustine drew purely me-
chanically on previous thinkers for his theories: he emphasised those lines which seemed to him best calculated to un-
derline nature's relation to and dependence on God.

1. A doctrine which was not developed by pagan thinkers,
but which was held by Augustine in common with other
Christian writers, was that of the creation of the world out
of nothing by God's free act. In the Plotinian emanation-
theory the world is depicted as proceeding in some way from
God without God becoming in any way diminished or altered
thereby, but for Plotinus God does not act freely (since such
activity would, he thought, postulate change in God) but
rather *necessitate naturae*, the Good necessarily diffusing itself. The doctrine of free creation out of nothing is not to be
found in neo-Platonism, if we except one or two pagan thinkers who had most probably been influenced by Christian
teaching. Augustine may have thought that Plato had taught
creation out of nothing in time, but it is improbable, in
spite of Aristotle's interpretation of the *Timaeus*, that Plato

really meant to imply this. However, whatever Augustine may
have thought about Plato's views on the matter, he himself
clearly states the doctrine of free creation out of nothing and
it is essential to his insistence on the utter supremacy of God
and the world's entire dependence on Him. All things owe
their being to God.[1]

2. But suppose that things were made out of some formless matter? Would not this formless matter be independent
of God? First of all, says Augustine, are you speaking of a
matter which is absolutely formless or of a matter which is
formless only in comparison with completely formed? If the
former, then you are speaking of what is equivalent to noth-
ingness. 'That out of which God has created all things is
what possesses neither species nor form; and this is nothing
other than nothing.' If, however, you are speaking of the
latter, of matter which has no completed form, but which
has inchoate form, in the sense of possessing the capacity to
receive form, then such matter is not altogether nothing indeed, but, as something, it has what being it has only from
God. 'Wherefore, even if the universe was created out of
some formless matter, this very matter was created from
something which was wholly nothing.'[2] In the *Confessions*[3]
Augustine identifies this matter with the mutability of bodies
(which is equivalent to saying that it is the potential element) and observes that if he could call it 'nothing' or assert
that it does not exist, he would do so; but if it is the capacity
of receiving forms, it cannot be called absolutely nothing.
Again, he remarks in the *De vera religione*[4] that not only
the possession of form but even the capacity to receive form
is a good, and what is a good cannot be absolute nothing.
Yet this matter, which is not absolutely nothing, is itself the
creation of God, not preceding formed things in time but
concreated with form,[5] and he identified the 'unformed matter which God made out of nothing' with the heaven and
earth mentioned in the first verse of the first chapter of
Genesis as the primary creation of God.[6] In other words, St.
Augustine is stating in rudimentary form the Scholastic doctrine that God created out of nothing not absolutely formless 'prime matter', apart from all form, but form and matter together, though, if we choose to think of Augustine's
statements as a rudimentary expression of the more elaborate
Scholastic doctrine, we should also remember that the Saint
is not so concerned with developing a philosophical doctrine

for its own sake as with emphasising the essential dependence of all creatures on God and the perishable nature of all corporeal creatures, even when once constituted in existence. They have their being from God, but their being is bound up with their mutability.

3. A theory which was dear to Augustine himself and to his followers, though it was rejected by St. Thomas, and which was calculated to exalt the divine agency at the expense of the causal activity of creatures, was that of the *rationes seminales* or 'seminal reasons', the germs of those things which were to develop in the course of time. Thus even man, as regards his body at least, to leave the origin of the soul out of account for the moment, was created in the *rationes seminales*, 'invisibly, potentially, causally, in the way that things are made which are to be but have not yet been made'.[7] The *rationes seminales* are germs of things or invisible powers or potentialities, created by God in the beginning in the humid element and developing into the objects of various species by their temporal unfolding. The idea of these germinal potentialities was to be found, and doubtless was found by Augustine, in the philosophy of Plotinus and ultimately it goes back to the *rationes seminales* or λόγοι σπερματικοί of Stoicism, but it is an idea of rather vague content. Indeed, St. Augustine never supposed that they were the object of experience, that they could be seen or touched: they are invisible, having inchoate form or a potentiality to the development of form according to the divine plan. The seminal reasons are not purely passive, but tend to self-development, though the absence of the requisite conditions and circumstances and of other external agencies may hinder or prevent their development.[8] St. Bonaventure, who maintained the theory of St. Augustine on this point, compared the *ratio seminalis* to the rosebud, which is not yet actually the rose but will develop into the rose, given the presence of the necessary positive agencies and the absence of negative or preventive agencies.

That St. Augustine asserted a rather vague theory regarding objects which are not the term of direct experience will appear less surprising if one considers *why* he asserted it. The assertion was the result of an exegetic, not a scientific problem, and the problem arose in this way. According to the book of Ecclesiasticus[9] 'He that liveth for ever created all things together', while on the other hand according to the book of Genesis the fishes and birds, for instance, appeared only on the fifth 'day' of creation, while the cattle and beasts of the earth appeared only on the sixth 'day'. (Augustine did not interpret 'day' as our day of twenty-four hours, since the sun was made only on the fourth 'day'.) How then can these two statements be reconciled, that God created all things together and that some things were made after others, that is to say, that *not* all things were created together? St. Augustine's way of solving the problem was to say that God did indeed create all things together in the beginning, but that He did not create them all in the same condition: many things, all plants, fishes, birds, animals, and man himself, He created invisibly, latently, potentially, in germ, in their *rationes seminales*. In this way God created in the beginning all the vegetation of the earth before it was actually growing on the earth,[10] and even man himself. He would thus solve the apparent contradiction between Ecclesiasticus and Genesis by making a distinction. If you are speaking of actual formal completion, then Ecclesiasticus is not referring to this, whereas Genesis is: if you are including germinal or seminal creation, then this is what Ecclesiasticus refers to.

Why did not Augustine content himself with 'seeds' in the ordinary sense, the visible seeds of plants, the grain and so on? Because in the book of Genesis it is implied that the earth brought forth the green herb *before* its seed,[11] and the same thing is implied in regard to the other living things which reproduce their kind. He found himself compelled, therefore, to have recourse to a different kind of seed. For example, God created in the beginning the *ratio seminalis* of wheat, which, according to God's plan and activity, unfolded itself at the appointed time as actual wheat, which then contained seed in the ordinary sense.[12] Moreover, God did not create all seeds or all eggs in act at the beginning, so that they too require a *ratio seminalis*. Each species, then, with all its future developments and particular members, was created at the beginning in the appropriate seminal reason.

From what has been said it should be clear that the Saint was not considering primarily a scientific problem but rather an exegetic problem, so that it is really beside the point to adduce him either as a protagonist or as an opponent of evolution in the Lamarckian or Darwinian sense.

4. St. Augustine made use of the Platonic number-theme, which goes back to Pythagoreanism. Naturally his treatment

of number sometimes appears to us as fanciful and even fantastic, as when he speaks of perfect and imperfect numbers or interprets references to numbers in the Scriptures; but, speaking generally, he looks on number as the principle of order and form, of beauty and perfection, of proportion and law. Thus the Ideas are the eternal numbers, while bodies are temporal numbers, which unfold themselves in time. Bodies indeed can be considered as numbers in various ways, as being wholes consisting of a number of ordered and related parts, as unfolding themselves in successive stages (the plant, for example, germinates, breaks into leaf, produces flower and fruit, seminates), or as consisting of a number of parts well disposed in space; in other words, as exemplifying intrinsic number, local or spatial number, and temporal number. The 'seminal reasons' are hidden numbers, whereas bodies are manifest numbers. Again, just as mathematical number begins from one and ends in a number which is itself an integer, so the hierarchy of beings begins with the supreme One, God, which brings into existence and is reflected in more or less perfect unities. This comparison or parallel between mathematical number and metaphysical number was derived, of course, from Plotinus, and in general Augustine's treatment of number adds nothing of substance to the treatment already accorded it in the Pythagorean-Platonic tradition.

5. The peak of the material creation is man, who consists of body and immortal soul. Augustine is quite clear about the fact that man does consist of soul and body, as when he says that 'a soul in possession of a body does not constitute two persons but one man'.[13] Why is it necessary to mention such an obvious point? Because Augustine speaks of the soul as a substance in its own right (*substantia quaedam rationis particeps, regendo corpori accomodata*)[14] and even defines man as 'a rational soul using a mortal and earthly body'.[15] This Platonic attitude towards the soul has its repercussions, as we have already seen, in Augustine's doctrine of sensation, which he represents as an activity of the soul using the body as an instrument, rather than as an activity of the total psycho-physical organism: it is, in fact, a temporary increase of intensity in the action by which the soul animates a certain part of the body. The soul, being superior to the body, cannot be acted on by the body, but it perceives the changes in the body due to an external stimulus.

6. The human soul is an immaterial principle, though, like the souls of brutes, it animates the body. A man may say or even think that his soul is composed of air, for example, but he can never know that it is composed of air. On the other hand he knows very well that he is intelligent, that he thinks, and he has no reason to suppose that air can think.[16] Moreover, the soul's immateriality and its substantiality assure it of immortality. On this point Augustine uses arguments which go back to Plato.[17] For example, Augustine utilises the argument of the *Phaedo* that, as the soul is the principle of life and as two contraries are incompatible, the soul cannot die. Apart from the fact that this argument is not very convincing in any case, it could not be acceptable to Augustine without modification, since it would seem to imply that the soul exists of itself or is a part of God. He adapted the argument, therefore, by saying that the soul participates in Life, holding its being and essence from a Principle which admits of no contrary, and by arguing that, as the being which the soul receives from this Principle (which admits no contrary) is precisely *life*, it cannot die. The argument, however, might clearly be taken to imply that the animal soul is immortal also, since it too is a principle of life, and so would prove too much. It must, then, be taken in conjunction with another argument, also derived from Plato, to the effect that the soul apprehends indestructible truth, which shows that it is itself indestructible. In the *De quantitate animae*[18] Augustine distinguishes the souls of beasts, which possess the power of sensation but not that of reasoning and knowing, from human souls, which possess both, so that this argument applies only to human souls. Plato had argued that the human soul, as capable of apprehending the Ideas, which are eternal and indestructible, shows itself to be akin to them, to be 'divine', that is to say, indestructible and eternal, and Augustine, without affirming pre-existence, proves the immortality of the soul in an analogous manner. In addition, he argues from the desire of beatitude, the desire for perfect happiness, and this became a favourite argument among Augustinians, with St. Bonaventure, for example.

7. Augustine clearly held that the soul is created by God,[19] but does not seem to have made up his mind as to the precise time and mode of its origin. He seems to have toyed with some form of the Platonic pre-existence theory while refusing to allow that the soul was put into the body as a

punishment for faults committed in a pre-earthly condition, but the chief question for him was whether God creates each individual soul separately or created all other souls in Adam's, so that the soul is 'handed on' by the parents (Traducianism). This second opinion would appear logically to involve a materialistic view of the soul, whereas in fact Augustine certainly did not hold any such view and insisted that the soul is not present in the body by local diffusion;[20] but it was for theological, not philosophical, reasons that he inclined towards traducianism, as he thought that in this way original sin could be explained as a transmitted stain on the soul. If original sin is looked on as something positive and not as in itself a privation, there is indeed a difficulty, even if not an insuperable difficulty, in affirming individual creation by God of each single human soul, but even apart from that it does not alter the fact that traducianism is inconsistent with a clear affirmation of the soul's spiritual and immaterial character.

Chapter Seven

ST. AUGUSTINE—V: MORAL THEORY

*Happiness and God—Freedom and Obligation—Need of grace
—Evil—the two Cities.*

1. St Augustine's ethic has this in common with what one
might call the typical Greek ethic, that it is eudaemonistic
in character, that it proposes an end for human conduct,
namely happiness; but this happiness is to be found only in
God. 'The Epicurean who places man's supreme good in the
body, places his hope in himself,'[1] but 'the rational creature
. . . has been so made that it cannot itself be the good by
which it is made happy':[2] the human being is mutable and
insufficient to itself, it can find its happiness only in the possession of what is more than itself, in the possession of an
immutable object. Not even virtue itself can be the end: 'it
is not the virtue of thy soul that maketh thee happy, but He
who hath given thee the virtue, who hath inspired thee to
will, and hath given thee the power to do.'[3] It is not the
ideal of the Epicurean that can bring happiness to man, nor
even that of the Stoic, but God Himself: 'the striving after
God is, therefore, the desire of beatitude, the attainment of
God is beatitude itself.'[4] That the human being strives after
beatitude or happiness, and that beatitude means the attainment of an object, Augustine knew well from his own experience, even if he found confirmation of this fact in philosophy; that this object is God, he learnt also from his personal
experience, even if he had been helped to realise the fact by
the philosophy of Plotinus. But when he said that happiness
is to be found in the attainment and possession of the eternal
and immutable Object, God, he was thinking, not of a purely

philosophic and theoretic contemplation of God, but of a
loving union with and possession of God, and indeed of the
supernatural union with God held up to the Christian as the
term of his grace-aided endeavour: one cannot well separate
out in Augustine's thought a natural and a supernatural ethic,
since he deals with man in the concrete, and man in the
concrete has a supernatural vocation: he regarded the neo-
Platonists as discerning something of that which was revealed
by Christ, neo-Platonism as an inadequate and partial realisation of the truth.

The ethic of Augustine is, then, primarily an ethic of love:
it is by the will that man reaches out towards God and finally
takes possession of and enjoys Him. 'When therefore the will,
which is the intermediate good, cleaves to the immutable
good . . . , man finds therein the blessed life';[5] 'for if God
is man's supreme good . . . it clearly follows, since to seek
the supreme good is to live well, that to live well is nothing
else but to love God with all the heart, with all the soul, with
all the mind.'[6] Indeed, after quoting the words of Christ, as
recorded by St. Matthew,[7] 'Thou shalt love the Lord thy
God with thy whole heart, and with thy whole soul, and with
thy whole mind' and 'thou shalt love thy neighbour as thy-
self', Augustine asserts that 'Natural philosophy is here, since
all the causes of all natural things are in God the Creator',
and that, 'Ethics are here, since a good and honest life is not
formed otherwise than by loving as they should be loved
those things which we ought to love, namely, God and our
neighbour.'[8] Augustine's ethic thus centres round the dynamism of the will, which is a dynamism of love (*pondus
meum, amor meus*),[9] though the attainment of beatitude,
'participation in the immutable good', is not possible for man
unless he be aided by grace, unless he receives 'the gratuitous
mercy of the Creator'.[10]

2. The will, however, is free, and the free will is subject to
moral obligation. The Greek philosophers had a conception
of happiness as the end of conduct, and one cannot say that
they had no idea of obligation; but owing to his clearer notion of God and of divine creation Augustine was able to
give to moral obligation a firmer metaphysical basis than the
Greeks had been able to give it.

The necessary basis of obligation is freedom. The will is
free to turn away from the immutable Good and to attach
itself to mutable goods, taking as its object either the goods

of the soul, without reference to God, or the goods of the body. The will necessarily seeks happiness, satisfaction, and *de facto* this happiness can be found only in God, the immutable Good, but man has not the vision of God in this life, he can turn his attention to and cling to mutable goods in place of God, and 'this turning away and this turning to are not forced but voluntary actions'.[11]

The human will is, then, free to turn to God or away from God, but at the same time the human mind must recognise the truth, not only that what it seeks, happiness, can be found only in the possession of the immutable Good, God, but also that the direction of the will to that good is implanted by God and willed by God, who is the Creator. By turning away from God the will runs counter to the divine law, which is expressed in human nature, made by God for Himself. All men are conscious to some extent of moral standards and laws: 'even the ungodly . . . rightly blame and rightly praise many things in the conduct of men.' How are they enabled to do so, save by seeing the rules according to which men ought to live, even if they do not personally obey these laws in their own conduct? Where do they see these rules? Not in their own minds, since their minds are mutable, whereas the 'rules of justice' are immutable; not in their characters, since they are *ex hypothesi* unjust. They see the moral rules, says Augustine, using his customary, if obscure, manner of speaking, 'in the book of that light which is called Truth'. The eternal laws of morality are impressed in the heart of man, 'as the impression of a ring passes into the wax, yet does not leave the ring'. There are indeed some men who are more or less blind to the law, but even they are 'sometimes touched by the splendour of the omnipresent truth'.[12] Thus, just as the human mind perceives eternal theoretic truths in the light of God, so it perceives, in the same light, practical truths or principles which should direct the free will. Man is by his nature, his nature considered in the concrete, set towards God; but he can fulfil the dynamism of that nature only by observing the moral laws which reflect the eternal law of God, and which are not arbitrary rules but follow from the Nature of God and the relationship of man to God. The laws are not arbitrary caprices of God, but their observance is willed by God, for He would not have created man without willing that man should be what He meant him to be. The will is free, but it is at the same time subject to moral obligations, and to love God is a duty.

3. The relationship of man to God, however, is the relationship of a finite creature to the infinite Being, and the result is that the gulf cannot be bridged without the divine aid, without grace: grace is necessary even to begin to will to love God. 'When man tries to live justly by his own strength without the help of the liberating grace of God, he is then conquered by sins; but in free will he has it in his power to believe in the Liberator and to receive grace.'[13] 'The law was therefore given that grace might be sought; grace was given that the law mght be fulfilled.'[14] 'Our will is by the law shown to be weak, that grace may heal its infirmity.'[15] 'The law of teaching and commanding that which cannot be fulfilled without grace demonstrates to man his weakness, in order that the weakness thus proved may resort to the Saviour, by whose healing the will may be able to do what in its feebleness it found impossible.'[16]

It would be out of place here to enter on the question of Augustine's doctrine of grace and its relation to the free will, which is in any case a difficult question; but it is necessary to grasp the fact that when Augustine makes the love of God the essence of the moral law, he is referring to that union of the will with God which requires the elevation effected by grace. This is only natural, once given the fact that he is considering and treating man in the concrete, man endowed with a supernatural vocation, and it means that he supplements and completes the wisdom of philosophy with the wisdom of the Scriptures. One can, for purposes of schematism, try to separate Augustine the philosopher and Augustine the theologian; but in his own eyes the true philosopher is a man who surveys reality in the concrete, as it is, and it cannot be seen as it is without taking into account the economy of redemption and of grace.

4. If moral perfection consists in loving God, in directing the will to God and bringing all other powers, e.g. the senses, into harmony with this direction, evil will consist in turning the will away from God. But what is evil in itself, moral evil? Is it something positive? It cannot, first of all, be something positive in the sense of something created by God: the cause of moral evil is not the Creator but the created will. The cause of good things is the divine goodness, whereas the cause of evil is the created will which turns away from the immuta-

ble Good:[17] evil is a turning-away of the created will from
the immutable and infinite Good.[18] But evil cannot strictly
be termed a 'thing', since this word implies a positive reality,
and if moral evil were a positive reality, it would have to be
ascribed to the Creator, unless one were willing to attribute
to the creature the power of positive creation out of nothing.
Evil, then, is 'that which falls away from essence and tends to
non-being. . . . It tends to make that which is cease to
be.'[19] Everything in which there is order and measure is to
be ascribed to God, but in the will which turns away from
God there is disorder. The will itself is good, but the absence
of right order, or rather the privation of right order, for
which the human agent is responsible, is evil. Moral evil is
thus a privation of right order in the created will.

This doctrine of evil as a privation was the doctrine of
Plotinus, and in it Augustine found the answer to the Mani-
chees. For if evil is a privation and not a positive thing, one
is no longer faced with the choice of either ascribing moral
evil to the good Creator or of inventing an ultimate evil principle responsible for evil. This doctrine was adopted by the
Scholastics generally from Augustine and finds adherents
among several modern philosophers of note, Leibniz, for
example.

5. If the principle of morality is love of God and the essence of evil is a falling-away from God, it follows that the
human race can be divided into two great camps, that of those
who love God and prefer God to self and that of those who
prefer self to God: it is by the character of their wills, by
the character of their dominant love, that men are ultimately
marked. Augustine sees the history of the human race as the
history of the dialectic of these two principles, the one in
forming the City of Jerusalem, the other the City of Babylon.
'Let each one question himself as to what he loveth; and he
shall find of which (city) he is a citizen.'[20] 'There are two
kinds of love; . . . These two kinds of love distinguish the
two cities established in the human race . . . in the so to
speak commingling of which the ages are passed.'[21] 'You
have heard and know that there are two cities, for the present
mingled together in body, but in heart separated.'[22]

To the Christian history is necessarily of profound importance. It was in history that man fell, in history that he
was redeemed: it is in history, progressively, that the Body
of Christ on earth grows and develops and that God's plan is

unfolded. To the Christian, history apart from the data of revelation is shorn of its significance: it is small wonder, then, that Augustine looked on history from the Christian stand-point and that his outlook was primarily spiritual and moral. If we speak of a philosophy of history in Augustine's thought, the word 'philosophy' must be understood in a wide sense as Christian wisdom. The knowledge of the facts of history may be mainly a natural knowledge, for example, knowledge of the existence and development of the Assyrian and Baby-lonian empires; but the principles by which the facts are in-terpreted and given meaning and judged are not taken from the facts themselves. The temporal and passing is judged in the light of the eternal. That Augustine's tendency to con-centrate on the aspect of Assyria under which it appeared to him as an embodiment of the City of Babylon (in the moral sense) would not commend itself to the modern historian is understandable enough; but Augustine was not concerned to play the part of an historian in the ordinary sense, but rather to give the 'philosophy' of history as he envisaged it, and the 'philosophy' of history, as he understood it, is the discern-ment of the spiritual and moral significance of historical phenomena and events. Indeed, so far as there can be a philosophy of history at all, the Christian at least will agree with Augustine that only a Christian philosophy of history can ever approach adequacy: to the non-Christian the posi-tion of the Jewish people, for example, is radically different from the position it occupies in the eyes of the Christian. If it were objected, as it obviously could be, that this involves a theological interpretation of history, a reading of history in the light of dogma, the objection would not cause Augustine any difficulty, since he never pretended to make that radical dichotomy between theology and philosophy which is implied in the objection.

Chapter Eight

ST. AUGUSTINE–VI: THE STATE

The State and the City of Babylon not identical—The pagan State does not embody true justice—Church superior to State.

1. As I have already remarked, Augustine saw in history, as he saw in the individual, the struggle between two principles of conduct, two loves, on the one hand the love of God and submission to His law, on the other hand love of self, of pleasure, of the world. It was only natural, then, that as he saw the embodiment of the heavenly city, Jerusalem, in the Catholic Church, so he should see in the State, particularly in the pagan State, the embodiment of the City of Babylon, and the result of Augustine's attitude in this matter is that one is tempted to assume that for him the City of God can be identified with the Church as a visible society and the City of Babylon with the State as such. Does he not ask, 'Without justice what are kingdoms but great bands of robbers? What is a band of robbers but a little kingdom?' And does he not approve the pirate's reply to Alexander the Great, 'Because I do it with a little ship, I am called a robber, and you, because you do it with a great fleet, are called an emperor'?[1] Assyria and pagan Rome were founded, increased and maintained by injustice, violence, rapine, oppression: is not this to affirm that the State and the City of Babylon are one and the same thing?

Undeniably Augustine thought that the most adequate historical embodiments of the City of Babylon are to be found in the pagan empires of Assyria and Rome, just as he certainly thought that the City of Jerusalem, the City of God, is manifested in the Church. None the less, the ideas of the heavenly and earthly cities are moral and spiritual ideas, the contents of which are not exactly coterminous with any actual organisation. For instance, a man may be a Christian and belong to the Church; but if the principle of his conduct is self-love and not the love of God, he belongs spiritually and morally to the City of Babylon. Again, if an official of the State is governed in his conduct by the love of God, if he pursues justice and charity, he belongs spiritually and morally to the City of Jerusalem. 'We see now a citizen of Jerusalem, a citizen of the kingdom of heaven, holding some office upon earth; as, for example, wearing the purple, serving as magistrate, as aedile, as proconsul, as emperor, directing the earthly republic, but he hath his heart above if he is a Christian, if he is of the faithful. . . . Let us not therefore despair of the citizens of the kingdom of heaven, when we see them engaged in the affairs of Babylon, doing something terrestrial in a terrestrial republic; nor again let us forthwith congratulate all men whom we see engaged in celestial matters, for even the sons of the pestilence sit sometimes in the seat of Moses. . . . But there will come a time of winnowing when they will be separated, the one from the other, with the greatest care. . . .'[2] Even if, then, the City of Babylon in the moral and spiritual sense tends to be identified with the State, particularly the pagan State, and the City of Jerusalem tends to be identified with the Church as a visible organisation, the identification is not complete: one cannot legitimately conclude that because a man is, for example, a Church official, he is necessarily a citizen of the spiritual City of Jerusalem, for as far as his spiritual and moral condition is concerned he may belong to the City of Babylon. Moreover, if the State were necessarily coincident with the City of Babylon, no Christian could legitimately hold office in the State, or even be a citizen, if he could help it, and St. Augustine certainly did not subscribe to any such opinion.

2. But if the State and the City of Babylon cannot simply be identified, St. Augustine certainly did not think that the State as such is founded on justice or that true justice is realised in any actual State, not at any rate in any pagan State. That there is some justice even in a pagan State is sufficiently obvious, but true justice demands that that worship should be paid to God which He requires, and pagan Rome did not pay that worship, indeed in Christian times she did her best to prevent its being paid. On the other hand

pagan Rome was obviously a State. How, then, is the conclusion to be avoided that true justice must not be included
within the definition of the State? For, if it is, one would
be reduced to the impossible position of denying that pagan
Rome was a State. Augustine accordingly defines a society as
a 'multitude of rational creatures associated in a common
agreement as to the things which it loves'.[3] If the things
which it loves are good, it will be a good society, while, if the
things which it loves are bad, it will be a bad society; but
nothing is said in the definition of a people as to whether
the objects of its love are good or bad, with the result that
the definition will apply even to the pagan State.

This does not mean, of course, that in Augustine's eyes the
State exists in a non-moral sphere: on the contrary, the same
moral law holds good for States as for individuals. The point
he wants to make is that the State will not embody true
justice, will not be a really moral State, unless it is a Christian State: it is Christianity which makes men good citizens.
The State itself, as an instrument of force, has its roots in
the consequences of original sin and, given the fact of original
sin and its consequences, is a necessary institution; but a
just State is out of the question unless it is a Christian State.
'No State is more perfectly established and preserved than
on the foundations, and by the bond, of faith and of firm
concord, when the highest and truest good, namely God, is
loved by all and men love each other in Him without dissimu-
lation because they love one another for His sake.'[4] The
State, in other words, is informed by love of this world, when
it is left to itself; but it can be informed by higher principles,
principles which it must derive from Christianity.

3. From this there follow two consequences of importance.
(1) The Christian Church will try to inform civil society
with its own celestial principles of conduct: it has a mission
to act as the leaven of the earth. Augustine's conception of
the Christian Church and her mission was essentially a dynamic and a social conception: the Church must permeate
the State by her principles. (2) The Church is thus the only
really perfect society and is definitely superior to the State,
for, if the State must take her principles from the Church,
the State cannot be above the Church nor even on a level
with the Church. In maintaining this view St. Augustine
stands at the head of the mediaeval exaltation of the Church
vis-à-vis the State, and he was only consistent in invoking the

help of the State against the Donatists, since, on his view, the Church is a superior society to which Christ has subjected the kingdoms of the world, and which has the right to make use of the powers of the world.[5] But if Augustine's view of the relation of Church to State was the one which became characteristic of western Christendom and not of Byzantium, it does not follow that his view necessarily tended to undermine the significance of civic and social life. As Christopher Dawson has pointed out,[6] although Augustine deprived the State of its aura of divinity, he at the same time insisted on the value of the free human personality and of moral responsibility, even against the State, so that in this way he 'made possible the ideal of a social order resting upon the free personality and a common effort towards moral ends'.

Chapter Nine

THE PSEUDO-DIONYSIUS

Writings and author—Affirmative way—Negative way—Neo-Platonic interpretation of Trinity—Ambiguous teaching on creation—Problem of evil—Orthodoxy or unorthodoxy?

1. During the Middle Ages the writings which were then ascribed to St. Paul's Athenian convert, Dionysius the Areopagite, enjoyed high esteem, not only among mystics and authors of works on mystical theology, but also among professional theologians and philosophers, such as St. Albert the Great and St. Thomas Aquinas. The reverence and respect paid to these writings were, of course, in great part due to the mistaken notion as to their authorship, a mistake which originated in the author's use of a pseudonym. 'Dionysius the Presbyter, to his fellow-presbyter Timothy.'[1] In 533 the Patriarch of Antioch, Severus, appealed to the writings of Dionysius, in support of his Monophysite doctrine, a fact which can be safely taken to mean that the writings were already regarded as possessed of authority. But, even if Severus appealed to the works in question in support of heretical doctrine, their ascription to St. Dionysius would free them from any suspicion as to their orthodoxy. In the Eastern Church they were widely circulated, being commented on by Maximus the Confessor in the seventh century and appealed to by the great Eastern Doctor, St. John Damascene, in the eighth century, though Hypatius of Ephesus attacked their authenticity.

In the West, Pope Martin I appealed to the writings as authentic at the first Lateran Council in 649, and about the year 858 John Scotus Eriugena, at the request of Charles the

Bald, made a translation from the Greek text which had been presented to Louis the Fair in 827 by the Emperor Michael Balbus. John Scotus, besides translating the writings of the Pseudo-Dionysius, also commented on them, thus furnishing the first of a series of commentaries in Western Christendom. For example, Hugh of St. Victor (d. 1141) commented on the *Celestial Hierarchy*, using Eriugena's translation, while Robert Grosseteste (d. 1253) and Albert the Great (d. 1280) also commented on the writings. St. Thomas Aquinas composed a commentary on the *Divine Names* about 1261. All these authors, as also, for example, Denis the Carthusian, accepted the authenticity of the writings; but in time it was bound to become clear that they embodied important elements taken from developed neo-Platonism and that they constituted in fact an attempt to reconcile neo-Platonism and Christianity, so that they would have to be attributed to an author of a much later date than the historic Dionysius the Areopagite. However, the question of the authenticity of the writings is not the same as the question of their orthodoxy from the Christian standpoint, and though in the seventeenth century, when critics began to attack the authenticity of the writings, their orthodoxy was also assailed, a recognition of their unauthentic character did not necessarily involve an admission of their incompatibility with Christian doctrine, though it was obviously no longer possible to maintain their orthodoxy on the *a priori* ground that they were composed by a personal disciple of St. Paul. Personally I consider that the writings are orthodox in regard to the rejection of monism; but that on the question of the Blessed Trinity it is highly questionable at least if they can be reconciled with orthodox Christian dogma. Whatever the intentions of the author may have been, his words, besides being obscure, as Aquinas admitted, are scarcely compatible, as they stand, with the Trinitarian teaching of Augustine and Thomas Aquinas. It may be objected that insufficient attention is paid to the dogma of the Incarnation, which is essential to Christianity, but the author clearly maintains this doctrine, and in any case to say little about one particular doctrine, even a central one, is not the same as to deny it. Taking the relevant passages of the Pseudo-Dionysius in the large, it does not seem possible to reject them as definitely unorthodox on this point, unless one is prepared also to reject as unorthodox, for example, the mystical doctrine of St. John of the Cross, who is a Doctor of the Church.

But though no one now supposes that the writings are actually the work of Dionysius the Areopagite, it has not proved possible to discover the real author. Most probably they were composed at the end of the fifth century, as they apparently embody ideas of the neo-Platonist Proclus (418–85), and it has been conjectured that the Hierotheus who figures therein was the Syrian mystic Stephen Bar Sadaili. If the writings of the Pseudo-Dionysius actually depend to any degree on the philosophy of Proclus, they cannot well have been composed before the closing decades of the fifth century, while as they were appealed to at the Council of 533, they can hardly have been composed much after 500. The ascription of about 500 as the date of their composition is, therefore, doubtless correct, while the supposition that they originated in Syria is reasonable. The author was a theologian, without doubt an ecclesiastic also; but he cannot have been Severus himself, as one or two writers have rashly supposed. In any case, though it would be interesting to know with certainty who the author was, it is probably unlikely that anything more than conjecture will ever be possible, and the chief interest of the writings is due, not to the personality of the author, but to the content and influence of the writings, these writings being the *Divine Names* (*De divinis Nominibus*), the *Mystical Theology* (*De mystica Theologia*), the *Celestial Hierarchy* (*De coelesti Hierarchia*) and the *Ecclesiastical Hierarchy* (*De ecclesiastica Hierarchia*), as well as ten letters. The works are printed in Migne's *Patrologia Graeca*, volumes 3–4; but a critical edition of the text has been begun.

2. There are two ways of approaching God, who is the centre of all speculation, a positive way (καταφατική) and a negative way (ἀποφατική). In the former way or method the mind begins 'with the most universal statements, and then through intermediate terms (proceeds) to particular titles',[2] thus beginning with 'the highest category'.[3] In the *Divine Names* the Pseudo-Dionysius pursues this affirmative method, showing how names such as Goodness, Life, Wisdom, Power, are applicable to God in a transcendental manner and how they apply to creatures only in virtue of their derivation from God and their varying degrees of participation in those qualities which are found in God not as inhering qualities but in substantial unity. Thus he begins with the idea or name of

goodness, which is the most universal name, inasmuch as all things, existent or possible, share in goodness to some degree, but which at the same time expresses the Nature of God: 'None is good save one, that is, God.'[4] God, as the Good, is the overflowing source of creation and its final goal, and 'from the Good comes the light which is an image of Goodness, so that the Good is described by the name of "Light", being the archetype of that which is revealed in the image'.[5] Here the neo-Platonic leitmotiv is brought in, and the Pseudo-Dionysius's dependence on neo-Platonism is particularly manifest in his language when he goes on to speak of the Good as Beauty, as the 'super-essential beautiful', and uses the phrases of Plato's *Symposium*, which reappear in the *Enneads* of Plotinus. Again, when in chapter 13 of the *Divine Names*[6] the Pseudo-Dionysius speaks of 'One' as 'the most important title of all', he is clearly writing in dependence on the Plotinian doctrine of the ultimate Principle as the One.

In brief, then, the affirmative method means ascribing to God the perfections found in creatures, that is, the perfections which are compatible with the spiritual Nature of God, though not existing in Him in the same manner as they exist in creatures, since in God they exist without imperfection and, in the case of the names which are ascribed to the Divine Nature, without real differentiation. That we start, in the affirmative way, with the highest categories, is, says the author,[7] due to the fact that we should start with what is most akin to God, and it is truer to affirm that He is life and goodness than that He is air or stone. The names 'Life' and 'Goodness' refer to something which is actually in God, but He is air or stone only in a metaphorical sense or in the sense that He is the cause of these things. Yet the Pseudo-Dionysius is careful to insist that, even if certain names describe God better than others, they are very far from representing an adequate knowledge and conception of God on our part, and he expresses this conviction by speaking of God as the super-essential Essence, the super-essential Beautiful, and so on. He is not simply repeating phrases from the Platonic tradition, but he is expressing the truth that the objective reference or content of these names as actually found in God infinitely transcends the content of the names as experienced by us. For example, if we ascribe intelligence to God, we do not mean to ascribe to Him human intelligence, the only intelligence of which we have immediate experience and from which we draw the name: we mean that God is *more*, infinitely more, than what we experience as intelligence, and this fact is best expressed by speaking of God as super-Intelligence or as the super-essential Intelligence.

3. The affirmative way was mainly pursued by the Pseudo-Dionysius in the *Divine Names* and in his (lost) *Symbolical Theology* and *Outlines of Divinity*, whereas the negative way, that of the exclusion from God of the imperfections of creatures, is characteristic of the *Mystical Theology*. The distinction of the two ways was dependent on Proclus, and as developed by the Pseudo-Dionysius it passed into Christian philosophy and theology, being accepted by St. Thomas Aquinas, for example; but the palm is given by the Pseudo-Dionysius to the negative way in preference to the affirmative way. In this way the mind begins by denying of God those things which are farthest removed from Him, e.g. 'drunkenness or fury,'[8] and proceeds upwards progressively denying of God the attributes and qualities of creatures, until it reaches 'the super-essential Darkness'.[9] As God is utterly transcendent, we praise Him best 'by denying or removing all things that are—just as men who, carving a statue out of marble, remove all the impediments that hinder the clear perception of the latent image and by this mere removal display the hidden statue itself in its hidden beauty'.[10] The human being is inclined to form anthropomorphic conceptions of the Deity, and it is necessary to strip away these human, all-too-human conceptions by the *via remotionis*; but the Pseudo-Dionysius does not mean that from this process there results a clear view of what God is in Himself: the comparison of the statue must not mislead us. When the mind has stripped away from its idea of God the human modes of thought and inadequate conceptions of the Deity, it enters upon the 'Darkness of Unknowing',[11] wherein it 'renounces all the apprehension of the understanding and is wrapped in that which is wholly intangible and invisible . . . united . . . to Him that is wholly unknowable';[12] this is the province of mysticism. The 'Darkness of Unknowing' is not due, however, to the unintelligibility of the Object considered in itself, but to the finiteness of the human mind, which is blinded by excess of light. This doctrine is doubtless partly influenced by neo-Platonism, but it is also to be found in the writings of Christian mystical theologians, notably St. Gregory of Nyssa, whose writings in turn, though influenced, as far as language and

presentation are concerned, by neo-Platonic treatises, were
also the expression of personal experience.

4. The neo-Platonic influence on the Pseudo-Dionysius
comes out very strongly in his doctrine of the Blessed Trinity,
for he seems to be animated by the desire to find a One
behind the differentiation of Persons. He certainly allows that
the differentiation of Persons is an eternal differentiation and
that the Father, for example, is not the Son, and the Son not
the Father, but so far as one can achieve an accurate interpretation of what he says, it appears that, in his opinion, the
differentiation of Persons exists on the plane of manifestation.
The manifestation in question is an eternal manifestation,
and the differentiation an eternal differentiation within God,
to be distinguished from the external manifestation of God
in differentiated creatures; but God in Himself, beyond the
plane of manifestation, is undifferentiated Unity. One can,
of course, attempt to justify the language of the Pseudo-
Dionysius by reference to the Nature of God which, according to orthodox Trinitarianism, is one and undivided and
with which each of the divine Persons is substantially identical; but it would seem most probable, not to say certain, that
the author was influenced, not only by Plotinus's doctrine of
the One, but also by Proclus's doctrine of the primary Principle which transcends the attributes of Unity, Goodness, Being. The super-essential Unity would seem to represent
Proclus's first Principle, and the distinction of three Persons
in unity of Nature would seem to represent the neo-Platonic
conception of emanation, being a stage, if an eternal stage,
in the self-manifestation or revelation of the ultimate Godhead or Absolute. When we speak of the all-transcendent
Godhead as a Unity and a Trinity, it is not a Unity or a
Trinity such as can be known by us . . . (though) 'we apply
the titles of "Trinity" and "Unity" to that which is beyond
all titles, expressing under the form of Being that which is
beyond being. . . . (The transcendent Godhead) hath no
name, nor can it be grasped by the reason. . . . Even the
title of "Goodness" we do not ascribe to it because we think
such a name suitable. . . .'[13] (The Godhead) 'is not unity
or goodness, nor a Spirit, not Sonship nor Fatherhood, . . .
nor does it belong to the category of non-existence or to that
of existence.'[14]

It is true that such phrases could be defended, as regards
the intention of the author if not as regards his actual words,

by pointing out that it is correct to say that the term 'Father',
for instance, belongs to the first Person as Person and not to
the Son, though the divine substance exists in numerical identity and without intrinsic real differentiation in each of the
three divine Persons, and also by allowing that the term 'Father', as applied to the first Person, though the best term
available in human language for the purpose, is borrowed
from a human relationship, and applied to God in an analogical sense, so that the content of the idea of 'Father' in
our minds is not adequate to the reality in God. Moreover,
the Pseudo-Dionysius certainly speaks of 'a differentiation in
the super-essential doctrine of God', referring to the Trinity
of Persons and the names applicable to each Person in particular,[15] and explicitly denies that he is 'introducing a confusion
of all distinctions in the Deity',[16] affirming that, while names
such as 'Super-vital' or 'Super-wise' belong to 'the entire Godhead', the 'differentiated names', the names of 'Father', 'Son'
and 'Spirit', 'cannot be interchanged, nor are they held in
common'.[17] Again, though there is a 'mutual abiding and
indwelling' of the divine Persons 'in an utterly undifferentiated and transcendent Unity', this is 'without any confusion'.[18] Nevertheless, though much of what the Pseudo-
Dionysius has to say on the subject of the Blessed Trinity can
be interpreted and defended from the standpoint of theological orthodoxy, it is hardly possible not to discern a strong
tendency to go behind, as it were, the distinction of Persons
to a super-transcendent undifferentiated Unity. Probably the
truth of the matter is that the Pseudo-Dionysius, though an
orthodox Trinitarian in intention, was so much influenced by
the neo-Platonic philosophy that a tension between the two
elements underlies his attempt to reconcile them and makes
itself apparent in his statements.

5. In regard to the relation of the world to God, the
Pseudo-Dionysius speaks of the 'emanation' (πρόοδος) of God
into the universe of things;[19] but he tries to combine the
neo-Platonic emanation theory with the Christian doctrine of
creation and is no pantheist. For example, since God bestows
existence on all things that are, He is said to become manifold
through bringing forth existent things from Himself; yet at
the same time God remains One even in the act of 'self-
multiplication' and without differentiation even in the process of emanation.[20] Proclus had insisted that the prior Principle does not become less through the process of emanation

and the Pseudo-Dionysius repeats his teaching on this matter; but the influence of neo-Platonism does seem to have
meant that he did not clearly realise the relation of creation
to the divine will or the freedom of the act of creation, for
he is inclined to speak as though creation were a natural and
even a spontaneous effect of the divine goodness, even though
God is distinct from the world. God exists indivisibly and
without multiplication of Himself in all individual, separate
and multiple things, and, though they participate in the
goodness which springs from Him and though they may in
a certain sense be thought of as an 'extension' of God, God
Himself is not involved in their multiplication: the world, in
short, is an outflowing of the divine goodness, but it is not
God Himself. On this point of God's transcendence as well
as on that of His immanence the Pseudo-Dionysius is clear;
but his fondness for depicting the world as the outflowing
of the over-brimming Goodness of God, as well as for drawing
a kind of parallel between the internal divine Processions
and the external procession in creation, lead him to speak as
though creation were a spontaneous activity of God, as if God
created by a necessity of nature.

That God is the transcendent Cause of all things, the
Pseudo-Dionysius affirms several times, explaining in addition
that God created the world through the exemplary or archetypal Ideas, the 'preordinations' (προορισμοί) which exist in
Him:[21] in addition, God is the final Cause of all things,
drawing all things to Himself as the Good.[22] He is, therefore,
'the Beginning and the End of all things',[23] 'the Beginning as
their Cause, the End as their Final Purpose'.[24] There is, then,
an outgoing from God and a return to God, a process of
multiplication and a process of intercommunion and return.
This idea became basic in the philosophy of the 'Areopagite's'
translator, John Scotus Eriugena.

6. As the Pseudo-Dionysius insisted so much on the divine
goodness, it was incumbent on him to give some attention to
the existence and the consequent problem of evil, and this he
gave in the *Divine Names*,[25] relying, partly at least, on
Proclus's *De subsistentia mali*. In the first place he insists
that, although evil would have to be referred to God as its
Cause, were it something positive, it is in fact not something
positive at all: precisely as evil it has no being. If it is objected that evil must be positive, since it is productive, sometimes even of good, and since debauchery, for example, which

is the opposite of temperance, is something evil and positive, he answers that nothing is productive precisely as evil, but only in so far as it is good, or through the action of good: evil as such tends only to destroy and debase. That evil has no positive being of itself is clear from the fact that good and being are synonymous: everything which has being proceeds from the Good and, as being, is good. Does this mean, then, that evil and non-existence are precisely the same? The Pseudo-Dionysius certainly tends to speak as if that were the case, but his real meaning is given in his statement that 'all creatures in so far as they have being are good and come from the Good, and in so far as they are deprived of the Good, neither are they good nor have they being'.[26] In other words, evil is a deprivation or privation: it consists, not simply in non-being or in the absence of being, but rather in the absence of a good that ought to be present. The sinner, for instance, is good in so far as he has being, life, existence, will; the evil consists in the deprivation of a good that ought to be there and actually is not, in the wrong relation of his will to the rule of morality, in the absence of this or that virtue, etc.

It follows that no creature, considered as an existent being, can be evil. Even the devils are good in so far as they exist, for they hold their existence from the Good, and that existence continues to be good: they are evil, not in virtue of their existence, their natural constitution, but 'only through a lack of angelic virtues':[27] 'they are called evil through the deprivation and the loss whereby they have lapsed from their proper virtues.' The same is true of bad human beings, who are called evil in virtue of 'the deficiency of good qualities and activities and in virtue of the failure and fall therefrom due to their own weakness'. 'Hence evil inheres not in the devils or in us as evil, but only as a deficiency and lack of the perfection of our proper virtues.'[28]

Physical, non-moral evil is treated in a similar manner. 'No natural force is evil: the evil of nature lies in a thing's inability to fulfil its natural functions.'[29] Again, 'ugliness and disease are a deficiency in form and a want of order', and this is not wholly evil, 'being rather a lesser good'.[30] Nor can matter as such be evil, since 'matter too has a share in order, beauty and form':[31] matter cannot be evil in itself, since it is produced by the Good and since it is necessary to Nature. There is no need to have recourse to two ultimate Principles, good and evil respectively. 'In fine, good comes from the one universal Cause; evil from many partial deficiencies.'[32]

If it be said that some people desire evil, so that evil, as the object of desire, must be something positive, the Pseudo-Dionysius answers that all acts have the good as their object, but that they may be mistaken, since the agent may err as to what is the proper good or object of desire. In the case of sin the sinner has the power to know the true good and the right, so that his 'mistake' is morally attributable to him.[33] Moreover, the objection that Providence should lead men into virtue even against their will is foolish, for 'it is not worthy of Providence to violate nature': Providence provides for free choice and respects it.[34]

7. In conclusion one may remark that, although Ferdinand Christian Baur[35] would seem to have gone too far in saying that the Pseudo-Dionysius reduced the Christian doctrine of the Trinity to a mere formal use of the Christian terms void of the Christian content and that his system will not allow of a special Incarnation, it must be admitted that there was a tension in his thought between the neo-Platonic philosophy which he adopted and the Christian dogmas, in which, we have no real reason to deny, he believed. The Pseudo-Dionysius meant to harmonise the two elements, to express Christian theology and Christian mysticism in a neo-Platonic philosophical framework and scheme; but it can scarcely be gainsaid that, when a clash occurred, the neo-Platonic elements tended to prevail. A specific and peculiar Incarnation was one of the major points in Christianity that pagan neo-Platonists, such as Porphyry, objected to, and though, as I have said, we cannot be justified in asserting that the Pseudo-Dionysius denied the Incarnation, his acceptance of it does not well adapt itself to his philosophical system, nor does it play much part in his extant writings. One may well doubt whether his writings would have exercised the influence they did on Christian mediaeval thinkers, had the latter not taken the author's pseudonym at its face value.

Chapter Ten

BOETHIUS, CASSIODORUS, ISIDORE

Boethius's transmission of Aristotelian ideas—Natural theology—Influence on Middle Ages—Cassiodorus on the seven liberal arts and the spirituality of the soul—Isidore's Etymologies *and* Sentences.

1. If one of the channels whereby the philosophy of the ancient world was passed on to the Middle Ages was the writings of the Pseudo-Dionysius, another channel, and in some respects a complementary one, was constituted by the writings of Boethius (*c.* A.D. 480–524/5), a Christian who, after studying at Athens and subsequently holding high magisterial office under the king of the Ostrogoths, Theodoric, was finally executed on a charge of high treason. I use the word 'complementary' since, while the Pseudo-Dionysius helped to impregnate early mediaeval philosophy, especially that of John Scotus Eriugena, with elements drawn from neo-Platonic speculation, Boethius transmitted to the early mediaevals a knowledge of at least the logic of Aristotle. His works I have listed in my volume on Greek and Roman philosophy,[1] and I shall not repeat them here; suffice it to recall that he translated into Latin the *Organon* of Aristotle and commented thereon, besides commenting on the *Isagoge* of Porphyry and composing original treatises on logic. In addition he wrote several theological opuscula and while in prison his celebrated *De Consolatione Philosophiae*.

It is uncertain whether or not Boethius translated, in accordance with his original plan, other works of Aristotle besides the *Organon*; but in his extant works mention is made of several salient Aristotelian doctrines. The earlier mediaeval thinkers were predominantly concerned with the discussion of the problem of universals, taking as their starting-point certain texts of Porphyry and Boethius, and they took little notice of the Aristotelian metaphysical doctrines to be found in Boethius's writings. The first great speculative thinker of the Middle Ages, John Scotus Eriugena, was more indebted to the Pseudo-Dionysius and other writers dependent on neo-Platonism than to any Aristotelian influence, and it was not until the Aristotelian *corpus* had become available to the West at the close of the twelfth and the beginning of the thirteenth centuries that a synthesis on Aristotelian lines was attempted. But that does not alter the fact that Aristotelian doctrines of importance were incorporated in the writings of Boethius. For instance, in his theological work against Eutyches[2] Boethius speaks clearly of 'matter', the common substrate of bodies, which is the basis for, and renders possible, substantial change in bodies, corporeal substances, while its absence in incorporeal substances renders impossible the change of one immaterial substance into another or the change of a corporeal substance into an incorporeal substance or *vice versa*. The discussion is carried on in a theological setting and with a theological purpose, for Boethius wishes to show that in Christ the divine Nature and the human Nature are distinct and both real, against Eutyches who held that 'the union with Godhead involved the disappearance of the human nature';[3] but within that theological setting a philosophical discussion is included and the categories employed are Aristotelian in character. Similarly, in the *De Trinitate*,[4] Boethius speaks of the correlative principle to matter, namely form. For instance, earth is not earth by reason of unqualified matter, but because it is a distinctive form. (For 'unqualified matter' Boethius uses the Greek phrase ἄποια ὕλη, taking it doubtless from Alexander of Aphrodisias.[5] On the other hand, God, the Divine Substance, is Form without matter and cannot be a substrate. As pure Form, He is one.

Again, in the *De Trinitate*,[6] Boethius gives the ten Categories or *Praedicamenta* and goes on to explain that when we call God 'substance', we do not mean that He is substance in the same sense in which a created thing is substance: He is 'a substance that is super-substantial'. Similarly, if we predicate a quality of God, such as 'just' or 'great', we do not mean that He has an inhering quality, for 'with Him to be just and to be God are one and the same', and while 'man is merely great, God is greatness'. In the *Contra Eutychen*[7] occurs Boethius's famous definition of person, *naturae rationalis individua substantia,* which was accepted by St. Thomas and became classical in the Schools.

2. In his doctrine of the Blessed Trinity, Boethius relied largely on St. Augustine; but in the *De Consolatione Philosophiae* he developed in outline a natural theology on Aristotelian lines, thus implicitly distinguishing between natural theology, the highest part of philosophy, and dogmatic theology which, in distinction from the former, accepts its premisses from revelation. In the third book[8] he at least mentions the rational argument for the existence of God as unmoved Mover, while in the fifth book[9] he treats of the apparent difficulty in reconciling human freedom with the divine foreknowledge. 'If God beholdeth all things and cannot be deceived, that must of necessity follow which His providence foreseeth to be to come. Wherefore, if from eternity He doth foreknow not only the deeds of men, but also their counsels and wills, there can be no free-will.'[10] To answer that it is not that future events will take place because God knows them, but rather that God knows them because they will take place is not a very satisfactory answer, since it implies that temporal events and the temporal acts of creatures are the cause of the eternal foreknowledge of God. Rather should we say that God does not, strictly speaking, 'foresee' anything: God is eternal, eternity being defined in a famous phrase as *interminabilis vitae tota simul et perfecta possessio,*[11] and His knowledge is the knowledge of what is eternally present to Him, of a never-fading instant, not a foreknowledge of things which are future to God. Now, knowledge of a present event does not impose necessity on the event, so that God's knowledge of man's free acts, which from the human viewpoint are future, though from the divine viewpoint they are present, does not make those acts determined and necessary (in the sense of not-free). The eternity of God's vision, 'which is always present, concurs with the future quality of an action'.

Boethius drew not merely on Aristotle, but also on Porphyry and other neo-Platonic writers, as well as on Cicero, for example, and it may be that the division of philosophy or speculative science into Physics, Mathematics and Theology was taken directly from the *Isagoge* of Porphyry; but it must be remembered that Porphyry himself was indebted to Aristotle. In any case, in view of the predominantly neo-Platonic character of foregoing Christian philosophy, the Aristotelian element in the thought of Boethius is more remarkable and significant than the specifically neo-Platonic elements. It is true that he speaks of the divine Goodness and its overflowing in a manner reminiscent of neo-Platonism (in the *De Consol. Phil.*[12] he says that 'the substance of God consisteth in nothing else but in goodness') and that he sometimes uses such terms as *defluere* in connection with the procession of creatures from God;[13] but he is quite clear about the distinction between God and the world and about the Christian doctrine of creation. Thus he expressly affirms that God, 'without any change, by the exercise of a will known only to Himself, determined of Himself to form the world and brought it into being when it was absolutely nothing, not producing it from His own substance',[14] denying that the divine substance *in externa dilabatur*[15] or that 'all things which are, are God'.[16]

3. Boethius, then, was of very considerable importance, for he transmitted to the earlier Middle Ages a great part of the knowledge of Aristotle then available. In addition, his application of philosophical categories to theology helped towards the development of theological science, while his use of and definition of philosophical terms was of service to both theology and philosophy. Lastly we may mention the influence exercised by his composition of commentaries, for this type of writing became a favourite method of composition among the mediaevals. Even if not particularly remarkable as an original and independent philosopher, Boethius is yet of major significance as a transmitter and as a philosopher who attempted to express Christian doctrine in terms drawn, not simply from the neo-Platonists, but also from the philosopher whose thought was to become a predominant influence in the greatest philosophical synthesis of the Middle Ages.

4. *Cassiodorus* (c. 477–c. 565/70) was a pupil of Boethius and, like his master, worked for a time in the service of Theodoric, King of the Ostrogoths. In his *De artibus ac disciplinis liberalium litterarum* (which is the second book of his *Institutiones*) he treated of the seven liberal arts, i.e. the three *scientiae sermocinales* (Grammar, Dialectic and Rhetoric) and the four *scientiae reales* (Arithmetic, Geometry,

Music and Astronomy). He did not aim at novelty or originality of thought, but rather at giving a synopsis of the learning he had culled from other writers,[17] and his book on
the arts, like that of Martianus Capella, was much used as a
text-book in the early Middle Ages. In his *De anima* Cassiodorus drew on St. Augustine and on Claudianus Mamertus
(died *c.* 474) in proving the spirituality of the human soul.
While the soul cannot be a part of God, since it is changeable
and capable of evil, it is not material and cannot be material,
since it can have what is spiritual as the object of its knowledge, and only that which is itself spiritual can know the
spiritual. As spiritual, the soul is wholly in the whole body
and wholly in each part, being indivisible and unextended;
but it operates in a given part of the body, e.g. a sense-organ,
now with greater, now with less intensity.[18]

5. Cassiodorus, then, was much more a 'transmitter' than
an original thinker, and the same can be said of *Isidore* (died
c. 636), who became Archbishop of Seville in the Visigothic
kingdom and whose encyclopaedia, the *Originum seu Ety-
mologiarum libri* XX, was very popular in the early Middle
Ages, being included in every monastic library of note. In
this work Isidore deals with the seven liberal arts, as also
with a great number of scientific or quasi-scientific facts and
theories on subjects from Scripture and jurisprudence and
medicine to architecture, agriculture, war, navigation, and so
on. He shows his conviction about the divine origin of
sovereignty and the paramount authority of morality, law and
justice in civil society, even in regard to the conduct and acts
of the monarch. In addition to his *Etymologies* Isidore's *Libri
tres sententiarum*, a collection of theological and moral theses
taken from St. Augustine and St. Gregory the Great, was also
widely used. His treatise on numbers, *Liber Numerorum*,
which treats of the numbers occurring in the Sacred Scriptures, is often fanciful in the extreme in the mystical meanings which it attaches to numbers.

Part Two

THE CAROLINGIAN RENAISSANCE

Chapter Eleven

THE CAROLINGIAN RENAISSANCE

Charlemagne—Alcuin and the Palatine School—Other schools, curriculum, libraries—Rhabanus Maurus.

1. In A.D. 771 the death of Carloman left Charles (Charlemagne) sole ruler of the Frankish dominions, and his subsequent destruction of the Lombard kingdom and his general policy made him, by the close of the century, the paramount sovereign in Western Christendom. His coronation as emperor by the Pope on December 25th, 800, symbolised the success of his imperial policy and the culmination of Frankish power. The Frankish Empire was later to break up and the imperial crown was to pass to Germany, but for the moment Charlemagne was undisputed master in Western Christendom and was enabled to set on foot the work of reorganisation and reform which had become a crying need under the Merovingian dynasty. The emperor was by no means simply a soldier nor even simply soldier and political organiser combined: he had also at heart the work of raising the cultural level of his subjects by the extension and improvement of education. For this purpose he needed scholars and educational leaders, and since these were not easily obtainable in the Frankish kingdom itself, he had to introduce them from abroad. Already in the fifth century the old culture of Romanised Gaul was fast on the wane and in the sixth and seventh centuries it was at a very low point indeed; what schools there were, were teaching only reading, writing and some rudimentary knowledge of Latin, besides, of course, giving religious instruction. It was to remedy this lamentable state of learning and education that Charlemagne made use

of foreign scholars like Peter of Pisa and Paul the Deacon, who were both Italians. The former appears to have been already advanced in age when he taught Latin at the Palace School of Charlemagne, while the latter (Paul Warnefrid, the Deacon), who had come to France in 782, in an attempt to obtain the freedom of his brother, a prisoner of war, taught Greek from 782 to 786, when he retired to Monte Cassino, where he composed his *History of the Lombards.* Another Italian teacher at the Palatine School was Paulinus of Aquileia, who taught from about 777 to 787.

In addition to the group of Italian grammarians one may mention two Spaniards who came to France as refugees: Agobard, who became Archbishop of Lyons in 816, and Theodulf, who became Bishop of Orleans and died in 821. The latter was familiar with the Latin classics and was himself a Latin poet. Incidentally the oldest known mediaeval manuscript of Quintilian comes from Theodulf's private library. From the point of view of practical importance in the educational work of Charlemagne, however, the Italians and the Spaniards are overshadowed by the celebrated English scholar, Alcuin of York.

2. *Alcuin* (c. 730–804) received his early education at York. Learning had been making progress in England since the year 669, when Theodore of Tarsus, a Greek monk, arrived in the country as Archbishop of Canterbury and, together with Abbot Hadrian, developed the school of Canterbury and enriched its library. This work was carried on by men like Benedict Biscop, who founded the monasteries of Wearmouth (674) and Jarrow (682), and Aldhelm, who, after studying under Theodore and Hadrian, organised the monastery of Malmesbury in Wiltshire, of which he became abbot. A more important figure in Anglo-Saxon scholarship was, however, that of the great exegete and historian Bede (674–735), a priest and monk of Jarrow. It was due to the labours of Bede's friend and pupil Egbert, who became Archbishop of York shortly before Bede's death, that the school of York became the leading cultural and educational centre of England and noted for the richness of its library.

At York Alcuin was more particularly under the care of Aelbert, in company with whom he travelled to Rome, meeting Charles on the way, and when Aelbert succeeded Egbert as Archbishop of York in 767, the chief work in the school devolved on Alcuin. However, in 781, Alcuin was sent by

Aelbert to Rome, and in Parma he met Charles for the second time, the king utilising the meeting to urge the English scholar to enter his service. After receiving the permission of his own king and his archbishop, Alcuin accepted the invitation and in 782 took over the direction of the Palatine School, which he maintained (save for a short visit to England in 786 and a longer one from 790 to 793) until 796, when he accepted the abbacy of St. Martin at Tours, where he spent the last years of his life.

Probably about the year 777 Charlemagne wrote a letter to Baugulf, Abbot of Fulda,[1] in which he exhorts the abbot and community to zeal for learning, and this is merely one of the examples of his constant solicitude in the cause of education. The school which is, however, particularly associated with the name of Charlemagne is the so-called Palace or Palatine School, which though not a new creation of the emperor, owed its development to him. Before its development under Charlemagne the school would seem to have existed for the purpose of training the royal princes and children of the higher nobility in the knightly way of life; but the emperor laid emphasis on intellectual training and, as a result of his reform, the pupils appear to have been drawn from a wider circle than the court. French writers have commonly claimed that the Palatine School was the origin of the University of Paris; but it must be remembered that the emperor's court was at Aachen or Aix-la-Chapelle, and not at Paris, though it would seem to have been later removed to Paris by Charles the Bald (d. 877). However, as the University of Paris eventually grew up out of an amalgamation of the Parisian schools, it may be said that the Palatine School was in some sense a remote ancestor of the University, even if the connection was somewhat loose.

Charlemagne's main instrument in the organisation of the Palatine School was Alcuin, from whose writings we can form some idea of the curriculum. Alcuin was certainly not an original thinker, and his educational works, written in dialogue form, rely for the most part on former authors. For example, the De Rhetorica makes use of Cicero, with additions from other authors, while in other treatises Alcuin draws on Donatus, Priscian, Cassiodorus, Boethius, Isidore, Bede. But, though Alcuin was unoriginal and mediocre as a writer and can hardly be held to merit the title of philosopher, he seems to have been eminent and successful as a teacher, and some of the best-known figures of the Carolingian renaissance, e.g. Rhabanus Maurus, were his pupils. When he retired to the abbey of St. Martin at Tours, he continued this work of teaching, as is clear from a celebrated letter to the emperor, in which Alcuin describes how he serves to some youths the honey of the Holy Scriptures, while others he tries to intoxicate with the wine of ancient literature: some are nourished on the apples of grammatical studies, while to others he displays the order of the shining orbs which adorn the azure heavens. (Charlemagne had a considerable personal interest in astronomy and the two men corresponded on this subject.)

At Tours Alcuin enriched the library with copies of manuscripts which he brought from York, the best library in western Europe. He also devoted his attention to improving the method of copying manuscripts. In a letter of 799[2] he speaks of his daily battle with the 'rusticity' of Tours, from which one may conclude that the path of reform was not always an easy one. It is certain that Alcuin also gave attention to the accurate copying and amending of the manuscripts of the Scriptures, since he speaks explicitly of this in letters to Charlemagne in 800[3] and 801;[4] but it is not certain exactly what part he took in producing the revision of the Vulgate which was ordered by the emperor, known as the 'Alcuinian revision'. However, in view of the important position occupied by the scholar in the implementation of the emperor's reforms, it would seem only reasonable to suppose that he took a leading part in this important work, which helped to arrest the progress of manuscript corruption.

3. As regards the development of other schools (i.e. other than the Palatine School and that of Tours), one may mention the schools attached to the monasteries of St. Gall, Corbie and Fulda. In the monasteries education was provided not only for those pupils who were destined to become members of the religious order, but also for other pupils, though it appears that two separate schools were maintained, the *schola claustri* for the former class of pupil, the *schola exterior* for the latter. Thus at St. Gall the *schola claustri* was within the precincts of the monastery, while the *schola exterior* was among the outer buildings. A capitulary of Louis the Pious (817) ordained that the monasteries should only possess schools for the 'oblates'; but it seems that not much notice was taken of this ordinance.

If one sets the Palatine School in a class by itself, the other schools fall, then, into two main classes, the episcopal or capitular schools and the monastic schools. As for the curriculum this consisted, apart from the study of theology and exegesis, especially in the case of those pupils who were preparing for the priesthood or the religious life, in the study of the *Trivium* (grammar, rhetoric and dialectic) and the *Quadrivium* (arithmetic, geometry, astronomy and music), comprising the seven liberal arts. There was, however, little fresh or original work done on these subjects. Thus grammar, which included literature, would be studied in the writings of Priscian and Donatus, and in the text-books of Alcuin, for example, though some commentaries were composed on the works of the ancient grammarians, by Smaragdus, for instance, on Donatus, and a few undistinguished grammatical works were written, such as the *Ars grammaticae* of Clemens Scotus, who began teaching at the Palatine School in the later years of Charlemagne. Logic too was studied in the handbooks of Alcuin or, if something more was required, in the works of the authors on whom Alcuin relied, e.g. Boethius. In geometry and astronomy little work was done in the ninth century, though the theory of music was advanced by the *Musica enchiriadis*, attributed to Hoger the Abbot of Werden (d. 902). Libraries, e.g. the library of St. Gall, received a considerable increase in the ninth century and they included, besides the theological and religious works which composed the bulk of the items listed, legal and grammatical works, as well as a certain number of classical authors; but it is clear that, as far as philosophy is concerned, logic or dialectic (which, according to Aristotle, is a propaedeutic to philosophy, not a branch of philosophy itself) was the only subject studied. There was only one real speculative philosopher in the ninth century, and that was John Scotus Eriugena. Charlemagne's renaissance aimed at a dissemination of existing learning and what it accomplished was indeed remarkable enough; but it did not lead to original thought and speculation, except in the one instance of John Scotus's system. If the Carolingian empire and civilisation had survived and continued to flourish, a period of original work would doubtless have eventuated at length; but actually it was destined to be submerged in the new Dark Ages and there would be need of another renaissance before the mediaeval period of positive, constructive and original work could be realised.

4. Because of his importance for education in Germany one must mention, in connection with the Carolingian renaissance, the name of Rhabanus Maurus, who was born about 776 and who, after having been a pupil of Alcuin, taught at the monastery of Fulda, where he became abbot in 822. In 847 he was appointed Archbishop of Mainz and continued in that post until his death in 856. Rhabanus concerned himself with the education of the clergy, and for this purpose he composed his work *De Institutione Clericorum* in three books. In addition to a treatment of the ecclesiastical grades, the liturgy, the training of the preacher and so on, this work also deals with the seven liberal arts, but Rhabanus showed no more originality in this work than in his *De rerum naturis*, an encyclopaedia which was derived very largely from that of Isidore. In general the author depended almost entirely on former writers like Isidore, Bede and Augustine. In regard to exegesis he favoured mystical and allegorical interpretations. In other words, the *Praeceptor Germaniae* was a faithful product of the Carolingian renaissance, a scholar with a real enthusiasm for learning and a lively zeal for the intellectual formation of the clergy, but markedly unoriginal in thought.

Chapter Twelve

JOHN SCOTUS ERIUGENA—I

Life and works

ne of the most remarkable phenomena of the ninth century
the philosophical system of John Scotus Eriugena, which
ands out like a lofty rock in the midst of a plain. We have
en that there was a lively educational activity in the course
f the century and, considering the standard, materials and
pportunities of the time, a growing interest in learning and
holarship; but there was little original speculation. This is
fact which need cause no surprise in regard to a period of
nservation and dissemination; but it is all the more remark-
ble that an isolated case of original speculation on the grand
ale should suddenly occur, without warning and indeed
ithout any immediate continuation. If John Scotus had con-
ned himself to speculation on one or two particular points,
e might not have been so surprised, but in point of fact he
roduced a system, the first great system of the Middle Ages.
may, of course, be said that he relied largely on the
rmer speculations of St. Gregory of Nyssa, for instance, and
articularly on the work of the Pseudo-Dionysius, and this is
uite true; but one can scarcely avoid the impression, when
ading his *De Divisione Naturae*, that one is watching a
gorous, profound and original mind struggling with the cat-
gories and modes of thought and ideas which former writers
ad bequeathed to him as the material on which and with
hich he had to work, moulding them into a system and
npregnating the whole with an atmosphere, a colour and a
ne peculiar to himself. It is indeed interesting, if not alto-
ther profitable, to wonder on what lines the thought of

John Scotus would have evolved, had he lived at a later and richer period of philosophical development: as it is, one is confronted with a mind of great power, hampered by the limitations of his time and by the poverty of the material at his disposal. Moreover, while it is, of course, a mistake to interpret the system of John Scotus in terms of a much later philosophy, itself conditioned by the previous development of thought and the historical circumstances of the time, for example, the Hegelian system, one is not thereby debarred from endeavouring to discern the peculiar characteristics of John's thought, which, to a certain extent, altered the meaning of the ideas and categories he borrowed from previous writers.

Of the life of John Scotus we do not know very much. He was born in Ireland about 810 and studied in an Irish monastery. 'Eriugena' means 'belonging to the people of Erin', while the term 'Scotus' need not be taken as indicating any near connection with Scotland, since in the ninth century Ireland was known as *Scotia Maior* and the Irish as *Scoti*. It was doubtless in an Irish monastery that he acquired his knowledge of the Greek language. In the ninth century the study of Greek was, speaking generally, peculiar to the Irish monasteries. Bede, it is true, attained to a working knowledge of the language, but neither Alcuin nor Rhabanus Maurus knew any Greek worth speaking of. The former used Greek phrases in his commentaries but, though he must have known at least the Greek alphabet, these *Graeca* were taken over from the writings of other authors, and, in general, it has been shown that the occurrence of Greek phrases in a manuscript points to Irish authorship or to some association with or influence from an Irish writer. The attention given to Greek at St. Gall, for instance, was due originally to Irish monks. However, even if the presence of *Graeca* in a manuscript indicates an Irish influence, direct or indirect, and even if the study of Greek in the ninth century was characteristic of the Irish monasteries, it would be extremely rash to conclude that all Irish writers who used Greek phrases, still less that all Irish monks, studied and knew Greek in any real sense. The use of a Greek phrase is, by itself, no more a proof of a real knowledge of the Greek language than the use of a phrase like *fait accompli* is, by itself, a proof of a real knowledge of French, and the number of even Irish monks who knew much more than the rudiments of Greek was doubtless small. John Scotus Eriugena at any rate was among their number, as is shown clearly by the fact that he was able, when in France, to translate from the Greek writings of St. Gregory of Nyssa and the works of the Pseudo-Dionysius, and even attempted the composition of Greek verse. It would be absurd to take John's knowledge of the language as typical of the century or even as typical of Irish monasteries: the truth of the matter is that he was, for the ninth century, an outstanding Greek scholar.

Sometime in the forties John Scotus crossed over to France. In any case he was at the court of Charles the Bald by 850 and occupied a prominent position in the Palatine School. There is no sure evidence that he was ever ordained priest; but, whether layman or not, he was induced by Hincmar, Bishop of Rheims, to intervene in a theological dispute concerning predestination and the result was his work De praedestinatione which pleased neither side and brought its author under suspicion of heresy. John thereupon turned his attention to philosophy and in 858 he undertook, at the request of Charles the Bald, the translation of the works of the Pseudo-Dionysius from Greek into Latin. These works had been presented to Louis the Fair in 827 by the Emperor Michael Balbus, but they had never been adequately translated. John, then, undertook not only to translate them, but also to comment on them, and in fact he published commentaries on the Pseudo-Dionysius's writings, except on the Mystical Theology, though Pope Nicholas I made it a subject of complaint that the publication had taken place without any reference to him. John Scotus also published translations of the Ambigua of Maximus the Confessor and the De Hominis Opificio of St. Gregory of Nyssa, and it appears that later he commented on St. John's Gospel and on Boethius's De Consolatione Philosophiae and theological opuscula.

The work for which John Scotus is celebrated, however, is the De Divisione Naturae, which he composed probably between 862 and 866. This work consists of five books and is written in dialogue form, a form of composition which was popular at the time and which was much used by Alcuin and others. It is not a very easy work to interpret, since the author's attempt to express Christian teaching and the philosophical doctrine of Augustine on lines suggested by the Pseudo-Dionysius and the neo-Platonic philosophy leaves room for dispute whether John Scotus was an orthodox Christian or very nearly, if not quite, a pantheist. Those scholars who maintain his orthodox intentions can point to such statements as that 'the authority of the Sacred Scriptures must be followed in all things',[1] while those who maintain that he regarded philosophy as superior to theology and anticipated the Hegelian rationalism can point, for example, to the statement[2] that 'every authority' (e.g. that of the Fathers) 'which is not confirmed by true reason seems to be weak, whereas true reason does not need to be supported by any authority'. However, one cannot profitably discuss the question of interpretation until the doctrine of the *De Divisione Naturae* has first been exposed, though it is as well to indicate beforehand the fact that there is a dispute about its correct interpretation.

John Scotus seems not to have outlived Charles the Bald, who died in 877. There are indeed various stories about his later life which are given by chroniclers, e.g. that he became Abbot of Athelney and was murdered by the monks, but there seems to be little evidence for the truth of such stories, and probably they are either legends or are due to a confusion with some other John.

Chapter Thirteen

JOHN SCOTUS ERIUGENA—II

*Nature—God and creation—Knowledge of God by affirmative
and negative ways; inapplicability of categories to God—How,
then, can God be said to have made the world?—Divine Ideas
in the Word—Creatures as participations and theophanies;
creatures are in God—Man's nature—Return of all things to
God—Eternal punishment in light of cosmic return—Interpretation of John Scotus's system.*

1. At the beginning of the first book of the *De Divisione
Naturae* John Scotus explains through the lips of the Master,
in a dialogue which takes place between a *Magister* and a
Discipulus, what he means by 'Nature', namely the totality
of the things that are and the things that are not, and he
gives various ways of making this general division. For example, things which are perceived by the senses or are pene-
trable by the intellect are the things that are, while the objects that transcend the power of the intellect are the things
that are not. Again, things which lie hid in their *semina*,
which are not actualised, 'are not', while the things which
have developed out of their seeds 'are'. Or again, the objects
which are objects of reason alone may be said to be the things
which are, while the objects which are material, subject to
space and time and to dissolution, may be called the things
which are not. Human nature, too, considered as alienated
from God by sin may be said 'not to be', whereas when it is
reconciled with God by grace, it begins to be.

The term 'Nature', then, means for John Scotus Eriugena,
not only the natural world, but also God and the supernatural
sphere: it denotes all Reality.[1] When, therefore, he asserts[2]

that nature is divided into four species, namely Nature which creates and is not created, Nature which is created and creates, Nature which is created and does not create, and Nature which neither creates nor is created, thus apparently making God and creatures species of Nature, it might well seem that he is asserting a monistic doctrine, and indeed, if these words be taken in their literal significance, we should have to conclude that he was. Nevertheless at the beginning of Book 2, in a long and somewhat complicated period, he makes it clear that it is not his intention to assert that creatures are actually a part of God or that God is a genus of which creatures are a species, although he retains the fourfold division of 'Nature' and says that God and creatures may be looked at as forming together a *universitas*, a 'universe' or totality. The conclusion is warranted that John Scotus did not intend to assert a doctrine of pantheistic monism or to deny the distinction between God and creatures, though his philosophic explanation or rationalisation of the egress of creatures from God and their return to God may, taken by itself, imply pantheism and a denial of the distinction.

2. 'Nature which creates and is not created' is, of course, God Himself, who is the cause of all things but is Himself without cause. He is the beginning or first principle, since all creatures proceed from Him, the 'middle' (*medium*); since it is in Him and through Him that creatures subsist and move; and the end or final cause, since He is the term of the creature's movement of self-development and perfection.[3] He is the first cause, which brought creatures into existence from a state of non-existence, out of nothing (*de nihilo*).[4] This doctrine of God is in accordance with Christian theology and contains a clear enunciation of the divine transcendence and self-existence; but John Scotus goes on to say that God may be said to be created in creatures, to be made in the things which He makes, to begin to be in the things which begin to be. It would, however, be an anachronism to suppose that he is asserting an evolutionary pantheism, and maintaining that nature, in the ordinary sense, is God-in-His-otherness, for he proceeds to explain[5] that when he says that God is made in creatures, he means that God 'appears' or manifests Himself in creatures, that creatures are a theophany. Some of the illustrations he uses are indeed somewhat unfortunate from the orthodox standpoint, as when he says that, just as the human intellect, when it proceeds into actuality in the sense of actu-

ally thinking, may be said to be made in its thoughts, so God may be said to be made in the creatures which proceed from Him, an illustration which would seem to imply that creatures are an actualisation of God; but, whatever illustrations John Scotus may use and however much he is influenced by the philosophical tradition which derived from neo-Platonism, it seems clear that his intention at least was to conserve the real distinction between God and creatures and that God, in relation to creation, is *Natura quae creat et non creatur*. On the truth of this formula he is emphatic.

3. In attaining to some knowledge of the *Natura quae creat et non creatur* one can use the affirmative (καταφατική) and negative (ἀποφατική) ways. When using the negative method one denies that the divine essence or substance is any of those things, 'which are', i.e. which can be understood by us: when using the affirmative method one predicates of God those things 'which are', in the sense that the cause is manifested in the effect.[6] This twofold method of theology was borrowed by John Scotus from the Pseudo-Dionysius, as he himself plainly affirms,[7] and it was from the same writer that he took the idea that God should not be called, e.g. Truth or Wisdom or Essence, but rather super-Truth, super-Wisdom and super-Essence, since no names borrowed from creatures can be applied to God in their strict and proper sense: they are applied to God *metaphorice* or *translative*. Moreover, in a succeeding passage[8] John Scotus indulges in a most ingenious piece of dialectic in order to show that the use of the affirmative method does not contradict the doctrine of the ineffable and incomprehensible character of the Godhead and that the negative method is the fundamental one. For example, by the affirmative method we say that God is Wisdom, while by the negative way we say that God is not wisdom, and this appears at first sight to be a contradiction; but in reality, when we say that God is Wisdom, we are using the word 'wisdom' in a 'metaphorical' sense (an 'analogical' sense, the Scholastic would say), while when we say that God is not wisdom, we are using the word in its proper and primary sense (i.e. in the sense of human wisdom, the only wisdom of which we have direct experience). The contradiction is, therefore, not real, but only verbal, and it is reconciled by calling God super-Wisdom. Now, as far as words go, to predicate super-Wisdom of God would seem to be an act of mind pursuing the affirmative way, but if we examine the matter

more closely we shall see that, although the phrase belongs formally and verbally to the *via affirmativa*, the mind has no content, no idea, corresponding to the word 'super', so that in reality the phrase belongs to the *via negativa*, and the addition of the word 'super' to the word 'wisdom' is equivalent to a negation. Verbally there is no negation in the predicate 'super-Wisdom', but in regard to the mind's content there is a negation. The *via negativa* is thus fundamental, and as we do not pretend to define *what* the 'super' is in itself, the ineffability and incomprehensibility of the Godhead is unimpaired. Of course, if we say that the use of the word 'super' is *simply and solely* equivalent to a negation, the obvious objection arises (and would be raised by a Logical Positivist) that there is no meaning in our minds when we use the phrase, that the phrase is non-significant. John Scotus, however, though he does not discuss this real difficulty, provides one answer when he indicates that when we say that God is, for example, super-Wisdom, we mean that He is *more than* wisdom. If this is so, then the addition of 'super' cannot be simply equivalent to a negation, since we can say that 'a stone is not wise' and we certainly mean something different when we say 'God is not wise' and 'a stone is not wise': we mean that if 'wise' be taken to refer to human wisdom, then God is not wise, in the sense that He is *more* than human wisdom, whereas a stone is not wise, in the sense that the stone is *less* than wise. This thought would seem to be indicated by John Scotus's concluding example. '(God) is essence', an affirmation; 'He is not essence', a negation; 'He is super-essential', an affirmation and negation at the same time.[9] The thesis and the antithesis are thus reconciled dialectically in the synthesis.

If, then, God cannot be properly termed wise, for this term is not predicated of purely material things, much less can we predicate of Him any of the ten categories of Aristotle, which are found in purely material objects. For example, quantity can certainly not be predicated of God, as quantity implies dimensions, and God has no dimensions and does not occupy space.[10] Properly speaking, God is not even substance or οὐσία, for He is infinitely more than substance, though He can be called substance *translative*, inasmuch as He is the creator of all substances. The categories are founded on and apply to created things and are strictly inapplicable to God: nor is the predicate 'God' a genus or a species or an accident. Thus God transcends the *praedicamenta* and the *praedica-*

bilia, and on this matter John Scotus is clearly no monist but he emphasises the divine transcendence in the way that the Pseudo-Dionysius had done. The theology of the Blessed Trinity certainly teaches us that relation is found in God, but it does not follow that the relations in God fall under the category of relation. The word is used *metaphorice* or *translative* and, as applied to the divine Persons, it is not used in its proper and intelligible sense: the divine 'relations' are more than relations. In fine, though we can learn from creatures *that* God is, we cannot learn *what* He is. We learn that He is more than substance, more than wisdom and so on; but what that more is, what substance or wisdom mean as applied to God, we cannot know, for He transcends every intellect, whether of angels or of men.

4. But though the doctrine of the inapplicability of the categories to God would seem to place the transcendence of God and the clear distinction between Him and creatures beyond all doubt, consideration of the categories of *facere* and *pati* seems to lead John Scotus to a very different conclusion. In a most ingenious discussion[11] he shows, what is obvious enough, that *pati* cannot be predicated of God and at the same time argues that both *facere* and *pati* involve motion. Is it possible to attribute motion to God? No, it is not. Then neither can making be attributed to God. But, how in this case, are we to explain the Scriptural doctrine that God made all things? In the first place, we cannot suppose that God existed before He made the world, for, if that were so, God would not only be in time but also His making would be an accident accruing to Him, and both suppositions are impossible. God's making, therefore, must be co-eternal with Himself. In the second place, even if the making is eternal and identical with God, and not an accident of God, we cannot attribute motion to God, and motion is involved in the category of making. What does it mean, then, to say that God made all things? 'When we hear that God makes all things, we should understand nothing else but that God is in all things, i.e. is the essence of all things. For He alone truly is, and everything which is truly said to be in those things which are, is God alone.'[12] Such a statement would seem to come very near, to put it mildly, to pantheism, to the doctrine of Spinoza, and it is small wonder that John Scotus prefaces his discussion with some remarks on the relation of reason to authority[13] in which he says that reason is prior to authority

and that true authority is simply 'the truth found by the power of reason and handed on in writing by the Fathers for the use of posterity'. The conclusion is that the words, expressions and statements of Scripture, however suited for the uneducated, have to be rationally interpreted by those capable of doing so. In other words, John Scotus does not think of himself as unorthodox or intend to be unorthodox, but his philosophic interpretation of Scripture sometimes seems equivalent to its rationalisation and to the setting of reason above authority and faith. However, this point of view should not be overstressed. For example, in spite of the pantheistic passage quoted he goes on to reaffirm creation out of nothing, and it is clear that when he refuses to say that God makes or made the world, he is not intending to deny creation but rather to deny of God making in the only sense in which we understand making, namely as an accident, as falling under a particular category. God's existence and essence and His act of making are ontologically one and the same,[14] and all the predicates we apply to God really signify the one incomprehensible super-Essence.[15]

The truth of the matter seems to be that John Scotus, while maintaining the distinction between God and creatures, wishes at the same time to maintain the conception of God as the one all-comprehensive Reality, at least when God is regarded *altiori theoria*. Thus he points out[16] that the first and fourth divisions of Nature (*Natura quae creat et non creatur* and *Natura quae nec creat nec creatur*) are verified only in God, as first efficient cause and final cause, while the second and third divisions (*Natura quae et creatur et creat* and *Natura quae creatur et non creat*) are verified in creatures alone; but he goes on to say[17] that inasmuch as every creature is a participation of Him who alone exists of Himself, all Nature may be reduced to the one Principle, and Creator and creature may be regarded as one.

5. The second main division of Nature (*Natura quae et creatur et creat*) refers to the 'primordial causes', called by the Greeks πρωτότυπα, ἰδέαι, etc.[18] These primordial causes or *praedestinationes* are the exemplary causes of created species and exist in the Word of God: they are in fact the divine ideas, the prototypes of all created essences. How, then, can they be said to be 'created'? John Scotus means that the eternal generation of the Word or Son involves the eternal constitution of the archetypal ideas or exemplary causes in

the Word. The generation of the Word is not a temporal but an eternal process, and so is the constitution of the *praedestinationes*: the priority of the Word, considered abstractly, to the archetypes is a logical and not a temporal priority. The emergence of these archetypes is thus part of the eternal procession of the Word by 'generation', and it is in this sense only that they are said to be created.[19] However, the logical priority of the Word to the archetypes and the dependence of the archetypes on the Word mean that, although there never was a time when the Word was without the archetypes, they are not *omnino coaeternae (causae)* with the Word.[20]

In what sense, then, can the primordial causes be said to create? If one were to press statements such as this, that the πρωτότυπον is diffused (*diffunditur*) through all things giving them essence, or again that it penetrates all the things which it has made,[21] one would naturally incline to a pantheistic interpretation; yet John Scotus repeats[22] that the Holy Trinity 'made out of nothing all things that it made', which would imply that the prototypes are causes only in the sense of exemplary causes. Nothing is created except that which was eternally pre-ordained, and these eternal *praeordinationes* or θεῖα θηλήματα are the prototypes. All creatures 'participate' in the archetypes, e.g. human wisdom in the Wisdom-in-itself.[23] He drew copiously on the Pseudo-Dionysius and Maximus for his doctrine and it would seem that he intended to reconcile his philosophic speculation with orthodox Christian theology; but his language rather gives the impression that he is straining at the leash and that his thought, in spite of his orthodox intentions, tends towards a form of philosophic pantheism. That his intentions were orthodox seems clear enough from the frequent *cautelae* he gives.

Is there actually and ontologically a plurality of *praedestinationes* in the Word? John Scotus answers in the negative.[24] Numbers proceed from the *monas* or unit, and in their procession they are multiplied and receive an order; but, considered in their origin, in the monad, they do not form a plurality but are undivided from one another. So the primordial causes, as existing in the Word, are one and not really distinct, though in their effects, which are an ordered plurality, they are multiple. The monad does not become less or undergo change through the derivation of numbers, nor does the primordial cause undergo change or diminution through the derivation of its effects, even though, from another point of view, they are contained within it. On this point John Scotus adheres to the neo-Platonic standpoint, according to which the principle undergoes no change or diminution through the emanation of the effect, and it seems that his philosophy suffers from the same tension that is observable in neo-Platonism, i.e. between a theory of emanation and a refusal to allow that emanation or procession impairs the integrity of the principle.

6. *Natura quae creatur et non creat* consists of creatures, exterior to God, forming the world of nature in the narrow sense, which was made by God out of nothing. John Scotus calls these creatures 'participations', and asserts that they participate in the primordial causes, as the latter participate immediately in God.[25] The primordial causes, therefore, look upwards towards the ultimate Principle and downwards towards their multiple effects, a doctrine which obviously smacks of the neo-Platonic emanation theory. 'Participation' means, however, derivation from, and, interpreting the Greek μετοχή or μετουσία as meaning μεταέχουσα or μεταουσία (*post-essentia* or *secunda essentia*), he says that participation is nothing else than the derivation of a second essence from a higher essence.[26] Just as the water rises in a fountain and is poured out into the river-bed, so the divine goodness, essence, life, etc., which are in the Fount of all things, flow out first of all into the primordial causes and cause them to be, and then proceed through the primordial causes into their effects.[27] This is clearly an emanation metaphor, and John Scotus concludes that God is everything which truly is, since He makes all things and is made in all things, 'as Saint Dionysius the Areopagite says'.[28] The divine goodness is progressively diffused through the universe of creation, in such a way that it 'makes all things, and is made in all things, and is all things'.[29] This sounds as if it were a purely pantheistic doctrine of the emanation type; but John Scotus equally maintains that the divine goodness created all things out of nothing, and he explains that *ex nihilo* does not imply the pre-existence of any material, whether formed or unformed, which could be called *nihil*: rather does *nihil* mean the negation and absence of all essence or substance, and indeed of all things which have been created. The Creator did not make the world *ex aliquo*, but rather *de omnino nihilo*.[30]

Here again, then, John Scotus tries to combine the Christian doctrine of creation and of the relation of creatures to God with the neo-Platonic philosophy of emanation, and it is this attempt at combination which is the reason for diversity of interpretation, according as one regards the one or other element in his thought as the more fundamental.

This tension became even clearer from the following consideration. Creatures constitute, not only a 'participation' of the divine goodness, but also the divine self-manifestation or theophany. All objects of intellection or sensation are 'the appearance of the non-appearing, the manifestation of the hidden, the affirmation of the negated (a reference to the *via negativa*), the comprehension of the incomprehensible, the speaking of the ineffable, the approach of the unapproachable, the understanding of the unintelligible, the body of the incorporeal, the essence of the super-essential, the form of the formless', etc.[31] Just as the human mind, itself invisible, becomes visible or manifest in words and writing and gestures, so the invisible and incomprehensible God reveals Himself in nature, which is, therefore, a true theophany. Now, if creation is a theophany, a revelation of the divine goodness, which is itself incomprehensible, invisible and hidden, does not this suggest a new interpretation of the *nihilum* from which creation proceeds? Accordingly John Scotus explains in a later passage[32] that *nihilum* means 'the ineffable and incomprehensible and inaccessible brightness of the divine goodness', for what is incomprehensible may, *per excellentiam*, be called 'nothing', so that when God begins to appear in His theophanies, He may be said to proceed *ex nihilo in aliquid*. The divine goodness considered in itself may be said to be *omnino nihil*, though in creation it comes to be, 'since it is the essence of the whole universe'. It would indeed be an anachronism to ascribe to John Scotus a doctrine of Absolutism and to conclude that he meant that God, considered in Himself apart from the 'theophanies', is a logical abstraction; but it does seem that two distinct lines of thought are present in his teaching about creation, namely the Christian doctrine of free creation 'in time' and the neo-Platonic doctrine of a necessary diffusion of the divine goodness by way of 'emanation'. Probably he intended to maintain the Christian doctrine, but at the same time considered that he was giving a legitimate philosophic explanation of it. Such an attitude would, of course, be facilitated by the fact

that there was at the time no clear distinction between theology and philosophy and their respective spheres, with the
result that a thinker could, without being what we would
nowadays call a rationalist, accept a revealed dogma like the
Trinity, and then proceed in all good faith to 'explain' or deduce it in such a way that the explanation practically changed
the dogma into something else. If we want to call John Scotus
an Hegelian before Hegel, we must remember that it is extremely unlikely that he realised what he was doing.

The precise relation of the created nature to God in the
philosophy of John Scotus is not an easy matter to determine.
That the world is eternal in one sense, namely in its *rationes*,
in the primordial causes, in God's will to create, occasions
no difficulty, and if the author, when he maintains that the
world is both eternal and created, meant simply that as fore-
seen and willed by God it is eternal, while as made it is
temporal and outside God, there would be no cause for surprise; but he maintains that the world is not outside God and
that it is both eternal and created *within* God.[33] As regards
the first point, that the world is not *extra Deum*, one must
understand it in terms of the theory of participation and 'as-
sumption' (*est igitur participatio divinae essentiae assump-
tio*).[34] As creatures are derived from God and owe all the
reality they possess to God, apart from God they are nothing,
so that in this sense it can be said that there is nothing outside God: if the divine activity were withdrawn, creatures
would cease to be. But we must go further.[35] God saw from
eternity all that He willed to create. Now, if He saw creatures
from all eternity, He also made them from all eternity, since
vision and operation are one in God. Moreover, as He saw
creatures in Himself, He made them in Himself. We must
conclude, therefore, that God and creatures are not distinct,
but one and the same (*unum et id ipsum*), the creature
subsisting in God and God being created in the creature 'in
a wonderful and ineffable manner'. God, then, 'contains and
comprehends the nature of all sensible things in Himself,
not in the sense that He contains within Himself anything
beside Himself, but in the sense that He is substantially all
that He contains, the substance of all visible things being
created in Him'.[36] It is at this point that John Scotus gives
his interpretation of the 'nothing' out of which creatures
proceed as the divine goodness,[37] and he concludes that
God is everything, that from the super-essentiality of His na-

ture (*in qua dicitur non esse*) He is created by Himself in the primordial causes and then in the effects of the primordial causes, in the theophanies.[38] Finally, at the term of the natural order, God draws all things back into Himself, into the divine Nature from which they proceeded, thus being first and final Cause, *omnia in omnibus*.

The objection may be raised that first of all John Scotus says that God is *Natura quae creat et non creatur* and then goes on to identify with God the *Natura quae creatur et non creat*: how can the two positions be reconciled? If we regard the divine Nature as it is in itself, we see that it is without cause, ἄναρχος and ἀναίτιος,[39] but at the same time it is the cause of all creatures: it is, then, rightly to be called 'Nature which creates and is not created'. From another point of view, looking on God as final Cause, as *term* of the rhythm of the cosmic process, He may be called 'Nature which neither creates nor is created'. On the other hand, considered as issuing out from the hidden depths of His nature and beginning 'to appear', He appears first of all in the primordial causes or *rationes aeternae*. These are identical with the Word, which contains them, so that, in 'creating' the primordial causes or principles of essences, God appears to Himself, becomes self-conscious, and creates Himself, i.e. as generating the Word and the *rationes* contained in the Word. God is thus 'Nature which both creates and is created'. In the second stage of the divine procession or theophany God comes to be in the effects of the primordial causes, and so is 'Nature which is created', while, since these effects have a term and include together all created effects, so that there are no further effects, He is also 'Nature which does not create'.[40]

7. John Scotus's allegorical explanation of the Biblical account of the six days of creation,[41] which he explains in terms of his own philosophy, brings him, in the fourth book, to his doctrine of man. We can say of man that he is an animal, while we can also say that he is not an animal,[42] since while he shares with the animals the functions of nutrition, sensation, etc., he has also the faculty of reason, which is peculiar to him and which elevates him above all the animals. Yet there are not two souls in man, an animal soul and a rational soul: there is a rational soul which is simple and is wholly present in every part of the body, performing its various functions. John Scotus is therefore willing to accept the definition of man as *animal rationale*, understanding by *ani-*

mal the genus and by *rationale* the specific difference. On the other hand the human soul is made in the image of God, is like to God, and this likeness to God expresses the true substance and essence of man. As it exists in any actual man it is an effect: as it exists in God it is a primordial cause, though these are but two ways of looking at the same thing.[43] From this point of view man can be defined as *Notio quaedam intellectualis in mente divina aeternaliter facta.*[44] That this substance of man, the likeness to God or participation in God, exists, can be known by the human mind, just as the human mind can know *that* God exists, but *what* its substance is the human mind cannot know, just as it cannot know *what* God is. While, then, from one point of view man is definable, from another point of view he is undefinable, since the mind or reason of man is made in the image of God and the image, like God Himself, exceeds our power of understanding. In this discussion of the definition of man we can discern Aristotelian elements and also neo-Platonic and Christian elements, which give rise to different attitudes and views on the matter.

John Scotus emphasises the fact that man is the microcosm of creation, since he sums up in himself the material world and the spiritual world, sharing with the plants the powers of growth and nutrition, with the animals the powers of sensation and emotional reaction, with the angels the power of understanding: he is in fact what Poseidonius called the bond or δέσμος, the link between the material and spiritual, the visible and invisible creation. From this point of view one can say that every genus of animal is in man rather than that man is in the genus animal.[45]

8. The fourth stage of the process of Nature is that of *Natura quae nec creat nec creatur*, namely of God as the term and end of all things, God all in all. This stage is that of the return to God, the corresponding movement to the procession from God, for there is a rhythm in the life of Nature and, as the world of creatures proceeded forth from the primordial causes, so will it return into those causes. 'For the end of the whole movement is its beginning, since it is terminated by no other end than by its principle, from which its movement begins and to which it constantly desires to return, that it may attain rest therein. And this is to be understood not only of the parts of the sensible world, but also of the whole world. Its end is its beginning, which it desires,

and on finding which it will cease to be, not by the perishing of its substance, but by its return to the ideas (*rationes*), from which it proceeds.'[46] The process is thus a cosmic process and affects all creation, though mutable and unspiritualised matter which John Scotus, following St. Gregory of Nyssa, represented as a complex of accidents and as appearance,[47] will perish.

Besides the cosmical process of creation as a whole, there is the specifically Christian theme (though John Scotus not infrequently does a little 'rationalising') of the return of man to God. Fallen man is led back to God by the incarnate Logos, who has assumed human nature and redeemed all men in that human nature, and John Scotus emphasises the solidarity of mankind both in Adam's fall and in Christ's resurrection. Christ brings mankind back to God, though not all are united to God in the same degree, for, though He redeemed all human nature, 'some He restores to the former state of human nature, while others He deifies beyond human nature', yet in no one except Himself is human nature substantially united with the Godhead.[48] John Scotus thus affirms the unique character of the Incarnation and of the relation of Christ's human nature to the Deity, though, when he gives the stages of the return of human nature to God, another—and less orthodox—point of view seems to show itself. These stages are:[49] (1) the dissolution of the human body into the four elements of the sensible world; (2) the resurrection of the body; (3) the change of body into spirit; (4) the return of human nature in its totality into the eternal and unchangeable primordial causes; and (5) the return of nature and the primordial causes to God. 'For God will be all in all, where nothing will exist but God alone.' Yet if at first sight this latter viewpoint seems quite inconsistent with orthodox theology and especially with the unique position of Christ, John Scotus clearly did not mean to assert a real pantheistic absorption in God, since he goes on to state that he does not mean to imply a perishing of individual substance but its elevation. He uses the illustration of the iron made white-hot in the fire and observes that, though the iron may be said to be transmuted into fire, the substance of the iron remains. Thus when, for example, he says that the human body is changed into spirit, what he refers to is the glorification or 'spiritualisation' of the human body, not to a kind of transubstantiation. Moreover, it must be remembered that

John Scotus expressly states that he is basing his teaching on the doctrine of St. Gregory of Nyssa and his commentator Maximus, and his teaching must accordingly be understood in the light of that statement. Lest it be thought, he says, that he is entirely neglecting the Latins in favour of the Greeks, he adds the testimony of St. Ambrose. Though the heavens and the earth will perish and pass away (their perishing being interpreted as a *reditus in causas*, which means the cessation of the generated material world), that does not mean that the individual souls of men, in their *reditus in causas*, will cease to exist: their *deificatio* no more means their substantial absorption in God than the permeation of the air by light means its destruction or transubstantiation. John Scotus is quite clear on that point.

The fact is that in the case of the cosmic 'return', as elsewhere, John Scotus tries to combine the teaching of the Scriptures and the Fathers with philosophical speculation of the neo-Platonic tradition or rather to express the Christian *Weltanschauung* in terms of such speculation. As the Christian wisdom is looked at as a totality, no clear distinction being made between revealed theology and philosophy, the application of John's speculative method necessarily means a *de facto* rationalisation on occasion, however orthodox his intentions may have been. For instance, though he insists on the fact that the return to God does not spell the annihilation or the complete absorption of the individual human being and though he expresses himself perfectly clearly on this point, yet his attitude towards matter as the term of the descending divine procession leads him to say[50] that before the Fall human beings were not sexually differentiated and that after the resurrection they will return to this state (in support of which views he appeals to St. Paul, St. Gregory and Maximus). Man, had he not fallen, would have been sexually undifferentiated and in the primordial cause human nature is sexually undifferentiated: the *reditus in causam* involves, therefore, a return to the state of human nature *in causa* and a liberation from the state consequent on the Fall. The *reditus in causam*, however, is a stage in the cosmic process of Nature, so that John Scotus has to maintain that the resurrection of the body takes place by nature, *natura et non per gratiam*,[51] though he appeals for support in this to St. Gregory of Nyssa, Maximus and St. Epiphanius. On the other hand, it is certain, theologically at least, that something is attributable to grace, and John Scotus accordingly attributes the *deificatio*, which is not attained by all human beings, to the free gift and disposition of God, to grace. This is an example of his attempt to combine revelation with the exigencies of his speculative system, an attempt for which, of course, he undoubtedly received support from the writings of earlier Christian authors. On the one hand John Scotus, owing to his Christian intentions, must attribute the resurrection in at least one aspect to God's free grace operating through Christ, while on the other hand, his philosophical doctrine of the return of all things to God means that he must make the resurrection in some degree a natural and necessary process, not only because human nature itself has to return into its cause, but because all creation has to return into its cause and endure eternally, and this it does effectively as being contained in man, the microcosm.[52]

9. But if there is to take place a cosmic return to God in and through human nature, so that God, as St. Paul says, will be 'all in all', how is it possible to maintain the theologically orthodox doctrine of the eternal punishment of the damned? The Scriptures teach that the fallen angels and human beings who are finally impenitent will be eternally punished, while on the other hand reason teaches that evil cannot be without end, since God will be all in all and evil is diametrically opposed to God, who is goodness.[53] How can one reconcile these two positions without rejecting either authority or reason? John Scotus's answer[54] is ingenious and affords a good example of his 'rationalisation'. Nothing that God has made can be evil: the substances or natures, therefore, of the devils and evil men must be good. On this point he quotes the Pseudo-Dionysius. The demons and evil men will never, then, suffer annihilation. All that God has made will return to God and all 'nature' will be contained in God, human nature included, so that it is impossible that human nature should undergo eternal punishment. What, then, of the punishments described in the Scriptures? In the first place they cannot be corporeal or material in character, while in the second place they can only affect what God has not made and what, in this sense, is outside 'nature'. Now, God did not make the perverse will of demons or evil men, and it is this which will be punished. But, if all things are to return to God and God will be all in all, how can punishment be contained in God? Moreover, if the malice has disappeared

and all impiety, what is there left to punish? The punishment must consist in the eternal prevention by God of the will's tendency to fix itself on the images, conserved in the memory, of the objects desired on earth. God, then, will be all in all, and all evil will have perished, but the wicked will be eternally punished. It is obvious, however, that from the viewpoint of orthodox theology 'wicked' and 'punished' must be placed in inverted commas, since John Scotus has rationalised the Scriptural teaching in order to satisfy the exigencies of his philosophical system.[55] All human nature, all men without exception, will rise with spiritualised bodies and the full possession of natural goods, though only the elect will enjoy 'deification'.[56]

The conclusion is, then, that the divine nature is the end and term of all things, which will return into their *rationes aeternae* and there abide, 'ceasing to be called by the name of creature', for God will be all in all, 'and every creature will be cast into the shade, i.e. changed into God, as the stars at the rising of the sun'.[57]

10. Although the *De Divisione Naturae* did not have the effect that its outstanding quality as a systematic metaphysic deserved, it was utilised by a succession of mediaeval writers from Remigius of Auxerre to Amalric of Bene, including Berengarius, Anselm of Laon, William of Malmesbury, who praised the work, though he disapproved of John Scotus's predilection for Greek authors, and Honorius of Autun, while the Pseudo-Avicenna borrowed from the work in his *De Intelligentiis*, written in the middle or later part of the twelfth century. However, the fact that the Albigensians appealed to the book, while Amalric of Bene (end of twelfth century) used the doctrine of John Scotus in a pantheistic sense, led to its condemnation in 1225 by Pope Honorius III, who ordered that the work should be burnt, though the order was by no means always fulfilled. This condemnation of the *De Divisione Naturae* and the interpretation which led to the condemnation naturally raises the question, whether John Scotus was or was not a pantheist.

That John Scotus was in intention orthodox has already been given as my opinion; but there are several points that might be mentioned by way of summary argument in support of this statement. First of all, he draws copiously on the writings and ideas of authors whom he certainly regarded as orthodox and with whose ideas he felt his own thought to be in harmony. For example, he makes extensive use of St. Gregory of Nyssa, of the Pseudo-Dionysius (whom he regarded as St. Dionysius the Areopagite), and, not to appear to neglect the Latins, quotes St. Augustine and St. Ambrose in favour of his views. Moreover, John Scotus considered his speculation to be founded on the Scriptures themselves. For instance, the theory of the fourth stage of Nature, *Deus omnia in omnibus*, has its foundation in the words of St. Paul:[58] 'And when all things shall be subdued unto him, then the Son also himself shall be subject unto him that put all things under him, that God may be all in all,' while the doctrine of the body 'becoming spirit' at the resurrection is based on the Pauline statement that the body is sown in corruption and raised in incorruption, that the risen body is a 'spiritual' body. Again, John Scotus draws from the first chapter of St. John's Gospel the conception of the Logos by whom all things were made, in his account of creation, while the theme of *deificatio* was common in the writings of the Fathers.

But, even if John Scotus wrote as though his system had a foundation in Scripture and Tradition, might it not be that he was consciously rationalising the text of Scripture, that he had, to put it crudely, 'his tongue in his cheek'? Does he not say[59] that authority proceeds from true reason and reason in no way from authority; that every authority which is not approved by true reason seems to be weak; that true reason does not need the confirmation of any authority and that authority is nothing else but the truth found by the power of reason and handed on by the Fathers in their writings for the use of posterity; and does not this indicate that he set no store by authority? It seems to me that, to judge by the context, when John Scotus speaks about 'authority' here, he is not referring to the words of Scripture but to the teaching of the Fathers and to the interpretation they had put on the words of the Scriptures. Of course, although it is true that authority must rest on reason, in the sense that the authority must have good credentials, the statement of John Scotus to the effect that authority is nothing else than the truth found by reason and handed on by the Fathers is, as it stands, unacceptable from the theological standpoint (I mean, if compared with the orthodox doctrine of Tradition); but what John Scotus apparently *means* is, not that the doctrine of the Trinity, for example, is simply a truth found by reason and not revealed, but that the attempted 'explanation' or development of the dogma by this or that Father is simply the result of the Father's rational effort and is not final. He does not mean to suggest that the bare dogma, as found in Scripture and preserved by, for example, St. Augustine, can legitimately be questioned, but rather that the intellectual development of the dogma given by St. Augustine, though worthy of respect, is the work of reason and cannot be placed on the same level as the dogma itself. His position is, therefore, this. If St. Paul says that God will be *omnia in omnibus*, this is a revealed truth, but when it comes to deciding what St. Paul meant by this statement and how precisely it is to be understood, reason is the final court of appeal. I am not trying to suggest that this attitude is theologically acceptable: my point is rather that, whether his actual view is acceptable or not, John Scotus is not questioning a dogma as such or claiming a right to deny it, but is claiming the right to interpret it, and that his 'rationalisation' consists in this. He has not got his tongue in his cheek when he appeals to Scripture, for he sincerely believed that the data of revelation have to be interpreted rationally and, as we would say, philosophically. This is partly due to the fact that he makes no clear-cut distinction between theology and philosophy. His system presupposes the 'Christian wisdom' (including truths discoverable by reason alone, e.g. God's existence, and truths which are revealed, but not discoverable by reason alone, e.g. the Trinity of Persons in the Godhead) and is a speculative attempt to exhibit the Christian wisdom as an organic and interconnected whole, without making any clear distinction between the spheres of philosophy and revelation, and this attempt inevitably involves some rationalisation. I repeat that I am not trying to defend John Scotus's rationalisation, but to explain his attitude, and my thesis is that it is a mistake to interpret his 'rationalisation' as if it post-dated the clear division of philosophy and theology: his attitude is not essentially different from that of later mediaeval theologians who attempted to prove the Trinity *rationibus necessariis*. If John Scotus had consciously been a 'philosopher' in the narrow sense and nothing more, we would have had to call him a rationalist in the modern sense; but he was both theologian and philosopher in combination (in confusion, if one prefers), and his rationalisation was, *psychologically*, quite compatible with a belief in revelation. Therefore, when he says[60] that he does not want to seem to resist the Apostle or the testimony *summae ac sanctae auctoritatis*, he is quite sincere. Indeed his true attitude is admirably indicated by his statement[61] that 'it is not for us to judge the opinions of the holy Fathers, but to accept them with piety and reverence, though we are not prohibited from choosing (among their opinions) that which appears to reason to agree better with the divine words'. John Scotus accepts, for instance, the doctrine of eternal punishment, because it is revealed, and he accepts it sincerely; but he does not consider that this prevents him from attempting to explain the doctrine in such a way that it will fit in with the rest of his system, a system which he regards as fundamentally based on revelation.

The discussion may seem to have strayed from the point at issue; but this is not so in reality. For instance, revelation, Christian dogma, teaches clearly that the world was made by God from nothing and that creatures are not God. Now John Scotus's general system demands that creatures should return to God and that God should be all in all. Regarding both truths as founded on divine teaching, John Scotus has to reconcile them rationally, in such a way that the *reditus in Deum* does not lead to the conclusion to which it might seem to lead, namely pantheistic absorption, and that the presentation of the distinction between God and creatures does not contradict the Pauline statement that God will be all in all. The process of reconciliation may involve him in what the Thomist theologians would call 'rationalisation', but his *cautelae*, e.g. that creatures return to God and 'become' God, not *ita ut non sint* but *'ut melius sint'*, are not sops thrown to the theologians with the writer's tongue in his cheek, but they are sincere expressions of John Scotus's desire to preserve Christian teaching or what he regards, rightly or wrongly, as Christian teaching.

That a tension develops between the Christian and neo-Platonic elements in John Scotus's thought has already been pointed out, but it is as well to emphasise it again, as it has a bearing on the question of his 'rationalism'. In accordance with the neo-Platonic tradition inherited through the Pseudo-Dionysius, John Scotus maintained[62] that God in Himself, *Natura quae creat et non creatur*, is impenetrable to Himself, unknown to Himself, as being infinite and super-essential, and that He becomes luminous to Himself only in His theophanies. This is, of course, an echo of the neo-Platonic doctrine that the One, the ultimate Godhead, is beyond thought, beyond self-consciousness, since thought and self-consciousness involve a duality of subject and object. Now, that God in Himself is incomprehensible to the created mind is certainly a Christian tenet, but that He is not self-luminous is not the teaching of Christianity. John Scotus, therefore, has to reconcile the two positions somehow, if he wishes to retain them both, and he attempts to do so by making the first 'theophany' the emergence of the Logos containing the primordial causes, so that in and through the Logos God becomes (though not temporally) self-conscious, appearing to Himself. The Logos thus corresponds to the neo-Platonic *Nous*, and a rationalisation arises out of the desire to preserve both the Christian doctrine and the principles of what John Scotus regards as true philosophy. The desire to preserve Christian doctrine is sincere enough, but a tension between the two elements is inevitable. If one takes a particular set of isolated statements of John Scotus one would have to say that he was either a pantheist or a theist. For example, the statement that the distinction between the second and third stages of Nature is due only to the forms of human reasoning[63] is in itself clearly pantheistic, while the statement that the substantial distinction between God and creatures is always preserved is clearly theistic. It might seem that we should opt for one or the other set in an unqualified manner, and it is this attitude which has given rise to the notion that John Scotus was a conscious pantheist who made verbal concessions to orthodoxy with his tongue in his cheek. But if one realises that he was a sincere Christian, who yet attempted to reconcile Christian teaching with a predominantly neo-Platonic philosophy or rather to express the Christian wisdom in the only framework of thought which was then at hand, which happened to be predominantly neo-Platonic, one should also be able to realise that, in spite of the tension involved and the tendency to rationalise Christian dogma, as far as the subjective standpoint of the philosopher was concerned a satisfactory reconciliation was effected. This does not, of course, alter the fact that not a few statements, if taken in isolation, affirm a pantheistic doctrine and that other statements are irreconcilable with orthodox theological teaching on such points as eternal punishment, and it was in view of such statements that the *De Divisione Naturae* was subsequently condemned by ecclesiastical authority. However, whether orthodox or not, the work bears testimony to a powerful and acute mind, the mind of a speculative philosopher who stands head and shoulders above any other thinker of his day.

Part Three

THE TENTH, ELEVENTH AND TWELFTH CENTURIES

Chapter Fourteen

THE PROBLEM OF UNIVERSALS

Situation following death of Charlemagne—Origin of discussion in texts of Porphyry and Boethius—Importance of the problem—Exaggerated realism—Roscelin's 'nominalism'—St. Peter Damian's attitude to dialectic—William of Champeaux —Abelard—Gilbert de la Porrée and John of Salisbury—Hugh of St. Victor—St. Thomas Aquinas.

1. One might have expected that the revival of letters and learning under Charlemagne would lead to a gradual and progressive development of philosophy and (the retention of what was already possessed having been provided for) that thinkers would be able to extend knowledge and pursue a more speculative path, especially as western Europe had been already supplied with an example of philosophical speculation and systematising by John Scotus Eriugena. In point of fact, however, this was not the case, since historical factors outside the sphere of philosophy plunged the empire of Charlemagne into a new Dark Age, the Dark Ages of the tenth century, and belied the promise of the Carolingian renaissance.

Cultural progress depended to some extent on the maintenance of the tendency to centralisation which had been apparent during the reign of Charlemagne; but after his death the empire was divided and the division of the empire among the descendants of Charlemagne was accompanied by the growth of feudalism, that is, by decentralisation. As nobles could be rewarded practically only through gifts of land, they tended, through the acquisition of land, to become more and more independent of the monarchy: their interests diverged or conflicted. Churchmen of the higher grades became feudal lords, monastic life was degraded (for example, through the common practice of the appointment of lay-abbots), bishoprics were used as means of honouring or rewarding servants of the king. The Papacy, which might have attempted to check and to remedy the worsening conditions in France, was itself at a very low ebb of spiritual and moral prestige, and, since education and learning were mainly in the hands of monks and ecclesiastics, the inevitable result of the break-up of the empire of Charlemagne was the decay of scholarship and educational activity. Reform did not begin until the establishment of Cluny in 910, and the influence of the Cluniac reform made itself felt only gradually, of course. St. Dunstan, who had been in the Cluniac monastery of Ghent, introduced the ideals of Cluny into England.

In addition to the internal factors which prevented the fruit of the Carolingian renaissance coming to maturity (such as the political disintegration which led in the tenth century to the transference of the imperial crown from France to Germany, the decay of monastic and ecclesiastical life, and the degradation of the Papacy), there were also operative such external factors as the attacks of the Norsemen in the ninth and tenth centuries, who destroyed centres of wealth and culture and checked the development of civilisation, as also the attacks of the Saracens and the Mongols. Internal decay, combined with external dangers and attacks, rendered cultural progress impossible. To conserve, or to attempt to do so, was the only practicable course: progress in scholarship and philosophy lay again in the future. Such interest in philosophy as existed, centred largely round dialectical questions, and particularly round the problem of universals, the starting-point or the discussion being supplied by certain texts of Porphyry and Boethius.

2. Boethius, in his commentary on the *Isagoge* of Porphyry,[1] quotes Porphyry as remarking that at present he refuses to state whether genera and species are subsistent entities or whether they consist in concepts alone; if subsisting, whether they are material or immaterial and, further, whether they are separate from sensible objects or not, on the ground that such exalted matters cannot be treated in an introduction. Boethius himself, however, goes on to treat of the matter, first of all remarking on the difficulty of the question and the need of care in considering it and then pointing out that there are two ways in which an idea may be so formed

that its content is not found in extramental objects precisely as it exists in the idea. For example, one may join together arbitrarily man and horse, to form the idea of a centaur, joining together objects which nature does not suffer to be joined together, and such arbitrarily constructed ideas are 'false'. On the other hand, if we form the idea of a line, i.e. a mere line as considered by the geometer, then, although it is true that no mere line exists by itself in extramental reality, the idea is not 'false', since bodies involve lines and all we have done is to isolate the line and consider it in abstraction. Composition (as in the composition of horse and man to form the centaur) produces a false idea, whereas abstraction produces an idea which is true, even though the thing conceived does not exist extramentally in a state of abstraction or separation.

Now, the ideas of genera and species are ideas of the latter type, formed by abstraction. The likeness of humanity is abstracted from individual men, and this likeness, considered by the mind, is the idea of the species, while the idea of the genus is formed by considering the likeness of diverse species. Consequently, 'genera and species are in individuals, but, as thought, are universals'. They 'subsist in sensible things, but are understood without bodies'. Extramentally there is only one subject for both genus and species, i.e. the individual, but that no more prevents their being considered separately than the fact that it is the same line which is both convex and concave prevents our having different ideas of the convex and concave and defining them differently.

Boethius thus afforded the material for an Aristotelian solution of the problem, though he goes on to say that he has not thought it proper to decide between Plato and Aristotle, but that he has been following out the opinions of Aristotle since his book is concerned with the *Categories* of which Aristotle was the author. But, though Boethius afforded material for a solution of the problem of universals on the lines of moderate realism and though his quotations from Porphyry and his comments on them started the discussion of the problem in the early Middle Ages, the first solution of the mediaevals was not on the lines suggested by Boethius but was a rather *simpliste* form of extreme realism.

3. The thoughtless might suppose that in occupying themselves with this problem the early mediaevals were canvassing a useless topic or indulging in a profitless dialectic juggling; but a short reflection should be sufficient to show the im-

portance of the problem, at least if its implications are considered.

Although what we see and touch are particular things, when we think these things we cannot help using general ideas and words, as when we say, 'This particular object which I see is a tree, an elm to be precise.' Such a judgement affirms of a particular object that it is of a certain kind, that it belongs to the genus tree and the species elm; but it is clear that there may be many other objects besides the actual one perceived to which the same terms may be applied, which may be covered by the same ideas. In other words, objects outside the mind are individual, whereas concepts are general, universal in character, in the sense that they apply indifferently to a multitude of individuals. But, if extramental objects are particular and human concepts universal, it is clearly of importance to discover the relation holding between them. If the fact that subsistent objects are individual and concepts general means that universal concepts have no foundation in extramental reality, if the universality of concepts means that they are mere ideas, then a rift between thought and objects is created and our knowledge, so far as it is expressed in universal concepts and judgements, is of doubtful validity at the very least. The scientist expresses his knowledge in abstract and universal terms (for example, he does not make a statement about this particular electron, but about electrons in general), and if these terms have no foundation in extramental reality, his science is an arbitrary construction, which has no relation to reality. In so far indeed as human judgements are of a universal character or involve universal concepts, as in the statement that this rose is red, the problem would extend to human knowledge in general, and if the question as to the existence of an extramental foundation of a universal concept is answered in the negative, scepticism would result.

The problem may be raised in various ways, and, historically speaking, it has taken various forms at various times. It may be raised in this form, for instance. 'What, if anything, in extramental reality corresponds to the universal concepts in the mind?' This may be called the ontological approach, and it was under this form that the early mediaevals discussed the matter. Or one may ask *how* our universal concepts are formed. This is the psychological approach and the emphasis is different from that in the first approach, though the two lines of approach are closely connected and one can scarcely treat the ontological question without answering in some way the psychological question as well. Then again, if one supposes a conceptualist solution, that universal concepts are simply conceptual constructions, one may ask how it is that scientific knowledge, which for all *practical* purposes is a fact, is *possible*. But, however the problem be raised and whatever form it takes, it is of fundamental importance. Perhaps one of the factors which may give the impression that the medievals were discussing a comparatively unimportant question is this, that they practically confined their attention to genera and species in the category of substance. Not that the problem, even in this restricted form, is unimportant, but if the problem is raised in regard to the other categories as well, its implications in regard to at least the greater part of human knowledge becomes more evident. It becomes clear that the problem is ultimately the epistemological problem of the relation of thought to reality.

4. The first solution to the problem given by the mediaevals was that known as 'Exaggerated Realism'. That it was chronologically the first solution is borne out by the fact that the opponents of this view were for some time known as the *moderni*, while Abelard, for instance, refers to it as the *antiqua doctrina*. According to this view, our generic and specific concepts correspond to a reality existing extramentally in objects, a subsistent reality in which individuals share. Thus the concept Man or Humanity reflects a reality, humanity or the substance of human nature, which exists extramentally in the same way as it is thought, that is, as a unitary substance in which all men share. If for Plato the concept Man reflects the ideal of human nature subsisting apart from and 'outside' individual men, an ideal which individual men embody or 'imitate' to a greater or less extent, the mediaeval realist believed that the concept reflects a unitary substance existing extramentally, in which men participate or of which they are accidental modifications. Such a view is, of course, extremely naïve, and indicates a complete misunderstanding of Boethius's treatment of the question, since it supposes that unless the object reflected by the concept exists extramentally in exactly the same way that it exists intramentally, the concept is purely subjective. In other words, it supposes that the only way of saving the objectivity of our knowledge is to maintain

a naïve and exact correspondence between thought and things.

Realism is already implied in the teaching of e.g. *Fredegisius* who succeeded Alcuin as Abbot of St. Martin's Abbey at Tours and maintained that every name or term supposes a corresponding positive reality (e.g. Darkness or Nothing). It is also implied in the teaching of *John Scotus Eriugena*. We find a statement of the doctrine in the teaching of *Remigius of Auxerre* (c. 841–908), who held that the species is a *partitio substantialis* of the genus and that the species, e.g. Man, is the substantial unity of many individuals (*Homo est multorum hominum substantialis unitas*). A statement of this kind, if understood as meaning that the plurality of individual men have a common substance which is numerically one, has as its natural consequence the conclusion that individual men differ only accidentally from one another, and *Odo of Tournai* (d. 1113) of the Cathedral School of Tournai (who is also called Odo of Cambrai, from the fact that he became Bishop of Cambrai) did not hesitate to draw this conclusion, maintaining that when a child comes into being God produces a new property of an already existing substance, not a new substance. Logically this ultra-realism should result in sheer monism. For example, we have the concepts of substance and of being, and, on the principles of ultra-realism, it would follow that all objects to which we apply the term substance are modifications of one substance and, more comprehensively, that all beings are modifications of one Being. It is probable that this attitude weighed with John Scotus Eriugena, in so far as the latter can justly be called a monist.

As Professor Gilson and others have pointed out, those who maintained ultra-realism in the early Middle Ages were philosophising as logicians, in the sense that they assumed that the logical and real orders are exactly parallel and that because the meaning of, for example, 'man' in the statements 'Plato is a man' and 'Aristotle is a man' is the same, there is a substantial identity in the real order between Plato and Aristotle. But it would, I think, be a mistake to suppose that the ultra-realists were influenced simply by logical considerations: they were influenced also by theological considerations. This is clear in the case of Odo of Tournai, who used ultra-realism in order to explain the transmission of original sin. If one understands by original sin a positive infection of the human soul, one is at once faced by an apparent dilemma:

either one has to say that God creates out of nothing a new human substance each time a child comes into being, with the consequence that God is responsible for the infection, or one has to deny that God creates the individual soul. What Odo of Tournai maintained was a form of traducianism, i.e. that the human nature or substance of Adam, infected by original sin, is handed on at generation and that what God creates is simply a new property of an already existing substance.

It is not always easy to assess the precise significance to be attached to the words of the early mediaevals, as we cannot always tell with certainty if a writer fully recognised the implications of his words or if he was making an emphatic point in controversy, perhaps as an *argumentum ad hominem*, without consciously wishing his statement to be understood according to its literal meaning. Thus when Roscelin said that the three Persons of the Blessed Trinity might well be called three gods, if usage permitted, on the ground that every existing being is an individual, St. Anselm (1033–1109) asked how he who does not understand how a multitude of men are specifically one man, can understand how several Persons, each of whom is perfect God, are one God.[2] On the strength of this statement St. Anselm has been called an ultra- or exaggerated realist, and indeed the natural interpretation of the statement, in the light of the theological dogma involved, is that, just as there is but one Substance or Nature in the Godhead, so there is but one substance or nature (i.e. numerically one) in all men. Yet it might be that St. Anselm was arguing *ad hominem* and that his question, as intended, amounts to asking how a man who does not realise the specific unity of men (supposing, rightly or wrongly, that Roscelin denied *all* reality to the universal) can possibly grasp the far greater union of the divine Persons in the one Nature, a Nature which is *numerically* one. St. Anselm may have been an ultra-realist, but the second interpretation of his question is supported by the fact that he obviously understood Roscelin to hold that universals have no reality but are mere *flatus vocis* and by the fact that in the *Dialogus de Grammatico*[3] he distinguished between primary and secondary substances, mentioning Aristotle by name.

5. If the implied principle of the ultra-realists was the exact correspondence of thought and extramental reality, the principle of the adversaries of ultra-realism was that only indi-

viduals exist. Thus *Eric* (Heiricus) *of Auxerre* (841–76) observed that if anyone tries to maintain that white or black exist absolutely and without a substance in which they adhere, he will be unable to point to any corresponding reality but will have to refer to a white man or a black horse. General names have no general or universal objects corresponding to them; their only objects are individuals. How, then, do universal concepts arise and what is their function and their relation to reality? Neither the understanding nor the memory can grasp all individuals, and so the mind gathers together (*coarctat*) the multitude of individuals and forms the idea of the species, e.g. man, horse, lion. But the species of animals or plants are themselves too many to be comprehended by the mind at once, and it gathers the species together to form the genus. There are, however, many genera and the mind takes a further step in the process of *coarctatio*, forming the still wider and more extensive concept of *usia* (οὐσία). Now, at first sight this seems to be a nominalist position and to remind one of the shorthand note theory of J. S. Mill; but, in the absence of more extensive evidence, it would be rash to affirm that this actually was Eric's consciously held view. Probably he merely meant to affirm emphatically that only individuals exist, that is, to deny ultra-realism, and at the same time to give attention to the psychological explanation of our universal concepts. We have not sufficient evidence to warrant an affirmation that he denied any real foundation to the universal concept.

A similar difficulty of interpretation arises in regard to the teaching of *Roscelin* (c. 1050–1120), who, after studying at Soissons and Rheims, taught at Compiègne, his birthplace, Loches, Besançon and Tours. His writings have been lost, except for a letter to Abelard, and we have to rely on the testimony of other writers like St. Anselm, Abelard and John of Salisbury. These writers make it perfectly clear indeed that Roscelin was an opponent of ultra-realism and that he maintained that only individuals exist, but his positive teaching is not so clear. According to St. Anselm,[4] Roscelin held that the universal is a mere word (*flatus vocis*) and accordingly he is numbered by St. Anselm among the contemporary heretics in dialectic. Anselm goes on to remark that these people think that colour is nothing else but body and the wisdom of man nothing else but the soul, and the chief fault of the 'dialectical heretics' he finds in the fact that their reason is so bound up with their imagination that they cannot free themselves from images and contemplate abstract and purely intelligible objects.[5] Now, that Roscelin said that universals are words, general words, we cannot call in question, since St. Anselm's testimony is quite clear; but it is difficult to assess precisely what he meant by this. If we interpret St. Anselm as more or less an Aristotelian, i.e. as no ultra-realist, then we should have to say that he understood Roscelin's teaching as involving a denial of any kind of objectivity to the universal; whereas if we interpret Anselm as an ultra-realist we can then suppose that Roscelin was merely denying ultra-realism in a very emphatic way. It is, of course, undeniable that the statement that the universal is a mere *flatus vocis* is, taken literally, a denial not only of ultra-realism and moderate realism but even of conceptualism and the presence of universal concepts in the mind; but we have not sufficient evidence to say what Roscelin held about the concept as such, if indeed he gave any attention to the matter: it might be that, in his determination to deny ultra-realism, the formal subsistence of universals, he simply opposed the *universale in voce* to the subsistent universal, meaning that only individuals exist and that the universal does not, as such, exist extramentally, but without meaning to say anything about the *universale in mente*, which he may have taken for granted or never have thought about. Thus it is clear from some remarks of Abelard in his letter on Roscelin to the Bishop of Paris[6] and in his *De divisione et definitione* that, according to Roscelin, a part is a mere word, in the sense that when we say that a whole substance consists of parts, the idea of a whole consisting of parts is a 'mere word', since the objective reality is a plurality of individual things or substances; but it would be rash to conclude from this that Roscelin, if called upon to define his position, would have been prepared to maintain that we have no *idea* of a whole consisting of parts. May he not have meant simply that our idea of a whole consisting of parts is purely subjective and that the only objective reality is a multiplicity of individual substances? (Similarly he appears to have denied the logical unity of the syllogism and to have dissolved it into separate propositions.) According to Abelard, Roscelin's assertion that the ideas of whole and part are mere words is on a par with his assertion that species are mere words; and if the above interpretation is tenable in regard to the whole-part relation, we could apply it also to his doctrine of genera and species and say that his identification of them with words is an affirmation of their subjectivity rather than a denial that there is such a thing as a general idea.

One has, of course, no axe to grind in interpreting Roscelin. He may indeed have been a nominalist in a naïve and complete sense, and I am certainly not prepared to say that he was not a nominalist pure and simple. John of Salisbury seems to have understood him in this sense, for he says that 'some have the idea that the words themselves are the genera and species, although this view was long ago rejected and has disappeared with its author',[7] an observation which must refer to Roscelin, since the same author says in his *Metalogicus*[8] that the view which identifies species and genera with words practically disappeared with Roscelin. But though Roscelin may have been a pure nominalist and though the fragmentary testimony as to his teaching, if taken literally, certainly supports this interpretation, still it does not seem possible to assert without doubt that he paid any attention to the question whether we have *ideas* of genera or species or not, still less that he denied it, even if his actual words imply this. All we are entitled to say with certainty is that, whether nominalist or conceptualist, Roscelin was an avowed anti-realist.

6. It has been remarked earlier that Roscelin proposed a form of 'Tritheism' which excited the enmity of St. Anselm and which led to his being condemned and having to retract his theory at a Council at Soissons in 1092. It was the fact of such incursions into theology on the part of the dialecticians which was largely responsible for the hostility shown towards them by men like St. Peter Damian. The peripatetic dialecticians or sophists, laymen who came from Italy and travelled from one centre of study to another, men like Anselmus Peripateticus of Parma, who attempted to ridicule the principle of contradiction, naturally put dialectic in a rather poor light through their verbal sophistry and jugglery; but as long as they restricted themselves to verbal disputes, they were probably little more than an irritating nuisance: it was when they applied their dialectic to theology and fell into heresy, that they aroused the enmity of theologians. Thus *Berengarius of Tours* (c. 1000–88), maintaining that accidents cannot exist without their supporting substance, denied the doctrine of Transubstantiation. Berengarius was a monk and not a *Peripateticus*, but his spirit of disregard of author-

ity seems to have been characteristic of a group of dialecticians in the eleventh century, and it was mainly this sort of
attitude which led St. Peter Damian to pronounce dialectics
a superfluity or Otloh of St. Emmeran (c. 1010–70) to say
that certain dialecticians put more faith in Boethius than in
the Scriptures.

St. Peter Damian (1007–72) had little sympathy with the
liberal arts (they are useless, he said) or with dialectics, since
they are not concerned with God or the salvation of the soul,
though, as theologian and writer, the Saint had naturally to
make use of dialectic himself. He was, however, convinced
that dialectic is a very inferior pursuit and that its use in
theology is purely subsidiary and subordinate, not merely because dogmas are revealed truths but also in the sense that
even the ultimate principles of reason may fail to apply in
theology. For instance God, according to St. Peter Damian,
is not only arbiter of moral values and the moral law (he
would have had some sympathy with Kierkegaard's reflections
on Abraham), but can also bring it about that an historical
event should be 'undone', should not have occurred, and if
this seems to go counter to the principle of contradiction,
then so much the worse for the principle of contradiction: it
merely shows the inferiority of logic in comparison with theology. In short, the place of dialectic is that of a handmaid,
velut ancilla dominae.[9]

The 'handmaid' idea was also employed by *Gerard of
Czanad* (d. 1046), a Venetian who became Bishop of Czanad
in Hungary. Gerard emphasised the superiority of the wisdom
of the Apostles over that of Aristotle and Plato and declared
that dialectic should be the *ancilla theologiae.* It is indeed
often supposed that this is the Thomist view of the province
of philosophy, but, given St. Thomas's delineation of the
separate provinces of theology and philosophy, the handmaid
idea does not fit in with his professed doctrine on the nature
of philosophy: it was rather (as M. De Wulf remarks) the
idea of a 'restricted group of theologians', men who had no
use for the newfangled science. However, they could not avoid
using dialectic themselves, and *Archbishop Lanfranc* (who
was born about the year 1010 and died as Archbishop of
Canterbury in 1089) was only talking common sense when
he observed that it is not dialectic itself, but the abuse of it,
which should be condemned.

7. The opposition of a saint and a rigorist theologian to

dialectic is also one of the motifs in the life of Abelard, whose controversy with William of Champeaux forms the next stage in the story of the discussion on universals, though it affected only Abelard's life, not the ultimate triumph of his fight against ultra-realism.

William of Champeaux (1070–1120), after studying at Paris and Laon, studied under Roscelin at Compiègne. He adopted, however, the very opposite theory to that of Roscelin, and the doctrine he taught at the Cathedral School of Paris was that of ultra-realism. According to Abelard, who attended William's lectures at Paris and from whom we have to derive our knowledge of William's teaching, the latter maintained the theory that the same essential nature is wholly present at the same time in each of the individual members of the species in question, with the inevitable logical consequence that the individual members of a species differ from one another, not substantially but only accidentally.[10] If this is so, says Abelard,[11] there is the same substance in Plato in one place and in Socrates in another place, being made Plato through one set of accidents and Socrates through another set of accidents. Such a doctrine is, of course, the form of ultra-realism current in the early Middle Ages, and Abelard had no difficulty in showing the absurd consequences it involved. For example, if the human species is substantially, and therefore wholly, present in both Socrates and Plato at the same time, then Socrates must be Plato and he must be present in two places at once.[12] Furthermore, such a doctrine leads ultimately to pantheism, since God is substance and all substances will be identical with the divine substance.

Under pressure of criticism of this kind William of Champeaux changed his theory, abandoning the identity-theory for the indifference-theory and saying that two members of the same species are the same thing, not essentially (*essentialiter*), but indifferently (*indifferenter*). We have this information from Abelard,[13] who evidently treated the new theory as a mere subterfuge, as though William were now saying that Socrates and Plato are not the same, but yet are not different. However, fragments from William's *Sententiae*[14] makes his position clear. He there says that the two words 'One' and 'same' can be understood in two ways, *secundum indifferentiam et secundum identitatem eiusdem prorsus essentiae*, and goes on to explain that Peter and Paul are 'indifferently' men or possess humanity *secundum indifferentiam* in that, as Peter is rational, so is Paul, and as Peter is mortal, so is Paul, etc., whereas their humanity is not the same (he means that their essence or nature is not numerically the same) but like (*similis*), since they are two men. He adds that this mode of unity does not apply to the divine Nature, referring, of course, to the fact that the divine Nature is identical in each of the three divine Persons. This fragment, then, in spite of somewhat obscure language, is clearly opposed to ultra-realism. When William says that Peter and Paul are one and the same in humanity *secundum indifferentiam* he means that their essences are alike and that this likeness is the foundation of the universal concept of man, which applies 'indifferently' to Peter or Paul or any other man. Whatever Abelard may have thought about this modified theory or under whatever interpretation he may have attacked it, it would seem to be in reality a denial of ultra-realism and not much different from Abelard's own view.

It should be mentioned that the above is somewhat of a simplification, in that the exact course of events in the dispute between Abelard and William is not clear. For instance, although it is certain that William, after being defeated by Abelard, retired to the Abbey of St. Victor and taught there, becoming subsequently Bishop of Châlons-sur-Marne, it is not certain at what point in the controversy he retired. It would seem probable that he changed his theory while teaching at Paris and then, under fresh criticism from Abelard, whether justified or not, retired from the fray to St. Victor, where he continued teaching and may have laid the foundation for the mystical tradition of the abbey; but, according to M. De Wulf, he retired to St. Victor and there taught the new form of his theory, the indifference-theory. It has also been held that William held three theories: (i) the identity-theory of ultra-realism; (ii) the indifference-theory, which was attacked by Abelard as indistinguishable from the first theory; and (iii) an anti-realist theory, in which case he would presumably have retired to St. Victor after teaching the first and second theories. This may be correct, and possibly it is supported by Abelard's interpretation and criticism of the indifference-theory; but it is questionable if Abelard's interpretation was anything more than polemical and I am inclined to agree with De Wulf that the indifference-theory involved a denial of the identity-theory, i.e. that it was not a mere verbal subterfuge. In any case the question is not one of much importance, since all are agreed that William of Champeaux eventually abandoned the ultra-realism with which he had begun.

8. The man who worsted William of Champeaux in debate, *Abelard* (1079–1142), was born at Le Pallet, Palet or Palais near Nantes, deriving thence his name of *Peripateticus Palatinus*, and studied dialectic under Roscelin and William, after which he opened a school of his own, first at Melun, then at Corbeil and subsequently at Paris, where he conducted the dispute with his former master. Later he turned his attention to theology, studied under Anselm of Laon and started teaching theology himself at Paris in 1113. As a result of the episode with Héloise Abelard had to withdraw to the abbey of St. Denis. In 1121 his book *De Unitate et Trinitate divina* was condemned at Soissons and he then founded the school of Le Paraclet near Nogent-sur-Seine, only to abandon the school in 1125, in order to become Abbot of St. Gildas in Brittany, though he left the monastery in 1129. From 1136 to 1149 at any rate, he was teaching at Ste. Geneviève at Paris, where John of Salisbury was one of his pupils. However, St. Bernard accused him of heresy and in 1141 he was condemned at the Council of Sens. His appeal to Pope Innocent II led to his further condemnation and an injunction against lecturing, after which he retired to Cluny and remained there until his death.

Abelard was, it is clear, a man of combative disposition and unsparing of his adversaries: he ridiculed his masters in philosophy and theology, William of Champeaux and Anselm of Laon. He was also, though somewhat sentimental, egoistic and difficult to get on with: it is significant that he left both the abbey of St. Denis and that of St. Gildas because he was unable to live in peace with the other monks. He was, however, a man of great ability, an outstanding dialectician, far superior in this respect to William of Champeaux; he was no mediocrity who could be ignored, and we know that his brilliance and dialectical dexterity, also no doubt his attacks on other teachers, won him great audiences. His incursions into theology, however, especially in the case of a brilliant man of great reputation, made him seem a dangerous thinker in the eyes of those who had little natural sympathy for dialectic and intellectual cleverness, and Abelard was pursued by the unremitting hostility of St. Bernard in particular, who appears to have looked on the philosopher as an agent of Satan; he certainly did everything he could to secure Abelard's condemnation. Among other charges he accused Abelard of holding an heretical doctrine of the Blessed Trinity, a charge the truth of which Abelard stoutly denied. Probably the philosopher was no rationalist in the usual sense, so far as intentions were concerned (he did not mean to deny revelation or explain away mystery); but at the same time, in his application of dialectic to theology he does seem to have offended against theological orthodoxy, in fact if not in intention. On the other hand it was the very application of dialectic to theology which made theological progress possible and facilitated the Scholastic systematisation of theology in the thirteenth century.

Abelard had no difficulty, as we have seen, in showing the absurdities to which William of Champeaux's ultra-realism logically led; but it was incumbent on him to produce a more satisfactory theory himself. Accepting Aristotle's definition of the universal, as given by Boethius (*quod in pluribus natum est praedicari, singulare vero quod non*), he went on to state that it is not a thing which is predicated but a name, and he concludes that 'it remains to ascribe universality of this sort to words alone'.[15] This sounds like the purely nominalistic view traditionally ascribed to Roscelin (under whom Abelard had studied), but the fact that he was willing to speak of universal and particular words shows that we cannot immediately conclude that Abelard denied any reality corresponding to the universal word, for he certainly did not deny that there is reality corresponding to the particular words, the reality in this case being the individual. Moreover, Abelard proceeded (in the *Logica nostrorum petitioni sociorum*) to distinguish *vox* and *sermo* and to say, not that *Universale est vox*, but that *Universale est sermo*. Why did he make this distinction? Because *vox* signifies the word as a physical entity (*flatus vocis*), a thing, and no thing can be predicated of another thing, whereas *sermo* signifies the word according to its relation to the logical content and it is this which is predicated.

What then is the logical content, what is the *intellectus universalis* or universal idea, which is expressed by the *nomen universale*? By universal ideas the mind 'conceives a common and confused image of many things . . . When I hear *man* a certain figure arises in my mind which is so related to individual men that it is common to all and proper to none.'

Such language suggests indeed that, according to Abelard, there are really no universal concepts at all, but only confused images, generic or specific according to the degree of confusion and indistinctness; but he goes on to say that universal concepts are formed by abstraction and that through these concepts we conceive what is *in* the object, though we do not conceive it *as* it is in the object. 'For, when I consider this man only in the nature of substance or of body, and not also of animal or of man or of grammarian, obviously I understand nothing except what is in that nature, but I do not consider all that it has.' He then explains that when he said that our idea of man is 'confused', he meant that by means of abstraction the nature is set free, as it were, from all individuality and is considered in such a way that it bears no special relation to any particular individual but can be predicated of all individual men. In fine, *that which* is conceived in specific and generic ideas is in things (the idea is not void of objective reference), but it is not in them, i.e. in individual things, *as* it is conceived. Ultra-realism, in other words, is false; but that does not mean that universals are purely subjective constructions, still less that they are mere words. When Abelard says that the universal is a *nomen* or *sermo*, what he means is that the logical unity of the universal concept affects only the predicate, that it is a *nomen* and not a *res* or individual thing. If we wish, with John of Salisbury, to call Abelard a 'nominalist', we must recognise at the same time that his 'nominalism' is simply a denial of ultra-realism and an assertion of the distinction between the logical and real orders, without involving any denial of the objective foundation of the universal concept. The Abelardian doctrine is an adumbration, in spite of some ambiguous language, of the developed theory of 'moderate realism'.

In his *Theologia Christiana* and *Theologia* Abelard follows St. Augustine, Macrobius and Priscian in placing in the mind of God *formae exemplares* or divine ideas, generic and specific, which are identical with God Himself, and he commends Plato on this point, understanding him in a neo-Platonic sense, as having placed the Ideas in the divine mind, *quam Graeci Noyn appellant.*

9. Abelard's treatment of the problem of universals was really decisive, in the sense that it gave a death-blow to ultra-realism by showing how one could deny the latter doctrine without at the same time being obliged to deny all objectivity

to genera and species, and, though the School of Chartres in the twelfth century (in contradistinction to the School of St. Victor) inclined to ultra-realism, two of the most notable figures connected with Chartres, namely Gilbert de la Porrée and John of Salisbury, broke with the old tradition.

(i) *Gilbert de la Porrée* or *Gilbertus Porretanus* was born at Poitiers in 1076, became a pupil of Bernard of Chartres and himself taught at Chartres for more than twelve years. Later he taught at Paris, though he became Bishop of Poitiers in 1142. He died in 1154.

On the subject of each man having his own humanity or human nature Gilbert de la Porrée was firm;[16] but he had a peculiar view as to the inner constitution of the individual. In the individual we must distinguish the individualised essence or substance, in which the accidents of the thing inhere, and the *formae substantiales* or *formae nativae*.[17] These native forms are common in the sense that they are alike in objects of the same species or genus, as the case may be, and they have their exemplars in God. When the mind contemplates the native forms in things, it can abstract them from the matter in which they are embodied or rendered concrete and consider them alone in abstraction: it is then attending to genus or species, which are *subsistentiae*, but not substantially existing objects.[18] For example, the genus is simply the collection (*collectio*) of *subsistentiae* obtained by comparing things which, though differing in species, are alike.[19] He means that the idea of the species is obtained by comparing the similar essential determinations or forms of similar individual objects and gathering them together into one idea, while the idea of the genus is obtained by comparing objects which differ specifically but which yet have some essential determinations or forms in common, as horse and dog have animality in common. The form, as John of Salisbury remarks apropos of Gilbert's doctrine,[20] is sensible in the sensible objects, but is conceived by the mind apart from sense, that is, immaterially, and while individual in each individual, it is yet common, or alike, in all the members of a species or genus.

His doctrines of abstraction and of comparison make it clear that Gilbert was a moderate realist and not an ultra-realist, but his curious idea of the distinction between the individual essence or substance and the common essence ('common' meaning alike in a plurality of individuals) landed him in difficulties when he came to apply it to the doctrine of the Blessed Trinity and distinguished as different things *Deus* and *Divinitas, Pater* and *Paternitas*, just as he would distinguish Socrates from humanity, that is, from the humanity of Socrates. He was accused of impairing the unity of God and teaching heresy, St. Bernard being one of his attackers. Condemned at the Council of Rheims in 1148, he retracted the offending propositions.

(ii) *John of Salisbury* (c. 1115–80) went to Paris in 1136 and there attended the lectures of, among others, Abelard, Gilbert de la Porrée, Adam Parvipontanus (Smallbridge) and Robert Pulleyn. He became secretary to the Archbishop of Canterbury, first to Archbishop Theobald and then to St. Thomas à Becket, being subsequently appointed Bishop of Chartres in 1176.

In discussing the problem of universals, says John, the world has grown old: more time has been taken up in this pursuit than was required by the Caesars for conquering and governing the world.[21] But anyone who looks for genera and species outside the things of sense is wasting his time:[22] ultra-realism is untrue and contradicts the teaching of Aristotle,[23] for whom John had a predilection in dialectical matters, remarking, apropos of the *Topics*, that it is of more use than almost all the books of dialectic which the moderns are accustomed to expound in the schools.[24] Genera and species are not things, but are rather the forms of things which the mind, comparing the likeness of things, abstracts and unifies in the universal concepts.[25] Universal concepts or genera and species abstractly considered are mental constructions (*figurata rationis*), since they do not exist as universals in extramental reality; but the construction in question is one of comparison of things and abstraction from things, so that universal concepts are not void of objective foundation and reference.[26]

10. It has been already mentioned that the School of St. Victor inclined to moderate realism. Thus *Hugh of St. Victor* (1096–1141) adopted more or less the position of Abelard and maintained a clear doctrine of abstraction, which he applied to mathematics and to physics. It is the province of mathematics to attend to *actus confusos inconfuse*,[27] abstracting, in the sense of attending to in isolation, the line or the plane surface, for example, although neither lines nor surfaces exist apart from bodies. In physics, too, the physicist

considers in abstraction the properties of the four elements, although in concrete reality they are found only in varying combinations. Similarly the dialectician considers the forms of things in isolation or abstraction, in a unified concept, though in actual reality the forms of sensible things exist neither in isolation from matter nor as universals.

11. The foundations of the Thomist doctrine of moderate realism had thus been laid before the thirteenth century, and indeed we may say that it was Abelard who really killed ultra-realism. When St. Thomas declares that universals are not subsistent things but exist only in singular things,[28] he is re-echoing what Abelard and John of Salisbury had said before him. Humanity, for instance, human nature, has existence only in this or that man, and the universality which attaches to humanity in the concept is a result of abstraction, and so is in a sense a subjective contribution.[29] But this does not involve the falsity of the universal concept. If we were to abstract the specific form of a thing and at the same time think that it actually existed in a state of abstraction, our idea would indeed be false, for a false judgement concerning the thing itself would be involved; but, though in the universal concept the mind conceives something in a manner different to its mode of concrete existence, our judgement about the thing itself is not erroneous; it is simply that the form, which exists in the thing in an individualised state, is abstracted, i.e. is made the object of the exclusive attention of the mind by an immaterial activity. The objective foundation of the universal specific concept is thus the objective and individual essence of the thing, which essence is by the activity of the mind set free from individualising factors, that is, according to St. Thomas, matter, and considered in abstraction. For example, the mind abstracts from the individual man the essence of humanity which is alike, but not numerically the same in the members of the human species, while the foundation of the universal generic concept is an essential determination which several species have in common, as the species of man, horse, dog, etc., have 'animality' in common.

St. Thomas thus denied both forms of ultra-realism, that of Plato and that of the early mediaevals; but, no more than Abelard was he willing to reject Platonism lock, stock and barrel, that is to say, Platonism as developed by St. Augustine. The ideas, exemplar ideas, exist in the divine mind, though not ontologically distinct from God nor really a plurality, and, as far as this truth is concerned, the Platonic theory is justified.[30] St. Thomas thus admits (i) the *universale ante rem*, while insisting that it is not a subsistent thing, either apart from things (Plato) or in things (early mediaeval ultra-realists), for it is God considered as perceiving His Essence as imitable *ad extra* in a certain type of creature; (ii) the *universale in re*, which is the concrete individual essence alike in the members of the species; and (iii) the *universale post rem*, which is the abstract universal concept.[31] Needless to say, the term *universale in re*, used in the *Commentary on the Sentences*, is to be interpreted in the light of St. Thomas's general doctrine, i.e. as the *foundation* of the universal concept, the foundation being the concrete essence or *quidditas rei*.[32]

In the later Middle Ages the problem of universals was to be taken up afresh and a different solution was to be given by William of Ockham and his followers; but the principle that only individuals exist as subsistent things had come to stay: the new current in the fourteenth century was set not towards realism but away from it. The history of this movement I shall consider in the next volume.

Chapter Fifteen

ST. ANSELM OF CANTERBURY

St. Anselm as philosopher—Proofs of God's existence in the Monologium—*The proof of God's existence in the* Proslogium—*Idea of truth and other Augustinian elements in St. Anselm's thought.*

1. St. Anselm was born at Aosta in Piedmont in 1033. After preliminary studies in Burgundy, at Avranches and afterwards at Bec he entered the Benedictine Order and later became Prior of Bec (1063), and subsequently abbot (1078). In 1093 he became Archbishop of Canterbury in succession to his former teacher, friend and religious superior Lanfranc, and in that post he died (1109).

In general the thought of St. Anselm is rightly said to belong to the Augustinian tradition. Like the great African Doctor, he devoted his chief intellectual effort to the understanding of the doctrine of the Christian faith and the statement of his attitude which is contained in the *Proslogium*[1] bears the unmistakable stamp of the Augustinian spirit. 'I do not attempt, O Lord, to penetrate Thy profundity, for I deem my intellect in no way sufficient thereunto, but I desire to understand in some degree Thy truth, which my heart believes and loves. For I do not seek to understand, in order that I may believe; but I believe, that I may understand. For I believe this too, that unless I believed, I should not understand.' This *Credo, ut intelligam* attitude is common to both Augustine and Anselm, and Anselm is in full accord with Augustine when he remarks in the *Cur Deus Homo*[2] that it is negligence if we make no attempt to understand what we believe. In practice, of course, this means for Anselm an application of dialectic or reasoning to the dogmas of faith, not in order to strip them of mystery but in order to penetrate them, develop them and discern their implications, so far as this is possible to the human mind, and the results of this process, for instance his book on the Incarnation and Redemption (*Cur Deus Homo*), make Anselm of importance in the history of theological development and speculation.

Now, the application of dialectic to the data of theology remains theology, and St. Anselm would scarcely earn a place in the history of philosophy through his theological speculation and developments, except indeed as the application of philosophical categories to revealed dogmas necessarily involves some treatment and development of those philosophical categories. In point of fact, however, the use of the *Credo, ut intelligam* motto was not confined by Anselm, any more than by Augustine, to the understanding of those truths exclusively which have been revealed and not discovered dialectically, but was extended to truths like the existence of God, which are indeed believed but which can be reached by human reasoning. Besides, then, his work as dogmatic theologian there is also his work as natural theologian or metaphysician to be considered, and on this count alone St. Anselm deserves a place in the history of philosophy, since he contributed to the development of that branch of philosophy which is known as natural theology. Whether his arguments for the existence of God are considered valid or invalid, the fact that he elaborated these arguments systematically is of importance and gives his work a title to serious consideration by the historian of philosophy.

St. Anselm, like St. Augustine, made no clear distinction between the provinces of theology and philosophy, and his implied attitude of mind may be illustrated as follows. The Christian should try to understand and to apprehend rationally all that he believes, so far as this is possible to the human mind. Now, we believe in God's existence and in the doctrine of the Blessed Trinity. We should, therefore, apply our understanding to the understanding of both truths. From the point of view of one who, like the Thomist, makes a clear distinction between philosophy and dogmatic theology the application of reasoning to the first truth, God's existence, will fall within the province of philosophy, while the application of reasoning to the second truth, the Trinity, will fall within the province of theology, and the Thomist will hold that the first truth is demonstrable by human reasoning, while the second truth is not demonstrable by human reasoning, even though the human mind is able to make true statements about the mystery, once revealed, and to refute the objections against it which human reasoning may raise. But, if one puts oneself in the position of St. Anselm, that is, in a state of mind anterior to the clear distinction between philosophy and theology, it is easy to see how the fact that the first truth is demonstrable, coupled with the desire to understand all that we believe, the attempt to satisfy this desire being regarded as a duty, naturally leads to an attempt to demonstrate the second truth as well, and in point of fact St. Anselm speaks of demonstrating the Trinity of Persons by 'necessary reasons'[3] and of showing in the same way that it is impossible for a man to be saved without Christ.[4] If one wishes to call this 'rationalism', as has been done, one should first of all be quite clear as to what one means by rationalism. If by rationalism one means an attitude of mind which denies revelation and faith, St. Anselm was certainly no rationalist, since he accepted the primacy of faith and the fact of authority and only then went on to attempt to understand the data of faith. If, however, one is going to extend the term 'rationalism' to cover the attitude of mind which leads to the attempt to prove mysteries, not because the mysteries are not accepted by faith or would be rejected if one could not prove them, but because one desires to understand all that one believes, without having first clearly defined the ways in which different truths are accessible to us, then one might, of course, call the thought of St. Anselm 'rationalism' or an approximation to rationalism. But it would show an entire misunderstanding of Anselm's attitude, were one to suppose that he was prepared to reject the doctrine of the Trinity, for example, if he was unable to find *rationes necessariae* for it: he believed the doctrine first of all, and only then did he attempt to understand it. The dispute about Anselm's rationalism or non-rationalism is quite beside the point, unless one first grasps quite clearly the fact that he had no intention of impairing the integrity of the Christian faith: if we insist on interpreting St. Anselm as though he lived after St. Thomas and had clearly distinguished the separate provinces of theology and philosophy, we shall only be guilty of an anachronism and of a misinterpretation.

2. In the *Monologium*[5] St. Anselm develops the proof of

God's existence from the degrees of perfection which are found in creatures. In the first chapter he applies the argument to goodness, and in the second chapter to 'greatness', meaning, as he tells us, not quantitative greatness, but a quality like wisdom, the more of which a subject possesses, the better, for greater quantitative size does not prove qualitative superiority. Such qualities are found in varying degrees in the objects of experience, so that the argument proceeds from the empirical observation of degrees of, for example, goodness, and is therefore an *a posteriori* argument. But judgement about different degrees of perfection (St. Anselm assumes, of course, that the judgement is objectively grounded) implies a reference to a standard of perfection, while the fact that things participate objectively in goodness in different degrees shows that the standard is itself objective, that there is, for example, an absolute goodness in which all good things participate, to which they approximate more or less nearly, as the case may be.

This type of argument is Platonic in character (though Aristotle also argued, in his Platonic phase, that where there is a better, there must be a best) and it reappears in the *Via quarta* of St. Thomas Aquinas. It is, as I have said, an *a posteriori* argument: it does not proceed from the idea of absolute goodness to the existence of absolute goodness but from observed degrees of goodness to the existence of absolute goodness and from degrees of wisdom to the existence of absolute wisdom, the absolute goodness and wisdom being then identified as God. The developed form of the argument would necessitate, of course, a demonstration both of the objectivity of the judgement concerning the differing degrees of goodness and also of the principle on which St. Anselm rests the argument, the principle, namely that if objects possess goodness in a limited degree, they must have their goodness from absolute goodness itself, which is good *per se* and not *per aliud*. It is also to be noted that the argument can be applied only to those perfections which do not *of themselves* involve limitation and finiteness: it could not be applied to quantitative size, for instance. (Whether the argument is valid and demonstrative or not, it is scarcely the province of the historian to decide.)

In the third chapter of the *Monologium* St. Anselm applies the same sort of argument to being. Whatever exists, exists either through something or through nothing. The latter supposition is absurd; so whatever exists, must exist through something. This means that all existing things exist either through one another or through themselves or through one cause of existence. But that X should exist through Y, and Y through X, is unthinkable: the choice lies between a plurality of uncaused causes or one such cause. So far indeed the argument is a simple argument from causality, but St. Anselm goes on to introduce a Platonic element when he argues that if there is a plurality of existent things which have being of themselves, i.e. are self-dependent and uncaused, there is a form of being-of-itself in which all participate, and at this point the argument becomes similar to the argument already outlined, the implication being that, when several beings possess the same form, there must be a unitary being external to them which *is* that form. There can, therefore, be but one self-existent or ultimate Being, and this must be the best and highest and greatest of all that is.

In chapters seven and eight St. Anselm considers the relation between the caused and the Cause and argues that all finite objects are made out of nothing, *ex nihilo*, not out of a preceding matter nor out of the Cause as matter. He explains carefully that to say that a thing is made *ex nihilo* is not to say that it is made out of nothing as its material: it means that something is created *non ex aliquo*, that, whereas before it had no existence outside the divine mind, it now has existence. This may seem obvious enough, but it has sometimes been maintained that to say that a creature is made *ex nihilo* is either to make nothing something or to lay oneself open to the observation that *ex nihilo nihil fit*, whereas St. Anselm makes it clear that *ex nihilo* does not mean *ex nihilo tamquam materia* but simply *non ex aliquo*.

As to the attributes of the *Ens a Se*, we can predicate of it only those qualities, to possess which is *absolutely* better than not to possess them.[6] For example, to be gold is better for gold than to be lead, but it would not be better for a man to be made of gold. To be corporeal is better than to be nothing at all, but it would not be better for a spirit to be corporeal rather than incorporeal. To be gold is better than not to be gold only *relatively*, and to be corporeal rather than non-corporeal is better only *relatively*. But it is *absolutely* better to be wise than not to be wise, living than non-living, just than not-just. We must, then, predicate wisdom, life, justice, of the supreme Being, but we cannot predicate corporeity or gold of the supreme Being. Moreover, as the supreme Being does not possess His attributes through participation, but through His own essence, He *is* Wisdom, Justice, Life, etc.,[7] and furthermore, since the supreme Being cannot be composed of elements (which would then be logically anterior, so that He would not be the supreme Being), these attributes are identical with the divine essence, which is simple.[8] Again, God must necessarily transcend space, in virtue of His simplicity and spirituality, and time, in virtue of His eternity.[9] He is wholly present in everything but not locally or *determinate*, and all things are present to His eternity, which is not to be conceived as endless time but as *interminabilis vita simul perfecte tota existens*.[10] We may call Him substance, if we refer to the divine essence, but not if we refer to the category of substance, since He is incapable of change or of sustaining accidents.[11] In fine, if we apply to Him any name that we also apply to creatures, *valde procul dubio intelligenda est diversa significatio*.

St. Anselm proceeds, in the *Monologium*, to give reasons for the Trinity of Persons in one Nature, without giving any clear indication that he is conscious of leaving the province of one science to enter that of another, and into this subject, interesting as it may be to the theologian, we cannot follow him. Enough has been said, however, to show that St. Anselm made a real contribution to natural theology. The Platonic element is conspicuous and, apart from remarks here and there, there is no considered treatment of analogy; but he gives *a posteriori* arguments for God's existence which are of a much more systematic character than those of St. Augustine and he also deals carefully with the divine attributes, God's immutability, eternity, etc. It is clear, then, how erroneous it is to associate his name with the 'Ontological Argument' in such a way as to imply that St. Anselm's only contribution to the development of philosophy was an argument the validity of which is at least questionable. His work may have not exercised any very considerable influence on contemporary thinkers and those who immediately followed him, because of their preoccupation with other matters (dialectical problems, reconciling the opinions of the Fathers, and so on), but looked at in the light of the general development of philosophy in the Middle Ages he must be acknowledged as one of the main contributors to Scholastic philosophy and theology, on account both of his natural theology and of his application of dialectic to dogma.

3. In the *Proslogium* St. Anselm develops the so-called 'ontological argument', which proceeds from the idea of God to God as a reality, as existent. He tells us that the requests of his brethren and consideration of the complex and various arguments of the *Monologium* led him to inquire whether he could not find an argument which would be sufficient, by itself alone, to prove all that we believe concerning the Divine Substance, so that one argument would fulfil the function of the many complementary arguments of his former *opusculum*. At length he thought that he had discovered such an argument, which for convenience sake may be put into syllogistic form, though St. Anselm himself develops it under the form of an address to God.

> God is that than which no greater can be thought:
> But that than which no greater can be thought must exist, not only mentally, in idea, but also extramentally:
> Therefore God exists, not only in idea, mentally, but also extramentally.
> The *Major Premiss* simply gives the idea of God, the idea which a man has of God, even if he denies His existence.
> The *Minor Premiss* is clear, since if that than which no greater can be thought existed only in the mind, it would not be that than which no greater can be thought. A greater could be thought, i.e. a being that existed in extramental reality as well as in idea.

This proof starts from the idea of God as that than which no greater can be conceived, i.e. as absolutely perfect: that is what is *meant* by God.

Now, if such a being had only ideal reality, existed only in our subjective idea, we could still conceive a greater being, namely a being which did not exist simply in our idea but in objective reality. It follows, then, that the idea of God as absolute perfection is necessarily the idea of an existent Being, and St. Anselm argues that in this case no one can at the same time have the idea of God and yet deny His existence. If a man thought of God as, for instance, a superman, he would be quite right to deny 'God's' existence in that sense, but he would not really be denying the objectivity of the idea of God. If, however, a man had the right idea of God, conceived the meaning of the term 'God', he could indeed deny

His existence with his lips, but if he realises what the denial involves (i.e. saying that the Being which must exist of its essence, the necessary Being, does not exist) and yet asserts the denial, he is guilty of a plain contradiction: it is only the fool, the *insipiens*, who has said *in his heart*, 'there is no God.' The absolutely perfect Being is a Being the essence of which is to exist or which necessarily involves existence, since otherwise a more perfect being could be conceived; it is the necessary Being; and a necessary being which did not exist would be a contradiction in terms.

St. Anselm wanted his argument to be a demonstration of all that we believe concerning the divine Nature, and, since the argument concerns the absolutely perfect Being, the attributes of God are contained implicitly in the conclusion of the argument. We have only to ask ourselves what is implied by the idea of a Being than which no greater can be thought, in order to see that God must be omnipotent, omniscient, supremely just and so on. Moreover, when deducing these attributes in the *Proslogium*, St. Anselm gives some attention to the clarification of the notions in question. For example, God cannot lie: is not this a sign of lack of omnipotence? No, he answers, to be able to lie should be called impotence rather than power, imperfection rather than perfection. If God could act in a manner inconsistent with His essence, that would be a lack of power on His part. Of course, it might be objected that this *presupposes* that we already know what God's essence is or involves, whereas what God's essence is, is precisely the point to be shown; but St. Anselm would presumably reply that he has already established that God is all-perfect and so that He is both omnipotent and truthful: it is merely a question of showing what the omnipotence of perfection really means and of exposing the falsity of a wrong idea of omnipotence.

The argument given by St. Anselm in the *Proslogium* was attacked by the monk Gaunilo in his *Liber pro Insipiente adversus Anselmi in Proslogio ratiocinationem*, wherein he observed that the idea we have of a thing is no guarantee of its extramental existence and that St. Anselm was guilty of an illicit transition from the logical to the real order. We might as well say that the most beautiful islands which are possible must exist somewhere, because we can conceive them. The Saint, in his *Liber Apologeticus contra Gaunilonem respondentem pro Insipiente*, denied the parity, and denied it with justice, since, if the idea of God is the idea of an all-perfect Being and if absolute perfection involves existence, this idea is the idea of an existent, and necessarily existent Being, whereas the idea of even the most beautiful islands is not the idea of something which must exist: even in the purely logical order the two ideas are not on a par. If God is possible, i.e. if the idea of the all-perfect and necessary Being contains no contradiction, God must exist, since it would be absurd to speak of a *merely possible necessary Being* (it is a contradiction in terms), whereas there is no contradiction in speaking of merely possible beautiful islands. The main objection to St. Anselm's proof, which was raised against Descartes and which Leibniz tried to answer, is that we do not know *a priori* that the idea of God, the idea of infinite and absolute Perfection, is the idea of a *possible* Being. We may not see any contradiction in the idea, but, say the objectors, this 'negative' possibility is not the same as 'positive' possibility; it does not show that there really is no contradiction in the idea. That there is no contradiction in the idea is clear only when we have shown *a posteriori* that God exists.

The argument of the *Proslogium* aroused little immediate interest; but in the thirteenth century it was employed by St. Bonaventure, with a less logical and more psychological emphasis, while it was rejected by St. Thomas. Duns Scotus used it as an incidental aid. In the 'modern' era it has had a distinguished, if chequered career. Descartes adopted and adapted it, Leibniz defended it in a careful and ingenious manner, Kant attacked it. In the Schools it is generally rejected, though some individual thinkers have maintained its validity.

4. Among the Augustinian characteristics of St. Anselm's philosophy one may mention his theory of truth. When he is treating of truth in the judgement,[12] he follows the Aristotelian view in making it consist in this, that the judgement or proposition states what actually exists or denies what does not exist, the thing signified being the cause of the truth, the truth itself residing in the judgement (correspondence-theory); but when, after treating of truth (rectitude) in the will,[13] he goes on to speak of the truth of being or essence[14] and makes the truth of things to consist in being what they 'ought' to be, that is, in their embodiment of or correspondence to their idea in God, the supreme Truth and standard

of truth, and when he concludes from the eternal truth of the judgement to the eternity of the cause of truth, God,[15] he is treading in the footsteps of Augustine. God, therefore, is the eternal and subsistent Truth, which is cause of the ontological truth of all creatures. The eternal truth is only cause and the truth of the judgement is only effect, while the ontological truth of things is at once effect (of eternal Truth) and cause (of truth in the judgement). This Augustinian conception of ontological truth, with the exemplarism it presupposes, was retained by St. Thomas in the thirteenth century, though he laid far more emphasis, of course, on the truth of the judgement. Thus, whereas St. Thomas's characteristic definition of truth is *adaequatio rei et intellectus,* that of St. Anselm is *rectitudo sola mente perceptibilis.*[16]

In his general way of speaking of the relation of soul to body and in the absence of a theory of hylomorphic composition of the two, Anselm follows the Platonic-Augustinian tradition, though, like Augustine himself, he was perfectly well aware that soul and body form one man, and he affirms the fact. Again, his words in the *Proslogium*[17] on the divine light recall the illumination-theory of Augustine: *Quanta namque est lux illa, de qua micat omne verum, quod rationali menti lucet.*

In general perhaps one might say that though the philosophy of Anselm stands in the line of the Augustinian tradition, it is more systematically elaborated than the corresponding elements of Augustine's thought, his natural theology, that is, and that in the methodic application of dialectic it shows the mark of a later age.

Chapter Sixteen

THE SCHOOL OF CHARTRES

Universalism of Paris, and systematisation of sciences in twelfth century—Regionalism, humanism—Platonism of Chartres—Hylomorphism at Chartres—Prima facie pantheism—John of Salisbury's political theory.

1. One of the greatest contributions made by the Middle Ages to the development of European civilisation was the university system, and the greatest of all mediaeval universities was unquestionably that of Paris. This great centre of theological and philosophical studies did not receive its definitive charter as a University in the formal sense until early in the thirteenth century; but one may speak, in an untechnical sense, of the Parisian schools as already forming a 'university' in the twelfth century. Indeed in some respects the twelfth century was more dominated by French learning than was the thirteenth century, since it was in the thirteenth century that other universities, such as Oxford, came into prominence and began to display a spirit of their own. This is true of northern Europe at least: as to the South, the University of Bologna, for instance, received its first charter in 1158, from Frederick I. But, though France was the great centre of intellectual activity in the twelfth century, a fact which led to the oft-quoted saying that 'Italy has the Papacy, Germany the Empire, and France has Knowledge', this does not mean, of course, that intellectual activity was pursued simply by Frenchmen: European culture was international, and the intellectual supremacy of France meant that students, scholars and professors came in large numbers to the French schools. From England came men like Adam Smallbridge and Alex-

ander Neckham, twelfth-century dialecticians, Adelard of
Bath and Robert Pulleyn, Richard of St. Victor (d. 1173)
and John of Salisbury; from Germany, Hugh of St. Victor
(d. 1141), theologian, philosopher and mystic; from Italy,
Peter Lombard (c. 1100–60), author of the celebrated *Sentences*, which were made the subject of so many commentaries
during the Middle Ages, by St. Thomas Aquinas and Duns
Scotus, for example. Thus the University of Paris may be
said to have represented the international character of mediaeval European culture, as the Papacy represented the international, or rather supra-national, character of mediaeval
religion, though the two were, of course, closely bound together, as the one religion gave a common intellectual outlook and the language of learning, the Latin tongue, was the
language of the Church. These two unities, the religious and
the cultural, so closely bound together, were what one might
call effective and real unities, whereas the political unity of
the Holy Roman Empire was rather theoretical than effective,
for, though the absolute monarchies were a development of
the future, nationalism was already beginning to increase,
even if its growth was checked by feudalism, by the local
character of mediaeval political and economic institutions and
by the common language and intellectual outlook.

This growing and expanding university life naturally found
an intellectual and academic expression in the attempt to
classify and systematise the science, knowledge and speculation of the time, an attempt which shows itself already in the
twelfth century. We may give two examples, the systematisa-
tions of Hugh of St. Victor and of Peter Lombard. The
former, in his *Didascalion*,[1] more or less follows the Aristotelian classification. Thus Logic is a propaedeutic or preamble
to science proper and deals with concepts, not with things.
It is divided into Grammar and into the *Ratio Disserendi*,
which in turn subdivides into *Demonstratio, Pars Probabilis*
and *Pars Sophistica* (Dialectic, Rhetoric and Sophistic). Science, to which Logic is a preamble and for which it is a necessary instrument, is divided under the main headings of
Theoretical Science, Practical Science and 'Mechanics'. Theoretical Science comprises Theology, Mathematics (Arithmetic,
dealing with the numerical aspect of things; Music, dealing
with proportion; Geometry, concerned with the extension of
things; Astronomy, concerned with the movement of things),
and Physics (which has as its subject-matter the inner nature

or inner qualities of things, and thus penetrates farther than Mathematics). Practical Science is subdivided into Ethics, 'Economics' and Politics, while Mechanics comprises the seven 'illiberal arts' or *scientiae adulterinae*, since the craftsman borrows his form from nature. These 'illiberal arts' are Wool-making, etc., Armoury and Carpentry, Navigation or Commerce, which, according to Hugh, 'reconciles peoples, quiets wars, strengthens peace, and makes private goods to be for the common use of all', Agriculture, Hunting (including cookery), Medicine and Theatricals. It is clear that Hugh's classification depended, not only on Aristotle, through Boethius, but also on the encyclopaedic work of writers like Isidore of Seville.

Peter Lombard, who was educated at the School of St. Victor, taught at the Cathedral School of Paris, and ultimately became bishop of that city between 1150 and 1152, composed his *Libri Quattuor Sententiarum*, a work which, although unoriginal in respect of content, exercised a tremendous influence, in that it stimulated other writers to the work of systematic and comprehensive exposition of dogma and became itself the subject of compendia and many commentaries, up to the end of the sixteenth century. The *Sentences* of the Lombard are admittedly a text-book[2] and were designed to gather the opinions or *sententiae* of the Fathers on theological doctrines, the first book being devoted to God, the second to creatures, the third to the Incarnation and Redemption and to the virtues, the fourth to the seven Sacraments and to the last things. The greatest number of quotations and the bulk of the doctrine are taken from St. Augustine, though other Latin Fathers are quoted, and even St. John Damascene makes an appearance, though it has been shown that the Lombard had seen only a small part of Burgundius of Pisa's Latin translation of the *Fons Scientiae*. Obviously enough the *Sentences* are predominantly a theological work, but the Lombard speaks of those things which are understood by the natural reason and can be so understood before they are believed, i.e. by faith:[3] such are the existence of God, the creation of the world by God and the immortality of the soul.

2. We have seen that the developing and expanding intellectual life of the twelfth century showed itself in the growing predominance of the 'university' of Paris and in the first attempts at classification and systematisation of knowledge; but the position of Paris did not mean that regional schools

were not flourishing. Indeed, vigour of local life and interests was a complementary feature in the mediaeval period to the international character of religious and intellectual life. For example, though some of the scholars who came to Paris to study remained there to teach, others returned to their own lands or provinces or became attached to local educational institutions. Indeed there was a tendency to specialisation, Bologna, for instance, being noted for its school of law and Montpellier for medicine, while mystical theology was a prominent feature of the School of St. Victor, outside Paris.

One of the most flourishing and interesting of the local schools of the twelfth century was that of Chartres, in which certain Aristotelian doctrines, to be noted presently, began to come into prominence, associated, however, with a very strong admixture of Platonism. This school was also associated with humanistic studies. Thus *Theodoric of Chartres* (Thierry), who, after being in charge of the school in 1121, taught at Paris, only to return to Chartres in 1141, where he became chancellor in succession to Gilbert de la Porrée, was described by John of Salisbury, himself a humanist, as *artium studiosissimus investigator*. His *Heptateuchon* was concerned with the seven liberal arts and he vigorously combated the anti-humanists, the 'Cornificians', who decried study and literary form. Similarly *William of Conches* (c. 1080–1154), who studied under Bernard of Chartres, taught at Paris and became tutor to Henry Plantagenet, attacked the Cornificians and himself paid attention to grammatical studies, thereby drawing from John of Salisbury the assertion that he was the most gifted grammarian after Bernard of Chartres.[4] But it was *John of Salisbury* (1115/20–1180) who was the most gifted of the humanist philosophers associated with Chartres. Though not educated at Chartres, he became, as we have seen earlier, Bishop of Chartres in 1176. A champion of the liberal arts and acquainted with the Latin classics, with Cicero in particular, he had a detestation for barbarity in style, dubbing those persons who opposed style and rhetoric on principle 'Cornificians'. Careful of his own literary style, he represents what was best in twelfth-century philosophic humanism, as St. Bernard, though not perhaps with full intention, represents humanism by his hymns and spiritual writings. In the next century, the thirteenth, one would certainly not go to the works of the philosophers as such for

Latinity, most of them being far more concerned with content than with form.

3. The School of Chartres, though its *floreat* fell in the twelfth century, had a long history, having been founded in 990 by *Fulbert*, a pupil of *Gerbert of Aurillac*. (The latter was a very distinguished figure of the tenth century, humanist and scholar, who taught at Rheims and Paris, paid several visits to the court of the German Emperor, became in turn Abbot of Bobbio, Archbishop of Rheims and Archbishop of Ravenna, and ascended the papal throne as Sylvester II, dying in 1003.) Founded in the tenth century, the School of Chartres preserved, even in the twelfth century, a certain conservative spirit and flavour, which shewed itself in its Platonist tradition, especially in its devotion to the *Timaeus* of Plato and also to the more Platonically inclined writings of Boethius. Thus *Bernard of Chartres*, who was head of the school from 1114 to 1119 and chancellor from 1119 to 1124, maintained that matter existed in a chaotic state before its information, before order was brought out of disorder. Called by John of Salisbury the 'most perfect among the Platonists of our time',[5] Bernard also represented Nature as an organism and maintained the Platonic theory of the World-Soul. In this he was followed by *Bernard of Tours (Silvestris)*, who was chancellor at Chartres about 1156 and composed a poem *De mundi universitate*, using Chalcidius's commentary on the *Timaeus* and depicting the World-Soul as animating Nature and forming natural beings out of the chaos of prime matter according to the Ideas existing in God or *Nous*. William of Conches went even further by identifying the World-Soul with the Holy Spirit, a doctrine which led to his being attacked by William of St. Theodoric. Retracting, he explained that he was a Christian and not a member of the Academy.

In conjunction with these speculations in the spirit of the *Timaeus* one may mention the inclination of the School of Chartres to ultra-realism, though, as we have seen, two of the most outstanding figures associated with Chartres, Gilbert de la Porrée and John of Salisbury, were not ultra-realists. Thus *Clarembald of Arras*, a pupil of Theodoric of Chartres, who became Provost of Arras in 1152 and Archdeacon of Arras in 1160, maintained, in his Commentary on the *De Trinitate* of Boethius, as against Gilbert de la Porrée, that there is but one and the same humanity in all men and that individual men differ only *propter accidentium varietatem*.[6]

4. In spite, however, of their fondness for the *Timaeus* of Plato, the members of the School of Chartres showed also an esteem for Aristotle. Not only did they follow Aristotle in logic, but they also introduced his hylomorphic theory: indeed it was at Chartres that this theory made its first appearance in the twelfth century. Thus, according to Bernard of Chartres, natural objects are constituted by form and matter. These forms he called *formae nativae* and he represented them as copies of the Ideas in God. This information we have from John of Salisbury, who tells us that Bernard and his disciples tried to mediate between or reconcile Plato and Aristotle.[7] For Bernard of Tours too the forms of things are copies of the Ideas in God, as we have already seen, while Clarembald of Arras represented matter as being always in a state of flux and as being the mutability or *vertibilitas* of things, the form being the perfection and integrity of the thing.[8] He thus interpreted the matter of Aristotle in the light of Plato's teaching about the mutability and evanescent character of material things. William of Conches indeed struck out on a line of his own by maintaining the atomic theory of Democritus;[9] but in general we may say that the members of the School of Chartres adopted the hylomorphic theory of Aristotle, though they interpreted it in the light of the *Timaeus*.[10]

5. The doctrine that natural objects are composed of matter and form, the form being a copy of the exemplar, the Idea in God, clearly makes a distinction between God and creatures and is non-pantheistic in character; but certain members of this School used terminology which, if taken literally and without qualification, would naturally be understood to imply pantheism. Thus Theodoric of Chartres, who was the younger brother of Bernard, maintained that 'all forms are one form; the divine form is all forms' and that the divinity is the *forma essendi* of each thing, while creation is depicted as the production of the many out of the one.[11] Again, Clarembald of Arras argued that God is the *forma essendi* of things and that, since the *forma essendi* must be present wherever a thing is, God is always and everywhere essentially present.[12] But, though these texts, taken literally and in isolation, are pantheistic or monistic in character, it does not appear that either Theodoric of Chartres or Clarembald of Arras meant to teach a monistic doctrine. For instance, immediately after saying that the divine form is all forms Theodoric

observes that, though the divine form is all forms by the fact that it is the perfection and integrity of all things, one may not conclude that the divine form is humanity. It would seem that Theodoric's doctrine must be understood in the light of exemplarism, since he says expressly that the divine form cannot be embodied, and cannot, therefore, be the actual concrete form of man or horse or stone. Similarly, Clarembald of Arras's general doctrine of exemplarism and his insistence that the forms of material things are copies, *imagines*, is incompatible with full pantheism. The phrases which seem to teach a doctrine of emanation are borrowed from Boethius, and it is probable that they no more express a literal understanding of emanation in Theodoric or Clarembald than they do in Boethius: in a sense they are stock phrases, canonised, as it were, by their antiquity, and they should not be pressed unduly.

6. Although John of Salisbury was not educated at Chartres, it is convenient to say something here of his philosophy of the State, as given in his *Polycraticus*. The quarrels between the Holy See and the Empire and the investiture controversies had naturally led to those writers who took part in the disputes having to express some view, even if only by the way, on the function of the State and its ruler. One or two writers went beyond mere asides, as it were, and gave a rude sketch of political theory. Thus *Manegold of Lautenbach* (eleventh century) even referred the power of the ruler to a pact with the people[13] and declared[14] that if the king forsakes rule by law and becomes a tyrant, he is to be considered to have broken the pact to which he owes his power and may be deposed by the people. Such ideas concerning the reign of law and justice as essential to the State and concerning the natural law, of which the civil law should be an expression, were based on texts of Cicero, the Stoics and the Roman jurists, and they reappear in the thought of John of Salisbury, who also made use of St. Augustine's *De Civitate Dei* and the *De Officiis* of St. Ambrose.

Although John of Salisbury did not put forward any compact theory after the fashion of Manegold of Lautenbach, he was insistent that the prince is not above law and declared that whatever the whitewashers of rulers might trumpet abroad to the contrary, he would never allow that the prince is free from all restrictions and all law. But what did he mean when he said that the prince is subject to law? Partly at least he had in mind (and this was indeed his main consideration) the natural law, in accordance with the Stoic doctrine that there is a natural law, to which all positive law does, or ought to, approximate. The prince, then, is not free to enact positive laws which go counter to, or are irreconcilable with, both the natural law and that *aequitas* which is *rerum convenientia, tribuens unicuique quod suum est*. The positive law defines and applies natural law and natural justice, and the attitude of the ruler on this matter shows whether he is prince or tyrant. If his enactments define, apply or supplement natural law and natural justice, he is a prince; if they infringe natural law and natural justice, he is a tyrant, acting according to caprice and not fulfilling the function of his office.

Did John of Salisbury understand anything else by law, when he maintained that the prince is subject to the law? Did he maintain that the prince is in any way subject to defined law? It was certainly the common opinion that the prince was subject in some way to the customs of the land and the enactments of his ancestors, to the local systems of law or tradition which had grown up in the course of time, and, although John of Salisbury's political writing shows little concern with feudalism, since he relied so largely on writers of the Roman period, it is only reasonable to suppose that he shared the common outlook on this matter. His actual judgements on the power and office of the prince express the common outlook, though his formal approach to the subject is through the medium of Roman law, and he would certainly not have envisaged the application in an absolutist sense to the feudal monarch of the Roman Jurist's maxim, *Quod principi placuit legis habet vigorem.*

Now, since John of Salisbury praised Roman law and regarded it as one of the great civilising factors of Europe, he was faced with the necessity of interpreting the maxim quoted above, without at the same time sacrificing his convictions about the restricted power of the prince. First of all, how did Ulpian himself understand his maxim? He was a lawyer and it was his aim to justify, to explain the legality of the Emperor's enactments and *constitutiones*. According to Republican lawyers the law governed the magistrate, but it was obvious that in the time of the Empire the Emperor was himself one of the sources of positive law, and the lawyers had to explain the legality of this position. Ulpian accordingly said that, though the Emperor's legislative authority is derived from the Roman people, the people, by the *lex regia*, transfers to him and vests in him all its own power and authority, so that, once invested with his authority, the will of the Emperor has the force of law. In other words, Ulpian was simply explaining the legality of the Roman Emperor's enactments: he was not concerned to establish a political theory by maintaining that the Emperor was entitled to disregard all natural justice and the principles of morality. When John of Salisbury observed, with express reference to Ulpian's dictum, that when the prince is said to be free from the law, this is not to be understood in the sense that he may do what is unjust, but in the sense that he ought to follow equity or natural justice out of a real love of justice and not from fear of punishment, which does not apply to him, he was expressing the general tradition of feudal lawyers and at the same time was not contradicting Ulpian's maxim. When in the late Middle Ages some political theorists detached Ulpian's maxim from the person of the Emperor, and transferring it to the national monarch interpreted it in an absolutist sense, they were forsaking the general mediaeval outlook and were at the same time changing the legal maxim of Ulpian into an abstract statement of absolutist political theory.

In conclusion it may be remarked that John of Salisbury accepted the supremacy of the ecclesiastical power (*Hunc ergo gladium de manu Ecclesiae accipit princeps*),[15] while he carried his distinction between prince and tyrant to its logical conclusion by admitting tyrannicide as legitimate. Indeed, since the tyrant is opposed to the common good, tyrannicide may sometimes be obligatory,[16] though he made the curious stipulation that poison should not be employed for this purpose.

Chapter Seventeen

THE SCHOOL OF ST. VICTOR

Hugh of St. Victor; proofs of God's existence, faith, mysticism—Richard of St. Victor; proofs of God's existence—Godfrey of St. Victor and Walter of St. Victor.

The Abbey of St. Victor outside the walls of Paris belonged to the Augustinian Canons. We have seen that William of Champeaux was associated with the abbey, retiring there after being worsted by Abelard, but the school is of note principally owing to the work of two men, one a German, Hugh of St. Victor, the other a Scotsman, Richard of St. Victor.

1. *Hugh of St. Victor* was born in Saxony in 1096 of noble parentage, and made his early studies in the monastery of Hamersleben near Halberstadt. After taking the habit he went to Paris in 1115 to continue his studies in the Abbey of St. Victor. In 1125 he started lecturing and from 1133 until his death in 1141 he was in charge of the school. One of the foremost theologians, dogmatic and mystical, of his time, he was yet no enemy to the cultivation of the arts, considering not only that the study of the arts, if rightly pursued, conduces to progress in theology, but also that all knowledge is of utility. 'Learn everything; you will see afterwards that nothing is superfluous.'[1] His chief work, from the philosophical viewpoint, is the *Didascalion* in seven books, in which he treats of the liberal arts (three books), theology (three books) and religious meditation (one book), but his writings on the theology of the Sacraments are also important to the theologian. He also compared exegetic and mystical works and a commentary on the *Celestial Hierarchy* of the Pseudo-Dionysius, using the Latin translation of John Scotus Eriugena.

Of Hugh's classification and systematisation of the sciences mention has already been made, in connection with the systematising tendency already discernible in the twelfth century and due partly to the application of dialectic in theology, as also of his theory of abstraction, in connection with the discussion on universals.[2] These two points bring out the Aristotelian aspects of his thought, whereas his psychology is distinctly Augustinian in character. 'No one is really wise who does not see that he exists; and yet, if a man begins truly to consider what he is, he sees that he is none of all those things which are either seen in him or can be seen. For that in us which is capable of reasoning, although it is, so to speak, infused into and mingled with the flesh, is yet distinguishable by reason from the substance of the flesh and is seen to be different therefrom.'[3] In other words, consciousness and introspection bear witness, not only to the existence of the soul, but also to its spirituality and immateriality. Moreover, the soul is of itself a person, having, as a rational spirit, personality of itself and through itself, the body forming an element in human personality only in virtue of its union with the rational spirit.[4] The mode of union is one of 'apposition' rather than of composition.[5]

Hugh contributed to the systematic advance of natural theology by giving *a posteriori* arguments both from internal and external experience. As regards the first line of proof, it rests upon the experiential fact of self-consciousness, the consciousness of a self which is 'seen' in a purely rational way and cannot be material. Regarding self-consciousness as necessary to the existence of a rational being, Hugh maintains that, as the soul has not always been conscious of its existence, there was a time when it did not exist. But it could not have given itself existence: it must, then, owe its existence to another being, and this being must be a necessary and self-existent being, God.[6] This proof is somewhat compressed, involving the premisses that the cause of a rational principle must itself be rational and that an infinite regress is impossible. Its 'interiority' certainly reminds one of Augustine, but it is not Augustine's proof from the soul's knowledge of eternal truths, nor does it presuppose religious, still less mystical, experience since it rests on the natural experience of the soul's self-consciousness, and it is this reliance on experience which characterises Hugh's proofs of God's existence.

The second proof, that from external experience,[7] rests on the experienced fact of change. Things are constantly coming into being and passing away, and the totality, which is composed of such changing things, must itself have had a beginning. It requires, therefore, a Cause. Nothing which lacks stability, which ceases to be, can have come into being without a Cause external to itself. The idea of such a proof is contained in the *De Fide Orthodoxa* of St. John Damascene;[8] but Hugh of St. Victor attempts to supply the deficiencies in St. John Damascene's procedure.

In addition to the proof from change Hugh gives a teleological proof in several parts.[9] In the world of animals we see that the senses and appetites find their satisfaction in objects: in the world in general we see a great variety of movements (the reference is to local motion), which, however, are ordered in harmony. Again, growth is a fact of experience, and growth, since it means the addition of something new, cannot be accomplished solely by the thing which grows. Hugh concludes that these three considerations exclude chance and postulate a Providence which is responsible for growth and guides all things according to law.[10] The proof is clearly somewhat unconvincing in the form given, but it is based on facts of experience, as the starting-point, and this is characteristic of Hugh's proofs in general. Hugh adopted the theory of William of Conches concerning the atomic structure of matter. These atoms are simple bodies, which are capable of increase and growth.[11]

Hugh was thus quite clear about the possibility of a natural knowledge of God's existence, but he was equally insistent on the necessity of faith. This faith is necessary, not only because the *oculus contemplationis*, whereby the soul apprehends God within herself *et ea quae in Deo erant*, has been completely darkened by sin, but also because mysteries which exceed the power of the human reason are proposed to man's beliefs. These mysteries are *supra rationem*, in that revelation and faith are required to apprehend them, but they are *secundum rationem*, not *contra rationem*: in themselves they are reasonable and can be the object of knowledge, but they cannot be the object of knowledge in the strict sense in this life, as man's mind is too weak, especially in its sin-darkened state. Knowledge, then, considered in itself, stands higher than faith, which is a certitude of the mind concerning absent things, superior to opinion but inferior to science or knowledge, since those who comprehend the object as immediately present (the *scientes*) are superior to those who believe on authority. We may say, therefore, that Hugh of St. Victor made a clear distinction between faith and knowledge and that, though he recognised the superiority of the latter, he did not thereby impugn the necessity of the former. His doctrine of the superiority of knowledge to faith is by no means equivalent to the Hegelian doctrine, since Hugh certainly did not consider that knowledge can, naturally at least, be substituted for faith in this life.

But, though the *oculus contemplationis* has been darkened by sin, the mind, under the supernatural influence of grace, can ascend by degrees to contemplation of God in Himself. Thus supernatural mysticism crowns the ascent of knowledge in this life as the beatific vision of God crowns it in heaven. To enter upon a discussion of Hugh's mystical teaching would scarcely be in place here; but it is worth pointing out that the mystical tradition of St. Victor was not simply a spiritual luxury; their mystical theology formed an integral part of their theologico-philosophical synthesis. In philosophy God's existence is proved by the natural use of reason, while in theology the mind learns about the Nature of God and applies dialectic to the data of revelation accepted on faith. But philosophical knowledge and theological (dialectical) knowledge are knowledge about God: higher still is the experience of God, the direct knowledge of God, which is attained in mystical experience, a loving knowledge or a knowing love of God. On the other hand, mystical knowledge is not full vision, and God's presence to the soul in mystical experience blinds by excess of light, so that above both knowledge about God by faith and direct mystical knowledge of God there stands the beatific vision of heaven.

2. *Richard of St. Victor* was born in Scotland but went to Paris early in life and entered the Abbey of St. Victor, where he became sub-prior about 1157 and prior in 1162. He died in 1173. The abbey passed through a difficult period during these years, as the abbot, an Englishman named Ervisius, wasted its goods and ruined its discipline, behaving in such an independent manner that Pope Alexander III called him 'another Caesar'. With some difficulty he was induced to resign in 1172, a year before the death of Richard. However, even if his abbot was a somewhat independent and high-handed individual, the prior, we are told by the abbey

necrology, left behind him the memory of a good example, a holy life and beautiful writings.

Richard is an important figure in mediaeval theology, his chief work being the *De Trinitate* in six books, but he was also a philosopher, as well as being a mystical theologian who published two works on contemplation, the *Beniamin minor*, on the preparation of the soul for contemplation, and the *Beniamin maior*, on the grace of contemplation. In other words, he was a worthy successor of Hugh of St. Victor, and like him he insisted on the necessity of using the reason in the pursuit and investigation of truth. 'I have frequently read that there is only one God, that He is eternal, uncreated, immense, omnipotent and Lord of all: . . . I have read concerning my God that He is one and three, one in Substance, three in Persons: all this I have read; but I do not remember that I have read how all these things are proved.'[12] Again, 'In all these matters authorities abound, but not arguments; in all these matters *experimenta desunt*, proofs are becoming rare; so I think that I shall have done something, if I am able to help the minds of the studious a little, even if I cannot satisfy them.'

The general attitude of St. Anselm is evident in the above quotations: *Credo, ut intelligam*. The data of the Christian religion presupposed, Richard of St. Victor sets out to understand them and to prove them. Just as St. Anselm had declared his intention of trying to prove the Blessed Trinity by 'necessary reasons', so Richard declares at the beginning of his *De Trinitate*[13] that it will be his intention in that work, so far as God grants, to adduce not only probable, but also necessary reasons for the things which we believe. He points out that there must be necessary reasons for what necessarily exists; so that, as God is necessarily Three in One, there must be a necessary reason for this fact. Of course, it by no means follows from the fact that God is necessarily Triune (God is the necessary Being) that we can discern this necessity, and Richard admits indeed that we cannot fully comprehend the mysteries of Faith, particularly that of the Blessed Trinity,[14] but that does not prevent his attempting to show that a plurality of persons in the Godhead necessarily follows from the fact that God is Love and to demonstrate the trinity of Persons in one Nature.

Richard's speculation on the Trinity had a considerable influence on later Scholastic theology; but from the philosophical viewpoint his proofs for the existence of God are of greater import. Such proofs, he insists, must rest on experience: 'We ought to begin from that class of things, of which we can have no manner of doubt, and by means of those things which we know by experience to conclude rationally what we must think concerning the objects which transcend experience.'[15] These objects of experience are contingent objects, things which begin to be and can cease to be. Such things we can come to know only through experience, since what comes into being and can perish cannot be necessary, so that its existence cannot be demonstrated *a priori*, but can be known only by experience.[16]

The starting-point of the argument is thus provided by the contingent objects of experience; but, in order that our reasoning on this basis may be successful, it is necessary to start from a clearly solid and, as it were, immovable foundation of truth;[17] that is, the argument needs a sure and certain principle on which it may rest. This principle is that every thing which exists or can exist has being either of itself or from another than itself, and that everything which exists or can exist either has being from eternity or begins to be in time. This application of the principle of contradiction allows us to form a division of being. Any existent thing must be either (i) from eternity and from itself, and so self-existent, or (ii) neither from eternity nor from itself, or (iii) from eternity, but not from itself, or (iv) not from eternity but yet from itself. This logical division into four admits immediately of a reduction to a threefold division, since a thing which is not from eternity but is *a se*, is impossible, for a thing which began to be obviously cannot either have given itself being or be a necessary existent.[18] A beginning in time and aseity are thus incompatible, and it remains to refer back to the things of experience and apply the general principle. The things of experience, as we observe them in the human, animal and vegetable kingdoms, and in nature in general, are perishable and contingent: they begin to be. If, then, they begin to be, they are not from eternity. But what is not from eternity cannot be from itself, as already said. Therefore it must be from another. But ultimately there must exist a being which exists of itself, i.e. necessarily, since, if there is no such being, there would be no sufficient reason for the existence of anything: nothing would exist, whereas in point of fact something does exist, as we know by experience. If it be objected that there must indeed be an *ens a se* but that this may very well be the world itself, Richard would retort that he has already excluded this possibility by pointing out that we experience the contingent character of the things of which the world is composed.

If in this first proof Richard's procedure shows a marked change from that of St. Anselm, in his next proof he adopts a familiar Anselmian position.[19] It is a fact of experience that there are different and varying degrees of goodness or perfection, the rational, for example, being higher than the irrational. From this experiential fact Richard proceeds to argue that there must be a highest, than which there is no greater or better. As the rational is superior to the irrational, this supreme substance must be intellectual, and as the higher cannot receive what it possesses from the lower, from the subordinate, it must have its being and existence from itself. This necessarily means that it is eternal. Something must be eternal and *a se*, as has been already shown, since otherwise nothing would exist, and experience teaches us that something does exist, and, if the higher cannot receive what it possesses from the lower, it must be the highest, the supreme Substance, which is the eternal and necessary Being.

In the third place Richard attempts to prove the existence of God from the idea of possibility.[20] In the whole universe nothing can exist, unless it has the possibility of being (the potentiality or power to be) from itself or receives it from another. A thing which lacks the possibility of being, which is completely impossible, is nothing at all, and in order that anything should exist, it must receive the ability to exist (*posse esse*) from the ground of possibility. (That the objects in the universe cannot receive their possibility from themselves, cannot be self-grounded, Richard here takes for granted: in his first proof he has already shown the incompatibility of aseity and temporality or beginning to be.) This ground of possibility, then, which is the source of the possibility and the existence of all things, must be self-dependent, ultimate. Every essence, every power, every wisdom, must depend on this Ground, so that the latter must itself be the supreme Essence as the ground of all essences, the supreme Power as source of all power, and supreme Wisdom as source of all wisdom, since it is impossible that a source should confer a gift greater than itself. But there can be no wisdom apart from a rational substance in which it is immanent: so there must be a rational and supreme Substance, in which supreme wisdom is immanent. The Ground of all possibility is, therefore, the supreme Substance.

These arguments are, of course, exercises of the rational, discursive intelligence, of the *oculus rationis*, superior to the *oculus imaginationis*, which views the corporeal world, but inferior to the *oculus intelligentiae*, by which God is contemplated in Himself.[21] On the inferior level the objects of sense are viewed immediately as present; on the middle level the mind thinks discursively about things not immediately visible, arguing, for example, from effect to cause or *vice versa*; on the superior level the mind views an invisible object, God, as immediately present.[22] The level of contemplation is thus, as it were, the spiritual analogue of sense-perception, being like to it in immediacy and concreteness in contrast with discursive thought, though it differs in that it is a purely spiritual activity, directed to a purely spiritual object. Richard's division of the six stages of knowledge, from the perception of God's beauty in the beauty of creation to the *mentis alienatio*, under the action of grace, influenced St. Bonaventure in the composition of his *Itinerarium mentis in Deum*.

3. Godfrey of St. Victor (d. 1194) wrote a *Fons Philosophiae*, in which he classifies the sciences and treats of such philosophers and transmitters as Plato, Aristotle, Boethius and Macrobius, devoting a special chapter to the problem of universals and the professed solutions of the problem. *Walter of St. Victor* (died after 1180) was the author of the celebrated diatribe *Contra Quattuor Labyrinthos Franciae*, Abelard, Peter Lombard, Peter of Poitiers and Gilbert de la Porrée, the representatives of dialectical theology, who, according to Walter, were puffed up with the spirit of Aristotle, treated with Scholastic levity of the ineffable things of the Blessed Trinity and the Incarnation, vomited out many heresies and bristled with errors. In other words, Walter of St. Victor was a reactionary who does not represent the genuine spirit of St. Victor, of Hugh the German and Richard the Scotsman, with its reasoned combination of philosophy, dialectical theology and mysticism. In any case the hands of the clock could not be put back, for dialectical theology had come to stay and in the following century it attained its triumph in the great systematic syntheses.

Chapter Eighteen

DUALISTS AND PANTHEISTS

Albigensians and Cathari—Amalric of Bene—David of Dinant.

1. In the thirteenth century St. Dominic preached against the Albigensians. This sect, as well as that of the Cathari, was already widespread in southern France and in Italy during the twelfth century. The principal tenet of these sects was a dualism of the Manichaean type, which came into western Europe by way of Byzantium. There exist two ultimate Principles, the one good and the other bad, of which the former caused the soul, the latter the body and matter in general. From this hypothesis they drew the conclusion that the body is evil and has to be overcome by asceticism and also that it is wrong to marry and propagate the human race. It may seem strange that a sect whose members held such doctrines should flourish; but it must be remembered that it was considered sufficient if the comparatively few *perfecti* led this ascetic existence, while their less exalted followers could safely lead a more ordinary life, if they received the blessing of one of the 'perfect' before death. It must also be remembered, when one is considering the attention which the Albigensians and Cathari received from the ecclesiastical and civil powers, that the condemnation of procreation and of marriage as evil leads naturally to the conclusion that concubinage and marriage are on much the same footing. Moreover, the Cathari denied the legitimacy of oaths and of all war. It was, then, only natural that the sects were looked on as constituting a danger to Christian civilisation. The sect of the Waldenses, which still exists, goes back to the Catharist movement and was originally a sect of dualists, though it was absorbed by the Ref-

ormation and adopted anti-Romanism and anti-sacerdotalism
as its chief tenets.[1]

2. *Amalric of Bene* was born near Chartres and died as a
professor of theology at Paris about 1206/7. St. Thomas
Aquinas[2] observes that 'others said that God is the formal
principle of all things, and this is said to have been the opinion of the Amalricians', while Martin of Poland says of
Amalric that he held God to be the essence of all creatures
and the existence of all creatures. Apparently he interpreted
in a pantheistic sense the teaching of John Scotus Eriugena,
as well as the phrases used by Theodoric of Chartres and
Clarembald of Arras, even going so far as to say that the
Persons of the Trinity are creatures, that all three became incarnate and that every single man is as much God as was
Christ. From this doctrine some of his followers seem to have
drawn the conclusion that sin is an unreal concept, on the
ground that, if every man is divine, there can be no question
of his sinning. Whether Amalric consciously upheld real
pantheism or not, he was in any case accused of heresy and
had to retract, his doctrines being condemned in 1210, after
his death, along with those of John Scotus Eriugena.

3. If for Amalric of Bene God is the form of all things, for
David of Dinant He was identified with prime matter, in the
sense of the potentiality of all things. Very little is known of
the life of David of Dinant, or of the sources from which he
derived his doctrines, or of the doctrines themselves, since his
writings, condemned in 1210 and forbidden at Paris in 1215,
have perished. St. Albert the Great[3] ascribes to him a *De
tomis, hoc est de divisionibus*, while the documents of the
Council of Paris (1210) ascribe to him a *Quaterni* or *Quater-
nuli*, though Geyer, for example, supposes that these two
titles refer to the same work, which consisted of a number of
sections or paragraphs (*quaterni*). In any case we have to rely
for our knowledge of his doctrine on quotations and reports by
St. Albert the Great, St. Thomas and Nicholas of Cusa.

In the *Summa Theologica*[4] St. Thomas states that David
of Dinant 'very foolishly affirmed that God is prime matter'.
Elsewhere[5] he says that David divided things into three
classes: bodies, souls and eternal substances, bodies being constituted of *Hyle*, souls of *Nous* or mind, and the eternal substances of God. These three constituent sources are the three
indivisibles, and the three indivisibles are one and the same.
Thus all bodies would be modes of one indivisible being,

Hyle, and all souls would be modes of one indivisible being, *Nous;* but these two indivisible beings are one, and were identified by David with God, who is the one Substance. 'It is manifest (according to David) that there is only one substance not only of all bodies, but also of all souls, and that this substance is nothing else but God himself. . . . It is clear, then, that God is the substance of all bodies and all souls, and that God and *Hyle* and *Mens* are one substance.'⁶

David of Dinant tried to prove this position dialectically. For two kinds of substances to differ from one another they must differ in virtue of a difference, and the presence of a difference implies the presence of a common element. Now, if matter differed from mind, there would have to be a *differentia* in prime matter, i.e. a form and a matter, and in this case we should go on to infinity.⁷ St. Thomas puts the argument this way.⁸ When things in no way differ from one another, they are the same. Now, whatever things differ from one another, differ in virtue of *differentiae,* and in this case they must be composite. But God and prime matter are altogether simple, not composite things. Therefore they cannot differ in any way from one another, and must consequently be the same. To this argument St. Thomas replies that composite things such as, for example, man and horse, do indeed differ from one another in virtue of *differentiae,* but that simple things do not: simple things should be said, strictly speaking, to be diverse (*diversa esse*), not to be different (*differre*). In other words he accuses David of playing with terms, of choosing, to express the diversity of God and matter, a term which implies composition in God and matter.

Why did St. Albert and St. Thomas think it worth while giving such attention to a pantheistic system, the theoretical support of which was more or less a dialectical quibble? Probably the reason was not so much that David of Dinant exercised an extensive influence as that they feared that the heresy of David might compromise Aristotle. The sources from which David drew his theories constitute a disputed point, but it is generally agreed that he drew on the exposition of ancient materialism given in the *Physics* and *Metaphysics,* and it is clear that he utilises the Aristotelian ideas of prime matter and form. In 1210 the same Council of Paris which condemned David's writings forbad also the public and private teaching of the natural philosophy of Aristotle in the University. Most probably, then, St. Thomas wished to show that David of Dinant's monism by no means followed from the teaching of Aristotle; and in his reply to the objection already cited he expressly refers to the *Metaphysics*.

Part Four

ISLAMIC AND JEWISH
PHILOSOPHY:
TRANSLATIONS

Chapter Nineteen

ISLAMIC PHILOSOPHY

Reasons for discussing Islamic philosophy—Origins of Islamic philosophy—Alfarabi—Avicenna—Averroes—Dante and the Arabian philosophers.

1. To come upon a chapter on the philosophy of the Arabs in a work devoted to mediaeval thought, in the sense of the thought of mediaeval Christendom, might astonish a reader who was making his first acquaintance with the philosophy of the Middle Ages; but the influence, positive and negative, of Islamic philosophy on that of Christendom is now a matter of common knowledge among historians, and one can scarcely avoid saying something on the subject. The Arabian philosophy was one of the principal channels whereby the complete Aristotle was introduced to the West; but the great philosophers of mediaeval Islam, men like Avicenna and Averroes, were more than mere transmitters or even commentators; they changed and developed the philosophy of Aristotle, more or less according to the spirit of neo-Platonism, and several of them interpreted Aristotle on important points in a sense which, whether exegetically correct or not, was incompatible with the Christian theology and faith.[1] Aristotle, therefore, when he appeared to mediaeval Christian thinkers in the shape given him by Averroes, for example, naturally appeared as an enemy of Christian wisdom, Christian philosophy in the wide sense. This fact explains to a large extent the opposition offered to Aristotelianism in the thirteenth century by many upholders of the Christian tra-

dition who looked on the pagan philosopher as the foe of Augustine, Anselm and the great philosophers of Christianity. The opposition varied in degree, from a rather crude dislike and fear of novelty, to the reasoned opposition of a thinker like St. Bonaventure; but it becomes easier to understand the opposition if one remembers that a Moslem philosopher such as Averroes claimed to give the right interpretation of Aristotle and that this interpretation was, on important questions, at variance with Christian belief. It explains too the attention paid to the Islamic philosophers by those (particularly, of course, St. Thomas Aquinas) who saw in the Aristotelian system not only a valuable instrument for the dialectical expression of Christian theology but also the true philosophy, for such thinkers had to show that Aristotelianism did not necessarily involve the interpretation given to it by the Moslems: they had to dissociate themselves from Averroes and to distinguish their Aristotelianism from his.

In order, then, fully to understand the polemics of St. Thomas Aquinas and others, it is necessary to know something of mediaeval Islamic philosophy; but it is also necessary for a connected reason, namely that there arose in Paris a School of philosophers who claimed to represent integral Aristotelianism, the chief figure of this School being the celebrated opponent of St. Thomas, Siger of Brabant. These 'integral' Aristotelians, the genuine Aristotelians as they thought themselves to be, meant by genuine Aristotelianism the system of Aristotle as interpreted by Averroes, the Commentator *par excellence*. In order, therefore, to understand this school and an important phase of the controversies at Paris, it is obviously necessary to be acquainted with the place of Averroes in the history of philosophy and with his doctrine.

But, though some treatment of mediaeval Islamic philosophy must be given, it does not come within the scope of this book to discuss the Islamic philosophy for its own sake. It has indeed its own peculiar interest (for example, its relations to Islamic theology, their attempted reconciliation and the tension between them, as well as the relation of Islamic thought to mysticism in the Islamic world, and of Islamic philosophy to Islamic culture in general, have their own intrinsic interest), but the reader must expect here no more than a brief sketch of Islamic philosophy in the mediaeval period, a treatment of it less for its own sake than in function of its influence on the thought of mediaeval Christendom. This perhaps rather one-sided treatment is not designed to belittle the achievements of Moslem philosophers, nor does it involve a denial of the intrinsic interest of Islamic philosophy for its own sake: it is simply dictated by the general purpose and scope of this book, as well as, of course, by considerations of space.

2. If Islamic philosophy was connected with the philosophy of Christendom in the way just mentioned, it was also connected with Christianity in its origins, owing to the fact that it was Christian Syrians who first translated Aristotle and other ancient philosophers into Arabic. The first stage consisted of the translation of Greek works into Syriac at the school of Edessa in Mesopotamia, which was founded by St. Ephrem of Nisibis in 363 and was closed by the Emperor Zeno in 489 because of the Nestorianism which prevailed there. At Edessa some of the works of Aristotle, principally the logical works, as well as Porphyry's *Isagoge*, were translated into Syriac, and this work was continued in Persia, at Nisibis and Gandisapora, whither the scholars betook themselves on the closure of the school. Thus works of Aristotle and Plato were translated into Persian. In the sixth century works of Aristotle and Porphyry and the writings of the Pseudo-Dionysius were translated into Syriac at the Monophysite schools of Syria.

The second stage consisted in the translation of the Syriac translations into Arabic. Even before the time of Mohammed (569–632) there had been a number of Nestorian Christians who worked among the Arabs, mainly as physicians, and when the 'Abbāsid dynasty replaced that of the Ommaiades in 750, Syrian scholars were invited to the Arab court at Baghdad. Medical works were translated first of all; but after a time philosophical works were also translated, and in 832 a school of translators was established at Baghdad, an institution which produced Arabic versions of Aristotle, Alexander of Aphrodisias, Themistius, Porphyry and Ammonius. Plato's *Republic* and *Laws* were also translated, as well as (in the first half of the ninth century) the so-called *Theology of Aristotle*, which consisted of a compilation of the *Enneads* (4–6) of Plotinus, erroneously attributed to Aristotle. To this must be added the fact that the *Liber de Causis*, really the *Institutio Theologica* of Proclus, was also attributed to Aristotle. These false attributions, as well as the translation into Arabic of neo-Platonic commentators on Aristotle, helped to popularise among the Arabs a neo-Platonic interpretation of the Aristotelian system, though other influences, as well as Aristotle and the neo-Platonists, contributed to the formation of Islamic philosophy, e.g. the Islamic religion itself and the influence of Oriental religious thought, such as that of Persia.

3. The Moslem philosophers may be divided into two groups, the eastern group and the western group. In this section I shall treat briefly of three thinkers belonging to the eastern group.

(i) *Alfarabi*, who belonged to the school of Baghdad and died about 950, is a good example of a thinker upon whom the influences mentioned above made themselves felt. Thus he helped to introduce the Islamic cultured world to the logic of Aristotle, while by his classification of the departments of philosophy and theology he made philosophy self-conscious, as it were, marking it off from theology. Logic is a propaedeutic and preparation for philosophy proper, which Alfarabi divided into physics, comprising the particular sciences (psychology being included and the theory of knowledge being treated of in psychology) and metaphysics (physics and metaphysics being the two branches of theoretical philosophy) and ethics or practical philosophy. His scheme for theology included as sections (1) omnipotence and justice of God; (2) the unity and other attributes of God; (3) the doctrine of sanctions in the next life; (4) and (5) the individual's rights and the social relations of the Moslem. By making philosophy a separate province, then, Alfarabi did not mean to supplant or undermine the Islamic theology: rather did he place schematisation and logical form at the service of theology.

In addition, Alfarabi utilised Aristotelian arguments in proving the existence of God. Thus, on the supposition that the things of the world are passively moved, an idea which fitted in well with Islamic theology, he argued that they must receive their movement from a first Mover, God. Again, the things of this world are contingent, they do not exist of necessity: their essence does not involve their existence, as is shown by the fact that they come into being and pass away. From this it follows that they have received their existence, and ultimately one must admit a Being which exists essentially, necessarily, and is the Cause of the existence of all contingent beings.

On the other hand, when it comes to the general system of

Alfarabi, the neo-Platonic influence is manifest. Thus the theme of emanation is employed to show how from the ultimate Deity or One there proceed the Intelligence and the World-Soul, from the thoughts or ideas of which proceeds the Cosmos, from the higher or outer spheres to the lower or inner spheres. Bodies are composed of matter and form. The intelligence of man is illuminated by the cosmic intelligence, which is the active intellect of man (the νοῦς ἐπίκτητος of Alexander of Aphrodisias). Moreover, the illumination of the human intellect is the explanation of the fact that our concepts 'fit' things, since the Ideas in God are at once the exemplar and source of the concepts in the human mind and of the forms in things.

This doctrine of illumination is connected, not only with neo-Platonism, but also with Oriental mysticism. Alfarabi himself became attached to the mystical school or sect of the Sufis, and his philosophy had a religious orientation. The highest task of man is to know God, and, just as the general process of the universe is a flowing out from God and a return to God, so should man, who proceeds from God in the emanative process and who is enlightened by God, strive after the return to and likeness with God.

(ii) The greatest Moslem philosopher of the eastern group is without a doubt *Avicenna* or *Ibn Sīnā* (980–1037), the real creator of a Scholastic system in the Islamic world.[2] A Persian by birth, born near Bokhara, he received his education in the Arab tongue, and most of his works, which were extremely numerous, were written in Arabic. A precocious boy, he learnt in succession the Koran, Arabic literature, geometry, jurisprudence, logic. Outstripping his instructors, he studied by himself theology, physics, mathematics and medicine, and at sixteen years of age he was already practising as a doctor. He then devoted a year and a half to the study of philosophy and logic, but it was only when he chanced upon a commentary by Alfarabi that he was able to understand to his satisfaction the *Metaphysics* of Aristotle, which he had read, he tells us, forty times without being able to understand it. The rest of his life was a busy and adventurous one, as he acted as Vizir to several Sultans and practised medicine, experiencing in his travels the ups and downs of life and the favour and disfavour of princes, but being always the philosopher, pursuing his studies and writings wherever he was, even in prison and on horseback. He died at Hamadan at the age of fifty-seven, after performing his ablutions, repenting of his sins, distributing abundant alms and freeing his slaves. His principal philosophical work is the *Aš-Šifā*, known in the Middle Ages as the *Sufficientiae*, which comprised logic, physics (including the natural sciences), mathematics, psychology and metaphysics. The *Najāt* was a collection of texts, taken from the first work and arranged in a different order.

Avicenna's division of philosophy in the wide sense into logic, the propaedeutic to philosophy, speculative philosophy (physics, mathematics and theology) and practical philosophy (ethics, economics and politics) offers no remarkable features, save that theology is divided into first theology (equivalent to ontology and natural theology) and second theology (involving Islamic themes), and this marks off Islamic theology from the Greek. But his metaphysic, in spite of its borrowing both from Aristotle and from neo-Platonism, shows features of its own, which make it plain that, however much he borrowed from former philosophers, Avicenna had thought out his system carefully and independently and had welded it into a system of a peculiar stamp. For instance, although he is at one with Aristotle in assigning the study of being as being to metaphysics, Avicenna employs an un-Aristotelian illustration to show that the mind necessarily apprehends the idea of being, though it is acquired normally through experience. Imagine a man suddenly created, who cannot see or hear, who is floating in space and whose members are so disposed that they cannot touch one another. On the supposition that he cannot exercise the senses and acquire the notion of being through sight or touch, will he thereby be unable to form the notion? No, because he will be conscious of and affirm his own existence, so that, even if he cannot acquire the notion of being through external experience, he will at least acquire it through self-consciousness.[3]

In Avicenna's eyes the notion of necessity is also a primary notion, for to him all beings are necessary. It is necessary, however, to distinguish two kinds of necessity. A particular object in the world is not necessary of itself: its essence does not involve existence necessarily, as is shown by the fact that it comes into being and passes away; but it is necessary in the sense that its existence is determined by the necessary action of an external cause. Accordingly a contingent being means, for Avicenna, a being the existence of which is due, not to the essence of the being itself, but to the necessary action of an external cause. Such beings are indeed caused and so 'contingent', but none the less the action of the cause is determined.

This leads him on to argue that the chain of causes cannot be infinite, since then there would be no reason for the existence of anything, but that there must be a first cause which is itself uncaused. This uncaused Being, the necessary Being, cannot receive its essence from another, nor can its existence form part of its essence, since composition of parts would involve an anterior uniting cause: essence and existence must therefore be identical in the necessary Being. This ultimate Being is necessary of itself, whereas 'contingent' beings are not necessary of themselves but necessary through another, so that the concept 'being', as applied to necessary and contingent being, has not the same sense. They are not, then, species of one genus; but rather does Being belong *par excellence*, properly and primarily, to the necessary Being and is predicated of contingent being only secondarily and analogically.

Closely allied with the distinction between the possible and the necessary is the distinction between potentiality and act. Potentiality, as Aristotle said, is the principle of change into another as other, and this principle may exist either in the agent (active potency) or in the patient (passive potency). Moreover, there are degrees of potency and act, ranging between the lower limit, pure potentiality, prime matter, and the upper limit, pure act, the necessary Being, though Avicenna does not use the phrase 'Pure Act' *quoad verbum*. From this position Avicenna proceeds to show that God is Truth, Goodness, Love and Life. For example, the Being which is always in act, without potentiality or privation, must be absolute Goodness, and since the divine attributes are ontologically indistinguishable, the divine Goodness must be identical with absolute Love.

As God is absolute Goodness, He necessarily tends to diffuse His goodness, to radiate it, and this means that He creates necessarily. As God is the necessary Being, all His attributes must be necessary: He is, therefore, necessarily Creator. This in turn involves the conclusion that creation is from eternity, for, if God is necessarily Creator and God is eternal, creation must be eternal. Moreover, if God creates by the necessity of His Nature, it follows also that there is no free choice in creation, that God could not create otherwise or create other things than He actually creates. But God can produce immediately only by a being like Himself: it is impossible for God to create material things directly. The logically first being to proceed from God is, therefore, the first Intelligence. This Intelligence is created, in the sense that it proceeds from God: it receives, then, its existence, and in this way duality begins. Whereas in the One there is no duality, in the primary Intelligence there is a duality of essence and existence, in that existence is received, while there is also a duality of knowledge, in that the primary Intelligence knows the One or God as necessary and itself as 'possible'. In this way Avicenna deduces the ten Intelligences which exhibit a growing multiplicity and so bridges the gap between the unity of God and the multiplicity of creation. The tenth Intelligence is the 'giver of forms', which are received in prime matter, pure potentiality (or rather potentiality 'deprived of' form, and so, in a sense, 'evil'), and so rendered capable of multiplication within the species. The separate Intelligences can differ from one another only specifically, in virtue of their greater or less proximity to the One and the decreasing simplicity in the process of emanation; but, as matter is the principle of individuation, the same specific form can be multiplied in a plurality of individual concrete objects, though prime matter has first to be taken out of its state of indetermination and disposed for the reception of specific form, first through the *forma corporeitatis* and then through the action of external causes which predispose matter for the reception of one particular specific form.

The tenth Intelligence has another function to perform besides that of *Dator formarum*, for it also exercises the function of the active intellect in man. In his analysis of abstraction Avicenna will not credit the human intellect as such with the final act of abstraction, the apprehension of the universal in a state of pure intelligibility, as this would mean that the intellect passes from a state of potentiality to act entirely by its own power, whereas no agent can proceed from passive potency to act except under the influence of an agent external to itself but like itself. He distinguished, therefore, the active and passive intellects, but made the active intellect a separate and unitary intelligence which illumines the human intellect or confers on it its intellectual and abstract grasp of essences (the essence or universal *post rem*, to be distinguished from the essence *ante rem* and *in re*).

Avicenna's idea of necessary creation and his denial that the One has direct knowledge of the multiplicity of concrete objects set him at variance with the theology of the Koran; but he tried, so far as he could, to reconcile his Aristotelian-neo-Platonist system with orthodox Islam. For example, he did not deny the immortality of the human soul, in spite of his doctrine concerning the separateness of the active intellect, and he maintained a doctrine of sanctions in the after life, though he interpreted this in an intellectualist manner, reward consisting in the knowledge of purely intelligible objects, punishment in the deprivation of such knowledge.[4] Again, though his analysis and explanation of creation and the relation of the world to God necessarily involved a theory of emanation and, in this respect, tended towards pantheism, he tried to safeguard himself from pantheism by affirming the distinction between essence and existence in all beings which proceed, immediately or mediately, from God. Possibly the Islamic doctrine of the divine omnipotence, when interpreted 'speculatively', tends to pantheism, and it may well be that some fundamental principles of Avicenna's system would favour pantheism; but he was certainly no pantheist by intention.

When portions of the writings of Avicenna were translated into Latin in the twelfth century, the Christian world found itself faced for the first time with a closely knit system which was bound to exercise a strong attraction on certain minds. Thus *Gundissalinus* (d. 1151) translated into Latin the Spanish translation made by Joannes Hispanus (Avendeath) and utilised the thought of Avicenna in his *De Anima*, following the Avicennian psychology (and citing the latter's allegory of the 'flying man'), though he left Avicenna for Augustine by making the active intellect, as source of illumination, identical with God. Moreover, in his *De Processione Mundi* he attempted to reconcile the cosmogony of Avicenna with Christian doctrine, though his example in this matter was not followed. Before the entire *Metaphysics* of Aristotle became available, uncertainty reigned as to which doctrines were to be attributed to Avicenna and which to Aristotle. Thus Roger Bacon thought that Avicenna must have followed Aristotle throughout, though he (Bacon) had not got books M and N

of the *Metaphysics* and so could not check the truth or un-
truth of this supposition. The result was that *William of
Auvergne* (died *c.* 1249), the first vigorous opponent of Avicenna, attributed the cosmogony of Avicenna to Aristotle
himself. This cosmogony, said William, was erroneous, in that
it admitted intermediaries in the process of creation, thus allowing to creatures a divine power, denied the divine freedom,
asserted the eternity of the world, made matter the principle
of individuation and regarded the separate active intellect
as the efficient cause of human souls. None the less William
himself followed Avicenna by introducing into Latin Scholasticism the distinction between essence and existence. Moreover, denying Avicenna's doctrine of the active intellect, he
pretty well identified it with God. Other thinkers, such as
Alexander of Hales, John of la Rochelle and St. Albert, while
denying the doctrine of a separate active intellect, made use
of Avicenna's theory of abstraction and of the necessity of
illumination, whereas Roger Bacon and Roger Marston found
Avicenna's error to consist only in not identifying the separate
and illuminating active intellect with God. Without going
any further into the question of Avicenna's influence, which
would require a distinct monograph, one can say that he influenced Latin Scholasticism in regard to at least three
themes, that of knowledge and illumination, that of the relation of essence and existence, and that of matter as the
principle of individuation.[5] Criticism of Avicenna by a Latin
Scholastic does not mean, of course, that the Scholastic learnt
nothing from Avicenna. For instance, St. Thomas found it
necessary to criticise the Moslem philosopher's treatment of
possibility,[6] but that does not mean that St. Thomas did not
develop his own position partly through a consideration of
Avicenna's doctrine, even if it is difficult to assess the precise
degree of influence exercised by the latter's writings on the
greatest of the Scholastics. Scotus, however, was much more
influenced by Avicenna than was St. Thomas, though he certainly could not be called with propriety a disciple of Avicenna.

(iii) *Algazel* (1058–1111), who lectured for a time at
Baghdad, opposed the views of Alfarabi and Avicenna from
the viewpoint of Mohammedan orthodoxy. In his *Maqāsid*
or *Intentiones Philosophorum* he summed up the views of
these two philosophers, and this exposition, translated into
Latin by Gundissalinus, gave the impression, when taken by

itself, that Algazel agreed with the opinions expressed. Thus
William of Auvergne coupled together as objects of attack
the 'followers of Aristotle', Alfarabi, Algazel and Avicenna,
being unaware of the fact that Algazel had proceeded to criticise the systems of the philosophers in his *Destructio philosophorum*,[7] which tried to show how the philosophers con-
tradicted themselves. This book elicited later from Averroes a
Destructio destructionis philosophorum. In his *Revivification
of the Religious Sciences* he gave his positive views, defend-
ing the orthodox doctrine of the creation of the world in
time and out of nothing against Avicenna's ideas of emanation and of the eternity of the world. He defended also the
doctrine of God's universal causality, making the connection
between cause and effect to depend on the divine power, not
on any causal activity on the part of creatures. The philosopher sees consequence or constant conjunction and concludes
to the relation of cause and effect, whereas in truth the following of one event on another is simply due to the power
and action of God. In other words he maintained an occa-
sionalistic doctrine.

Algazel was very far from being simply a philosopher who
wished to counteract the unorthodox tendencies of his Hel-
lenising predecessors: he was also an eminent Sufi, a mystic
and spiritual writer. Leaving his work at Baghdad he retired
into Syria, where he lived a life of asceticism and contemplation. Sometimes indeed he emerged from his retirement and
in any case he had disciples: he even founded a kind of
theological college and a school of Sufism at his place of
retirement, Tūs; but the major interest of his life was the
revival of religion, in the sense of mysticism. Drawing not
only on previous Islamic sources, but utilising neo-Platonic
ideas, and even ideas from Judaism and Christianity, he built
up a system of spirituality which was personalist, i.e. non-
pantheistic, in character. Some of Algazel's expressions would
seem at first sight to imply or involve pantheism, but his
neo-Platonism was put at the service of religious mysticism
rather than of speculation. It is not that he tends to identify
the world with God, but rather that his fusion of the Islamic
doctrines of predestination and divine omni-causality with
strongly emphasised religious mysticism leads him into a kind
of panentheism. The Semitic monotheism, when seen in the
light of neo-Platonism and fused with mysticism, could lead
him probably in no other direction. In the field of purely

philosophical speculation he shows a somewhat sceptical attitude, and he represents the protest of religious mysticism against rationalism as well as that of Islamic theology against Aristotelian philosophy.

4. The background of the Moslem philosophers of the West was provided by the brilliant Islamic civilisation which grew up in Spain in the tenth century and which, at that period, was so greatly superior to what western Christendom had to offer. The first philosopher of the western group was *Ibn Masarrah* (d. 931), who adopted ideas from the Pseudo-Empedocles, while *Avempace* or *Ibn Bājja* (d. 1138) and *Abubacer* or *Ibn Tufail* (d. 1185) represented mystical tendencies; but the greatest figure of this group is undoubtedly Averroes, who occupies that prominent position in the western group which Avicenna represents in the eastern group.

Averroes or *Ibn Rušd* (the *Commentator* of the Latin Scholastics) was born at Córdoba in 1126, the son of a judge. After studying theology, jurisprudence, medicine, mathematics and philosophy, he occupied judicial posts, first at Seville and afterwards at Córdoba, becoming physician to the Caliph in 1182. Subsequently he fell into disfavour with the Caliph al-Mansūr and was banished from court. He later crossed to Morocco, dying there in 1198.

Being convinced that the genius of Aristotle was the final culmination of the human intellect, Averroes naturally devoted a great deal of energy to the composition of commentaries. These fall into three classes: (i) the lesser or 'middle' commentaries, in which Averroes gives the content of Aristotle's doctrine, adding his own explanations and developments in such a way that it is not always easy to distinguish what comes from Aristotle and what from Averroes; (ii) the greater commentaries, in which Averroes gives first a portion of the actual text of Aristotle and then adds his own commentary; and (iii) the little commentaries (paraphrases or compendia), in which he gives the conclusions arrived at by Aristotle, omitting proofs and historical references, and which were designed for students unable to go to the sources or larger commentaries. (Apparently he composed the middle commentaries and the compendia before the greater commentaries.) The entire *Organon* of Aristotle, in the lesser commentary and in the compendium, is extant, as also Latin translations of all three classes of commentary for the *Posterior Analytics*, the *Physics*, the *De Caelo*, the

De Anima and the *Metaphysics*. In addition to these and other commentaries in Latin translations the Christian Scholastics possessed Averroes's answer to Algazel (i.e. the *Destructio destructionis philosophorum*), several logical works, a letter on the connection between the abstract intelligence and man, a work on the beatitude of the soul, etc.

The metaphysical scale reaches from pure matter as the lowest limit to pure Act, God, as the highest limit, between these limits being the objects composed of potency and act, which form *Natura naturata*. (The phrases of the Latin translation, *Natura naturans* and *Natura naturata*, reappear eventually in the system of Spinoza.) Prime matter, as equivalent to non-being, as pure potentiality and the absence of all determination, cannot be the term of the creative act: it is, therefore, co-eternal with God. God, however, draws or educes the forms of material things from the potency of pure matter, and creates the Intelligences, ten in number, connected extrinsically with the spheres, so that the Avicennian emanation-theory is avoided and real pantheism is excluded. The order of the creation or generation of things is, however, determined.

Nevertheless, even if Averroes's rejection of emanation makes him in a sense more orthodox than Avicenna, he did not follow Avicenna in accepting personal immortality. Averroes did indeed follow Themistius and other commentators in holding that the *intellectus materialis* is the same substance as the *intellectus agens* and that both survive death, but he followed Alexander of Aphrodisias in holding that this substance is a separate and unitary Intelligence. (It is the Intelligence of the moon, the lowest sphere.) The individual passive intellect in the individual man becomes, under the action of the active intellect, the 'acquired intellect', which is absorbed by the active intellect in such a way that, although it survives bodily death, it does so not as a personal, individual existent, but as a moment in the universal and common intelligence of the human species. There is, therefore, immortality, but there is no personal immortality. This view was earnestly combated by St. Thomas Aquinas and other Scholastics, though it was maintained by the Latin Averroists as a philosophical truth.

More interesting, however, than Averroes's particular philosophical doctrine is his notion of the general relation of philosophy to theology. Holding, as he did, that Aristotle was

the completer of human science,[8] the model of human perfection and the author of a system which is the supreme
truth, interpreting Aristotle as holding the unicity of the
active intellect and accepting the doctrine of the eternity of
matter, Averroes had necessarily to attempt a reconciliation
of his philosophical ideas with orthodox Islamic theology, especially as those were not wanting who were ready to accuse
him of heresy because of his devotion to a pagan thinker. He
accordingly attempted this reconciliation by means of the
so-called 'double truth' theory. This does not mean that,
according to Averroes, a proposition can be true in philosophy
and false in theology or *vice versa*: his theory is that one
and the same truth is understood clearly in philosophy and
expressed allegorically in theology. The scientific formulation
of truth is achieved only in philosophy, but the same truth
is expressed in theology, only in a different manner. The
picture-teaching of the Koran expresses the truth in a manner
intelligible to the ordinary man, to the unlettered, whereas
the philosopher strips away the allegorical husk and attains
the truth 'unvarnished', free from the trappings of *Vorstel-
lung*. Averroes's idea of the relation of philosophy to theology
resembles somewhat that of Hegel, and it would be unacceptable, and was unacceptable, to the orthodox Islamic theologian; but it was not the absurd idea that one proposition
can be true in philosophy and the diametrically opposite
proposition true in theology. What Averroes did was to make
theology subordinate to philosophy, to make the latter the
judge of the former, so that it belongs to the philosopher to
decide what theological doctrines need to be allegorically
interpreted and in what way they should be interpreted. This
view was accepted by the Latin Averroists, and it was this
view, moreover, which drew upon Averroes, and upon philosophy generally, the hostility of the Islamic theologians. In
regard to statements attributed to Averroes which taken literally imply that one proposition, for example, that the active
intellect is numerically single, is true in philosophy and false
in theology, it has been suggested that this was simply a
sarcastic way of saying that the theological doctrine is non-
sense. When Averroes says that some proposition is true in
the fideistic theology of the conservatives, who rejected philosophy, he means that it is 'true' in the School of the enemies
of science, i.e. that it is simply false. He had no use for the

traditionalists as the traditionalists had no use for him, and his attitude in this matter led to the prohibition in Islamic Spain of the study of Greek philosophy and to the burning of philosophic works.

5. Of the influence of Averroes in Latin Christendom I shall speak later; but it may be of interest to add a word here on the attitude of Dante (1265-1321) towards the Arabian philosophers.[9] The question of Dante's attitude to the Arab philosophers arose when scholars began to ask themselves seriously and without prejudice why Dante, who in the *Divina Commedia* places Mohammed in hell, not only placed Averroes and Avicenna in Limbo, but also placed the Latin Averroist Siger of Brabant in heaven and even went so far as to put his eulogium into the mouth of St. Thomas Aquinas, who was a doughty opponent of Siger. Obviously Dante was treating these men as philosophers, and it was because of this fact that he placed the two Islamic thinkers as high in the scale as he could: as they were not Christians, he did not consider that he could release them from *Inferno* altogether, and so he placed them in Limbo. Siger on the other hand was a Christian, and so Dante placed him in heaven. That he made St. Thomas speak his praises and that he put him on the left of St. Thomas, while St. Albert the Great was on Aquinas's right, is explicable if we remember that the Thomist system presupposes a philosophy which is built up by natural reason alone and that to build up a philosophy by reason alone was precisely what Siger of Brabant professed to do: it is not necessary to suppose that Dante approved all Siger's notions, but he takes him as the symbol of 'pure philosophy'.

However, why did Dante single out Avicenna, Averroes and Siger of Brabant? Was it simply because they were philosophers or did Dante owe something himself to the Moslems? It has been shown by Bruno Nardi,[10] and the theme has been resumed by Asín Palacios,[11] that Dante owed to the systems of Alfarabi, Avicenna, Algazel and Averroes important points in his philosophy, for example, the light-doctrine of God, the theory of the Intelligences, the influence of the celestial spheres, the idea that only the intellectual part of the soul is directly and properly created, the need of illumination for intellection, etc. Some of these ideas were found in the Augustinian tradition, it is true; but it has been shown that Dante, far from being a Thomist pure and simple, owed a considerable debt to the Moslems and to Averroes in particular. This will explain why he singles out for special treatment the most eminent of the Islamic philosophers, and why he places in heaven the greatest of the Latin Averroists.

Chapter Twenty

JEWISH PHILOSOPHY

The Cabala—Avicebron—Maimonides.

1. Philosophy among the Jews really owes its origin to intercourse with other nations and cultures. Thus in the first volume of this history I have already treated of Philo, the Alexandrian Jew (*c.* 25 B.C.–*c.* A.D. 40), who attempted a reconciliation of the Jewish Scriptural theology and Greek philosophy, producing a system in which elements of the Platonic tradition (the theory of Ideas), of Stoicism (doctrine of the Logos) and of Oriental thought (intermediary beings) were combined. In the philosophy of Philo the transcendence of God was strongly emphasised, and this insistence on the divine transcendence was characteristic of the doctrine of the *Cabala*, as modified by Greek, particularly by Platonic, theories. The *Cabala* consisted of two works, the *Jezîrah* (creation), which was probably composed after the middle of the ninth century A.D., and the *Sohar* (brightness), which was built up from the beginning of the thirteenth century and committed to writing by a Spanish Jew about the year 1300. Additions and commentaries were subsequently made. The Cabalistic philosophy shows the influence of neo-Platonism in its doctrine of emanation and intermediary beings between God and the world, and one of the channels by which neo-Platonism influenced the construction of the emanationist philosophy of the *Sohar* was the thought of the Spanish Jew who was known to the Latin Scholastics as Avicebron.

2. *Salomon Ibn Gabirol* or *Avicebron* (so called by the Latin Scholastics, who thought that he was an Arab) was born

at Malaga about 1021, was educated at Saragossa and died in 1069/70. He was naturally influenced by the Arabian philosophy and his chief work, the *Fons Vitae*, was originally composed in Arabic. The Arabic original is, however, no longer extant, though we possess the work in the Latin translation of Joannes Hispanus (Avendeath) and Dominicus Gundissalinus. The work consists of five books and had a considerable influence on the Christian Scholastics.

The neo-Platonic influence shows itself in the emanationist scheme of Avicebron's philosophy. The summit of the hierarchy of being and the source of all limited being is, of course, God, who is one and unknowable by the discursive reason, apprehensible only in the intuition of ecstasy. To this Avicebron added a peculiar doctrine concerning the divine will by which are created, or from which emanate, all lesser beings. The divine will, like God Himself, transcends the composition of matter and form and can be apprehended only in mystical experience; but the exact relation of the divine will to God is not easy to determine. The distinction drawn between the divine essence and the divine will would appear to make of the latter a distinct hypostasis, though on the other hand the divine will is depicted as being God Himself as active *ad extra*, as God in His appearance. In any case there is a substitution of Will for Logos. From God, *via* the divine will, whether God under one aspect or a distinct hypostasis, proceeds the cosmic spirit or World-Soul, which is inferior to God and is composed of matter and form, *materia universalis* and *forma universalis*. From the World-Soul in turn proceed pure spirits and corporeal things.

The interesting point about Avicebron's system is, however, not his emanationist scheme, but rather his doctrine of universal hylomorphic composition in all beings inferior to God, a doctrine which was derived, at least indirectly, from Plotinus and which influenced one tradition of Christian Scholasticism. Just as from the World-Soul proceed the individual forms, so from the World-Soul proceed also spiritual matter, which is present in the Intelligence and in the rational soul, and corporeal matter. Matter, then, which does not *of itself* involve corporeality, is the principle of limitation and finiteness in all creatures: it is the hylomorphic composition in creatures which marks them off from God, for in God there is no composition. This doctrine of universal hylomorphic composition in creatures was maintained by St.

Bonaventure, for example, the great Franciscan contemporary of St. Thomas Aquinas. Moreover, there is a plurality of forms in every being which possesses in itself a plurality of grades of perfection, as the human being, for example, the microcosm, possesses the perfections of corporeality, vegetative life, sensitive life and intellectual life. Every corporeal being possesses the *forma corporeitatis*, but it has further to be given its determinate place in the hierarchy of being, and this is accomplished by the reception of the form or forms by which it becomes, e.g. living thing, animal, dog. It has been maintained that the doctrine of Avicebron was the real origin of the Augustinian School's theory of the plurality of forms, but, even granting this, it must also be remembered that the doctrine fitted well into the scheme of the Augustinians' philosophy, since Augustine had himself taught that the function of the lower forms is to lead on to the higher forms and that this is true also of these forms as represented in human knowledge, i.e. that contemplation of the lower stages of being should lead the mind to higher stages.

3. The most interesting of the Jewish mediaeval philosophers is, however, *Moses Maimonides*, who was born at Córdoba in 1135 and died in Cairo in 1204, having had to abandon Moorish Spain, which was no longer favourable to philosophers. In his *Guide of the Doubting* he attempted to give to theology its rational basis in philosophy, which for him meant the philosophy of Aristotle, whom he reverenced as the greatest example of human intellectual power apart from the Prophets. We must hold fast to what is given us in sense-perception and what can be strictly demonstrated by the intellect: if statements contained in the Old Testament plainly contradict what is plainly established by reason, then such statements must be interpreted allegorically. This view, however, did not mean that Maimonides discarded the teaching of theology whenever Aristotle held something different to that which the Scripture taught. For example, theology teaches the creation of the world in time out of nothing, and this means both that God must be the author of matter as well as of form and that the world cannot be eternal. If the eternity of the world could be demonstrated by reason in such a way that the opposite was clearly seen to be an impossibility, then we should have to interpret the Scriptural teaching accordingly; but, as a matter of fact, the Scriptural teaching is clear and the philosophical arguments adduced to

prove the eternity of the world are inconclusive: we must, then, reject Aristotle's teaching on this point. Plato came nearer to the truth than Aristotle, but even he accepted an uncreated matter. The creation out of nothing of both matter and form is also necessary, according to Maimonides, if the fact of miracles, plainly taught in the Old Testament, is to be allowed, since, if God is able to suspend the operation of natural laws, He must be the absolute Sovereign of nature and He would not be that unless He were Creator in the full sense of the word. To the fanatics Maimonides's allegorical interpretation of some of the Scriptural pictures of God seemed to be a selling of the Holy Scripture to the Greeks, and some Jews in France even went so far as to try to enlist the aid of the Inquisition against this 'heresy'; but in point of fact he was merely saying that there can be a fountain of certain truth besides theology. In other words, he gave a charter to philosophy, and he thus influenced the growth of philosophical interest among the Jews in Spain, even if his chief influence lay in the province of theology. That he was no blind worshipper of Aristotle has been shown already. Aristotle, thought Maimonides, went wrong in teaching the eternity of the world, and even if philosophy cannot demonstrate creation in time, it can at least show that the arguments brought up in favour of the Aristotelian position are inconclusive and unsound.

Relying partly on the natural theology of Alfarabi and Avicenna, Maimonides proved the existence of God in various ways, arguing from creatures to God as first Mover, as necessary Being and as first Cause. These arguments he supported from statements of Aristotle in the *Physics* and *Metaphysics*. But if Maimonides anticipated most of the types of proof given later by St. Thomas, he was more insistent than the latter on the inapplicability of positive predicates to God. God is pure Act, without matter and without potency, infinitely removed from creatures, and, in regard to 'qualities', we can say what God is *not*, rather than what He is. He is one and transcendent (between God and the world there is a hierarchy of Intelligences or pure spirits), but we cannot form any adequate positive idea of God. St. Thomas, of course, would admit this, but Maimonides was rather more insistent on the *via negativa*. We can, however, ascribe to God activities, the activities of creation and providence, for example, provided that we realise that the difference of names does not correspond to any difference in God Himself and that God Himself is unchangeable. Unlike Avicebron, Maimonides admitted a special providence on God's part in regard to particular creatures, though this is true only of men, so far as the material world is concerned. The active intellect is the tenth Intelligence (the Intelligences are without 'matter'), but the passive intellects of the just are immortal. Immortality, then, he admitted only in a limited extension, for the just; but he maintained the freedom of the will, whereby men become just, and he denied the determining influence of the celestial bodies and spheres in regard to human conduct. In fine, Moses Maimonides made a better business of reconciling Greek philosophy with Jewish orthodoxy than Avicebron had made of it, and it is noteworthy that the influence of the Aristotelian system is more in evidence in the former's philosophy than in the latter's.

Chapter Twenty-one

THE TRANSLATIONS

The translated works—Translations from Greek and fr[o]
Arabic—Effects of translations and opposition to Aristo[
lianism.

1. Before the twelfth century part of the *Organon* of Ar[i]
totle (the *Categories* and the *De Interpretatione*) had be[en]
available to mediaeval philosophers in the Latin version [of]
Boethius (*Logica vetus*), but the entire *Organon* becam[e]
available fairly early in the twelfth century. Thus about 11[
James of Venice translated the *Analytics*, the *Topics* and t[he]
Sophistical Arguments from Greek into Latin, the new[ly]
translated books of the *Organon* being known as the *Log[ica]
nova*. It appears that portions at least of other books of t[he]
Organon besides the *Categories* and the *De Interpretatio[ne]
had survived into the twelfth century in the translation [of]
Boethius; but in any case a complete translation of the C[r-]
ganon into Latin had been effected by the middle of t[he]
century. It is to be noted that the translation by James [in]
Spain was made from the Greek, as was also the translati[on]
of the fourth book of the *Meteorologica* made by Henric[us]
Aristippus before 1162. Henricus Aristippus was Archdeac[on]
of Catania in Sicily, an island which was an important cen[tre]
in the work of translation. Thus it was in twelfth-centu[ry]
Sicily that Ptolemy's μεγάλη σύνταξις and the *Optics*, so[me]
of the works of Euclid and Proclus's *Elementatio physi[ca]*
were translated from Greek into Latin.

Sicily was one centre of the work of translation; Spain w[as]
another, the most famous school of translators being that [of]
Toledo. Thus under Archbishop Raymond (1126–51) J[

nnes Hispanus (Avendeath) translated from the Arabic into Latin (*via* Spanish) the Logic of Avicenna, while Dominicus Gundissalinus translated (with help from other scholars) the *Metaphysics* of Avicenna, parts of his *Physics*, his *De Sufficientia, De Caelo et Mundo* and *De Mundo*, the *Metaphysics* of Algazel and the *De Scientiis* of Alfarabi. Dominicus Gundissalinus and John of Spain also translated from Arabic into Latin the *Fons Vitae* of Avicebron.

A distinguished member of this group of scholars was Gerard of Cremona, who took up work at Toledo in 1134 and died in 1187. He translated from Arabic into Latin Aristotle's *Posterior Analytics* (together with the commentary of Themistius), *Physics, De Caelo et Mundo, De Generatione et Corruptione, Meteorologica* (first three books); Alkindi's *De Intellectu, De Somno et Visione, De quinque Essentiis*; the *Liber de Causis* and some other works.

The Toledo school of translators was still of importance in the thirteenth century. Thus Michael Scot (Michael Scotus, died c. 1235) translated at Toledo the *De Caelo et Mundo*, the *De Anima*, the zoological writings and also (probably) the *Physics of Aristotle*, as well as Averroes's commentaries on the *De Caelo et Mundo* and the *De Anima*, Avicenna's compendium of the *De Animalibus*, while Herman the German, who died in 1272, as Bishop of Astorga, translated Averroes's 'middle commentary' on the *Nicomachean Ethics* and also his compendium of the same work and his commentaries on the *Rhetoric* and the *Poetics*.

2. It will be seen from what has already been said that it is a mistake to imagine that the Latin Scholastics were entirely dependent on translations from Arabic or even that translation from the Arabic always preceded translation from the Greek. Thus Henricus Aristippus's translation of the fourth book of the *Meteorologica* from the Greek preceded Gerard of Cremona's translation of the first three books of the same work from the Arabic. Moreover, some of the *Metaphysics* had been translated from the Greek before the Arabic translation was made. The translation from the Greek,[1] which did not comprise simply the first three books and a small part of book four, as was formerly supposed, was in use at Paris by 1210 and was known as the *Metaphysica vetus*, in distinction from the translation from the Arabic, which was made by Gerard of Cremona or Michael Scot and was known (in the first half of the thirteenth century) as the

Metaphysica nova. Books K, M, N, as well as smaller passages
were missing in this translation. In the second half of th
century the title *Metaphysica nova* or *Translatio nova* wa
given to the translation from the Greek by William of Moer
beke (after 1260), upon which translation St. Thomas base
his commentary. It has also been shown that there was
translatio media from the Greek, on which St. Albert th
Great based his commentary and which was known to St
Thomas.

As regards the ethical writings of Aristotle, a translatio
of Books 2 and 3 of the *Nicomachean Ethics* was available b
the end of the twelfth century. This translation had bee
made from the Greek (possibly it was the work of Boethiu
himself) and was known as the *Ethica vetus*, while a late
translation (of Book 1) was known as the *Ethica nova*. A ful
translation, generally ascribed to Robert Grosseteste (d
1253), was then made from the Greek, the first three book
being a recension of the *Ethica vetus* and the *Ethica nova*
The *Magna Moralia* were translated by Bartholomew of Mes
sina in the reign of King Manfred (1258–66); but only th
seventh book of the *Eudemian Ethics* was known in the thir
teenth century.

The *De Anima* was translated from the Greek before 1215
the translation from the Arabic by Michael Scot being some
what later. William of Moerbeke produced a further versio
from the Greek or a corrected edition of the first translatio
from the Greek. Similarly there was a translation of the *Phys
ics* from the Greek before the two translations from th
Arabic by Gerard of Cremona and Michael Scot, while
translation of the *De Generatione et Corruptione* from th
Greek preceded the translation from the Arabic by Gerar
of Cremona. The *Politics* were translated from the Gree
about 1260 by William of Moerbeke (there was no transla
tion from the Arabic), who probably also translated the *Ecc
nomics* about 1267. This eminent man, who was born abou
1215 and died in 1286, as Archbishop of Corinth, not onl
translated Aristotle's works from the Greek and re-edite
earlier translations (thus enabling his friend, St. Thoma
Aquinas, to write his commentaries), but also translated fron
the Greek some commentaries by Alexander of Aphrodisias
Simplicius, Joannes Philoponus and Themistius, as also som
works of Proclus and the latter's exposition of the *Timaeu*
of Plato.[2] His translation of Proclus's *Elementatio theologic*

brought to St. Thomas the realisation that the *Liber de Causis* was not the work of Aristotle, as it was previously supposed to be, but was based on the work of Proclus. It was also William of Moerbeke who translated the *Rhetoric* of Aristotle. As to the *Poetics*, the mediaevals possessed only Herman the German's translation of Averroes's commentary.[3]

As modern investigation has shown that translations from the Greek generally preceded translations from the Arabic, and that, even when the original translation from the Greek was incomplete, the Arabic-Latin version soon had to give place to a new and better translation from the Greek, it can no longer be said that the mediaevals had no real knowledge of Aristotle, but only a caricature of his doctrine, a picture distorted by the hand of Arabian philosophers. What can, however, be said is that they were not always able to distinguish what was to be ascribed to Aristotle from what was not to be ascribed to Aristotle. A great step forward was taken when St. Thomas came to realise that the *Liber de Causis* was not the work of Aristotle. He was already quite conscious of the fact that Averroes's commentaries were not to be taken as the unquestionable interpretation of Aristotle's philosophy, but even he seems to have thought, at least for a time, that the Pseudo-Dionysius was not far from being a follower of Aristotle. The fact of the matter is, not that the mediaevals had no reliable texts of Aristotle, but that they were deficient in historical knowledge: they did not, for example, adequately realise the relation of Aristotle to Plato or of neo-Platonism to Plato and Aristotle. That St. Thomas was an able commentator on Aristotle can be denied only by those unacquainted with his commentaries; but it would be foolish to claim even for St. Thomas a knowledge of the history and development of Greek philosophy such as is open to the modern scholar. He made good use of the information available to him; but that information was rather limited.

3. The translation of works of Aristotle and his commentators, as well as of the Arabian thinkers, provided the Latin scholastics with a great wealth of intellectual material. In particular they were provided with the knowledge of philosophical systems which were methodologically independent of theology and which were presented as the human mind's reflection on the universe. The systems of Aristotle, of Avicenna, of Averroes, opened up a wide vista of the scope of the human reason and it was clear to the mediaevals that the

truth attained in them must have been independent of Christian revelation, since it had been attained by a Greek philosopher and his Greek and Islamic commentators. In this way the new translations helped to clarify in the minds of the mediaevals the relation between philosophy and theology and contributed very largely to the delimitation of the provinces of the two sciences. It is, of course, true that Aristotle's system not unnaturally took the limelight in preference to those of his commentators, and his philosophy tended to appear in the eyes of those Latins who were favourably impressed as the *ne plus ultra* of human intellectual endeavour, since it constituted the most sustained and extensive effort of the human mind with which they were acquainted; but they were quite well aware that it was the work of reason, not a set of revealed dogmas. To us, looking back from a long way off, it may seem that some of the mediaevals exaggerated the genius of Aristotle (we also know that they did not realise the existence of different strata or periods in Aristotle's thought), but we should put ourselves for a moment in their place and try to imagine the impression which would be made on a mediaeval philosopher by the sight of what in any case is one of the supreme achievements of the human mind, a system which, in regard to both completeness and close reasoning, was unparalleled in the thought of the early Middle Ages.

However, the system of Aristotle did not meet with universal welcome and approbation, though it could not be ignored. Largely because the *Liber de Causis* (until St. Thomas discovered the truth), the so-called *Theologia Aristotelis* (extracts from the *Enneads* of Plotinus) and the *De secretis secretorum* (composed by an Arab philosopher in the eleventh or beginning of the twelfth century) were wrongly attributed to Aristotle, the latter's philosophy tended to appear in a false light. Moreover, the attribution of these books to Aristotle naturally made it appear that the Arab commentators were justified in their neo-Platonic interpretation. Hence it came about that in 1210 the Provincial Council of Paris, meeting under the presidency of Peter of Corbeil, Archbishop of Sens, forbad the public or private teaching of Aristotle's 'natural philosophy' or of the commentaries on them. This prohibition was imposed under pain of excommunication and applied to the University of Paris. In all probability 'natural philosophy' included the metaphysics of Aristotle, since when the statutes of the university were sanctioned by Robert de Courçon, Papal Legate, in 1215 Aristotle's works on metaphysics and natural philosophy, as well as compendia of these works and the doctrines of David of Dinant, Amalric of Bene and Maurice of Spain (probably Averroes, the Moor or *Maurus*) were prohibited, though the study of Aristotle's logic was ordered. The study of the *Ethics* was not forbidden.

The reason for the prohibition was, as already indicated, largely due to the ascription to Aristotle of works which were not by him. Amalric of Bene, whose writings were included in the prohibition of 1215, maintained doctrines which were at variance with Christian teaching and which would naturally appear to find some support in the philosophy of Aristotle, if the latter were interpreted in the light of all the books attributed to him, while David of Dinant, the other heretical philosopher whose writings were prohibited, had actually appealed to the *Metaphysics*, which had been translated into Latin from the Greek version brought from Byzantium before 1210. To these considerations must be added the undoubted fact that Aristotle maintained the eternity of the world. It was, therefore, not unnatural that the Aristotelian system, especially when coupled with the philosophies of David of Dinant, Amalric of Bene and Averroes, should appear as a danger to orthodoxy in the eyes of the traditionalists. The logic of Aristotle had long been in use, even if the full *Organon* had come into circulation only comparatively recently, but the complete metaphysical and cosmological teaching of Aristotle was a novelty, a novelty rendered all the more dangerous through association with heretical philosophies.

However, in 1231 Pope Gregory IX, while maintaining the prohibition, appointed a commission of theologians, William of Auxerre, Stephen of Provins and Simon of Authie, to correct the prohibited books of Aristotle, and as this measure obviously implied that the books were not fundamentally unsound, the prohibition tended to be neglected. It was extended to Toulouse in 1245 by Innocent IV, but by that date it was no longer possible to check the spread of Aristotelianism and from 1255 all the known works of Aristotle were officially lectured on in the University of Paris. The Holy See made no move against the university, though in 1263 Urban IV renewed the prohibition of 1210, probably out of fear of Averroism, the renewed prohibition remaining a dead letter. The Pope must have known perfectly well that

William of Moerbeke was translating the prohibited works o
Aristotle at his own court, and the prohibition of 1263 mus
have been designed as a check to Averroism, not as a seriousl
meant attempt to put an end to all study of the Aristotelia
philosophy. In any case the prohibition was of no effect, an
finally in 1366 the Legates of Urban V required from a
candidates for the Licentiate of Arts at Paris a knowledge o
all the known works of Aristotle. It had by then long bee
clear to the mediaevals that a work like the *Liber de Caus*
was not Aristotelian and that the philosophy of Aristotle wa
not, except, of course, in the eyes of the Latin Averroist
bound up with the interpretation given it by Averroes bu
could be harmonised with the Christian faith. Indeed th
dogmas of faith themselves had by then been expressed b
theologians in terms taken from the Aristotelian system.

This brief summary of the official attitude to Aristotle o
the part of ecclesiastical and academic authority shows tha
Aristotelianism triumphed in the end. This does not mear
however, that all mediaeval philosophers of the thirteenth an
fourteenth centuries extended an equal welcome to Aristotl
or that they all understood him in the same way: the vigou
and variety of mediaeval thought will be made clear in suc
ceeding chapters. There is truth in the statement that th
shadow of Aristotle hung over and dominated the philosophi
thought of the Middle Ages, but it is not the whole trutl
and we would have a very inadequate idea of mediaeval ph
losophy in the thirteenth and fourteenth centuries if we im
agined that it was inspired and characterised by a slavish a
ceptance of every word of the great Greek philosopher.

Chapter Twenty-two

INTRODUCTION

The University of Paris—Universities closed and privileged corporations—Curriculum—Religious Orders at Paris—Currents of thought in the thirteenth century.

1. The leading philosophers and theologians of the thirteenth century were all associated, at some period, with the University of Paris, which arose out of the body of professors and students attached to the Cathedral School of Notre Dame and the other schools of Paris, the statutes of the university being sanctioned by Robert de Courçon, Papal Legate, in 1215. Alexander of Hales, St. Bonaventure, St. Albert the Great, St. Thomas Aquinas, Matthew of Aquasparta, Roger Marston, Richard of Middleton, Roger Bacon, Giles of Rome, Siger of Brabant, Henry of Ghent, Raymond Lull, Duns Scotus (d. 1308), all either studied or taught (or both) at Paris. Other centres of higher education were, however, growing in importance and acquiring a tradition of their own. Thus with the University of Oxford were associated the names of men like Robert Grosseteste, Roger Bacon and Duns Scotus, and whereas Paris was the scene of the triumph of Aristotelianism, the name of Oxford recalls a characteristic mingling of the Augustinian tradition with 'empiricism', as in the philosophy of Roger Bacon. Yet in spite of the importance of Oxford, Bologna and, at times, the Papal Court, the University of Paris was easily the most important centre of higher studies in the Christendom of the thirteenth century. Scholars might come to Paris for their studies and then return to Oxford or Bologna to teach, thus carrying with them the spirit and ideals of the great university, and even those scholars who never

themselves set foot in Paris were subject to Parisian influence. Robert of Grosseteste, for instance, who possibly never studied at Paris, was certainly influenced by professors of Paris.

The international character of the University of Paris, with its consequent importance in the intellectual expression and defence of Christianity, naturally made the maintenance of religious orthodoxy within its precincts one of the interests of the Holy See. Thus the Averroistic controversy must be seen in the light of the university's international standing: it represented in itself the intellectual culture of the Middle Ages, as far as philosophy and theology were concerned, and the spread within its walls of a system of thought which was irreconcilable with Christianity could not be a matter of indifference to Rome. On the other hand it would be a mistake to suppose that there was any rigid imposition of one particular tradition. St. Thomas Aquinas met with difficulties, it is true, in his acceptance and propagation of Aristotelianism; but such difficulties did not last, and even if the philosophy of Aristotle came in the end to dominate the intellectual life of the university, in the thirteenth and fourteenth centuries there was still plenty of room for different philosophical outlooks.

2. The universities, to be constituted as such, had to receive a formal charter, either from pope or emperor (the University of Naples received its charter from Frederick II) or, later, from kings. These charters conferred considerable privileges on professors and students, privileges which were jealously guarded. The two most important privileges were those of internal jurisdiction (which still survives at Oxford, for example) and of power to give the degree, which carried with it licence to teach. The students were exempt from military service, except in special circumstances, and the university was generally exempt from a great deal of taxation, particularly local taxation. In northern Europe the professors controlled the university, the rector being elected, whereas the universities of southern Europe were often distinctly democratic in their governmental arrangements, but in either case the university was a largely independent and closed corporation, which maintained its privileges against Church and State. In this respect the universities of Oxford and Cambridge represent more faithfully the mediaeval tradition and

practice than do those continental universities where rectors and professors are appointed by the State.

3. In mediaeval times, and the same is true of a much later period as well, students entered the university at a much earlier age than they do at present. Thus boys of thirteen or fourteen might begin attending the university, and if one remembers this fact, the number of years required in order to obtain the doctorate will not appear so surprising. The course in arts lasted some four and a half to six years, according to the university (though at Oxford some seven years were required), and for a time at least the student had to qualify in the faculty of arts before he could proceed to theology. In the theological course he had to spend four years in attending lectures on the Bible and then two more years in attending lectures on the *Sentences*, after which, if by then twenty-six years of age, he became a Baccalaureate and lectured for the two following years on two books of the Bible. He could then lecture on the *Sentences* and finally, after several years spent in study and disputations, he could take the doctorate and teach theology, the minimum age for this being thirty-four. For teaching the arts the minimum age required was twenty. At Paris the tendency was to increase the number of years required for obtaining the doctorate, though at Oxford the arts course was longer and the theological course shorter than at Paris.

Those students who took the doctorate and left the university were known as *magistri non regentes*, whereas those who remained to teach were known as *magistri regentes*; but, however many students there may have been who fell into the first class, it is clear that the long university course was designed to produce professors and teachers by career.

As for the curriculum, the general practice in the university of the thirteenth century was to lecture or listen to lectures on certain texts. Thus, apart from the writings of the grammarians like Priscian and Donatus and certain other classical texts, the writings of Aristotle came to dominate the arts school altogether in the course of time, and it is significant that 'Latin Averroism' was represented principally by professors in that faculty. In theology the Bible and the *Sentences* of Peter Lombard dominated the scene, and the professor gave his own views by way of commentary. Besides the lectures there was another essential feature of the curriculum, namely the disputation, which took the form either of an 'ordinary' disputation (*disputatio ordinaria*) or the 'general' disputation (*de quolibet*). The *disputationes de quolibet*, in which a choice was made from a great variety of topics, were held at solemn feasts, and after the disputation in the strict sense, that is, between a defendant or *respondens* and the objectors, *opponentes*, the professor summed up the whole matter, arguments, objections and replies, and finished by giving his considered solution (*determinatio*) of the point at issue, in which he began with the words, *Respondeo dicendum*. The final result, arranged by the professor, was then published as a *Quodlibet*. (St. Thomas left some eleven or twelve *Quodlibets*.) The *disputatio ordinaria* was also followed by a *determinatio* and was published as a *quaestio disputata*. There were other forms of disputation as well; but these two, the *disputatio ordinaria* and the *disputatio de quolibet*, were the most important. They were designed to increase the student's understanding of a particular theme, and his power of argument and of refuting objections. In fact, generally speaking, mediaeval university education aimed rather at imparting a certain body of knowledge and dexterity in dealing with it than at increasing factual knowledge as in a modern research institute. Of course, scholars certainly aimed at increasing knowledge speculatively; but the increase of scientific knowledge, for example, had little place in mediaeval education, though in the fourteenth century science made some progress at Paris and at Vienna.

4. Of considerable importance in the life of Paris and Oxford were the religious Orders, particularly the two mendicant Orders founded in the thirteenth century, the Dominicans and the Franciscans. The former Order established itself in Paris in 1217, the latter a few years later, and both Orders then proceeded to claim chairs of theology in the university, i.e. they claimed that their chairs of theology should be incorporated in the university and that their professors and students should enjoy the university privileges. There was considerable opposition to this claim from the teaching body of the university; but in 1229 the Dominicans received one chair and in 1231 a second, in the same year that the Franciscans obtained their first chair (they did not receive a second). Roland of Cremona and John of St. Giles were the first Dominican professors, Alexander of Hales the first Franciscan professor. In 1248 the General Chapter of the Dominican Order decreed the erection of *studia generalia* (houses of

study for the whole Order, distinct from the houses of study of particular provinces) at Cologne, Bologna, Montpellier and Oxford, while the Franciscans meanwhile erected *studia generalia* at Oxford and Toulouse. In 1260 the Augustinians opened a house at Paris, the first official doctor being Giles of Rome, while the Carmelites opened houses at Oxford in 1253 and at Paris in 1259. Other Orders also followed suit.

The religious Orders, particularly the Dominicans and Franciscans, accomplished a great work in the intellectual field and produced men of outstanding eminence (we have only to think of St. Albert the Great and St. Thomas Aquinas in the Dominican, of Alexander of Hales and St. Bonaventure in the Franciscan Order); but they had to put up with a good deal of opposition, doubtless inspired in part by jealousy. Not only did their opponents demand that no religious Order should occupy more than one chair at one time, but they even set about attacking the religious state itself. Thus in 1255 William of St. Amour published a pamphlet, *De periculis novissimorum temporum*, which drew from St. Thomas's pen the *Contra impugnantes Dei cultum*. William of St. Amour's pamphlet was condemned and in 1257 the seculars were forbidden to publish writings against the regulars; but in spite of this prohibition Gerard of Abbeville restarted the opposition with his *Contra adversarium perfectionis christianae*. St. Bonaventure and St. Thomas, however much they might disagree on matters philosophical, were united in a determination to defend the religious Orders, and both published replies to Gerard's work, and these in their turn evoked a counterblast from Nicholas of Lisieux, writing on behalf of the seculars. The quarrel between regulars and seculars broke out again on various later occasions, but, as far as the main point was concerned, the incorporation into the university of the regular chairs, judgement had been given in favour of the regulars and it was not revoked. One result followed, however, which is worthy of mention, and that is the founding of the College of the Sorbonne in 1253 by Robert de Sorbon, chaplain to Louis IX, for the education of students in theology, secular students being admitted. If I call the founding of the College of the Sorbonne and similar colleges a 'result' of the controversy between seculars and regulars, all I mean is that such colleges were founded partly perhaps to counterbalance the influence and position of the regulars and certainly in order to extend to a wider field the benefits of the type of education and training provided by the religious.

5. In the thirteenth century one can distinguish various currents of thought which tended eventually, in the religious Orders, to become more or less fixed in traditional schools. First of all there is the Augustinian current of thought, conservative in character and generally reserved in its attitude towards Aristotelianism, its attitude varying from marked hostility to partial acceptance. This current is characteristic of the Franciscan thinkers (and indeed of the first Dominicans), represented by Grosseteste, Alexander of Hales and St. Bonaventure. Secondly there is the Aristotelian current of thought, which became characteristic of the Dominicans, represented by St. Albert the Great (in part) and (fully) by St. Thomas Aquinas. Thirdly there are the Averroists, represented by Siger of Brabant. Fourthly one has to take into consideration the independent and eclectic thinkers like Giles of Rome and Henry of Ghent. Fifthly, at the turn of the century, there is the great figure of Duns Scotus who revised the Franciscan tradition in the light of Aristotelianism and who, rather than St. Bonaventure, became the accepted Doctor of his order. I cannot enter in detail into the thought of all the philosophers of the thirteenth century; but I shall endeavour to put in clear relief their salient characteristics, show the variety of thought within a more or less common framework and indicate the formation and development of the different traditions.

Chapter Twenty-three

WILLIAM OF AUVERGNE

*Reasons for treating of William of Auvergne—God and crea-
tures; essence and existence—Creation by God directly and in
time—Proofs of God's existence—Hylomorphism—The soul—
Knowledge—William of Auvergne a transition-thinker.*

1. William of Auvergne (or William of Paris), author of a
De Trinitate or *De primo principio* (*c.* 1225), a *De Anima*
(1230), a *De universo creaturarum* (*c.* 1231) and other
smaller treatises, was Bishop of Paris from 1228 to 1249, the
year in which he died. He is not, it is true, one of the best-
known thinkers of the Middle Ages; but he claims our attention as a philosopher and theologian who was Bishop of
Paris at the time when Gregory IX appointed the commission of theologians to amend the works of Aristotle and thus
tacitly modified the Church's attitude towards the pagan philosopher. Indeed William of Auvergne represents the attitude
adopted by Gregory IX when he (William) says in his *De
Anima* that although Aristotle often contradicts the truth and
so must be rejected, his teaching should be accepted when it
conforms to the truth, that is, when it is compatible with
Christian doctrine. In his fundamental line of thought William continues the tradition of Augustine, Boethius and Anselm, but he knew not only the works of Aristotle, but also
the writings of the Arabian and Jewish philosophers and he
did not hesitate to utilise their ideas extensively. In general,
therefore, one may say that in William of Auvergne we see an
intelligent and open-minded adherent of the old tradition
who was willing to utilise the new currents of thought but
who was perfectly conscious of the points in which the Ara-

bians and Aristotle himself were at variance with Christian doctrine. He is, then, an embodiment of the meeting of the twelfth and thirteenth centuries and has a title to be considered when one is treating of the earlier thinkers of the latter century. Moreover, he was a secular priest who occupied the episcopal see of Paris at the time when the mendicant Orders obtained their first chairs, and on this count too there is justification for discussing his philosophical ideas before proceeding to deal with the thinkers of the Franciscan and Dominican Orders. Nor is he himself a negligible figure: on the contrary, his thought is vigorous, original and systematic.

2. From Avicenna, William of Auvergne adopted the distinction between essence and existence and made it the explanation of the creature's finitude and dependence. *Esse*, existence, does not belong to the *ratio* or essence of any object save that one object (God) in which it is identical with the essence; of all other objects existence is predicated only 'accidentally', i.e. it belongs to them by participation (*per participationem*). If we consider any finite object, we realise that there is a distinction between its *ratio* or essential nature and its existence, it is not necessary that it should exist; but if we consider the necessary Being, we realise that its essence cannot be conceived without existence. In fine, 'in everything (other than God) *ens* is one thing, *esse* or *entitas* another'.[1] This means that God alone is pure existence, existence being His essence, whereas objects do not exist essentially, because they must, but because their existence is acquired, received. The relation, then, of objects other than God to God must be one of creature to Creator, from which it follows that the theory of emanation is false:[2] God is absolutely simple. Things did not pre-exist in God as parts of God, as they would have had to do if they flowed from God as the waters from a fountain, but only in the *formae exemplares*, which are identical with God. God sees Himself as the exemplary cause of all creatures.[3]

3. If William of Auvergne rejects the neo-Platonist-Arabian theory of emanation, he rejects also the notion of creation by way of intermediaries. The hierarchy of Intelligences posited by Aristotle and his followers has no foundation in reality:[4] God created the world directly. From this it follows that He exercises providence in regard to individual things and William appeals at length to the instinctive activities of the brutes as an illustration of the operation of divine provi-

dence.[5] Again, the Aristotelian doctrine of the eternity of the world is rejected. Whatsoever people may say and however much they may try to excuse Aristotle, it is a certain fact that he held that the world is eternal and that it did not begin to be, and Avicenna followed him in this opinion.[6] Accordingly William not only gives the reasons why Aristotle and Avicenna held this opinion, but he even tries to put them in the best light by improving on their arguments, after which he refutes the arguments. For example, the idea that if God preceded the creation of the world, an infinite duration would have to be passed through before creation, and the idea that there would be empty time before creation both rest on a confusion of time with eternity. The idea of infinite duration elapsing before creation would have significance only if eternity were the same as time, i.e. if it were not eternity, if God were in time; and the idea of empty time before creation is also meaningless, since before creation there can be no time. We have to speak of God preceding creation, of existing before the world, it is true, but at the same time we must remember that such phrases are borrowed from temporal duration and that when applied to what is eternal, they are used in an analogical, not in a univocal sense.

However, as William of Auvergne remarks,[7] it is not sufficient to contradict one's opponents and to show the insufficiency of their arguments unless one goes on to prove one's own position positively. He, therefore, gives various arguments for the creation of the world in time, some of which appear again in St. Bonaventure and are declared inconclusive by St. Thomas. For example, William argues, taking the words out of his adversary's mouth, as it were, that if the world had been eternally in existence, an infinite time would have been passed through before the present moment. But it is impossible to pass through an infinite time. Therefore the world cannot have existed from eternity. Therefore it was created in time, that is, a first moment of time is assignable. Again, supposing that the revolutions of Saturn stand to the revolutions of the sun in a proportion of one to thirty, the sun will have made thirty times as many revolutions since creation as Saturn. But if the world exists from eternity, both Saturn and the sun will have made an infinite number of revolutions. Now, how can an infinity be thirty times greater than another infinity?

From what has been already said it is clear that William of

Auvergne did not simply deny the neo-Platonic conception of emanation and the Aristotelian idea of an eternal world, while maintaining the Augustinian doctrine of direct and free creation by God in time. On the contrary, he vigorously and exactly detailed and refuted the arguments of his opponents and elaborated systematic proofs of his own thesis. That he was able to do this was largely due to the fact that he was acquainted at first hand with the writings of Aristotle and the Arabians and did not hesitate to utilise not only the Aristotelian logic and the Aristotelian categories but also the ideas of Aristotle, Avicenna and others, when they were acceptable. His utilisation of Avicenna's distinction between essence and existence, for instance, has been already mentioned, and indeed he was the first mediaeval Scholastic to make this distinction an explicit and fundamental point in his philosophy. To this distinction, which enabled him to develop clearly the relation of creature to Creator, William added the doctrine of analogy. Apropos of the statement that finite things possess *esse* 'by participation', he observes that the reader is not to be upset or troubled by the fact that the same word or concept is applied to both God and creatures, since it is not applied in the same sense (*univoce*) or equally: it is applied primarily to God, who *is esse*, and only secondarily to creatures who *have esse*, who participate, that is, in existence in virtue of receiving it through God's creative act. Health, he comments, is predicated of man, of urine, of medicine and of food, but it is not predicated in the same sense or in the same way.[8] The illustration of health is somewhat hackneyed, but it shows that William of Auvergne had apprehended the doctrine of analogy, which is essential to a theistic philosophy.

4. In regard to proofs of God's existence it is a curious fact that William of Auvergne made little use of the proofs used by Aristotle or even by Maimonides. The Aristotelian proof of God as first unmoved mover is not given, and although William certainly looks on God as the first efficient cause, his characteristic proof is one that recalls at least the line of argument adopted by St. Anselm, even though Anselm's argument is not reproduced. The argument in question is from the being which exists by participation to the being which exists essentially, *per essentiam*. This immediately suggests the proof from contingency, which appears in the Arabian and Jewish philosophy, but William prefers to argue from

the one concept to the other. For example, the concept *esse adunatum* has as its correlative concept *esse non causatum*, *esse causatum* involves *esse non causatum*, *esse secundarium*, *esse primum*, and so on.[9] William speaks of the *analogia oppositorum* and points out how the one concept or word necessarily involves its correlative concept or word, so that Grunwald[10] can say that William prefers a purely logical or even grammatical mode of proof, in that from one word he concludes to another word which is contained in or presupposed by the first word. That the argument does tend to give this impression is true, and, if it were a purely verbal argument, it would be open to the retort that the words, or concepts, *esse participatum* or *esse causatum* certainly involve the words, or concepts, *esse per essentiam* or *esse non causatum*, but this is no proof that *esse per essentiam* or *esse non causatum* actually exists, unless it has first been shown that there is an *esse participatum* or an *esse causatum*. Otherwise the proof would be no more a demonstration of God's existence than is St. Anselm's *a priori* argument. However, although William does not sufficiently develop the experiential character of the proof in regard to its starting-point, his argument is by no means purely verbal, since he shows that the object which comes into being cannot be self-dependent or self-caused. *Esse indigentiae* demands *esse sufficientiae* as the reason for its existence, just as *esse potentiale* requires being in act to bring it into a state of actuality. The whole universe requires necessary Being as its cause and reason. In other words, though one may often get the impression that William is simply analysing concepts and hypostasising them, he gives a proof which is not merely logical or verbal but also metaphysical.

5. William of Auvergne accepted the Aristotelian doctrine of hylomorphic composition, but he refused to admit Avicebron's notion that the Intelligences or angels are hylomorphically composed.[11] It is clear that Aristotle did not think that the rational soul contains *materia prima*, since he clearly asserts that it is an immaterial form, and the account of prime matter given by Averroes, according to which prime matter is the potentiality of sensible substance and sensible substance the final act of prime matter, clearly implies the same, that is, that prime matter is the matter of sensible substance only. Moreover, what could be the use of prime matter in the angels, what function could it serve? Matter in itself is some-

thing dead; it cannot contribute in any way to intellectual and spiritual operations or even receive them. As he had already utilised the distinction between essence and existence to explain the finitude of creatures and their radical difference from God, William did not require universal hylomorphic composition for this purpose, and as he considered that to postulate the presence of prime matter in the angels would hinder rather than facilitate the explanation of their purely spiritual operations, he restricted prime matter to the sensible world, as St. Thomas did after him.

6. In his psychology, as set forth in the *De Anima,* William of Auvergne combines Aristotelian and Augustinian themes. Thus he expressly adopts the Aristotelian definition of the soul as *perfectio corporis physici organici potentia vitam habentis,*[12] though he warns the reader that he is not quoting Aristotle as an unquestionable authority, but proposes to show the truth of the definition. That he has a soul should be clear to every man, since he is conscious that he understands and judges;[13] but the soul is not the whole of man's nature. If it were, then a human soul joined to an aerial body, for example, would still be a man, whereas in point of fact it would not be. Aristotle, then, was correct in saying that the soul is to the body, as form is to matter.[14] However, that does not prevent him from saying that the soul is a substance on the ground that it must be either substance or accident and cannot be an accident, and he uses the Augustinian comparison of the soul with a harpist, the body being the harp. It might appear that in man there are three souls, one being the principle of life (vegetative soul), the second being the principle of sensation (animal or sensitive soul) and the third being the principle of intellection (rational soul); but a little reflection will show that this cannot be so. If there was an animal soul in man, distinct from the rational or human soul, then humanity, human nature, would not involve animality, whereas in point of fact a man is an animal because he is man, animality belonging to human nature.[15] There is, then, one soul in man, which exercises various functions. It is created and infused by God alone, neither generated by the parents nor educed from the potentiality of matter,[16] and it is, moreover, immortal, as William proceeds to show by arguments, some of which are of Platonic origin. For example, if the malice of an evil soul does not injure or destroy its *esse,* how can bodily death destroy it?[17] Again, since the body

receives life from the soul and the soul's power is such that it vivifies a body which, considered in itself, is dead, that is, lacking life, the fact that the body ceases to live cannot destroy the vital power inherent in the soul.[18] Further, the soul can communicate with *substantiae separatae* and is thus like to them, immortal; but as the human soul is indivisible and one, it follows that the whole human soul is immortal, not simply a rational part.[19]

But though he accepts the Peripatetic doctrine of the soul as form of the body (one must make the reservation that he sometimes uses Platonic-Augustinian expressions in regard to the soul's union with the body), William of Auvergne follows St. Augustine in refusing to recognise a real distinction between the soul and its faculties.[20] Only a substance can understand or will, an accident could not do so. Therefore it is the soul itself which understands or wills, though it exercises itself in regard to different objects, or to the same objects, in different ways, now by apprehending them, now by desiring them. From this it would naturally follow that the Aristotelian distinction between the active and the passive intellects must be rejected, and indeed William of Auvergne rejects the doctrines of the active intellect and of the *species intelligibilis* altogether. The followers of Aristotle and of his commentators swallow the theory of the active intellect without any real reflection, whereas not only are the arguments adduced to prove the theory insufficient, but also very good arguments can be adduced to prove the contrary, the argument from the simplicity of the soul, for example. The active intellect is, then, to be rejected as a useless fiction.[21] A *fortiori*, of course, William rejects the Arabian idea of a *separate* active intellect, an idea which, following Averroes, he ascribed (and probably rightly) to Aristotle himself.

7. In regard to the active intellect, then, William of Auvergne parts company with Aristotle and the Arabians in favour of Augustine, and the Augustinian influence is observable also in his theory of knowledge. Like Augustine he emphasises the soul's knowledge of itself, its direct self-consciousness, and, again like Augustine, he minimises the importance of the senses. It is true that man is inclined to concentrate on bodily things, the objects of the senses; that is why a man may neglect the data of self-consciousness and even be so foolish as to deny the very existence of the immaterial soul. It is also true that for sense-perception the

senses are necessary, obviously enough, and that corporeal objects produce a physical impression on the organs of sense. But the intelligible forms, abstract and universal, by which we know the objects of the corporeal world, cannot arise either from the objects themselves or from the phantasms of such objects, since both the objects and the images are particular. How, then, are our abstract and universal ideas of sensible objects produced? They are produced by the understanding itself, which is not purely passive, but active, *effectrix earum (scientiarum quae a parte sensibilium ei advenire videntur) apud semetipsam et in semetipsa*.[22] This activity is an activity of the soul itself, though it is exercised on the occasion of sense-impressions.

What guarantee is there, then, of the objective character of abstract and universal ideas? The guarantee is the fact that the intellect is not merely active but also passive, though it is in regard to God that it is passive, not in regard to the things of sense. God impresses on the intellect not only the first principles, but also our abstract ideas of the sensible world. In the *De Anima*[23] William teaches explicitly that it is not only the first principles (*regulae primae et per se notae*) and the laws of morality (*regulae honestatis*) which are known in this way, but also the intelligible forms of sensible objects. The human soul occupies a position on the bounds of two worlds (*velut in horizonte duorum mundorum naturaliter esse constitutam et ordinatam*), the one being the world of sensible objects, to which it is joined by the body, the other being, not Plato's universal Ideas or Aristotle's separate Intelligence, but God Himself, *creator ipse*, who is the *exemplar*, the *speculum*, the *liber vivus*, so present to the human intellect that the latter reads off, as it were, in God (*absque ullo alio medio*) the principles and rules and intelligible forms. In this way William of Auvergne makes the active intellect of Aristotle and the Arabians to be God Himself, combining this theory with the Augustinian theory of illumination, interpreted ideogenetically.

8. It may cause surprise that a special chapter has been dedicated to a man whose name is not among the most famous of mediaeval thinkers; but William of Auvergne is of interest not only as a vigorous and systematic philosopher, but also as an illustration of the way in which the metaphysical, cosmological and psychological ideas of Aristotle and the Arabians could affect an open-minded man who stood, gen-

erally speaking, in the line of the older tradition. William of Auvergne was quite ready to accept ideas from the Aristotelians; he adopted Aristotle's definition of the soul, for instance, and utilised Avicenna's distinction between essence and existence; but he was first and foremost a Christian philosopher and, apart from any personal predilection for Augustine, he was not the type of man to adopt Aristotelian or supposedly Aristotelian doctrines when these seemed to him to be incompatible with the Christian faith. Thus the Aristotelian doctrine of the eternity of the world, the neo-Platonic-Arabian notions of emanation and of 'creation' by intermediaries, the theory of a separate, unitary and infra-divine active intellect, he unhesitatingly rejected. It would, however, be a mistake to suppose that he rejected these ideas as incompatible with Christianity and left it at that, for he was clearly satisfied in his own mind that the arguments for the offending positions were inconclusive and insufficient, while the arguments for his own tenets were conclusive. In other words, he was a philosopher and wrote as a philosopher, even though in his works we find theological and philosophical themes treated together in the same book, a feature common to most other mediaeval thinkers.

One may say, then, that William of Auvergne was a transition-thinker. He helped, through his intimate acquaintance with the writings of Aristotle and of the Arabian and Jewish philosophers, and through his limited acceptance of their theories, to pave the way for the completer Aristotelianism of St. Albert and St. Thomas, while, on the other hand, his clear rejection of some leading notions of Aristotle and his followers paved the way for the explicitly anti-Aristotelian attitude of an Augustinian like St. Bonaventure. He is, as I have said earlier, the embodiment of the meeting of the twelfth and thirteenth centuries: he is, one might say, the twelfth century meeting the thirteenth century sympathetically, yet by no means with uncritical admiration or acceptance.

But though we are entitled to regard William of Auvergne as a transition-thinker in respect of the rising influence and growing acceptance of Aristotelianism, i.e. as a stage in the development of thought from the older Augustinianism to the Christian Aristotelianism of St. Thomas, we are also entitled to look upon his philosophy as a stage in the development of Augustinianism itself. St. Anselm had made comparatively little use of Aristotelianism, of which he had but a very restricted knowledge; but later Augustinians were forced to take account of Aristotle, and we find Duns Scotus in the thirteenth century attempting the construction of a synthesis in which Augustinianism would be expounded and defended with the help of Aristotle. Of course, whether one should regard these thinkers as Augustinians who modified and enriched Augustinianism under the influence of Aristotle or as incomplete Aristotelians, is disputable, and one's estimate of William's philosophy will differ, according as one adopts the one or the other point of view, but unless one is determined to view mediaeval philosophy simply in function of Thomism, one should be prepared to admit that William of Auvergne could be regarded as preparing the way for Duns Scotus just as well as preparing the way for St. Thomas. Probably both judgements are true, though from different viewpoints. In a sense any pre-Thomistic mediaeval philosopher who made some use of Aristotle was preparing the way for a more complete adoption of Aristotelianism, and there can be no difficulty in admitting it; yet it is also legitimate to ask whether Aristotelian elements were employed in the service of the Augustinian tradition, so that the resulting philosophy was one in which characteristic Augustinian themes predominated, or whether they were employed in the construction of a philosophy which was definitely orientated towards Aristotelianism as a system. If one asks this question, there can be little doubt about the answer so far as William of Auvergne is concerned; so that M. Gilson can affirm that 'the complex Augustinian of the thirteenth century is almost completely represented by the doctrine of William of Auvergne' and that while nothing could stop the invasion of the Schools by Aristotle, 'the influence of William certainly did much to retard and limit its progress'.[24]

Chapter Twenty-four

ROBERT GROSSETESTE AND ALEXANDER OF HALES

(a) *Robert Grosseteste's life and writings—Doctrine of light —God and creatures—Doctrine of truth and of illumination.* (b) *Alexander of Hales's attitude to philosophy—Proofs of God's existence—The divine attributes—Composition in creatures—Soul, intellect, will—Spirit of Alexander's philosophy.*

When one is treating of mediaeval philosophy, it is not easy to decide in what way one will group the various thinkers. Thus one might very well treat Oxford and Paris separately. At Oxford the general tendency in metaphysics and psychology was conservative, Augustinian, while at the same time an interest was developed in empirical studies, and the combination of these two factors would afford some reason for tracing the course of philosophy at Oxford from Robert Grosseteste to Roger Bacon in a continuous line; while as regards Paris the Augustinianism of Alexander of Hales and St. Bonaventure on the one hand and the Aristotelianism of St. Albert and St. Thomas on the other hand, together with the relation between the two Schools, might make it desirable to treat them in close proximity. However, such a method has its disadvantages. For example, Roger Bacon died (c. 1292) long after Alexander of Hales (1245), in regard to whose writings he made some slighting remarks, and also after St. Albert the Great (1280), towards whom he seems to have felt a special hostility, so that it would seem desirable to consider Roger Bacon after considering these two thinkers. One might, even then, leave over Robert Grosseteste for consideration with Roger Bacon, but the fact remains that Grosseteste

died (1253) well before the Oxford condemnation of series
of theses, among which figured some of those maintained by
St. Thomas (1277 and 1284), whereas Roger Bacon was alive
at the time of the condemnations and criticised that of 1277,
in so far as he felt that it concerned him personally. While
admitting, then, that there would be a great deal to say in
favour of another mode of grouping, in which more attention would be paid to spiritual affinities than to chronology,
I decided to treat first of Robert Grosseteste at Oxford and
Alexander of Hales at Paris, then of Alexander's disciple St.
Bonaventure, the greatest representative of the Augustinian
tradition in the thirteenth century, then of the Aristotelianism of St. Albert and St. Thomas and of the ensuing controversies, and only afterwards to consider Roger Bacon, in
spite of his spiritual affinity with Grosseteste.

(a) ROBERT GROSSETESTE

1. Robert Grosseteste was born in Suffolk about 1170 and
became Chancellor of Oxford University about 1221. From
1229 to 1232 he was Archdeacon of Leicester and in 1235 he
became Bishop of Lincoln, a post which he occupied until
his death in 1253. Besides translations (it has already been
mentioned that he probably translated the *Ethics* directly
from the Greek), Robert Grosseteste composed commentaries on the *Posterior Analytics*, the *Sophistical Arguments*, the
Physics, though the 'commentary' on the *Physics* was rather
a compendium than a commentary, and on the writings of
the Pseudo-Dionysius. The statement by Roger Bacon to the
effect that Grosseteste *neglexit omnino libros Aristotelis et
vias eorum*[1] cannot, therefore, be taken as meaning that he
was ignorant of the writings of Aristotle, but must be understood in the sense that, though acquainted with the thought
of Aristotle, Grosseteste approached philosophical problems
in a different manner. Bacon's further words make this clear,
as he says that Grosseteste was dependent on other authors
than Aristotle and that he also relied on his own experience.

Of original works Robert Grosseteste published books: *De
unica forma omnium, De Intelligentiis, De statu causarum,
De potentia et actu, De veritate, De veritate propositionis,
De scientia Dei, De ordine emanandi causatorum a Deo* and
De libero arbitrio, the authenticity of the *De Anima* not
being certain. In works such as those just named it is quite

clear that Grosseteste stood in the Augustinian tradition, although he knew the philosophy of Aristotle and utilised some of his themes. But with his Augustinianism he combined an interest in empirical science which influenced Roger Bacon and excited his admiration, so that Bacon was led to say of his master that he knew the sciences better than other men[2] and was able to explain causes by the aid of mathematics.[3] Thus Grosseteste wrote *De utilitate artium, De generatione sonorum, De sphaera, De computo, De generatione stellarum, De cometis, De impressione aeris, De luce, De lineis, angulis et figuris, De natura locorum, De iride, De colore, De calore solis, De differentiis localibus, De impressionibus elementorum, De motu corporali, De motu super-caelestium, De finitate motus et temporis* and *Quod homo sit minor mundus.*

2. The philosophy of Robert Grosseteste centres round the idea of light, so dear to the mind of the Augustinian. In the *De luce*[4] Grosseteste remarks that the first corporeal form, which some call corporeity, is in his judgement light. Light unites with matter, that is, with Aristotelian prime matter, to form a simple substance without dimensions. Why does Grosseteste make light the first corporeal form? Because it is the nature of light to diffuse itself and he uses this property of light to explain how a substance composed of non-dimensional form and non-dimensional matter acquires tridimensionality. If we suppose that the function of light is to multiply itself and to diffuse itself and so to be responsible for actual extension, we must conclude that light *is* the first corporeal form, since it would not be possible for the first corporeal form to produce extension through a secondary or consequent form. Moreover, light is the noblest of all forms and bears the greatest resemblance to the separate intelligences, so that on this title also it is the first corporeal form.

Light (*lux*) diffuses itself in all directions, 'spherically', forming the outermost sphere, the firmament, at the farthest point of its diffusion, and this sphere consists simply of light and prime matter. From every part of the firmament light (*lumen*) is diffused towards the centre of the sphere, this light (the light of experience) being *corpus spirituale, sive mavis dicere spiritus corporalis.*[5] This diffusion takes place by means of a self-multiplication and generation of light, so that at intervals, so to speak, there arises a new sphere, until the nine celestial and concentric spheres are complete, the innermost being the sphere of the moon. This sphere in turn produces light, but the rarefaction or diffusion is less as the light approaches the centre, and the four infra-lunar spheres, of fire, air, water and earth are produced. There are, then, thirteen spheres in all in the sensible world, the nine celestial spheres, which are incorruptible and changeless, and the four infra-celestial spheres, which are corruptible and capable of change.

The degree of light possessed by each kind of body determines its place in the corporeal hierarchy, light being the *species et perfectio corporum omnium*.[6] Grosseteste also explains colour in terms of light, declaring that it is *lux incorporata perspicuo*.[7] An abundance of light *in perspicuo puro* is whiteness, while *lux pauca in perspicuo impuro nigredo est*, and he explains in this sense the statement of Aristotle[8] and Averroes that blackness is a privation. Light again is the principle of motion, motion being nothing else but the *vis multiplicativa lucis*.[9]

3. So far light has been considered as something corporeal, as a component of the corporeal; but Grosseteste extends the conception of light to embrace the spiritual world as well. Thus God is pure Light, the eternal Light (not in the corporeal sense, of course), and the angels are also incorporeal lights, participating in the eternal Light. God is also the 'Form of all things', but Grosseteste is careful to explain that God is not the form of all things as entering into their substance, uniting with their matter, but as their exemplary form.[10] God precedes all creatures, but 'precedes' must be understood as meaning that God is eternal, the creature temporal: if it is understood as meaning that there is a common duration in which both God and creatures exist, the statement will be incorrect, since the Creator and the creature do not share any common measure.[11] We naturally *imagine* a time in which God existed before creation, just as we naturally imagine space outside the universe; but reliance on the imagination in such matters is a source of error.

4. In the *De veritate propositionis*[12] Grosseteste says that *veritas sermonis vel opinionis est adaequatio sermonis vel opinionis et rei*, but he concentrates more on 'ontological truth', on the Augustinian view of truth. He is willing to accept the Aristotelian view of the truth of enunciation as *adaequatio sermonis et rei* or *adaequatio rei ad intellectum*, but truth really means the conformity of things to the eternal Word *quo dicuntur* and consists in their conformity to the

divine Word.[13] A thing is true, in so far as it is what it ought to be, and it is what it ought to be when it is conformed to the Word, that is, to its exemplar. This conformity can be perceived only by the mind, so that truth may also be defined with St. Anselm as *rectitudo sola mente perceptibilis*.[14]

From this it follows that no created truth can be perceived except in the light of the supreme Truth, God. Augustine bore witness to the fact that a created truth is visible only in so far as the light of its *ratio eterna* is present to the mind.[15] How is it, then, that the wicked and impure can attain truth? They cannot be supposed to see God, who is seen only by the pure of heart. The answer is that the mind does not perceive the Word or the *ratio eterna* directly, but perceives truth in the light of the Word. Just as the bodily eye sees corporeal objects in the light of the sun without looking directly at the sun or even perhaps adverting to it at all, so the mind perceives truth in the light of the divine illumination without thereby perceiving God, the *Veritas summa*, directly or even without necessarily realising at all that it is only in the divine light that it sees truth.[16] Thus Grosseteste follows the Augustinian doctrine of divine illumination, but explicitly rejects any interpretation of the doctrine which would involve a vision of God.

Into Grosseteste's views on mathematics, perspective, etc., I cannot enter: enough has been said to show how Grosseteste's philosophy was built upon Augustinian lines by a man who yet knew and was willing to utilise Aristotelian ideas.

(b) ALEXANDER OF HALES

5. There was within the Franciscan Order a party of zealots who adopted a hostile attitude towards learning and other accommodations to the needs of life, which they regarded as treason to the simple idealism of the Seraphic Father; but these 'Spirituals' were frowned upon by the Holy See, and in point of fact the Franciscan Order produced a long line of distinguished theologians and philosophers, the first eminent figure being that of the Englishman, Alexander of Hales, who was born in Gloucestershire between 1170 and 1180, entered the Franciscan Order about 1231 and died in 1245. He was the first Franciscan professor of theology at Paris and

occupied the chair until within a few years of his death, having as his successor John of la Rochelle.

It is difficult to ascertain exactly what contributions to philosophy are to be ascribed to Alexander of Hales in person, since the *Summa theologica* which passes under his name, and which drew caustic comments from Roger Bacon, comprises elements, particularly in the latter portion, taken from the writings of other thinkers and seems to have attained its final form some ten years or more after Alexander's death.[17] In any case, however, the work represents a stage in the development of western philosophy and a tendency in that development. It represents a stage, since the Aristotelian philosophy as a whole is clearly known and utilised: it represents a tendency, since the attitude adopted towards Aristotle is critical, in the sense that Alexander not only attacks certain doctrines of Aristotle and the Aristotelians but also considers that the pagan philosophers were unable to formulate a satisfactory 'philosophy', in the wide sense, owing to the fact that they did not possess the Christian revelation: a man on a hill can see more even of the valley than the man at the foot of the hill can see. He followed, therefore, his Christian predecessors (the Fathers, especially St. Augustine, Boethius, the Pseudo-Dionysius, St. Anselm, the Victorines) rather than Aristotle.

6. The doctrine of the Blessed Trinity cannot be attained by man's unaided reason, owing to the weakness of the human intellect,[18] but God's existence can be known by all men, whether they are good or bad.[19] Distinguishing God's existence (*quia est*) from His nature (*quid est*) Alexander teaches that all can know God's existence by means of creatures, recognising God as efficient and final cause.[20] Moreover, though the natural light of reason is insufficient to attain to a knowledge of the divine nature as it is in itself, that does not mean that all knowledge of God's nature is barred to the natural intellect, since it can come to know something of God, for example, His power and wisdom, by considering His operation in creatures, a degree of knowledge open to those who are not in a state of grace.[21] This type of knowledge is not univocal but analogical.[22] For example, goodness is predicated of God and of creatures, but while it is predicated of God *per naturam*, as being identical with His nature and as the self-existent source of all goodness, it is predicated of creatures *per participationem*, inasmuch as creatures depend on

God, are God's effects, and receive a limited degree of goodness from Him.

In proving God's existence Alexander makes use of a variety of arguments. Thus he uses Richard of St. Victor's proof from contingency, St. John Damascene's argument from causality and Hugh of St. Victor's argument from the soul's knowledge that it had a beginning; but he also employs St. Augustine's and St. Anselm's proof from the eternity of truth and accepts the latter's proof from the idea of the Perfect, as given in the *Proslogium*.[23] In addition he maintains that it is impossible to be ignorant of God's existence.[24] This is a startling proposition, but it is necessary to bear in mind certain distinctions. For instance, we must distinguish habitual knowledge and actual knowledge (*cognitio habitu, cognitio actu*). The former, says Alexander, is a habit naturally impressed on the intellect, enabling the intellect to know God, and would seem to be little more than implicit knowledge, if 'implicit knowledge' can be called knowledge at all. St. Albert the Great comments, rather sarcastically, that this distinction is a *solutio mirabilis*.[25] Actual knowledge itself must also be distinguished, since it may comprise the soul's recognition that it is not *a se* or it may mean a concentration on creatures. In so far as actual knowledge of the first sort is concerned, the soul cannot fail to know God's existence, though it would appear that the actual recognition of God may even here be 'implicit', but in so far as the soul is turned away from God by sin and error and rivets its attention on creatures, it may fail to realise God's existence. In this latter case, however, a further distinction must be introduced between knowledge of God *in ratione communi* and knowledge of God *in ratione propria*. For example, the man who places his happiness in riches or sensual pleasures knows God in a sense, since God is Beatitude, but he does not have a true notion of God, *in ratione propria*. Similarly the idolater recognises God *in communi*, for example, as 'Something', but not as He really is, *in ratione propria*. Such distinctions may indeed appear somewhat far-fetched, but Alexander is taking into account such facts as St. Paul's[26] saying that the heathen know God but have not glorified Him as God or St. John Damascene's declaration that the knowledge of God is naturally impressed on the mind.[27] The view that the human mind cannot be without any knowledge of God is characteristic of the Augustinian School; but, in view of the fact that idolaters and, at least, professed atheists exist, any writer who wishes to maintain such a view is bound to introduce the distinction between implicit and explicit knowledge or between knowledge of God *in ratione communi* and knowledge of God *in ratione propria*.

7. Alexander treats of the divine attributes of immutability, simplicity, infinity, incomprehensibility, immensity, eternity, unity, truth, goodness, power and wisdom, giving objections, his own reply to the general question and answers to the objections. Appeals to former writers and quotations from authorities like Augustine and Anselm are frequent, nor is the doctrine developed in a particularly original fashion, but the arrangement is systematic and careful, and a considerable amount of general philosophical reflection is included. For instance, when treating of the unity of the divine nature, Alexander begins by considering unity in general, defining *unitas* as *indivisio entis* and *unum* as *ens indivisum in se, divisum autem ab aliis*,[28] and goes on to consider the relation of unity to being, truth and goodness.[29] As regards the divine knowledge, Alexander maintains, following Augustine and Anselm, that God knows all things in and through Himself. The exemplar or eternal 'ideas' of creatures are in God, though, considered in themselves, they do not form a plurality but are identical with the one divine essence, so that it is by knowing Himself that God knows all things. How, then, does He know evil and sin? Only as defect, i.e. a defect from goodness. If light, says Alexander, following the Pseudo-Dionysius, were gifted with the power of knowing, it would know that this or that object was unreceptive of its action: it would not know darkness in itself without any relation to light. This involves, of course, the view that evil is nothing positive but rather a privation,[30] for, if evil were something positive, it would be necessary either to maintain dualism or to say that evil has an exemplar in God.

In treating of the divine will Alexander raises the question whether or not God can order actions which are against the natural law. The immediate origin of the question is a problem of Scriptural exegesis; how, for example, to explain God's order to the Israelites to despoil the Egyptians, but the question has, of course, a much wider significance. God, he answers, cannot order an action which would be formally contrary to the natural law, since this would be to contradict Himself; He cannot, for instance, will that man should have any other end but God, since God is essentially the final end.

Nor could God order the Israelites to steal in the proper sense of the word, as implying an act directed against God Himself, a sin. God can, however, deprive the Egyptians of their property and so order the Israelites to take it. He can also order the Israelites to take something that belongs to another, since this affects only the *ordo ad creaturam*, but cannot order them to take it *ex cupiditate*, since this affects the *ordo ad Deum* and would involve self-contradiction on God's part.[31] Similarly, God could order the prophet Osee to have intercourse with a woman who was not his wife, in so far as this act involved the *ordo ad creaturam*, but He could not order Osee to do this *ex libidine*, since this would invove the *ordo ad Deum*. Alexander's distinctions on this matter are somewhat obscure and not always satisfactory, but it is in any case clear that he did not believe that the moral law depends on God's arbitrary *fiat*, as Ockham was later to maintain.

8. God is the immediate Creator of the world, in regard both to matter and form, and the non-eternity of the world can be proved.[32] Thus Alexander rejects the Aristotelian notion of the eternity of the world, but he accepts the doctrine of hylomorphic composition. This composition is found in every creature, since 'matter' equals potentiality, but a more fundamental composition, also found in every creature, is that between the *quo est* and the *quod est*.[33] It may appear that this is the distinction between essence and existence, but it seems rather that the *quod est* refers to the concrete being, a man, for instance, and the *quo est* to the abstract essence, humanity, for example. In any case the distinction is a 'rational' distinction, since we can predicate the *quo est* of the *quod est*, in a certain sense at least, as when we say that this being is a man. There is no real distinction between a man and his humanity; yet the humanity is received. In God there is no dependence, no reception, and so no composition between the *quod est* (*Deus*) and the *quo est* (*Deitas*).

9. In accordance with his general spirit of reliance on tradition, Alexander of Hales gives and defends seven definitions or descriptions of the human soul.[34] For example, the soul may be defined as *Deiforme spiraculum vitae*,[35] or as *substantia quaedam rationis particeps, regendo corpori accommodata*[36] or as *substantia spiritualis a Deo creata, propria sui corporis vivificatrix*.[37] Other definitions are taken from St. Augustine, St. John Damascene and Seneca. The soul, insists Alexander, is not a substance simply in the sense that

it is a substantial form, but it is an *ens in se*, a substance *simpliciter*, composed of 'intellectual' matter and form. If in this respect he follows the Platonic-Augustinian tradition, even suggesting that the soul must be a substance since it stands to the body as the sailor to the ship, he also insists that the soul vivifies the body. An angel is also *spiraculum vitae*, but an angel is not *spiraculum vitae corporis*, whereas the soul is the principle of the body's life.

Each human soul is created by God out of nothing.[38] The human soul is not an emanation of God, part of the divine substance,[89] nor is it propagated in the manner postulated by the traducianists. Original sin can be explained without recourse to a traducianist theory.[40] The soul is united with the body after the manner of the union of form with matter (*ad modum formae cum materia*),[41] but this must be interpreted in an Augustinian sense, since the rational soul is joined to its body *ut motor mobili et ut perfectio formalis suo perfectibili*.[42] The soul has the three powers of the *vis vegetativa*, the *vis sensitiva* and the *vis intellectiva*, and though these powers are not to be called parts of the soul, in the strict sense of the word 'part',[43] they are yet distinct from one another and from the essence of the soul. Alexander, therefore, explains Augustine's assertion of the identity of the soul and its powers by saying that this identity is to be referred to the substance, not to the essence of the soul.[44] The soul cannot subsist without its powers nor are the powers intelligible apart from the soul, but just as *esse* and *operari* are not identical, so are *essentia* and *potentia* not identical.

The active and passive intellects are *duae differentiae* of the rational soul, the former referring to the spiritual form of the soul, the latter to its spiritual matter, and the active intellect is not separate from the soul but belongs to it.[45] But together with the Aristotelian classification of the rational powers of the soul Alexander gives also the classifications of St. Augustine and St. John Damascene and attempts to reconcile them. For example, 'intellect' in the Aristotelian philosophy refers to our power of acquiring knowledge of intelligible forms by means of abstraction,[46] and it corresponds, therefore, to the Augustinian *ratio*, not to the Augustinian *intellectus* or *intelligentia*, which has to do with spiritual objects. Intellect in the Aristotelian sense has to do with embodied forms and abstracts them from the *phantasmata*, but intellect in the Augustinian sense has to do with non-embodied, spiritual forms, and when there is question of knowing those forms which are superior to the human soul, the intellect is powerless unless it is illuminated by God.[47] Alexander provides no clear explanation of what this illumination precisely is, but he at least makes it clear that he accepts the Aristotelian doctrine of abstraction in regard to the corporeal world, though in regard to the spiritual world the doctrine of Aristotle has to be supplemented by that of Augustine. One may also remark that Alexander was quite right in seeing in the Peripatetic classification a psychological analysis and in the Augustinian classification a division according to the objects of knowledge.

Alexander gives three definitions of free will, that of St. Anselm (*potestas servandi rectitudinem propter se*), that of St. Augustine (*facultas rationis et voluntatis, qua bonum eligitur gratia assistente et malum eadem desistente*) and that of St. Bernard (*consensus ob voluntatis inamissibilem libertatem et rationis indeclinabile iudicium*) and attempts to reconcile them.[48] *Liberum arbitrium* is common to God and the soul, but it is predicated neither universally nor equivocally, but analogically, primarily of God, secondarily of the creature.[49] In man it is one faculty or function of reason and will in union, and it is in this sense only that it may be termed distinct from reason and will: it is not in reality a separate power of the soul. Moreover, inasmuch as it is bound up with the possession of reason and will, it is inseparable from the soul, that is, as far as natural liberty is concerned. Following St. Bernard, Alexander distinguishes *libertas arbitrii* and *libertas consilii et complaciti* and declares that, while the latter may be lost, the former cannot.

10. Alexander of Hales is of interest, since his main work is a sustained effort of systematic thought, being a Scholastic presentation of the Christian theology and philosophy. In regard to form it belongs to the mediaeval period of the *Summas*, sharing in the merits and defects of that type of compilation, in their succinctness and orderly arrangement as in their aridity and absence of developments which, from our point of view, might be desirable. As regards content, on the one hand Alexander's *Summa* stands in close connection with the past, as the author is determined to be faithful to tradition and very frequently quotes Augustine or Anselm, Bernard or John Damascene, instead of developing his own arguments. This does not mean that he appeals simply to au-

thority, in the sense of merely citing famous names, since he often quotes the arguments of his predecessors; but it does mean that the developed arguments which would have been desirable even at the time he wrote, are absent. However, his work is, of course, a *Summa*, and a *Summa* is admittedly a summary. On the other hand the work shows a knowledge of Aristotle, though he is not often explicitly mentioned, and it makes some use of the Peripatetic doctrine. There is always present, however, the desire to harmonise the elements taken from Aristotle with the teaching of Augustine and Anselm, and the general tendency is towards a contrast between the God-enlightened Christian thinkers on the one hand and the Philosophers on the other hand. It is not that Alexander gives the impression of being a polemical writer nor that he confuses philosophy and theology,[50] but he is chiefly concerned with the knowledge of God and of Christ. To say that, is simply to say that he was faithful to the tradition of the Augustinian School.

Chapter Twenty-five

ST. BONAVENTURE—I

Life and works—Spirit—Theology and philosophy—Attitude to Aristotelianism.

1. St. Bonaventure, Giovanni Fidanza, was born at Bagnorea in Tuscany in the year 1221. Healed of a sickness while a child, through his mother's invocation of St. Francis of Assisi, he entered the Franciscan Order at a date which cannot be exactly determined. It may have been shortly before or after 1240, but in any case Bonaventure must have become a Franciscan in time to study under Alexander of Hales at Paris before the latter's death in 1245. The teaching of Alexander evidently made a great impression on his pupil, for in his *Praelocutio prooemio in secundum librum Sententiarum praemissa* Bonaventure declares that just as in the first book of the *Sentences* he has adhered to the common opinions of the masters, and especially to those of 'our master and father of happy memory Brother Alexander', so in the following books he will not stray from their footsteps.[1] In other words Bonaventure imbibed the Franciscan, i.e. the Augustinian, tradition, and he was determined to keep to it. It might perhaps be thought that this determination indicated simply a pious conservatism and that Bonaventure was ignorant of or at least ignored and adopted no definite and positive attitude towards the new philosophical tendencies at Paris; but the Commentary on the *Sentences* dates from 1250-1 (he started lecturing in 1248, on St. Luke's Gospel) and at that date Bonaventure cannot have made his studies at Paris and yet have been ignorant of the Aristotelian philosophy. Moreover, we shall see later that he adopted a very definite attitude

towards that philosophy, an attitude which was not simply the fruit of ignorance but proceeded from reflection and reasoned conviction.

St. Bonaventure was involved in the same difficulties between regulars and seculars in which St. Thomas Aquinas was involved, and in 1255 he was excluded from the university, that is, he was refused recognition as a doctor and professor of the university staff. He may have been readmitted in 1256, but in any case he was accepted, along with Aquinas, in October 1257, as a result of Papal intervention. He was then a professor of theology at the university, as far as acceptance was concerned, and would doubtless have proceeded to exercise that office had he not been elected Minister General of his Order on February 2nd, 1257. The fulfilment of the normal functions of his office would by itself have prevented his living the settled life of a university professor, but in addition there were differences of opinion at the time within the Order itself in regard to its spirit, practice and function, and Bonaventure was faced with the difficult task of maintaining or restoring peace. However, in 1259 he wrote the *Itinerarium mentis in Deum*, in 1261 his two lives of St. Francis, in 1267 or 1268 the *Collationes de decem praeceptis* (Lenten sermons), the *De decem donis Spiritus sancti* (about 1270), the *Collationes in Hexaëmeron* in 1273. The *Breviloquium* was written before 1257. The Commentaries on the Scriptures, short mystical treatises, sermons, and letters on points connected with the Franciscan Order make up his other writings at various periods of his life.

Although in 1265 Bonaventure had succeeded in inducing the Pope to rescind his appointment to the Archbishopric of York, he was appointed Bishop of Albano and Cardinal in 1273. In 1274 he was present at the Council of Lyons, where he preached on the reunion of the Eastern Church with Rome, but on the conclusion of the Council he died (July 15th, 1274) and was buried at Lyons in the presence of Pope Gregory X.

2. St. Bonaventure was not only himself a man of learning, but he also encouraged the development of studies within the Franciscan Order, and this may appear strange in the case of a Franciscan saint, when it can hardly be said that the founder had envisaged his friars devoting themselves to erudition. But it is, of course, perfectly clear to us, as it was to Bonaventure, that an order consisting largely of priests, with

a vocation which involved preaching, could not possibly fulfil its vocation unless its members, at least those who were destined for the priesthood, studied the Scriptures and theology. But it was impossible to study Scholastic theology without acquiring a knowledge of philosophy, so that philosophical and theological studies were both necessary. And once this general principle was admitted, as admitted it must be, it was hardly practicable to set a limit to the degree of study. If the students were to be trained in philosophy and theology, they had to have professors and the professors had not only to be competent themselves but to educate their successors. Moreover, if apostolic work might involve contact with learned men, perhaps also with heretics, one could not set on *a priori* grounds a limit to the study which might be advisable.

One might indeed multiply such practical considerations, which justified the development of studies within the Franciscan Order; but, as far as Bonaventure is concerned, there is an equally important consideration to be mentioned. St. Bonaventure was perfectly faithful to the spirit of St. Francis in regarding union with God as the most important aim in life; but he saw very well that this would scarcely be attained without knowledge of God and the things of God, or at least that such knowledge, so far from being a hindrance to union with God, should predispose the soul to closer union. After all, it was the study of the Scriptures and of theology which he recommended and himself pursued, not the study of questions which had no connection with God, and this was one of the reasons why he disliked and mistrusted the metaphysical philosophy of Aristotle, which had no place for personal communion with the Godhead and no place for Christ. There is, as M. Gilson has pointed out, a certain parallel between the life of St. Francis and the teaching of St. Bonaventure. For just as the former's personal life culminated in mystical communion with God, so the latter's teaching culminated in his mystical doctrine, and just as Francis had approached God through Christ and had seen, *concretely*, all things in the light of the divine Word, so Bonaventure insisted that the Christian philosopher must see the world in its relation to the creative Word. Christ, as he expressly says, is the *medium* or Centre of all sciences, and so he could not accept the Aristotelian metaphysic, which, so far from knowing anything of Christ, had rejected even the exemplarism of Plato.

In the end the Franciscan Order accepted Duns Scotus as its doctor *par excellence;* but though it was doubtless right in so doing and though Scotus was undoubtedly a man of genius, a thinker of great speculative and analytic ability, one may perhaps say that it was St. Bonaventure who stood nearer in thought, as in time, to the spirit of the Seraphic Father. Indeed, it is not without reason that he was accorded the title of the Seraphic Doctor.

3. St. Bonaventure's view of the purpose and value of study, determined as much by his own inclinations and spiritual tendencies as by his intellectual training under Alexander of Hales and his membership of the Franciscan Order, naturally placed him in the Augustinian tradition. St. Augustine's thought centred round God and the soul's relation to God, and, since the man who is related to God is the concrete and actual man of history, who has fallen from grace and who has been redeemed by grace, Augustine dealt with man in the concrete and not with the 'natural man', not, that is, with man considered apart from his supernatural vocation and in abstraction from the operation of supernatural grace. This meant that St. Augustine could make no very rigid distinction between philosophy and theology, even though he distinguished between the natural light of reason and supernatural faith. There is, of course, adequate justification for treating in philosophy of man in 'the state of nature', since the order of grace is super-natural and one can distinguish between the order of grace and the order of nature; but the point I want to make is simply this, that if one is principally interested in the soul's advance to God, as Augustine and Bonaventure were, then one's thought will centre round man in the concrete, and man in the concrete is man with a supernatural vocation. Man considered in the 'state of nature', is a legitimate abstraction; but this legitimate abstraction will not appeal to one whose thought centres round the actual historical order. It is largely a question of approach and method. Neither Augustine nor Bonaventure would deny the distinction between the natural and the supernatural, but since they were both primarily interested in the actual historical man, who, be it repeated, is man with a supernatural vocation, they naturally tended to mingle theological and philosophical themes in one Christian wisdom rather than to make a rigid, methodological distinction between philosophy and theology.

It may be objected that in this case St. Bonaventure is simply a theologian and not a philosopher at all; but one can give a similar answer in the case of Bonaventure as in that of Augustine. If one were to define a philosopher as one who pursues the study of Being or the ultimate causes, or whatever other object one is pleased to assign to the philosopher, without any reference to revelation and prescinding *completely* from dogmatic theology, the Christian dispensation and the supernatural order, then of course neither Augustine nor Bonaventure could be termed a philosopher; but if one is willing to admit into the ranks of the philosophers all those who pursue what are generally recognised as philosophical themes, then both men must be reckoned philosophers. Bonaventure may sometimes treat, for instance, of the stages of the soul's ascent from knowledge of God through creatures to immediate and interior experience of God and he may speak of the stages without any clear demarcation of what is proper to theology and what is proper to philosophy; but that does not alter the fact that in treating of knowledge of God through creatures, he develops proofs of God's existence and that these proofs are reasoned arguments and so can be termed philosophical arguments. Again, Bonaventure's interest in the material world may be principally an interest in that world as the manifestation of God and he may delight to see therein *vestigia* of the Triune God, but that does not alter the fact that he holds certain opinions about the nature of the world and its constitution which are cosmological, philosophical, in character. It is true that to isolate Bonaventure's philosophical doctrines is in a sense to impair the integrity of his system; but there are philosophical doctrines in his system and this fact entitles him to a place in the history of philosophy. Moreover, as I shall mention shortly, he adopted a very definite attitude towards philosophy in general and the Aristotelian system in particular, and on this count alone he merits a place in the history of philosophy. One could hardly exclude Kierkegaard from the history of philosophy, although his attitude towards philosophy, in his understanding of the term, was hostile, for he philosophised about philosophy: still less can one exclude Bonaventure whose attitude was less hostile than that of Kierkegaard and who represents a particular standpoint in regard to philosophy, the standpoint of those who maintain not only that there is such a thing as Christian philosophy, but also that every independent philosophy is bound to be deficient and even partly erroneous as philosophy. Whether this standpoint is right or wrong, justified or unjustified, it deserves consideration in a history of philosophy.

Bonaventure was, then, of the Augustinian tradition; but it must be remembered that a great deal of water had flowed under the bridge since the time of Augustine. Since that time Scholasticism had developed, thought had been systematised, the Aristotelian metaphysic had been fully made known to the western Christian world. Bonaventure commented on the *Sentences* of Peter Lombard and he was acquainted with the thought of Aristotle: we would only expect, then, to find in his writings not only far more elements of Scholasticism and of the Scholastic method than in Augustine but also an adoption of not a few Aristotelian ideas, for Bonaventure by no means rejected Aristotle lock, stock and barrel: on the contrary he respected him as a natural philosopher, even if he had no high opinion of his metaphysics, of his theology at least. Thus from the point of view of the thirteenth century the Bonaventurian system was a modern Augustinianism, an Augustinianism developed through the centuries and rethought in relation to Aristotelianism.

4. What then was Bonaventure's view of the general relation of philosophy to theology and what was his view of Aristotelianism? The two questions can be taken together, since the answer to the first determines the answer to the second.

As has already been remarked, Augustine distinguished faith and reason, and Bonaventure naturally followed him, quoting Augustine's words to the effect that what we believe we owe to authority, what we understand to reason.[2] It follows from this, one might think, that philosophy and theology are two separate sciences and that an independent philosophy of a satisfactory character is, at least theoretically, possible. Indeed Bonaventure actually makes an explicit and clear distinction between dogmatic theology and philosophy. For example, in the *Breviloquium*[3] he says that theology begins with God, the supreme Cause, with whom philosophy ends. In other words, theology takes its data from revelation and proceeds from God Himself to His effects, whereas philosophy starts with the visible effects and argues to God as cause. Again, in the *De Reductione Artium ad Theologiam*[4] he divides 'natural philosophy' into physics, mathematics and metaphysics, while in the *In Hexaëmeron*[5] he divides philosophy into physics, logic and ethics.

In view of the above, how can it be maintained that St. Bonaventure did not admit of any rigid distinction between philosophy and theology? The answer is that he admitted a methodological distinction between the sciences and also a distinction of subject-matter, but insisted that no satisfactory metaphysic or philosophical system can be worked out unless the philosopher is guided by the light of faith and philosophises in the light of faith. For instance, he was well aware that a philosopher can arrive at the existence of God without the aid of revelation. Even if he had not been convinced of this by his own reason and by the testimony of the Scriptures, the philosophy of Aristotle would have been sufficient to persuade him of the fact. But he was not content to say that the knowledge of God so attained is incomplete and stands in need of the completion provided by revelation: he went further and stated that such purely rational knowledge is, and must be, in important points erroneous. This point he proved empirically. For example, 'the most noble Plotinus of the sect of Plato and Tully of the academic sect', in spite of the fact that their views on God and the soul were preferable to those of Aristotle, fell into error since they were unaware of the supernatural end of man, of the true resurrection of the body and of eternal felicity.[6] They could not know these things without the light of faith, and they fell into error precisely because they had not got the light of faith. Similarly, a mere metaphysician may come to the knowledge of the supreme Cause, but if he is a mere metaphysician he will stop there, and if he stops there he is in error, since he thinks of God otherwise than He is, not knowing that God is both one and three. 'Philosophical science is the way to other sciences; but he who wishes to stop there, falls into darkness.'[7] In other words, Bonaventure is not denying the power of the philosopher to attain truth, but he maintains that the man who is satisfied with philosophy, who is a mere philosopher, necessarily falls into error. It is one thing if a man comes by reason to know that there exists one God and then goes on to recognise, in the light of faith, that this unity is a unity of Nature in Trinity of Persons, and quite another thing if a man stops short at the unity of God. In the latter case the man affirms the unity of Nature to the exclusion of the Trinity of Persons, and to do this is to fall into error. If it is objected that it is not necessary to exclude the Trinity, since a philosopher may prescind from revelation altogether, so that his philosophical knowledge, though incomplete, remains valid and true, Bonaventure would doubtless answer that if the man is simply a philosopher and rests in philosophy, he will be convinced that God is one in Nature and not three in Persons. In order to make due allowance for the completion, he must already possess the light of faith. The light of faith does not supply the rational arguments for God's existence (there is such a thing as philosophy), but it ensures that the philosophy remains 'open' and that it does not close in on itself in such a way that error results.

Bonaventure's view of Aristotelianism follows easily enough from these premises. That Aristotle was eminent as a natural philosopher, that is, in regard to sensible objects, Bonaventure admits: what he will not admit is that Aristotle was a true metaphysician, that is, that the metaphysics of Aristotle are satisfactory. Some people, seeing that Aristotle was so eminent in other sciences, have imagined that he must also have attained truth in metaphysics; but this does not follow, since the light of faith is necessary in order to form a satisfactory metaphysical system. Moreover, Aristotle was so competent in other sciences precisely because his mind and interests were of such a kind that he was not inclined to form a philosophy which should point beyond itself. Thus he refused to find the principle of the world outside the world: he rejected the ideas of Plato[8] and made the world eternal.[9] From his denial of the Platonic theory of ideas there followed not only the denial of creationism, but also the denial of God's knowledge of particulars, and of divine foreknowledge and providence.[10] Again, the doctrine of the unicity of the intellect is at least attributed to Aristotle by Averroes, and from this there follows the denial of individual beatitude or punishment after death.[11] In short, though all pagan philosophers have fallen into error, Aristotle was more involved in error than Plato or Plotinus.

Possibly one may obtain a clearer view of Bonaventure's notion of the relation of philosophy to theology if one bears in mind the attitude of the Catholic philosopher in practice. The latter works out arguments for the existence of God, for example, but he does not make himself an atheist for the time being nor does he deny his faith in the dogma of the Trinity: he philosophises in the light of what he already believes and he will not conclude to a unity in God of such a kind that it will exclude the Trinity of Persons. On the other hand his arguments for God's existence are rational arguments: in them he makes no reference to dogma, and the value of the proofs as such rests on their philosophical merits or demerits. The philosopher pursues his arguments, psychologically speaking, in the light of the faith which he already possesses and which he does not discard during his philosophical studies, and his faith helps him to ask the right questions and to avoid untrue conclusions, though he does not make any formal use of the faith in his philosophic arguments. The Thomist would, of course, say that the faith is to the philosopher an extrinsic norm, that the philosopher prescinds from his faith, even though he does not deny it, and that a pagan could, theoretically at least, reach the same conclusions in philosophy. St. Bonaventure, however, would reply that, even though the philosopher may make no formal use of dogma in this or that metaphysical argument, he certainly philosophises in the light of faith and that this is something positive: the action of faith is a positive influence on the mind of the philosopher and without it he will inevitably fall into error. One cannot exactly say that St. Bonaventure believed only in a total Christian wisdom comprising indifferently philosophical and theological truths, since he admitted a classification of the sciences in which philosophy figures; but, this latter point once admitted, one can say that his ideal was the ideal of a Christian wisdom in which the light of the Word is shed not only on theological but also on philosophical truths, and without which those truths would not be attained.

I have argued that since St. Bonaventure certainly treated of philosophical questions, he has a claim to be included in a history of philosophy, and I do not see how this contention can be seriously disputed; but it remains true that he was a theologian, that he wrote as a theologian and that he did not really consider philosophical questions and problems for their own sake. St. Thomas Aquinas was also primarily a theologian, and he wrote primarily as a theologian; but he did consider philosophical problems at length and even composed some philosophical works, which St. Bonaventure did not do. The Commentary on the *Sentences* was not what we would to-day call a philosophical work. It seems, therefore, to constitute something of an exaggeration when M. Gilson maintains, in his magnificent study of St. Bonaventure's philosophical thought, that there is a Bonaventurian philosophical system, the spirit and content of which can be sharply defined. We have seen that St. Bonaventure recognised philosophy as a definite science, separate from theology; but as far as he himself is concerned, he might be called a philosopher *per accidens*. In a sense the same is true, of course, of any mediaeval thinker who was primarily a theologian, even of St. Thomas; but it is most relevant in the case of a thinker who was chiefly concerned with the soul's approach to God. Moreover, M. Gilson probably tends to exaggerate St. Bonaventure's hostility to pagan philosophy and to Aristotle in particular. I have indeed admitted that St. Bonaventure attacked the Aristotelian metaphysic (this is a fact which cannot be denied) and that he considered that any philosopher who is merely a philosopher will inevitably fall into error; but it is desirable in this connection to call to mind the fact that St. Thomas himself insisted on the moral necessity of revelation. On that point St. Bonaventure and St. Thomas were in agreement. They both rejected pagan philosophy where it was incompatible with Christianity, though they differed as to what precise points were to be rejected and how far one could go in following Aristotle.

However, though I think that M. Gilson's genius for capturing the peculiar spirit of the individual thinker and for setting it in clear relief leads him to exaggerate the systematic aspect of St. Bonaventure's philosophy and to find a greater opposition between the views of Bonaventure and Thomas in regard to the pagan philosophers than probably exists in actual fact, I cannot subscribe to the judgement of M. Fernand Van Steenberghen[12] that 'the philosophy of St. Bonaventure is an eclectic and neo-Platonising Aristotelianism, put at the service of an Augustinian theology'. That Bonaventure made considerable use of Aristotelianism is perfectly true; but the inspiration of his philosophy is, in my opinion, what for want of a better word we call 'Augustinian'. As I remarked in regard to William of Auvergne, it depends to a large extent on one's point of view whether one calls those Augustinian theologians who adopted selected Aristotelian doctrines in philosophy incomplete Aristotelians or modified Augustinians; but in the case of a man whose whole interest centred round the soul's ascent to God, who laid such stress on the illuminative action of God and who, as M. Van Steenberghen himself states when criticising M. Gilson, never worked out a philosophy for its own sake, it seems to me that 'Augustinian' is the only fit word for describing his thought, if for no better reason than the principle that *maior pars trahit minorem* and that the spirit must take precedence of the letter.

Chapter Twenty-six

ST. BONAVENTURE–II: GOD'S EXISTENCE

Spirit of Bonaventure's proofs of God's existence—Proofs from sensible world—A priori knowledge of God—The Anselmian argument—Argument from truth.

1. We have seen that St. Bonaventure, like St. Augustine, was principally interested in the soul's relation to God. This interest had an effect on his treatment of the proofs for God's existence; he was chiefly concerned to exhibit the proofs as stages in the soul's ascent to God or rather to treat them in function of the soul's ascent to God. It must be realised that the God to whom the proofs conclude is not, then, simply an abstract principle of intelligibility, but is rather the God of the Christian consciousness, the God to whom men pray. I do not, of course, mean to suggest that there is, ontologically, any discrepancy or any irreconcilable tension between the God of the 'philosophers' and the God of experience; but since Bonaventure is primarily interested in God as Object of worship and prayer and as goal of the human soul, he tends to make the proofs so many acts of drawing attention to the self-manifestation of God, whether in the material world or within the soul itself. Indeed, as one would expect, he lays more emphasis on proofs from within than on proofs from the material world, from without. He certainly does prove God's existence from the external sensible world (St. Augustine had done this) and he shows how from the knowledge of finite, imperfect, composite, moving and contingent beings man can rise to the apprehension of the infinite, perfect, simple, unchanging and necessary Being; but the proofs are

ot systematically elaborated, the reason for this being, not
ny inability on Bonaventure's part to develop the proofs
ialectically, but rather his conviction that the existence of
God is so evident to the soul through reflection on itself that
xtramental creation serves mainly to remind us of it. His
ttitude is that of the Psalmist, when he says: *Coeli enar-
ant gloriam Dei, et opera manuum eius annuntiat firmamen-
um.* Thus it is quite true that the imperfection of finite and
ontingent things demands and proves the existence of abso-
ite perfection, God; but, asks St. Bonaventure in a truly
Platonic manner, 'how could the intellect know that this be-
ıg is defective and incomplete, if it had no knowledge of
Being without any defect?'[1] In other words, the idea of im-
erfection presupposes the idea of perfection, so that the idea
f perfection or the perfect cannot be obtained simply by way
f negation and abstraction, and consideration of creatures
ı their finiteness and imperfection and dependence serves
imply to remind the soul or to bring the soul to a clearer
wareness of what is in some sense already evident to it, al-
eady known to it.

2. St. Bonaventure does not deny for a moment that God's
xistence can be proved from creatures: on the contrary he
ffirms it. In the Commentary on the *Sentences*[2] he declares
ıat God can be known through creatures as Cause through
ffect, and he goes on to say that this mode of cognition is
atural to man inasmuch as for us sensible things are the
ıeans by which we arrive at the knowledge of '*intelligibilia*',
ıat is, objects transcending sense. The Blessed Trinity can-
ot be proved in the same way, however, by the natural light
f reason, since we cannot conclude to the Trinity of Persons
ther by denying certain properties or limitations of crea-
ires or by the positive way of attributing to God certain
ualities of creatures.[3] St. Bonaventure thus teaches clearly
1ough the possibility of a natural and 'philosophic' knowl-
dge of God, and his remark on the psychological natural-
ess of this approach to God through sensible objects is
ristotelian in character. Again, in the *In Hexaëmeron*[4] he
rgues that if there exists being which is produced, there
iust be a first Being, since there must be a cause: if there
being *ab alio*, there must be Being *a se*: if there is a com-
osite being, there must be simple Being: if there is change-
ɔle being, there must be unchanged Being, *quia mobile re-
ucitur ad immobile*. The last statement is obviously a

reference to the Aristotelian proof of the existence of the unmoved mover, though Bonaventure mentions Aristotle only to say that he argued on these lines to the eternity of the world and that on this point the Philosopher was wrong.

Similarly in the *De Mysterio Trinitatis*[5] Bonaventure gives a series of brief arguments to show how clearly creatures proclaim the existence of God. For instance, if there is *ens ab alio*, there must exist *ens non ab alio*, because nothing can bring itself out of a state of non-being into a state of being, and finally there must be a first Being which is self-existent. Again, if there is *ens possibile*, Being which can exist and cannot exist, there must be *ens necessarium*, being which has no possibility of non-existence, since this is necessary in order to explain the eduction of possible being into a state of existence; and if there is *ens in potentia*, there must be *ens in actu*, since no potency is reducible to act save through the agency of what is itself in act; and ultimately there must be *actus purus*, a Being which is pure Act, without any potentiality, God. Again, if there is *ens mutabile*, there must be *ens immutabile* because, as the Philosopher proves, motion has as its principle an unmoved being and exists for the sake of unmoved being, which is its final cause.

It might indeed appear from such passages, where Bonaventure employs Aristotelian arguments, that the statement to the effect that Bonaventure regarded the witness of creatures to God's existence in function of the soul's ascent to God and that he regarded the existence of God as a self-evident truth, cannot stand. But he makes it quite clear in various places[6] that he regards the sensible world as the mirror of God and sense-knowledge or knowledge obtained through sense and reflection on sensible objects as, formally, the first step in the stages of the soul's spiritual ascent, the highest stage of which in this life is the experimental knowledge of God by means of the *apex mentis* or *synderesis scintilla* (on this point he shows himself faithful to the tradition of Augustine and the Victorines), while in the very article of the *De Mysterio Trinitatis* where he gives the proofs cited he affirms emphatically that God's existence is indubitably a truth naturally implanted in the human mind (*quod Deum esse sit menti humanae indubitabile, tanquam sibi naturaliter insertum*). He goes on to declare that, in addition to what he has already said on this matter, there is a second way of showing that the existence of God is an indubitable truth. The

cond way consists in showing that what every creature pro-
aims is an indubitable truth, and it is at this point that he
ves his succession of proofs or rather of indications that
ery creature really does proclaim God's existence. Subse-
lently he adds that there is a third way of showing that
od's existence cannot be doubted and proceeds to give his
rsion of St. Anselm's proof in the *Proslogium*. There can,
en, be no doubt at all that Bonaventure affirmed that God's
istence is self-evident and cannot be doubted: the question
rather what exactly he meant by this, and we will consider
is in the next section.

3. In the first place St. Bonaventure did not suppose that
eryone has an explicit and clear knowledge of God, still
ss that he has such a knowledge from birth or from the first
e of reason. He was well aware of the existence of idola-
rs and of the *insipiens*, the fool who said in his heart that
ere is no God. The existence of idolaters does not, of course,
use much difficulty since idolaters and pagans do not so
uch deny the existence of God as possess a wrong idea of
od; but what of the *insipiens*? The latter sees, for example,
at the impious are not always punished in this world or at
ast that they sometimes appear to be better off in this
orld than many good people, and he concludes from this
at there is no divine Providence, no divine Ruler of the
orld.[7] Moreover, he explicitly affirms,[8] in answer to the
jection that it is useless to prove the existence of that
hich is self-evident, of that concerning which no one doubts,
at though the existence of God is indubitable so far as ob-
ctive evidence is concerned, it can be doubted *propter de-
ctum considerationis ex parte nostra* because of want of due
nsideration and reflection on our part. Does not this look
if Bonaventure is saying no more than that objectively
eaking, the existence of God is indubitable (i.e. the evi-
nce, when considered, is indubitable and conclusive), but
at subjectively speaking it may be doubted (i.e. because
is or that human being does not give sufficient attention
the objective evidence); and if this is what he means when
e says that God's existence is indubitable and self-evident,
ow does his position differ from that of St. Thomas?
The answer seems to be this. Although St. Bonaventure
d not postulate an explicit and clear idea of God in every
man being, still less any immediate vision or experience of
od, he certainly postulated a dim awareness of God in ev-

ery human being, an implicit knowledge which cannot b
fully denied and which can become an explicit and clea
awareness through interior reflection alone, even if it ma
sometimes need to be supported by reflection on the sensibl
world. The universal knowledge of God is, therefore, im
plicit, not explicit; but it is implicit in the sense that it ca
at least be rendered explicit through interior reflection alon
St. Thomas admitted an implicit knowledge of God, but b
this he meant that the mind has the power of attaining t
the knowledge of God's existence through reflection on th
things of sense and by arguing from effect to cause, where:
St. Bonaventure meant something more by implicit know
edge, that is, virtual knowledge of God, a dim awarene
which can be rendered explicit without recourse to the se
sible world.

Application of this view to Bonaventure's concrete i
stances may make the understanding of it easier. For instanc
every human being has a natural desire for happiness (a,
petitus beatitudinis). But happiness consists in the possessic
of the supreme Good, which is God. Therefore every huma
being desires God. But there can be no desire without son
knowledge of the object (sine aliquali notitia). Therefore th
knowledge that God or the supreme Good exists is natural
implanted in the soul.[9] Similarly, the rational soul has
natural knowledge of itself, because it is present to itself an
is knowable by itself. But God is most present to the so
and is knowable. Therefore a knowledge of its God is ir
planted in the soul. If it be objected that while the soul
an object proportionate to its own power of knowing, God
not, the reply can be made that, if that were true, the so
could never come to the knowledge of God, which is ob
ously false.[10]

According to the above line of argument, then, the huma
will is naturally orientated towards the supreme Good, whic
is God, and not only is this orientation of the will inexplic
ble unless the supreme Good, God, really exists, but it al
postulates an a priori knowledge of God.[11] This knowled,
is not necessarily explicit or clear, since if it were there cou
be no atheists, but it is implicit and vague. If it is object
that an implicit and vague knowledge of this kind is n
knowledge at all, it may be answered that an unprejudic
man who reflects on the orientation of his will towards ha
piness can come to realise that the direction of his will i

plies the existence of an adequate object and that this object, the complete Good, must exist and is what we call God. He will realise not only that in seeking happiness he is seeking God, but that this search implies an inkling, as it were, of God, since there can be no search for what is *entirely* unknown. Therefore, by reflecting on itself, on its own dependence and on its own desires for wisdom, peace or felicity, the soul can recognise God's existence and even God's presence, God's activity within it: it is not necessary for it to seek without, it has only to follow Augustine's advice and enter within itself, when it will see that it was never without some inkling, some dim awareness, a 'virtual' knowledge of God. To seek for happiness (and every human being must seek for happiness) and to deny God's existence is really to be guilty of a contradiction, to deny with the lips what one affirms with the will and, in the case of wisdom at least, with the intellect. Whether this line of argument is valid or not, I do not propose to discuss here. It is obviously open to the objection, cogent or otherwise, that if there were no God, then the desire for happiness might be *frustra* or might have some other cause than the existence of God. But it is at least clear that St. Bonaventure did not postulate an innate idea of God in the crude form under which Locke later attacked innate ideas. Again, when St. Bonaventure declares that the soul knows God as most present to it, he is not affirming ontologism or saying that the soul sees God immediately: he means that the soul, recognising its dependence, recognises, if it reflects, that it is the image of God: it sees God in His image. As it necessarily knows itself, is conscious of itself, it necessarily knows God in at least an implicit manner. By contemplating itself it can make this implicit awareness explicit, without reference to the external world. Whether the absence of reference to the external world is more than formal, in the sense that the external world is not explicitly mentioned, is perhaps disputable.

4. We have seen that for St. Bonaventure the very arguments from the external world presuppose some awareness of God, for he asks how the mind can know that sensible things are defective and imperfect if it has no previous awareness of perfection, in comparison with which it recognises the imperfections of creatures. This point of view must be borne in mind when considering his statement of St. Anselm's proof, which he adopted from the *Proslogium*.

In the Commentary on the *Sentences*[12] St. Bonaventure resumes the Anselmian argument. God is that than which no greater can be thought. But that which cannot be thought not to exist is greater than that which can be thought not to exist. Therefore, since God is that than which no greater can be thought, God cannot be thought not to exist. In the *De Mysterio Trinitatis*[13] he quotes and states the argument at somewhat greater length and points out[14] that doubt may arise if someone has an erroneous notion of God and does not realise that He is that than which no greater can be thought. Once the mind realises what the idea of God is, then it must also realise not only that the existence of God cannot be doubted, but also that His non-existence cannot even be thought. As regards Gaunilo's objection about the best of all possible islands St. Bonaventure answers[15] that there is no parity, for while there is no contradiction involved in the concept of a Being than which no greater can be thought the idea of an island than which no better can be thought is a contradiction in terms (*oppositio in adiecto*), since 'island' denotes an imperfect being whereas 'than which no better can be thought' denotes a perfect being.

This method of argument may appear to be purely dialectical, but, as already mentioned, Bonaventure did not regard the idea of the perfect as obtained simply through a negation of the imperfection of creatures, but as something presupposed by our recognition of the imperfection of creatures, at least in the sense that man's desire of the perfect implies a previous awareness. In accordance with the Platonic-Augustinian tradition Bonaventure presupposed, then, a virtual innate idea of the perfect, which can be nothing else but God's imprint on the soul, not in the sense that the soul is perfect but in the sense that the soul receives the idea of the perfect or forms the idea of the perfect in the light of God through the divine illumination. The idea is not something negative, the realisation of which in concrete existence can be denied, for the presence of the idea itself necessarily implies God's existence. On this point we may note the resemblance at least between St. Bonaventure's doctrine and that of Descartes.[16]

5. St. Augustine's favourite argument for the existence of God had been that from truth and the existence of eternal truths: St. Bonaventure utilised this argument as well. For example, every affirmative proposition affirms something

true; but the affirmation of any truth affirms also the cause of all truth.[17] Even if someone says that a man is an ass, this statement, whether correct or not, affirms the existence of the primal truth, and even if a man declares that there is no truth, he affirms this negation as true and so implies the existence of the foundation and cause of truth.[18] No truth can be seen save through the first truth, and the truth through which every other truth is seen, is an indubitable truth: therefore, since the first Truth is God, God's existence is indubitable.[19]

But here again St. Bonaventure is not pursuing a merely verbal and dialectical argument. In a passage of the *In Hexaëmeron*,[20] where he points out that the man who says there is no truth contradicts himself, since he affirms it as true that there is no truth, he remarks that the light of the soul is truth, which so enlightens the soul that it cannot deny truth's existence without contradicting itself, and in the *Itinerarium mentis in Deum*[21] he maintains that the mind can apprehend eternal truths and draw certain and necessary conclusions only in the divine light. The intellect can apprehend no truth with certainty save under the guidance of Truth itself. To deny God's existence, then, is not simply to be guilty of a dialectical contradiction; it is also to deny the existence of the Source of that light which is necessary for the mind's attainment of certitude, the light *quae illuminat omnem hominem venientem in hunc mundum*: it is to deny the Source in the name of that which proceeds from the Source.

Chapter Twenty-seven

ST. BONAVENTURE—III:
RELATION OF CREATURES TO GOD

Exemplarism—The divine knowledge—Impossibility of creation from eternity—Errors which follow from denial of exemplarism and creation—Likeness of creatures to God, analogy—Is this world the best possible world?

1. We have seen that the lines of proof adopted by St. Bonaventure lead, not to the transcendent and self-enclosed unmoved Mover of Aristotle (though he does not hesitate to
utilise the Philosopher's thought and to cite him when he considers it apposite), but to the God, at once transcendent and
immanent, who is the Good which draws the will, the Truth
which is not only foundation of all particular truths but also
the Light which through its radiation within the soul makes
the apprehension of certain truth possible, the Original
which is mirrored in the human soul and in nature, and the
Perfect which is responsible for the idea of the perfect within
the human soul. In this way the arguments for God's existence stand in close relation to the spiritual life of the soul,
revealing to it the God whom it has always sought, if only in
a semi-conscious fashion, and the God who has always operated within it. The further knowledge of God which is given
by revelation crowns the philosophic knowledge and opens
up to the soul higher levels of spiritual life and the possibility
of a closer union with God. Philosophy and theology are thus
integrated together, the former leading on to the latter, the
latter shedding light on the deeper meaning of the former.
    A similar integration of philosophy and theology is seen in
Bonaventure's doctrine of exemplarism, which in his eyes was

a matter of the greatest importance. In the *In Hexaëmeron*[1] he makes exemplarism the central point of metaphysics. The metaphysician, he says, proceeds from the consideration of created, particular substance to the uncreated and universal substance (not in the pantheistic sense, of course), and so, in so far as he deals in general with the originating Principle of all things, he is akin to the natural philosopher who also considers the origins of things, while in so far as he considers God as final end he shares his subject-matter to some degree with the moral philosopher, who also considers the supreme Good as the last end, giving his attention to happiness in the practical or speculative order. But in so far as the metaphysician considers God, the supreme Being, as exemplary cause of all things, he shares his subject-matter with no one else (*cum nullo communicat et verus est metaphysicus*). The metaphysician, however, if he will attain the truth concerning exemplarism, cannot stop at the mere fact that God is the exemplary Cause of all things, for the *medium* of creation, the express image of the Father and the exemplar of all creatures, is the divine Word. Precisely as a philosopher he cannot come to a certain knowledge of the Word, it is true;[2] but then if he is content to be a mere philosopher, he will fall into error: he must, enlightened by faith, proceed beyond mere philosophy and realise that the divine Word is the exemplary Cause of all things. The purely philosophic doctrine of exemplarism thus prepares the way for the theology of the Word and, conversely, the theology of the Word sheds light on the truth attained by philosophy, and in this sense Christ is the *medium* not only of theology, but also of philosophy.

An obvious conclusion in regard to Aristotle follows from this position. Plato had maintained a doctrine of archetypal ideas or essences and, whatever Plato himself may or may not have thought, the neo-Platonists at least 'located' these ideas in the divine mind, so that St. Augustine was enabled to praise Plato and Plotinus on this account; but Aristotle rejected the ideas of Plato and attacked his theory with bitterness (*in principio Metaphysicae et in fine et in multis aliis locis exsecratur ideas Platonis*).[3] In the *Ethics* too he attacks the doctrine, though the reasons he gives are worthless (*nihil valent rationes suae*).[4] Why did he attack Plato? Because he was simply a natural philosopher, interested in the things of the world for their own sake, and gifted with the *sermo scientiae* but not with the *sermo sapientiae*. In refusing to despise the sensible world and in refusing to restrict certainty to knowledge of the transcendent Aristotle was right as against Plato, who, in his enthusiasm for the *via sapientiae*, destroyed the *via scientiae*, and he rightly censured Plato on this point, but he himself went to the opposite extreme and destroyed the *sermo sapientiae*.[5] Indeed, by denying the doctrine of exemplarism, Aristotle necessarily involved himself also in a denial of divine creation and divine providence, so that his error was worse than that of Plato. Now, exemplarism, on which Plato insisted, is, as we have seen, the key to and centre of metaphysics, so that Aristotle, by rejecting exemplarism, excluded himself from the rank of metaphysicians, in Bonaventure's understanding of the term.

But we have to go beyond Plato and learn from Augustine, to whom was given both the *sermo sapientiae* and the *sermo scientiae*,[6] for Augustine knew that the ideas are contained in the divine Word, that the Word is the archetype of creation. The Father knows Himself perfectly and this act of knowledge is the image and expression of Himself: it is His Word, His *similitudo expressiva*.[7] As proceeding from the Father the Word is divine, the divine Son (*filius* denotes the *similitudo hypostatica*, the *similitudo connaturalis*),[8] and as representing the Father, as *Imago*, as *similitudo expressa*, the Word expresses also, represents, all that the Father can effect (*quidquid Pater potest*).[9] If anyone could know the Word, he would know all knowable objects (*si igitur intelligis Verbum, intelligis omnia scibilia*).[10] In the Son or Word the Father expressed all that He could make (i.e. all possible beings are ideally or archetypally represented in the Word) and all that He would make.[11] The 'ideas' of all creatures, therefore, possible and actual, are contained in the Word, and these ideas extend not only to universals (*genera* and *species*), but also to singular or individual things.[12] They are infinite in number, as representing all possibles, as representing the infinite power of God.[13] But when it is said that there is an infinity of ideas in the Word, it is not meant that the ideas are really distinct in God, for there is no distinction in God save the distinctions of Persons: considered as existent in God, they are not distinct from the divine Essence or from one another (*ideae sunt unum secundum rem*).[14] It follows that, not being distinct from one another, they cannot form a real hierarchy.[15] However, although the ideas are ontologically one and there is no real distinction between them, there is a distinction of reason, so that they are *plures secundum rationem intelligendi*.[16] The foundation of the distinction cannot be any real distinction in the divine Essence, since not only are the ideas ontologically identical with the simple divine Essence, but also there is no real relation on the part of God to creatures, for He is in no way dependent on creatures, though there is a real relation on the part of creatures to God and God and creatures are not the same, so that from the point of view of the things signified or connoted the ideas are distinct *secundum rationem intelligendi*. In God the ideas are one, but from our point of view they stand midway, as it were, between God the knower and the thing known, the distinction between them being, not a distinction in what they are (i.e. not a real distinction) but a distinction in what they connote, and the foundation of the distinction being the real multiplicity of the things connoted (i.e. creatures), not any real distinction in the divine Essence or in the divine knowledge.

Plato was working towards this theory of ideas, but as he lacked the light of faith, he could not ascend to the true doctrine but necessarily stopped short: in order to possess the true doctrine of ideas, it is necessary to have knowledge of the Word. Moreover, just as creatures were produced through the medium of the Word and could not have been produced save through the Word, so they cannot be truly known save in the light of their relation to the Word. Aristotle may have been, indeed was, an eminent natural philosopher, but he could not know truly even the selected objects of his studies, since he did not see them in their relation to the Word, as reflections of the divine Image.

2. God, then, in knowing Himself knows also all ways in which His divine essence can be mirrored externally. He knows all the finite good things which will be realised in time, and this knowledge Bonaventure calls the *cognitio approbationis*, the knowledge of those things to which His *beneplacitum voluntatis* extends. He knows too, not only all the good things which have been, are and will be in the course of time, but also all the evil things, and this knowledge Bonaventure calls the *cognitio visionis*. Needless to say St. Bonaventure does not mean to imply that evil has its exemplary idea in God: evil is rather the privation in the creature of that which it ought to have according to its idea in God. God knows too all possible things, and this knowledge Bonaven-

ture terms *cognitio intelligentiae*. Its objects, the possibles, are infinite in number, whereas the objects of the two former types of knowledge are finite.[17] The three types of knowledge are, however, not accidents in God, distinct from one another: considered ontologically, as in God, they are one act of knowledge, identical with the divine essence.

God's act of knowledge is infinite and eternal, so that all things are present to Him, even future events: there is no succession in the divine knowledge, and if we speak of God's 'foreknowledge' we must understand the futurity as concerning the objects themselves (in the sense that they succeed one another in time and are known by God to succeed one another in time), not as concerning the divine knowledge itself. God knows all things by one eternal act and there is no temporal succession in that act, no before and after; but God knows eternally, through that one act, things as succeeding one another in time. Bonaventure therefore makes a distinction in regard to the statement that God knows all things *praesenter*, pointing out that this *praesentialitas* must be understood in reference to God (*a parte cognoscentis*), not in reference to the objects known (*a parte cognitorum*). If it were understood in the latter sense, the implication would be that all things are present to one another, which is false, for they are not all present to one another, though they are all present to God.[18] Imagine, he says,[19] an eye fixed and motionless on a wall and observing the successive movements of all persons and things down below with a single act of vision. The eye is not changed, nor its act of vision, but the things under the wall are changed. This illustration, remarks Bonaventure, is really in no way like what it illustrates, for the divine knowledge cannot be pictured in this way; but it may help towards an understanding of what is meant.

3. If there were no divine ideas, if God had no knowledge of Himself and of what He can effect and will effect, there could be no creation, since creation demands knowledge on the Creator's part, knowledge and will. It is not a matter for surprise, then, that Aristotle, who rejected the ideas, rejected also creation and taught the eternity of the world, a world uncreated by God. At least he is judged to have held this by all the Greek Doctors, like Gregory of Nyssa, Gregory Nazianzen, Damascene and Basil, and by all the Arabian commentators, while you will never find Aristotle himself saying that the world had a beginning: indeed he censures

Plato, the only Greek philosopher who seems to have declared that time had a beginning.[20] St. Bonaventure need not have spoken so cautiously, since Aristotle certainly did not believe in a divine creation of the world out of nothing.

St. Thomas saw no incompatibility, from the philosophical standpoint, between the idea of creation on the one hand and of the world's eternity on the other, so that for him the world might have had no beginning in time and yet have been created, that is, God might have created the world from eternity; but St. Bonaventure considered that the eternity of the world is impossible and that God could not have created it from eternity: if it is created, then time necessarily had a beginning. It follows that to deny that time had a beginning is to deny that the world was created, and to prove that eternal motion or time without a beginning is impossible is to prove that the world was created. St. Bonaventure, therefore, regarded the Aristotelian idea of the world's eternity as *necessarily* bound up with a denial of creation, and this opinion, which Aquinas did not share, sharpened his opposition to Aristotle. Both Bonaventure and Aquinas naturally accepted the *fact* of the world having had a beginning in time, since this is taught by theology; but they differed on the question of the abstract possibility of creation from eternity, and Bonaventure's conviction of its impossibility naturally made him resolutely hostile to Aristotle, since the latter's assertion of it as a fact, and not merely as a possibility, necessarily seemed to him an assertion of the independence of the world in relation to God, an assertion which he thought was primarily due to the Philosopher's rejection of exemplarism.

For what reasons did Bonaventure hold eternal motion or time without a beginning to be impossible? His arguments are more or less those which St. Thomas treats as objections to his own position. I give some examples.

(i) If the world had existed from eternity, it would follow that it is possible to add to the infinite. For instance, there would have been already an infinite number of solar revolutions, yet every day another revolution is added. But it is impossible to add to the infinite. Therefore the world cannot have always existed.[21]

St. Thomas answers[22] that if time is supposed eternal, it is infinite *ex parte ante*, but not *ex parte post*, and there is no cogent objection to an addition being made to the infinity at the end at which it is finite, that is, terminates in the present. To this St. Bonaventure retorts that, if one considers simply the past, then one would have to admit an infinite number of lunar revolutions. But there are twelve lunar revolutions to one solar revolution. Therefore we are faced with two infinite numbers, of which the one is twelve times greater than the other, and this is an impossibility.

(ii) It is impossible to pass through an infinite series, so that if time were eternal, that is, had no beginning, the world would never have arrived at the present day. But it is clear that it has.[23] To this St. Thomas answers[24] that every passing through or *transitus* requires a beginning term and a final term. But if time is of infinite duration, there was no first term and consequently no *transitus*, so that the objection cannot arise. St. Bonaventure retorts, however, that there is either a revolution of the sun which is infinitely distant, in the past, from to-day's revolution or there is not. If there is not, then the distance is finite and the series must have had a beginning. If there is, then what of the revolution immediately following that which is infinitely distant from to-day's? Is this revolution also infinitely distant from to-day's or not? If not, then the hypothetically infinitely distant revolution cannot be infinitely distant either, since the interval between the 'first' and second revolution is finite. If it is, then what of the third and fourth revolutions, and so on? Are they also infinitely distant from to-day's revolution? If they are, then to-day's revolution is no less distant from them than from the first. In this case there is no succession and they are all synchronous, which is absurd.

(iii) It is impossible for there to be in existence at the same time an infinity of concrete objects. But, if the world existed from eternity, there would be in existence now an infinity of rational souls. Therefore the world cannot have existed from eternity.[25]

To this Aquinas answers[26] that some say that human souls do not exist after the death of the body, while others maintain that only a (common) intellect remains: others again hold a doctrine of reincarnation, while certain writers maintain that an infinite number in act is possible in the case of things which are not ordered (*in his quae ordinem non habent*). St. Thomas naturally held none of the first three positions himself; as to the fourth position his own final attitude seems to be doubtful, so that Bonaventure was able to remark rather caustically that the theory of reincarnation is an error in philosophy and is contrary to the psychology of Aristotle, while the doctrine that a common intellect alone survives is an even worse error. As to the possibility of an infinite number in act he believed that it was an erroneous notion, on the ground that an infinite multitude could not be ordered and so could not be subject to divine providence, whereas in fact all that God has created is subject to His providence.

Bonaventure was thus convinced that it can be philosophically proved, as against Aristotle, that the world had a beginning and that the idea of creation from eternity involves a 'manifest contradiction', since, if the world was created from nothing, it has being after not-being (*esse post non-esse*)[27] and so cannot possibly have existed from eternity. St. Thomas answers that those who assert creation from eternity do not say that the world was made *post nihilum*, but that it was made out of nothing, the opposite of which is 'out of something'. The idea of time, that is to say, is in no way implicated. In Bonaventure's eyes it is bad enough to say that the world is eternal and is uncreated (that is an error which can be philosophically disproved), but to say that it was created eternally out of nothing is to be guilty of a glaring contradiction, 'so contrary to reason that I should not have believed that any philosopher, of however little understanding, could have asserted it'.[28]

4. If the doctrine of exemplarism is denied, and if God did not create the world, it is only natural to conclude that God knows only Himself, that He moves only as final Cause, as object of desire and love (*ut desideratum et amatum*) and that He knows no particular thing outside Himself.[29] In this case God can exercise no providence, not having in Himself the *rationes rerum*, the ideas of things, by which He may know them.[30] The doctrine of St. Bonaventure is, of course, that God knows things other than Himself, but that He knows them in and through Himself, through the exemplary ideas. If he did not hold this, he would have to say that the divine knowledge receives a complement or perfection from things outside of God, depends in some way on creatures. In reality it is God who is completely independent: creatures are dependent on Him and cannot confer on His Being any perfection.[31] But if God is wrapped up in Himself, in the sense of having no knowledge of creatures and exercising no providence, it follows that the changes or movements of

the world proceed either from chance, which is impossible, or from necessity, as the Arabian philosophers held, the heavenly bodies determining the movements of things in this world. But if this be so, then all doctrine of reward or punishment in this life disappears, and in point of fact you will never find Aristotle speaking of a beatitude after the present life.[32] All these erroneous conclusions follow, then, from a denial of exemplarism, and it is more than ever clear that exemplarism is the key to a true metaphysic and that without it a philosopher will inevitably fall into errors if he discusses metaphysical themes.

5. From the doctrine of exemplarism it follows that there is some resemblance between creatures and God; but we have to distinguish various kinds of resemblance (*similitudo*) in order to attain to a correct idea of the relation of creatures to God, in order to avoid pantheism on the one hand and an independent world on the other hand. In the Commentary on the *Sentences*[33] Bonaventure says that *similitudo* may mean the agreement of two things in a third (and this he calls *similitudo secundum univocationem*), or it may mean the likeness of one thing to another without any agreement in a third thing being implied, and it is in this sense that the creature is said to be a likeness of God. In the same *conclusio* (*ad* 2) he distinguishes *similitudo univocationis sive participationis* and *similitudo imitationis, et expressionis*, going on to remark that the former does not hold good of the relation between creatures and God, because there is no common term (*quia nihil est commune*, because there is nothing common to God and the creature, that is). What he means is that God and the creature do not participate in Being, for example, *univocally* (precisely in the same sense), for if they did, the creature would be God and pantheism would result. The creature is, however, an imitation of God, of the idea of it in God, and God expresses the idea externally in the finite creature. Therefore, when Bonaventure rejects *similitudo participationis*, we must understand participation as referring here to participation in something common to both God and creatures in a univocal sense, in a *tertium commune* as he puts it.

It may be objected that if there is nothing common between God and creatures, there can be no likeness; but the community which St. Bonaventure wishes to exclude is *univocal* community, to which he opposes *analogy*. The likeness of the creature to God or of God to the creature (*exemplaris ad exemplatum*) is one kind of analogy, the other being that of *proportionalitas* (*habitudo duorum ad duo*), which exists between sets of things belonging to different genera, though in the case of the relation between creatures and God it is only the creature which is a member of a generic class. Thus a teacher is to his school what a pilot is to his ship, since both direct.[34] In the latter place Bonaventure distinguishes proportion in a wide sense, which includes proportionality, from proportion in a strict sense, which exists between members of the same class, arithmetical numbers, for example. Proportion in this strict sense cannot, of course, exist between God and creatures.

But though Bonaventure speaks of analogy of proportionality, the analogies to which he gives most attention are those of likeness, for he loved ever to find expressions, manifestations, images and *vestigia* of God in the world of creatures. Thus in the Commentary on the *Sentences*,[35] after excluding *similitudo per convenientiam omnimodam in natura*, which holds good between the three divine Persons, each of whom is identical with the divine Nature, and *similitudo per participationem alicuius naturae universalis*, which holds good between man and ass, in virtue of their common sharing in the *genus* animal, he admits proportionality, *similitudo secundum proportionalitatem* (giving here the example of the pilot and the charioteer in relation to the objects they direct) and *similitudo per convenientiam ordinis* (*sicut exemplatum assimilatur exemplari*), and proceeds to discuss these latter types of analogy, both of which, as already mentioned, hold good between the creature and God.

Every creature, says Bonaventure, is a *vestigium* of God, and the two types of analogy (that of the *exemplatum* to the *exemplar* and that of proportionality) apply to every creature, the first inasmuch as every creature is the effect of God and is conformed to God through the divine idea, the second inasmuch as the creature also produces an effect, although not in the same way as God produces His effect (*sicut enim Deus producit suum effectum, sic et agens creatum, licet non omnino*—for the creature is not the total cause of its effect). But though every creature is a *vestigium Dei*, this general conformity of the creature to God is comparatively remote (*magis de longinquo*): there is another type of likeness which is closer (*de proximo*) and more express and which applies only to certain creatures. All creatures are ordered to God, but only rational creatures are directed immediately (*immediate*) to God, the irrational creatures being directed to God mediately (*mediante creatura rationali*). The rational creature alone can know God, can praise God and serve God consciously, and so has a greater conformity to God, a greater *convenientia ordinis* than the irrational creature. Now, the greater the *convenientia ordinis*, the greater and closer and more express is the resemblance or *similitudo*. This closer resemblance is called by Bonaventure *imago*. Every creature is, then, a *vestigium Dei*, but only the rational creature is an *imago Dei*, for it resembles God in the possession of spiritual powers through which it can become ever more and more conformed to God.

A similar difference between the rational creature and the irrational creature can be observed if we consider the analogy of proportionality. We can say, if we make the due allowances and reservations, that as God is to the creature, as Cause, that is, to His effect, so is the creature to its effect, and this holds good of all creatures in so far as they are active agents: but the effect considered is *extrinsic* to the agent, whereas in the case of rational creatures, and of them alone, there is an *intrinsic* proportion. In God there is a unity of Nature in a Trinity of Persons, and in man there is a unity of essence with a trinity of powers which are ordered to one another, the relation between them resembling in some way the relations in God (*quasi consimili modo se habentium, sicut se habent personae in divinis*). Bonaventure does not mean that we can prove the doctrine of the Trinity by the natural light of reason from a consideration of human nature, for he denies the possibility of any strict philosophical proof of the mystery, but rather that, guided by the light of faith, we can find an analogy to the Trinity in human rational nature. As the divine Nature is to the three divine Persons, so (*quasi consimili modo*) is the human nature or essence to its three powers. This is an 'express' resemblance of proportion and on this count, too, man is to be called the image of God. The word 'express' means that the Blessed Trinity has expressed itself, manifested itself to some degree in the constitution of human nature, and it is clear that for Bonaventure the analogy of resemblance (i.e. *exemplati ad exemplar*) is more fundamental than the analogy of proportionality, the latter being really treated in function of the former and having no concrete value or meaning apart from it.

In this way Bonaventure is enabled to order the hierarchy of being according to the closeness or remoteness of the likeness of the creature to God. The world of purely sensible things is the *vestigium* or *umbra Dei*, though here too he finds analogies of the Trinity; it is the *liber scriptus forinsecus*. When considered by the natural philosopher who is nothing else but a natural philosopher it is simply *natura*: such a man cannot read the book of nature, which is to him no *vestigium Dei* but something considered for its own sake and without reference to God.[36] The rational creation stands above the purely sensible creation and is *imago Dei*, God's image in a special sense. But the phrase 'image of God' is itself of wide application, for it covers not only the natural substance of men and angels, but also that supernatural likeness which is the result of the possession of grace. The soul in grace is the image of God in a higher sense than is the purely natural essence of man, and the soul in heaven, enjoying the beatific vision, is God's image in a yet deeper sense. Thus there are many grades of analogy, of likeness to God, and every grade must be seen in the light of the Word, who is the consubstantial image of the Father and the Exemplar of all creation, reflected in creatures according to various degrees of 'expression'. We may note not only the constant integration of theology and philosophy, but also the fact that the various degrees of likeness stand in close relation to the intellectual and spiritual life of man. The ascent to God on the part of the individual involves a turning from the *umbra* or pure *vestigium*, contemplated by the senses, from the *liber scriptus forinsecus*, to the interior reflection of God, the *imago Dei*, the *liber scriptus intrinsecus*, in obedience to the command of Augustine to go within oneself, and so ultimately to the contemplation of God in Himself, the *exemplatum*. The fact that St. Bonaventure does not treat theology and philosophy in watertight compartments of their own enables him to link up his vision of the universe with the ascetical and mystical life and so to deserve the name of a specifically Christian thinker.

6. Is this world, which reflects so admirably the Divine Creator, the best of all possible worlds? We must first of all distinguish two questions. Could God make a better world than this world? Could God have made this world better

than it is? Bonaventure answers to the first question that God could have made a better world than this one, by creating nobler essences, and that this cannot be denied without thereby limiting the divine power. As to the second question, it all depends on what you mean by 'world' and by 'better'. If you refer to the substances which go to make up the world, are you asking if God could make these substances better in the sense of making them nobler essences or substances, that is, of a higher kind, or are you asking if God could make these substances accidentally better, that is, while remaining within their own class? If the former, then the answer is that God could indeed change the substances into nobler ones, but it would not be the same world and God would not be making *this* world better. If the latter, then God could make this world better. To take an example. If God changed a man into an angel, the man would no longer be a man and God would not be making the man better; but God could make a man better by increasing his intellectual power or his moral qualities.[37] Again, while God could make *this* man or *this* horse a better man or horse, we must make another distinction if it is asked whether or not God could make man as such better, in the sense of placing him in better conditions. Absolutely speaking He could; but if one takes into consideration the purpose for which He has placed man in these conditions or allowed him to be in these conditions it may very well be that He could not make man better. For instance, if God brought it about that all men served Him well, He would be making man better, from the abstract viewpoint; but if you consider the purpose for which God has permitted man to serve Him well or ill, He would not be making man better by practically overriding his free will. Finally, if anyone asks why, if God could have made or could make the world better, He has not done so or does not do so, no answer can be given save this, that He so willed and that He Himself knows the reason (*solutio non potest dari nisi haec, quia voluit, et rationem ipse novit*).[38]

Chapter Twenty-eight

ST. BONAVENTURE—IV:
THE MATERIAL CREATION

Hylomorphic composition in all creatures—Individuation—
Light—Plurality of forms—Rationes seminales.

1. St. Bonaventure accepted from his master, Alexander of
Hales, the doctrine of the hylomorphic composition of all
creatures, the doctrine, that is, that all creatures are composed of matter and form. By 'matter' he naturally meant in
this connection the principle of potentiality in the widest
sense, not 'matter' in the sense in which matter is opposed
to spirit. 'Matter *considered in itself* is neither spiritual nor
corporeal', and so in itself it is indifferent to the reception
either of a spiritual or of a corporeal form; but as matter
never exists on its own, apart from a definite form, and as,
once united with a corporeal or a spiritual form, it always
remains corporeal or spiritual as the case may be, it follows
that the matter actually present in a corporeal substance is
different in kind from that in a spiritual substance.[1] 'Matter'
may be regarded in more than one way. If one considers it
from the point of view of 'privation' (*per privationem*), abstracting from all forms, whether substantial or accidental,
one must admit that it is essentially the same in all creatures,
'for if either kind of matter is separated from all forms and
all accidents, no difference at all will be seen.' But if matter
is looked at 'analogically' (*secundum analogiam*), that is, as
potentiality, as a foundation for form, one must make a distinction. In so far as matter is looked on as providing a foundation for form in regard simply to being (*in ratione entis*),
it is essentially the same in both spiritual and material crea-

tures, since both spiritual and material creatures exist and subsist, and one can consider their existence by itself, without going on to consider the precise way in which they exist or the kind of things they are. This is the way in which the metaphysician considers matter, and so in the eyes of the metaphysician matter is similar in the spiritual and in the material creation. If, however, matter is simply looked on in its relation to motion in the wide sense, understood, that is, as change, then it is not the same in creatures which cannot undergo substantial change or receive corporeal forms and in creatures which can undergo substantial change and receive corporeal forms, though it can be considered as *analogically* similar, inasmuch as angels are susceptible of, for example, divine influence. It is the natural philosopher or *physicus* who considers matter in this light.

Without going into the further distinctions made by Bonaventure and without attempting a judgement on his doctrine, one can say, then, that his teaching on the hylomorphic composition of all creatures is this, that matter is the principle of potentiality as such. Both spiritual creatures and material creatures are dependent beings, not self-existent beings, so that if one considers potentiality in abstraction from all form, looking on it as a co-principle of being, one can say with the metaphysician that it is essentially the same in both. If, however, one considers it as actually existent, as standing in relation to a concrete form, spiritual or material, it is not the same in both. The natural philosopher considers bodies and is concerned with matter, not its abstract essence but as existent in a particular type of being, as standing in a concrete relation to a certain kind of form, material form; and matter considered in this light is not to be found in spiritual beings. One might, of course, object that if matter as concretely existing, as united with form, is of different kinds and remains different, there must be something in the matter itself which makes it of different kinds so that its similarity in the spiritual and material created orders cannot be more than analogical; but Bonaventure admits that matter never actually exists apart from form and only states that if it is considered, as it can be considered, in abstraction from all form, as mere potentiality, then it can justly be said to be essentially the same. If the angels have an element of possibility, of potency in them, as they have, they must possess matter, for matter, considered in itself, is simply possibility or potency. It is only in the Being who is pure Act, without any potency or possibility, that there is no matter.

2. Is matter the principle of individuation? Some thinkers, says St. Bonaventure,[2] have held this, relying on the words of Aristotle, but it is very difficult to see how that which is common to all can be the principal cause of distinction, of individuality. On the other hand, to say that form is the principle of individuation and to postulate an individual form, following on that of the species, is to go to the opposite extreme and forget that every created form is capable of having another like it. It is better to hold that individuation arises from the actual union of matter and form, which appropriate one another, as it were, through their union. Seals are made by different impressions in wax, and without the wax there would be no plurality of seals, but without the different impressions the wax would not become many. Similarly, matter is necessary if there is to be distinction and multiplicity, number, but form is also necessary, for distinction and multiplication presuppose the constitution of a substance through the elements composing it. That an individual substance is something definite, of a definite kind, it owes to the form; that it is *this* something, it owes principally to matter, by which the form acquires position in place and time. Individuation denotes principally something substantial, a substance composed of matter and form, but it also denotes something which can be considered an accident, namely number. Individuality (*discretio individualis*) denotes two things: individuation, which arises from the union of the two principles, matter and form, and secondly distinction from other things, which is the origin of number; but the former, individuation, is the more fundamental.

Personality (*discretio personalis*) arises when the form united with matter is a rational form, and it thus adds to individuality the dignity of rational nature, which holds the highest place among created natures and is not in potency to a higher substantial form. But there is something more needed to constitute personality, namely that within the *suppositum* there should be no other nature of a greater eminence and dignity, that within the *suppositum* rational nature should possess *actualem eminentiam*. (In Christ the human nature, though perfect and complete, does not possess *actualem eminentiam* and so is not a person.) 'We must say, then, that just as individuality arises from the existence of a natural form in matter, so personality arises from the existence of a noble and supereminent nature in the substance.'[3]

As St. Bonaventure attributes matter, that is, a spiritual matter, to the angels, he is able to admit a plurality of individual angels within the same species without being compelled like St. Thomas to postulate as many angelic species as there are angels. The Scriptures show us some angels as exercising similar functions and this argues similarity of being, while the 'love of charity' also demands the multiplicity of angels within the same species.[4]

3. In the corporeal creation there is one substantial form which all bodies possess, and that is the form of light.[5] Light was created on the first day, three days before the production of the sun, and it is corporeal in Bonaventure's opinion, although St. Augustine interpreted it as meaning the angelic creation. It is not, properly speaking, a body but the form of a body, the first substantial form, common to all bodies and the principle of their activity, and the different kinds of body form a graded hierarchy according as they participate more or less in the form of light. Thus the 'empyrean' stands at one end of the scale, while the earth stands at the other, the lower end. In this way the light-theme, so dear to the Augustinian School and going back to Plotinus and to Plato's comparison of the Idea of the Good with the sun, finds a prominent place in the philosophy of St. Bonaventure.

4. Obviously if Bonaventure holds that light is a substantial form, possessed by all bodies, he must also hold that there can be a plurality of substantial forms in one substance. For him there was no difficulty in holding this, since he looked on form as that which prepares the body for the reception of other and higher perfections. While for St. Thomas substantial form was limitative and definitive, so that there could not be more than one substantial form in a body, for St. Bonaventure form looked forward and upward, so to speak, not so much rounding off the body and confining it as preparing it for fresh possibilities and perfections. In the In Hexaëmeron[6] he went so far as to say that it is mad (insanum) to say that the final form is added to prime matter without there being something which is a disposition for it or in potency to it, without there being any intermediate form, and he loved to trace a parallel between the order of grace and that of nature. Just as the gift of knowledge disposes for the gift

of wisdom and is not itself annulled by the gift of wisdom, and as the gifts do not annul the theological virtues, so one form predisposes for a higher form and the latter, when received, does not expel the former but crowns it.

5. It is only to be expected that St. Bonaventure, who avowedly walked in the path of the Augustinian tradition, would accept the doctrine of *rationes seminales*, especially as this doctrine lays emphasis on the work of the Creator and diminishes the independence of the natural agent, though it was no more a 'scientific' doctrine in the modern sense of the word with St. Bonaventure than it was with St. Augustine: for both men it was required by true Scriptural exegesis or rather by a philosophy which took account of the data of revelation, with the added reason in the case of Bonaventure that it was held by his great predecessor, the Christian philosopher *par excellence*, who was endowed with both the *sermo sapientiae* and the *sermo scientiae*. 'I believe that this position should be held, not only because reason inclines us to it, but also because the authority of Augustine, in his literal commentary on Genesis, confirms it.'[7]

Bonaventure thus maintained a certain *latitatio formarum* of things in matter; but he refused to accept the view that the forms of things which appear in time were originally in matter in an *actual* state, like a picture covered with a cloth, so that the particular agent only uncovers them, like the man who takes away the cloth from the picture and lets the painting appear. On this view contrary forms, which exclude one another, would have been together at the same time in the same subject, which is impossible. Nor will he accept the view that God is the only efficient cause in the eduction of forms, for this would mean that God creates all forms in the way in which He creates the rational human soul and that the secondary agent really does nothing at all, whereas it is clear that its activity really does contribute something to the effect. The second of these two views would reduce or do away altogether with the activity of the created agent, while the first would reduce it to a minimum, and Bonaventure is unwilling to accept either of them. He prefers the view 'which seems to have been that of Aristotle, and which is now commonly held by the doctors of philosophy and theology' that 'almost all the natural forms, corporeal forms at least, such as the forms of the elements and the forms of mixtures, are contained in the potency of matter and are reduced to act

(*educuntur in actum*) through the action of a particular
agent.' But this may be understood in two ways. It may mean
that matter has both the potency to receive the form and
the inclination to co-operate in the production of the form
and that the form to be produced is in the particular agent
as in its effective and original principle, so that the eduction
of the form takes place by the multiplication of the form of
the agent, as one burning candle may light a multitude of
candles, or it may mean that matter contains the form to be
educed not only as that in which and, to a certain extent, by
which the form is produced, but also as that from which it
is produced, though in the sense that it is concreated with
matter and in matter, not as an actual, but as a virtual form.
On the first hypothesis the forms are not indeed said to be
created by the agent, since they do not come out of nothing,
though all the same a new essence would seem to be produced
in some way, whereas on the second hypothesis no new essence or quiddity is produced, but the form which existed in
potency, virtually, is reduced to act, is given a new *dispositio*.
The second hypothesis, therefore, attributes less to the
created agent than does the first, since the created agent simply brings it about that what formerly existed in one way
now exists in another way, whereas on the first hypothesis
the created agent would produce something positively new,
even if not by way of creation out of nothing. If a gardener
tends the rose-tree so that the rose-buds can blossom into
roses he does something, it is true, but less than he would do,
were he to produce a rose-tree from some other form of tree.
Bonaventure, then, anxious to avoid attributing even the sem-
blance of creative powers to a created agent, chooses the hypothesis which attributes less to the work of the created agent
and more to the work of the Creator.

The forms which are educed were, therefore, originally in
matter in a virtual state. These virtual forms are the *rationes
seminales*. A *ratio seminalis* is an active power, existing in
matter, the active power being the essence of the form to be
educed, standing to the latter in the relation of *esse incom-
pletum* to *esse completum* or of *esse in potentia* to *esse in
actu*.[8] Matter is thus a *seminarium* or seed-bed in which God
created in a virtual state corporeal forms which would be suc-
cessively educed therefrom. This applies not only to the forms
of inorganic things, but also to the souls of brutes and vege-
tables. Needless to say, Bonaventure is aware that the activity

of particular agents is necessary for the birth of an animal, but he will not admit the traducianist theory, according to which the soul of a new animal is produced by 'multiplication' of the soul of the parent, yet without any diminution on the latter's part, as this theory implies that a created form can produce a similar form out of nothing.[9] What happens is that the parent animals act upon what they have themselves received, the seminal principle, the seminal principle being an active power or potency containing the new soul in germ, though the activity of the parents is necessary in order that the virtual should become actual. Bonaventure thus steers a middle course between attributing too little or nothing to the created agent and attributing what seemed to him too much, his general principle being that while God produces things out of nothing, a created agent can only produce something which already existed in potency, by which he means in a virtual state.[10] It is, however, useless to look for an exact description and explanation of the concrete working of his theory of *rationes seminales*, since it is founded partly on authority and partly on *a priori* philosophic reasoning, not on empirical observation or scientific experiment.

Chapter Twenty-nine

ST. BONAVENTURE—V:
THE HUMAN SOUL

Unity of human soul—Relation of soul to body—Immortality of the human soul—Falsity of Averroistic monopsychism —Knowledge of sensible objects and of first logical principle —Knowledge of spiritual realities—Illumination—The soul's ascent to God—Bonaventure as philosopher of the Christian life.

1. We have seen that, according to St. Bonaventure, the souls of animals are produced *seminaliter*; but this does not, of course, apply to the human soul, which is produced immediately by God, created by Him out of nothing. The human soul is the image of God, called to union with God, and on this count (*propter dignitatem*) its production was fittingly reserved by God to Himself. This reasoning involves theology, but Bonaventure also argues that since the human soul is immortal, incorruptible, its production can be effected only by that Principle which has life and perpetuity of itself. The immortality of the human soul implies a 'matter' in the soul which is incapable of being an element in substantial change; but the activity of created agents is confined to working on transmutable matter and the production of a substance with unchangeable matter transcends the power of such agents. It follows that the traducianist view must be rejected, even if Augustine inclined to it on occasion because he thought that thereby he could explain the transmission of original sin.[1]

What is it that God creates? It is the entire human soul, not the rational faculty alone. There is one soul in man, endowed with rational and sensitive faculties, and it is this soul which God creates. The body was contained *seminaliter* in the body of Adam, the first man, and it is transmitted by means of the seed, but this does not mean that the body has a sensitive soul, educed from the potency of matter and distinct from the created and infused rational soul. The seed contains, it is true, not only the superfluity of the father's nourishment, but also something of his *humiditas radicalis*, so that there is in the embryo, before the infusion of the soul, an active disposition towards the act of sensation, a kind of inchoate sensibility; but this disposition is a disposition to accomplishing the act of sensation through the power of the soul, once it has been infused: at the complete animation of the embryo by the infusion of the soul this inchoate sensibility ceases or rather it is subsumed under the activity of the soul, which is the principle of sensation as well as of intellection. In other words, St. Bonaventure is careful to maintain the continuity of life and the reality of parentage while avoiding any splitting of the human soul into two.[2]

2. The human soul is the form of the body: St. Bonaventure uses the Aristotelian doctrine against those who hold that the souls of all men are one substance. 'The rational soul is the act and entelechy of the human body: therefore since human bodies are distinct, the rational souls which perfect those bodies will also be distinct':[3] the soul is an existent, living, intelligent form, endowed with liberty.[4] It is present wholly in every part of the body, according to the judgement of St. Augustine, which Bonaventure approves as preferable to the theory that the soul is primarily present in a determinate part of the body, the heart for instance. 'Because it is the form of the whole body, it is present in the whole body; because it is simple, it is not present partly here and partly there; because it is the sufficient moving principle (*motor sufficiens*) of the body, it has no particular situation, is not present at one point or in a determinate part.'[5]

But though Bonaventure accepts the Aristotelian definition of the soul as the form of the body, his general tendency is Platonic and Augustinian in character, inasmuch as he insists that the human soul is a spiritual substance, composed of spiritual form and spiritual matter. It is not enough to say that there is in the soul composition of *ex quo est* and *quod est*, since the soul can act and be acted upon, move and be moved, and this argues the presence of 'matter', the principle of passivity and mutability, though this matter transcends extension and corruptibility, being spiritual and not corporeal matter.[6] This doctrine may seem to contradict the admitted simplicity of the human soul, but Bonaventure points out[7] that 'simplicity' has various meanings and degrees. Thus 'simplicity' may refer to absence of quantitative parts, and this the soul enjoys, being simple in comparison with corporeal things; or it may refer to absence of constitutive parts, and this the soul does not enjoy. The main point, however, is that the soul, though form of the body and moving principle of the body, is also much more than this, and can subsist by itself, being *hoc aliquid*, though as a *hoc aliquid* which is partly passive and mutable it must have in it spiritual matter. The doctrine of the hylomorphic composition of the human soul is thus calculated to ensure its dignity and its power of subsistence apart from the body.

If the soul is composed of form and spiritual matter, it follows that it is individuated by its own principles.[8] If this is so, however, why is it united with the body, for it is an individual spiritual substance in its own right? The answer is that the soul, even though a spiritual substance, is so constituted that it not only can inform a body but also has a natural inclination to do so. Conversely, the body, though also composed of matter and form, has an *appetitus* for being informed by the soul. The union of the two is thus for the perfection of each and is not to the detriment of either soul or body.[9] The soul does not exist simply, or even primarily, to move the body[10] but to enjoy God; yet it exercises its powers and potentialities fully only in informing the body and it will one day, at the resurrection, be reunited with the body. Aristotle was ignorant of this, and it is not to be wondered at that he was ignorant of it, for 'a philosopher necessarily falls into some error, unless he is aided by the light of faith'.[11]

3. The doctrine of the hylomorphic composition of the human soul naturally facilitates the proof of its immortality, since Bonaventure does not link the soul so closely to the body as does the Aristotelian doctrine; but his favourite proof is the one drawn from the consideration of the ultimate purpose of the soul (*ex consideratione finis*). The soul seeks for perfect happiness (a fact which no one doubts, 'unless his reason is entirely perverted'). But no one can be perfectly happy if he is afraid of losing what he possesses: on the contrary, it is this very fear which makes him miserable. Therefore, as the

soul has a natural desire for perfect happiness, it must be naturally immortal. This proof presupposes the existence of God, of course, and the possibility of attaining perfect happiness, as also the existence of a natural desire for human happiness; but it was Bonaventure's favourite proof because of its spiritual character, because of its connection with the movement of the soul towards God: it is for him the *ratio principalis*, the principle argument.[12]

In a rather similar way he argues[13] from consideration of the formal cause, from the nature of the soul as the image of God. Because the soul has been made for the attainment of happiness, which consists in the possession of the supreme Good, God, it must be capable of possessing God (*capax Dei*) and so must be made in His image and likeness. But it would not be made in the likeness of God if it were mortal. Therefore it must be immortal. Again (arguing *ex parte materiae*), Bonaventure declares that the form of the rational soul is of such dignity that it makes the soul like to God, with the result that the matter which is united to this form (i.e. the spiritual matter) finds its satisfaction and completion in union with this form alone, so that it must be likewise immortal.

Bonaventure gives other arguments, such as that from the necessity of sanctions in an after life[14] and from the impossibility of God's bringing the good to frustration. In the latter proof he argues that it would be against divine justice for that which has been well done to tend towards evil and frustration. Now, according to all moral teaching a man ought to die rather than commit injustice. But if the soul were mortal, then its adhesion to justice, lauded by all moral philosophers, would come to nothing, and this is contrary to divine justice. More Aristotelian in character are the arguments drawn from the soul's power of reflection on itself and from its intellectual activity, which has no intrinsic dependence on the body, to prove its superiority to corporeal matter and its incorruptibility.[15] But though these Aristotelian proofs are probably more acceptable to us, as presupposing less and as involving no theology, in Bonaventure's eyes it was the proofs borrowed from Augustine or dependent on his line of thought which were more telling, especially that from the desire of beatitude. The Augustinian proof from the soul's apprehension of and assimilation to abiding truth is given by Bonaventure,[16] but it does not appear as a *potissimus modus* of proving the soul's immortality. This qualification is reserved for the proofs drawn from the desire for beatitude.

If it were objected against Bonaventure that this form of proof presupposes the desire for union with God, for beatitude in the full sense, and that this desire is elicited only under the action of grace and so belongs to the supernatural order and not to the order of nature, which is the object of the philosopher's study, the Saint would doubtless answer that he had not the slightest intention of denying the work of grace or its supernatural character, but that, on the other hand, the true philosopher considers the world and human life as they are and that one of the data is precisely the desire for complete happiness. Even though the desire may imply the operation of grace, it is a datum of experience and so can be taken into account by the philosopher. If the philosopher cannot explain it without recourse to theology, that is only another proof of Bonaventure's principle that no philosophy can be satisfactory unless it is illumined by the light of faith. In other words, whereas the 'Thomist' systematically eliminates from the data of experience all he knows to be supernatural and then, as philosopher, considers the resulting 'nature', the Bonaventurian philosopher starts from nature in the sense of the given. It is perfectly true that grace is not something 'given' in the sense of visible or apprehensible with certainty by unaided reason, but some of its effects are given in experience and these the philosopher will take into account, though he cannot explain them without reference to theology. The Thomist approach and the Bonaventurian approach are therefore different and one cannot force them into the same mould without thereby distorting one or the other.

4. All that has been said on the human soul implies the individuality of the soul, but Bonaventure was quite aware of the Averroistic interpretation of Aristotle and argued explicitly against it. Averroes maintained that both the active and passive intellects survive death, and, whatever Aristotle himself may have taught, his commentator, Averroes, certainly held that these intellects are not individual to each man, are not parts or faculties of individual men, but rather unitary substances, cosmic intelligences. Such a position, however, is not only heretical and contrary to the Christian religion, but also against reason and experience.[17] It is against reason since it is clear that the intellectual soul is a perfection of man as man, and men differ from one another, are individual per-

sons, as men and not merely as animals, which would be the case if the rational soul were numerically one in all men. It is against experience, since it is a matter of experience that different men have different thoughts. And it is no good saying that this difference of thoughts comes simply from the diversity of *species* in the imaginations of different men, that is, that it is only the perishable imagination, fed by the senses, which is different in different individuals, since men differ in ideas, for example, of the virtues, which are not founded on sense-perception and which are not abstracted from imaginative *species*. Nor, from the point of view of Bonaventure, is it a good argument to say that the intellectual soul is independent of the body and cannot therefore be individuated by it, for the soul is not individuated by the body but by the union of its two constitutive principles, spiritual matter and spiritual form.

5. In regard to the content of the soul's knowledge of sensible objects, this is dependent on sense-perception, and St. Bonaventure agrees with Aristotle that the soul does not of itself have either knowledge or species of sensible objects: the human intellect is created in a state of 'nudity' and is dependent on the senses and imagination.[18] The sensible object acts upon the sense organ and produces therein a sensible species, which in turn acts upon the faculty of sensation, and then perception takes place. It will be noted that St. Bonaventure, in admitting a passive element in sensation, departs from the teaching of St. Augustine; but at the same time he holds that the faculty of sensation or sensitive power of the soul judges the content of sensation, for example, that this is white, the passive reception of the species being attributed primarily to the organ, the activity of the judgement to the faculty.[19] This judgement is not, of course, a reflective judgement, it is rather a spontaneous awareness; but it is possible because the faculty of sensation is the sensitive faculty of a rational soul, for it is the soul which communicates to the body the act of sensation.[20] The separate sensations, for example, of colour and touch, are unified by the 'common sense' and preserved in the imagination, which is not the same as 'memory' if the latter is taken as meaning *recordatio* or recalling at will.[21] Finally the active and passive intellects, working in co-operation, abstract the species from the imagination. The active and passive intellects are not two powers, one of which can work without the other, but are two 'differences'

of the same intellectual faculty of the soul. We can indeed say that the active intellect abstracts and the passive intellect receives, but Bonaventure qualifies this statement by affirming that the passive intellect has the power of abstracting the species and judging it, though *only* with the help of the active intellect, while the active intellect is dependent for its activity of knowing on the information of the passive intellect by the species. There is, in fact, only one complete act of intellection and the active and passive intellects co-operate inseparably in that act.[22]

Clearly, then, apart from various 'Augustinianisms', such as the refusal to make a real distinction between the faculties of the soul, Bonaventure's view of the way in which we acquire our knowledge of sensible objects approximates more or less closely to the Aristotelian theory. He admits that the soul, in regard to knowledge of such objects, is originally a *tabula rasa*,[23] and he has no place for innate ideas. Moreover, this rejection of innate ideas applies also to our knowledge of first principles. Some people have said that these principles are innate in the active intellect, though acquired as far as the possible intellect is concerned; but such a theory agrees neither with the words of Aristotle nor with the truth. For if these principles were innate in the active intellect, why could it not communicate them to the possible intellect without the help of the senses, and why does it not know these principles from the very beginning? A modified version of innatism is that the principles are innate in their most general form while the conclusions or particular applications are acquired, but it would be difficult on such a view to show why a child does not know the first principles in their general form. Moreover, even this modified innatism contradicts both Aristotle and Augustine. Bonaventure doubtless considered that a theory which united against it both Aristotle and Augustine could not possibly be true. It remains then to say that the principles are innate only in the sense that the intellect is endowed with a natural light which enables it to apprehend the principles in their universality when it has acquired knowledge of the relevant species or ideas. For example, no one knows what a whole is or a part until he has acquired the species or idea in dependence on sense-perception; but once he has acquired the idea, the light of the intellect enables him to apprehend the principle that the whole is greater than the part.[24] On this matter, therefore, St. Bonaventure is at one with St. Thomas.

6. But though we have no innate knowledge of sensible objects or of their essences or of the first principles, logical or mathematical, it does not follow that our knowledge of purely spiritual realities is acquired through sense-perception. 'God is not known by means of a likeness drawn from sense',[25] but rather by the soul's reflection on itself. It has no intuitive vision of God, of the divine Essence, in this life, but it is made in the image of God and is orientated towards God in desire and will, so that reflection on its own nature and on the direction of the will enables the soul to form the idea of God without recourse to the external sensible world. In this sense the idea of God is 'innate', though not in the sense that every man has from the beginning a clear, explicit and accurate knowledge of God. The direction of the will, its desire for complete happiness, is the effect of the divine action itself, and reflection on this desire manifests to the soul the existence of the Object of the desire, which indeed it already knows in a kind of vague awareness, though not necessarily in an explicit idea. 'The knowledge of this truth (God's existence) is innate in the rational mind, inasmuch as the mind is an image of God, by reason of which it has a natural appetite and knowledge and memory of Him in whose image it has been made and towards whom it naturally tends, that it may find its beatitude in Him.'[26] The knowledge of God is of various kinds: God has a comprehensive knowledge of Himself, the Blessed know Him clearly (*clare et perspicue*), we know Him partly and in a hidden way (*ex parte et in aenigmate*), this last knowledge being contained implicitly in or implied by the knowledge which each soul has that it did not always exist and must have had a beginning.[27]

The knowledge of the virtues too must be 'innate' in the sense that it is not derived from sense-perception. An unjust man can know what justice is; but obviously he cannot know justice through its presence in his soul, since he does not possess it, nor can he know it through abstraction from sensible species, since it is not an object of sense and has no likeness in the world of sense. He cannot know it by its effects, since he would not recognise the effects of justice unless he previously knew what justice is, just as one cannot recognise the effects of a man's activity as the effects of a man's activity unless one previously knows what a man is.[28] There must, therefore, be some *a priori* or innate knowledge of the virtues. In what sense is it innate? There is no innate idea (*species innata*) in the sense of a clear idea or intellectual likeness of the virtue in the mind from its beginning; but there is present in the soul a natural light by which it can recognise truth and rectitude, and there is present also an affection or inclination of the will. The soul knows, therefore, what rectitude is and what an affection or inclination of the will is, and in this way it recognises what *rectitudo affectionis* is. As this is charity, it knows what charity is, even though it does not actually possess the virtue of charity.[29]

Thus the knowledge of the virtues is innate in much the same sense as knowledge of God is innate, not as an innate explicit species or idea, but in the sense that the soul has in itself all the material needed to form the explicit idea, without its being necessary for it to have recourse to the sensible world. The innate idea of Bonaventure is a virtually innate idea. Of course, there is one big difference between our knowledge of the virtues and our knowledge of God, for while we can never apprehend the essence of God in this life, it is possible to apprehend the essence of the virtues. However, the ways in which we arrive at the knowledge of the virtues and of God are similar, and we can say that the soul possesses an innate knowledge of the principles necessary to its conduct. It knows by self-reflection what God is, what fear is and what love is, and so it knows what it is to fear and to love God.[30] If anyone quotes in opposition the Philosopher's dictum *nihil est in intellectu, quod prius non fuerit in sensu,* the answer is that the dictum must be understood as having reference only to our knowledge of sensible objects or to the acquisition of ideas which are capable of being formed by abstraction from sensible species.[31]

7. But though Bonaventure will not admit that the first principles relating to the world about us or indeed even the first principles of conduct are explicit in the mind from the beginning or infused into it from outside apart from any activity on the part of the mind itself, it does not follow that he is prepared to dispense with the Augustinian doctrine of illumination; on the contrary, he regards it as one of the cardinal truths of metaphysics.

Truth is the *adaequatio rei et intellectus,*[32] involving the object known and the knowing intellect. In order that truth in this sense, truth apprehended, may exist, conditions are required on the part of both subject and object, immutability on the part of the latter and infallibility on the part of the former.[33] But if Bonaventure is prepared to echo in this way the words of the *Theaetetus*, demanding these two conditions in order that *cognitio certitudinalis*, certain knowledge, may exist, he is necessarily faced by problems similar to those with which Plato and Augustine were faced, since no created object is strictly immutable and all sensible objects are perishable, while the human mind is not *of itself* infallible in regard to any class of object. It must, therefore, receive help from outside, and naturally Bonaventure had recourse to the Augustinian theory of illumination, which commended itself to him, not only because St. Augustine had held it but also because it emphasised both the dependence of the human intellect on God and the interior activity of God in the human soul. For him it was both an epistemological truth and a religious truth, something that could be established as a necessary conclusion from a study of the nature and requirements of certainty and also something upon which one could profitably meditate in the religious sense. Indeed for him the intellectual life and the spiritual life cannot properly be separated.

The human mind, then, is subject to change, doubt, error, while the phenomena which we experience and know are also changeable. On the other hand it is an indubitable fact that the human mind does possess certainties and knows that it does so and that we apprehend unchanging essences and principles. It is only God, however, who is unchanging, and this means that the human mind is aided by God and that the object of its certain knowledge is seen in some way as rooted in God, as existing in the *rationibus aeternis* or divine ideas. But we do not apprehend these divine ideas directly, in themselves, and Bonaventure points out with Augustine that to follow the Platonic doctrine is to open the door to scepticism, since if the only certain knowledge attainable is direct knowledge of the eternal archetypes or exemplars and if we have no direct knowledge of these archetypes, the necessary conclusion is that true certainty is unattainable by the human mind.[34] On the other hand it is not sufficient to say that the *ratio aeterna* influences the mind in this sense only, that the knowing mind attains not the eternal principle itself but only its influence, as a *habitus mentis*, for the latter would be itself created and subject to the same conditions as the mind of which it is a disposition.[35] The *rationes aeternae*, then, must have a direct regulative action on the human mind, though remaining themselves unseen. It is they which move the mind and rule the mind in its certain judgements, enabling it to apprehend the certain and eternal truths in the speculative and moral orders and to make certain and true judgements even concerning sensible objects: it is their action (which is the divine illumination) which enables the mind to apprehend the unchanging and stable essences in the fleeting and changing objects of experience. This does not mean that Bonaventure contradicts the approval he has given to Aristotle's doctrine about our knowledge of the sensible world, but it does mean that he considers it insufficient. Without sense-perception we would never indeed know sensible objects and it is quite true that the intellect abstracts, but the divine illumination, the direct action of the *ratio aeterna*, is necessary in order that the mind should see in the object the reflection of the unchanging *ratio* and be able to make an infallible judgement concerning it. Sense-perception is required in order that our ideas of sensible objects should arise, but the stability and necessity of our judgements concerning them are due to the action of the *rationes aeternae*, since neither are the sensible objects of our experience unchanging nor are the minds which know them infallible of themselves. The dim (*obtenebratae*) species of our minds, affected by the obscurity of *phantasmata*, are thus illumined in order that the mind should know. 'For if to have real knowledge means to know that a thing cannot possibly be otherwise, it is necessary that He alone should cause us to know, who knows the truth and has the truth in Himself.'[36] Thus it is through the *ratio aeterna* that the mind judges all those things which we know by the senses.[37]

In the *Itinerarium Mentis in Deum*[38] St. Bonaventure describes how the exterior sensible objects produce a likeness of themselves (*similitudo*) first in the medium and then through the medium on the organ of sense, and so on the interior sense. The particular sense, or the faculty of sensation acting through the particular sense, judges that this object is white or black or whatever it is, and the interior sense that it is pleasing, beautiful, or the reverse. The intellectual faculty, turning itself towards the species, asks why the object represented is beautiful and judges that it is beautiful because it possesses certain characteristics. But this judgement implies a reference to an idea of beauty which is stable and unchanging, not bound to place or time. This is where the divine illumination comes in, namely to explain the judgement in its unchanging and supertemporal aspect by reference to the directing and regulating *ratio aeterna*, not to supersede or annul the work of the senses or the activity of abstraction. All sensible objects which are known enter the mind through the three psychical operations of *apprehensio*, *oblectatio* and *diiudicatio*, but the latter operation, to be true and certain, must be a judgement made in the light of the *rationes aeternae*.

Now, as we have seen earlier, the *rationes aeternae* are ontologically identified and are in fact identical with the Word of God. It follows then that it is the Word which illuminates the human mind, that Word which enlightens every man who comes into the world. 'Christ is the interior teacher and no truth is known except through Him, not by His speaking as we speak, but by His enlightening us interiorly. . . . He is intimately present to every soul and by His most clear ideas He shines upon the dark ideas of our minds.'[39] We have no vision of the Word of God and though the light is so intimately within us, it is invisible, *inaccessibilis*: we can only reason to its presence from observation of its effects.[40] Thus Bonaventure's doctrine of illumination and his interpretation of Augustine do not involve ontologism. His doctrine completes his seemingly Aristotelian affirmation of abstraction and his denial of the properly innate character of even the first principles, giving to his teaching a peculiar and non-Aristotelian, an Augustinian flavour and colour. We abstract, yes, but we could not seize the intelligible and stable merely through abstraction, we need also the divine illumination: we can attain knowledge of moral principles by interior reflection, yes, but we could not apprehend their unchanging and necessary character without the regulative and guiding action of the divine light. Aristotle failed to see this, he failed to see that as we cannot know creatures fully unless we see them as *exemplata* of the divine *exemplar*, so we cannot form certain judgements about them without the light of the divine Word, of the *Ratio Aeterna*. Exemplarism and illumination are closely connected, the true metaphysician recognises them both: Aristotle recognised neither.

8. There are only four faculties of the soul, the vegetative and sensitive powers, the intellect and the will; but Bona-

venture distinguishes various 'aspects' of the soul and, in particular, of the intellect or mind according to the objects to which its attention is directed and according to the way in which it is directed. It would, then, be a mistake to suppose that he meant that *ratio*, *intellectus*, *intelligentia* and *apex mentis* or *synderesis scintilla*[41] are all different faculties of the soul: they denote rather different functions of the rational soul in its upward ascent from sensible creatures to God Himself. In the Commentary on the *Sentences*[42] he says expressly that the division of the reason into lower and higher (*ratio inferior* and *ratio superior*) is not a division into different faculties: it is a division into *officia* and *dispositiones*, which is something more than a division into aspects (*aspectus*). The lower reason is reason turned towards sense-objects, the higher reason is reason turned towards intelligible objects, and the term 'lower' and 'higher' thus refer to different functions or *officia* of the same faculty; but there is this further point to be added, that the reason as directed to intelligibles is strengthened and invigorated, whereas, directed to sensibles, it is in a manner weakened and drawn down, so that although there is only one *ratio*, the distinction between higher and lower reason corresponds not only to different functions, but also to different dispositions of the one reason.

The stages of the upward ascent of the mind scarcely need much elaboration, as they are more connected with ascetical and mystical theology than with philosophy in our sense; but since they are connected with philosophy in Bonaventure's understanding of the term, it is as well to touch very briefly on them, as they illustrate his tendency to integrate philosophy and theology as closely as possible. Walking in the footsteps of Augustine and the Victorines Bonaventure traces the ascending stages of the soul's life, stages which correspond to different potentialities in the soul and lead him from the sphere of nature into that of grace. Starting from the soul's sensitive powers (*sensualitas*) he shows how the soul may see in sensible objects the *vestigia Dei*, as it contemplates sensible things first as God's effects, then as things wherein God is present, and he accompanies it, with Augustine, as it retires within itself and contemplates its natural constitution and powers as the image of God. The intelligence is then shown contemplating God in the soul's faculties renewed and elevated by grace, being enabled to do so by the Word of God. In this stage, however, the soul still contemplates God in

His image, which is the soul itself, even if elevated by grace, and it can proceed yet further, to the contemplation of God *supra nos*, first as Being, then as the Good. Being is good, and the contemplation of God as Being, the perfection of being, leads to the realisation of Being as the Good, as *diffusivum sui*, and so to the contemplation of the Blessed Trinity. Further than this the intellect cannot go: beyond lies the luminous darkness of mystical contemplation and ecstasy, the *apex affectus* outstripping the mind. The will, however, is a faculty of the one human soul and, though issuing from the substance of the soul, it is not a distinct accident, so that to say that the affection of the will outruns the intellect is simply to say that the soul is united to God by love so closely that the light infused into it blinds it. There can be but one higher stage, reserved for the next life, and that is the vision of God in heaven.

9. It will be remembered that the three cardinal points of metaphysics for Bonaventure are creation, exemplarism and illumination. His metaphysical system is thus a unity in that the doctrine of creation reveals the world as proceeding from God, created out of nothing and wholly dependent on Him, while the doctrine of exemplarism reveals the world of creatures as standing to God in the relation of imitation to model, of *exemplatum* to *exemplar*, while the doctrine of illumination traces the stages of the soul's return to God by way of contemplation of sensible creatures, of itself and finally of Perfect Being. The divine action is always emphasised. Creation out of nothing can be proved, as also God's presence and activity in creatures and especially in the soul itself: God's action enters into the apprehension of every certain truth, and even though for the establishment of the higher stages of the soul's ascent the data of theology are required, there is in a sense a continuity of divine action in increasing intensity. God acts in every man's mind when he attains truth, but at this stage the activity of God is not all-sufficient, man is also active through the use of his natural powers: in the higher stages God's action progressively increases until in ecstasy God takes possession of the soul and man's intellectual activity is superseded.

Bonaventure may thus be termed the philosopher of the Christian life, who makes use of both reason and faith in order to produce his synthesis. This integration of reason and faith, philosophy and theology, is emphasised by the place he accords to Christ, the Word of God. Just as creation and exemplarism cannot be properly understood apart from the realisation that it is through the Word of God that all things are created and that it is the Word of God, the consubstantial image of the Father, whom all creatures mirror, so illumination in its various stages cannot be properly understood apart from the realisation that it is the Word of God who illumines every man, the Word of God who is the door through which the soul enters into God above itself, the Word of God who, through the Holy Spirit whom He has sent, inflames the soul and leads it beyond the limitations of its clear ideas into the ecstatic union. Finally it is the Word of God who shows us the Father and opens to us the beatific vision of heaven. Christ in fact is the *medium omnium scientiarum*,[43] of metaphysics as of theology, for though the metaphysician as such cannot attain to knowledge of the Word through the use of the natural reason, he can form no true and certain judgements without the illumination of the Word, even if he is quite unaware of this, and in addition his science is incomplete and vitiated by its incompleteness unless it is crowned by theology.

APPENDIX I

Honorific titles applied in the Middle Ages to philosophers treated of in this volume.

RHABANUS MAURUS:	Praeceptor Germaniae.
ABELARD:	Peripateticus Palatinus.
ALAN OF LILLE:	Doctor universalis.
AVERROES:	Commentator.
ALEXANDER OF HALES:	Doctor irrefragibilis.
ST. BONAVENTURE:	Doctor seraphicus.
ST. ALBERT THE GREAT:	Doctor universalis.
ST. THOMAS AQUINAS:	Doctor angelicus and Doctor communis.
ROGER BACON:	Doctor mirabilis.
RICHARD OF MIDDLETON:	Doctor solidus.
RAYMOND LULL:	Doctor illuminatus.
GILES OF ROME:	Doctor fundatissimus.
HENRY OF GHENT:	Doctor solemnis.
DUNS SCOTUS:	Doctor subtilis.

APPENDIX II

A SHORT BIBLIOGRAPHY

General Works on Mediaeval Philosophy

Bréhier, E. Histoire de la philosophie: tome 1, l'antiquité et le moyen âge. Paris, 1943.

Carlyle, R. W. & A. J. A History of Mediaeval Political Theory in the West. 4 vols. London, 1903–22.

Dempf, A. Die Ethik des Mittelalters. Munich, 1930.
Metaphysik des Mittelalters. Munich, 1930.

De Wulf, M. Histoire de la philosophie médiévale. 3 vols. Louvain, 1934–47 (6th edition). English translation of first two vols. by E. C. Messenger, London, 1935–8 (3rd edition).

Geyer, B. Die patristische und scholastische Philosophie. Berlin, 1928. (This is the second volume of the revised edition of Ueberweg.)

Gilson, E. La philosophie au moyen âge. Paris, 1944 (2nd edition, revised and augmented). English translation, 1936.
L'esprit de la philosophie médiévale. 2 vols. Paris, 1944 (2nd edition).
Études de philosophie médiévale. Strasbourg, 1921.
The Unity of Philosophical Experience. London, 1938.
Reason and Revelation in the Middle Ages. New York, 1939.

Grabmann, M. Die Philosophie des Mittelalters. Berlin, 1921.
Mittelalterliches Geistesleben. 2 vols. Munich, 1926 and 1936.

GRUNWALD, G. Geschichte der Gottesbeweise im Mittelalter bis zum Ausgang der Hochscholastik. Münster, 1907. (Beiträge zur Geschichte der Philosophie und Theologie des Mittelalters, 6, 3.)

HAURÉAU, B. Histoire de la philosophie scolastique. 3 vols. Paris, 1872–80.

HAWKINS, D. J. B. A Sketch of Mediaeval Philosophy. London, 1946.

LOTTIN, O. Psychologie et morale aux XIIe et XIIIe siècles. Tome 1: Problèmes de Psychologie. Louvain, 1942. Tome 2: Problèmes de Morale. 1948.

Le droit naturel chez S. Thomas d'Aquin et ses prédécesseurs. Bruges, 1931 (2nd edition).

PICAVET, F. Esquisse d'une histoire générale et comparée des philosophies médiévales. Paris, 1907 (2nd edition).

Essais sur l'histoire générale et comparée des théologies et des philosophies médiévales. Paris, 1913.

ROMEYER, B. La philosophie chrétienne jusqu'à Descartes. 3 vols. Paris, 1935–7.

RUGGIERO, G. DE. La filosofia del cristianesimo. 3 vols. Bari.

STÖCKL, A. Geschichte der Philosophie des Mittelalters. 3 vols. Mainz, 1864–6.

VIGNAUX, P. La pensée au moyen âge. Paris, 1938.

Chapter II: The Patristic Period

(a) Texts: General collections of

Migne (edit.), Patrologia Graeca. Paris.

Migne (edit.), Patrologia Latina. Paris.

Die griechischen christlichen Schriftsteller der ersten drei Jahrhunderte. Leipzig.

Corpus scriptorum ecclesiasticorum Latinorum. Vienna.

Ante-Nicene Christian Library, Translations of the writings of the Fathers down to A.D. 325. Edinburgh.

A Library of the Fathers (English translations). Oxford.

Ancient Christian Writers: the works of the Fathers in Translation. Westminster, Maryland, U.S.A., 1946 (edit. J. Quasten and J. C. Plumpe).

(b) Particular Texts

ARISTIDES. Apology. In Zwei griechische Apologeten, J. Geffcken. Leipzig, 1907.

Apology. In Texte und Untersuchungen, IV. E. Hennecke (edit.). Leipzig, 1893.

ARNOBIUS. Libri 7 adversus gentes. Appended to *Lactantii opera omnia* (L. C. Firmiani). Paris, 1845.

ATHENAGORAS. Apology. In *Zwei griechische Apologeten*. J. Geffcken. Leipzig, 1907.

  Libellus pro Christianis and Oratio de resurrectione cadaverum in *Texte und Untersuchungen*, IV. E. Schwartz (edit.). Leipzig, 1891.

CLEMENT OF ALEXANDRIA. The Exhortation to the Greeks, etc. G. W. Butterworth (edit.). London, 1919.

EUSEBIUS. The Proof of the Gospel (*Demonstratio Evangelica*). 2 vols. W. J. Ferrar (edit.). London, 1920.

GREGORY OF NYSSA, ST. The Cathechetical Oration of St. Gregory of Nyssa. J. H. Srawley (edit.). London, 1917.

  La Création de l'homme. J. Laplace and J. Daniélou. Paris, 1943.

HIPPOLYTUS. Philosophumena. 2 vols. F. Legge (edit.). London, 1921.

IRENAEUS, ST. The Treatise of Irenaeus of Lugdunum against the Heresies. F. R. Montgomery Hitchcock (edit.). London, 1916.

JUSTIN MARTYR, ST. The Dialogue with Trypho. A. L. Williams (edit.). London, 1930.

LACTANTIUS. Opera omnia. L. C. Firmiani. Paris, 1843.

MINUCIUS FELIX. The Octavius of Minucius Felix. J. H. Freese (edit.). London (no date).

ORIGEN. Homélies sur la Genèse. L. Doutreleau (edit.). Paris, 1943.

  Origen on First Principles. G. W. Butterworth (edit.). London, 1936.

TATIAN. Oratio ad Graecos. In *Texte und Untersuchungen*, IV. E. Schwartz (edit.). Leipzig, 1888.

TERTULLIAN. Tertullian concerning the Resurrection of the Flesh. A. Souter (edit.). London, 1922.

  Tertullian against Praxeas. A. Souter (edit.). London, 1920.

  Tertullian's Apology. J. E. B. Mayer (edit.). Cambridge, 1917.

Other Works

ARNOU, R. De 'platonismo' Patrum. Rome, 1935.

BALTHASAR, HANS VON. Présence et pensée. Essai sur la philosophie religieuse de Grégoire de Nysse. Paris, 1943.

BARDY, G. Clément d'Alexandrie. Paris, 1926.

BAYLIS, H. J. Minucius Felix. London, 1928.

DANIÉLOU, J. Platonisme et théologie mystique. Essai sur la doctrine spirituelle de saint Grégoire de Nysse. Paris, 1944.

DIEKAMP, F. Die Gotteslehre des heiligen Gregor von Nyssa. Münster, 1896.

ERMONI, V. Saint Jean Damascène. Paris, 1904.

FAIRWEATHER, W. Origen and the Greek Patristic Philosophy. London, 1901.

FAYE, E. DE. Gnostiques et gnosticisme. Paris, 1925 (2nd edition).

HITCHCOCK, F. R. MONTGOMERY. Irenaeus of Lugdunum. Cambridge, 1914.

LEBRETON, J. Histoire du dogme de la Trinité. Paris, 1910.

MONDÉSERT, C. Clément d'Alexandrie. Lyons, 1944.

MORGAN, J. The Importance of Tertullian in the development of Christian dogma. London, 1928.

PICHON, R. Étude sur les mouvements philosophiques et religieux sous le règne de Constantin. Paris, 1903.

PRESTIGE, G. L. God in Patristic Thought. London, 1936.

PUECH, A. Histoire de la littérature grecque chrétienne depuis les origines jusqu'à la fin du IVe siècle. 3 vols. Paris, 1928–30.

RIVIÈRE, J. Saint Basile, évêque de Césarée. Paris, 1930.

THAMIN, R. Saint Ambroise et la morale chrétienne au IVe siècle. Paris, 1895.

Chapters III–VIII: St. Augustine

Texts

Patrologia Latina (Migne), vols. 32–47.

Corpus scriptorum ecclesiasticorum latinorum, vols. 12, 25, 28, 33, 34, 36, 40, 41–4, 51–3, 57, 58, 60, 63 . . .

City of God. 2 vols. (Everyman Edition). London, 1945.

Confessions. F. J. Sheed. London, 1943.

The Letters of St. Augustine. W. J. Sparrow-Simpson (edit.). London, 1919.

Studies on Augustine

BARDY, G. Saint Augustin. Paris, 1946 (6th edition).

BOURKE, V. J. Augustine's Quest of Wisdom. Milwaukee, 1945.

BOYER, C. Christianisme et néo-platonisme dans la forma-
    tion de saint Augustin. Paris, 1920.
    L'idée de vérité dans la philosophie de saint Augustin.
    Paris, 1920.
    Essais sur la doctrine de saint Augustin. Paris, 1932.
COMBES, G. La doctrine politique de saint Augustin. Paris,
    1927.
FIGGIS, J. N. The Political Aspects of St. Augustine's City
    of God. London, 1921.
GILSON, E. Introduction à l'étude de saint Augustin. Paris,
    1943 (2nd edition).
GRABMANN, M. Der göttliche Grund menschlicher Wahrheit-
    serkenntnis nach Augustinus and Thomas von Aquin.
    Cologne, 1924.
    Die Grundgedanken des heiligen Augustinus über Seele
    und Gott. Cologne, 1929 (2nd edition).
HENRY, P. L'extase d'Ostie. Paris, 1938.
HESSEN, J. Augustins Metaphysik der Erkenntnis. Berlin,
    1931.
LE BLOND, J. M. Les conversions de saint Augustin. Paris,
    1948.
MARTIN, J. La doctrine sociale de saint Augustin. Paris, 1912.
    Saint Augustin. Paris, 1923 (2nd edition).
MAUSBACH, J. Die Ethik des heiligen Augustinus. 2 vols.
    Freiburg, 1929 (2nd edition).
MESSENGER, E. C. Evolution and Theology. London, 1931.
    (For Augustine's theory of rationes seminales.)
MUÑOZ VEGA, P. Introducción a la síntesis de San Augustin.
    Rome, 1945.
PORTALIÉ, E. Augustin, saint. Dictionnaire de théologie
    catholique, vol. 1. Paris, 1902.
SWITALSKI, B. Neoplatonism and the Ethics of St. Augus-
    tine. New York, 1946.

Publications for 15th centenary of St. Augustine

A Monument to St. Augustine. London, 1930.
Aurelius Augustinus. Cologne, 1930.
S. Agostino. Milan, 1931.
Études sur S. Augustin. Archives de Philosophie, vol. 7,
    cahier 2. Paris, 1930.
Religion y Cultura. XV Centenario de la Muerte de San
    Augustin. Madrid, 1931.

Mélanges augustiniens. Paris, 1930.
Miscellanea agostiniana. 2 vols. Rome, 1930–1.

Chapter IX: The Pseudo-Dionysius

Texts

Patrologia Graeca, vols. 3–4.
Dionysius the Areopagite on the Divine Names and the Mystical Theology. C. E. Rolt (edit.). London, 1920.

Chapter X: Boethius, Cassiodorus, Isidore

Texts

Patrologia Latina (Migne); vols. 63–4 (Boethius), 69–70 (Cassiodorus), 81–4 (Isidore).
BOETHIUS. The Theological Tractates and The Consolation of Philosophy. H. F. Stewart and E. K. Rand (edit.). London, 1926.
    De Consolatione Philosophiae. A. Fortescue (edit.). London, 1925.

Studies

BARRETT, H. M. Boethius: Some Aspects of his Times and Work. Cambridge, 1940.
PATCH, H. R. The Tradition of Boethius, a Study of his Importance in Medieval Culture. New York, 1935.
RAND, E. K. Founders of the Middle Ages; ch. 5, Boethius the Scholastic. Harvard U.P., 1941.

Chapter XI: The Carolingian Renaissance

Texts

Patrologia Latina (Migne); vols. 100–1 (Alcuin), 107–12 (Rhabanus Maurus).

Studies

BUXTON, E. M. WILMOT. Alcuin. London, 1922.
LAISTNER, M. L. W. Thought and Letters in Western Europe, A.D. 500–900. London, 1931.
TAYLOR, H. O. The Mediaeval Mind, vol. 1. London, 1911.
TURNAU, D. Rabanus Maurus praeceptor Germaniae. Munich, 1900.

Chapters XII–XIII: John Scotus Eriugena

Texts

Patrologia Latina (Migne); vol. 122.
Selections (in English) in *Selections from Mediaeval Philosophers*, vol. 1, by R. McKeon. London, 1930.

Studies

BETT, H. Johannes Scotus Eriugena, a Study in Mediaeval Philosophy. Cambridge, 1925.
CAPPUYNS, M. Jean Scot Erigène, sa vie, son œuvre, sa pensée. Paris, 1933.
SCHNEIDER, A. Die Erkenntnislehre des Johannes Eriugena im Rahmen ihrer metaphysischen und anthropologischen Voraussetzungen. 2 vols. Berlin, 1921–3.
SEUL, W. Die Gotteserkenntnis bei Johannes Skotus Eriugena unter Berücksichtigung ihrer neo-platonischen und augustinischen Elemente. Bonn, 1932.

Chapter XIV: The Problem of Universals

Texts

Patrologia Latina (Migne); vols. 105 (Fredegisius), 139 (Gerbert of Aurillac), 144–5 (St. Peter Damian), 158–9 (St. Anselm), 160 (Odo of Tournai), 163 (William of Champeaux), 178 (Abelard), 188 (Gilbert de la Porrée), 199 (John of Salisbury), 175–7 (Hugh of St. Victor).
B. GEYER. Die philosophischen Schriften Peter Abelards. 4 vols. Münster, 1919–33.
Selections from Abelard in *Selections from Mediaeval Philosophers*, vol. 1, by R. McKeon. London, 1930.

Studies

BERTHAUD, A. Gilbert de la Porrée et sa philosophie. Poitiers, 1892.
CARRÉ, M. H. Realists and Nominalists. Oxford, 1946.
COUSIN, V. Ouvrages inédits d'Abélard. Paris, 1836.
DE WULF, M. Le problème des universaux dans son évolution historique du IXe au XIIIe siècle. Archiv für Geschichte der Philosophie, 1896.
LEFÈVRE, G. Les variations de Guillaume de Champeaux et la question des universaux. Lille, 1898.

OTTAVIANO, C. Pietro Abelardo, La vita, le opere, il pensiero. Rome, 1931.

PICAVET, F. Gerbert ou le pape philosophe. Paris, 1897. Roscelin philosophe et théologien, d'après la légende et d'après l'histoire. Paris, 1911.

REINERS, J. Der aristotelische Realismus in der Frühscholastik. Bonn, 1907. Der Nominalismus in der Frühscholastik. Münster, 1910 (Beiträge, 8, 5).

REMUSAT, C. DE. Abaelard. 2 vols. Paris, 1845.

SICKES, J. G. Peter Abaelard. Cambridge, 1932.

Chapter XV: St. Anselm of Canterbury

Texts

Patrologia Latina (Migne); vols. 158–9.

Studies

BARTH, K. Fides quaerens intellectum. Anselms Beweis der Existenz Gottes im Zusammenhang seines theologischen Programms. Munich, 1931.

FISCHER, J. Die Erkenntnislehre Anselms von Canterbury. Münster, 1911 (Beiträge, 10, 3).

FILLIÂTRE, C. La philosophie de saint Anselme, ses principes, sa nature, son influence. Paris, 1920.

GILSON, E. Sens et nature de l'argument de saint Anselme, in Archives d'histoire doctrinale et littéraire du moyen âge, 1934.

KOYRÉ, A. L'idée de Dieu dans la philosophie de saint Anselme. Paris, 1923.

LEVASTI, A. Sant' Anselmo, Vita e pensiero. Bari, 1929.

Chapter XVI: The School of Chartres

Texts

Patrologia Latina (Migne); vols. 199 (John of Salisbury, containing also fragments of Bernard of Chartres, columns 666 and 938), 90 (William of Conches's Philosophia, among works of Bede).

JANSSEN, W. Der Kommentar des Clarembaldus von Arras zu Boethius De Trinitate. Breslau, 1926.

BARACH, C. S. & WROBEL, J. Bernardus Silvestris, De mundi universitate libri duo. Innsbruck, 1896.

WEBB, C. C. J. Metalogicon. Oxford, 1929.
  Policraticus. 2 vols. Oxford, 1909.

Studies

CLERVAL, A. Les écoles de Chartres au moyen âge du Ve au
  XVIe siècle. Paris, 1895.
FLATTEN, H. Die Philosophie des Wilhelm von Conches.
  Coblenz, 1929.
SCHARSCHMIDT, C. Joannes Saresberiensis nach Leben und
  Studien, Schriften und Philosophie. Leipzig, 1862.
WEBB, C. C. J. John of Salisbury. London, 1932.

Chapter XVII: The School of St. Victor

Texts

Patrologia Latina (Migne); vols. 175–7 (Hugh), 196 (Richard and Godfrey).

Studies

EBNER, J. Die Erkenntnislehre Richards von Sankt Viktor.
  Münster, 1917 (Beiträge, 19, 4).
ETHIER, A. M. Le De Trinitate de Richard de Saint-Victor.
  Paris, 1939.
KILGENSTEIN, J. Die Gotteslehre des Hugo von Sankt Vik-
  tor. Würzburg, 1897.
MIGNON, A. Les origines de la scolastique et Hugues de Saint-
  Victor. 2 vols. Paris, 1895.
OSTLER, H. Die Psychologie des Hugo von Sankt Viktor.
  Münster, 1906 (Beiträge, 6, 1).
VERNET, F. Hugues de Saint-Victor. Dictionnaire de théol-
  ogie catholique, vol. 7.

Chapter XVIII: Dualists and Pantheists

ALPHANDÉRY, P. Les idées morales chez les hétérodoxes latins
  au début du XIIIe siècle. Paris, 1903.
BROEKX, E. Le catharisme. Louvain, 1916.
CAPELLE, G. C. Autour du décret de 1210: III, Amaury de
  Bène, Étude sur son panthéisme formel. Paris, 1932
  (Bibliothèque thomiste, 16).
RUNCIMAN, S. The Mediaeval Manichee. Cambridge, 1947.
THÉRY, G. Autour du décret de 1210: I, David de Dinant,
  Étude sur son panthéisme matérialiste. Paris, 1925
  (Bibliothèque thomiste, 6).

Chapter XIX: Islamic Philosophy

Texts

ALFARABI. Alpharabius de intelligentiis, philosophia prima. Venice, 1508.

Alfarabis philosophische Abhandlungen, aus dem arabischen übersetzt. Fr. Dieterici. Leiden, 1892.

Alfarabi über den Ursprung der Wissenschaften. Cl. Baeumker. Münster, 1933.

Alfarabius de Platonis Philosophia. Edited by F. Rosenthal and R. Walzer. Plato Arabus, vol. 2. London, Warburg Institute, 1943.

ALGAZEL. Alagazel's Metaphysics, a Mediaeval Translation. Toronto, 1933.

AVICENNA. Avicennae Opera. Venice, 1495–1546.

Avicennae Metaphysices Compendium. Rome, 1926 (Latin).

AVERROES. Aristotelis opera omnia, Averrois in ea opera commentaria. 11 vols. Venice.

Die Epitome der Metaphysik des Averroës. S. Van den Bergh. Leiden, 1924.

Accord de la religion et de la philosophie, traité d'Ibn Rochd (Averroes), traduit et annoté. L. Gauthier. Algiers, 1905.

Studies: General

BOER, T. J. DE. History of Philosophy in Islam. Translated by E. R. Jones. London, 1903.

CARRA DE VAUX, B. Les penseurs d'Islam. 5 vols. Paris, 1921–6.

GAUTHIER, L. Introduction à l'étude de la philosophie musulmane. Paris, 1923.

MUNK, S. Mélanges de philosophie juive et arabe. Paris, 1927.

O'LEARY, DE LACY. Arabic Thought and its place in History. London, 1922.

The Legacy of Islam. T. Arnold and A. Guillaume (edit.). Oxford, 1931.

Particular

ALONSO, M. Teologia de Averroes. Madrid-Granada, 1947.

ASÍN Y PALACIOS, M. Algazel: Dogmatica, moral, ascética. Saragossa, 1901.

CARRA DE VAUX, B. Gazali. Paris, 1902.
  Avicenne. Paris, 1900.
GAUTHIER, L. La théorie d'Ibn Rochd sur les rapports de la religion et de la philosophie. Paris, 1909.
  Ibn Roschd (Averroès). Paris, 1948.
GOICHON, A. M. Introduction à Avicenne. Paris, 1933.
  La distinction de l'essence et de l'existence d'après Ibn Sīnā (Avicenna). Paris, 1937.
  La philosophie d'Avicenne. Paris, 1944.
HORTEN, M. Die Metaphysik des Averroës. Halle, 1912.
KLEINE, W. Die Substanzlehre Avicennas bei Thomas von Aquin. Fribourg, 1933.
RENAN, E. Averroès et l'averroisme. Paris, 1869 (3rd edition).
SALIBA, D. Étude sur la métaphysique d'Avicenne. Paris, 1927.
SMITH, M. Al-Ghazālī, the Mystic. London, 1944.
SWEETMAN, J. W. Islam and Christian Theology, vol. 1. London, 1945.
WENSINCK, A. J. La Pensée de Ghazzālī. Paris, 1940.

Chapter XX: Jewish Philosophy

Texts

Avencebrolis Fons Vitae, ex arabico in latinum translatus ab Johanne Hispano et Dominico Gundissalino. Münster, 1892–5.
MAIMONIDES. Le guide des égarés, traité de théologie et de philosophie. 3 vols. Paris, 1856–66.

Studies

GUTTMANN, J. Die Philosophie des Judentums. Munich, 1933.
HUSIK, I. A History of Mediaeval Jewish Philosophy. New York, 1918.
LEVY, L. G. Maïmonide. Paris, 1932 (2nd edition).
MUNK, S. Mélanges de philosophie juive et arabe. Paris, 1927.
MUNZ, J. Moses ben Maimon, sein Leben und seine Werke. Frankfurt am M., 1912.
ROHNER, A. Das Schöpfungsproblem bei Moses Maimonides, Albertus Magnus und Thomas von Aquin. Münster, 1913 (Beiträge, 11, 5).
ROTH, L. Spinoza, Descartes and Maimonides. Oxford, 1924.

Chapter XXI: The Translations

See the bibliography in M. De Wulf's *Histoire de la philosophie médiévale*, vol. 2, 6th French edition. (In the English translation by Dr. E. C. Messenger the bibliography and the sections by A. Pelzer on the translations have been abridged.) See also B. Geyer's *Die patristische und scholastische Philosophie* (1928), pp. 342–51, with the corresponding bibliography, p. 728.

Chapter XXII: Introduction (to Thirteenth Century)

BONNEROT, J. La Sorbonne, sa vie, son rôle, son œuvre à travers les siècles. Paris, 1927.

DENIFLE, H. and CHATELAIN, A. Chartularium Universitatis Parisiensis. 4 vols. Paris, 1889–97.
Auctuarium Chartularii Universitatis Parisiensis. 2 vols. Paris, 1894–7.
Les universités françaises au moyen âge. Paris, 1892.

GLORIEUX, P. Répertoire des maîtres en théologie de Paris au XIIIe siècle. 2 vols. Paris, 1933–4.

GRABMANN, M. I divieti ecclesiastici di Aristotele sotto Innocenzo e Gregorio IX. Rome, 1941.

LITTLE, A. G. The Grey Friars in Oxford. Oxford, 1892.

RASHDALL, H. The Universities of Europe in the Middle Ages. New edition, edited by F. M. Powicke and A. B. Emden. 3 vols. Oxford, 1936.

SHARP, D. E. Franciscan Philosophy at Oxford in the Thirteenth Century. Oxford, 1936.

Chapter XXIII: William of Auvergne

Texts

Opera. 2 vols. Paris, 1674.

Studies

BAUMGARTNER, M. Die Erkenntnislehre des Wilhelm von Auvergne. Münster, 1895 (Beiträge, 2, 1).

MASNOVO, A. Da Guglielmo d'Auvergne a San Tommaso d'Aquino. Milan, vol. 1 (1930 and 1945); vol. 2 (1934 and 1946); vol. 3 (1945).

Chapter XXIV: Robert Grosseteste and Alexander of Hales

Texts

Die philosophischen Werke des Robert Grosseteste, Bischof von Lincoln. L. Baur. Münster, 1912 (Beiträge, 9).

THOMSON, S. H. The Writings of Robert Grosseteste, Bishop of Lincoln, 1175–1253. Cambridge, 1940 (Bibliographical).

Doctoris irrefragabilis Alexandri de Hales, O.M. Summa Theologica. 3 vols. Quaracchi, 1924–30.

Studies

BAUR, L. Die Philosophie des Robert Grosseteste. Münster, 1917 (Beiträge, 18, 4–6).

For Alexander of Hales, see introduction to Quaracchi critical edition (*supra*).

Chapters XXV–XXIX: St. Bonaventure

Text

Opera omnia. 10 vols. Quaracchi, 1882–1902.

Studies

BISSEN, J. M. L'exemplarisme divin selon saint Bonaventure. Paris, 1929.

DE BENEDICTIS, M. M. The Social Thought of Saint Bonaventure. Washington, 1946.

GILSON, E. The Philosophy of St. Bonaventure. London, 1938.

GRÜNEWALD, S. Franziskanische Mystik. Versuch zu einer Darstellung mit besonderer Berücksichtigung des heiligen Bonaventura. Munich, 1931.

LUTZ, E. Die Psychologie Bonaventuras. Münster, 1909 (Beiträge, 6, 4–5).

LUYCKX, B. A. Die Erkenntnislehre Bonaventuras. Münster, 1923 (Beiträge, 23, 3–4).

O'DONNELL, C. M. The Psychology of St. Bonaventure and St. Thomas Aquinas. Washington, 1937.

ROBERT, P. Hylémorphisme et devenir chez S. Bonaventure. Montreal, 1936.

ROSENMÖLLER, B. Religiöse Erkenntnis nach Bonaventura. Münster, 1925 (Beiträge, 25, 3–4).

NOTES

Chapter One

1. A *History of Philosophy*, Vol. I, Greece and Rome, Image Books, 1961.
2. This bald statement, however, though sponsored by M. Gilson, requires a certain modification. See Vol. II, Pt. I, pp. 274–9.

Chapter Two

1. Quotations from the edition published in *Texts and Studies*, Vol. I.   2. 2, 1.   3. 2, 3.   4. 2, 4–6.   5. 3, 1 ff.
6. E.g. *Apol.*, I, 8, 2.   7. *Ibid.*, I, 8, 4.   8. *Ibid.*, I, 5, 3 ff.
9. *Ibid.*, II, 6 (7), 3.   10. *Against the Heresies*, I, 28.
11. E.g. *Adv. Jovin.*, 1, 3; *Comm. in Amos*.
12. Iren., *Against the Heresies*, I, 28.   13. *On the Resurrection*.
14. *Ad Autol.*, 3, 6.   15. 2, 9, 1.   16. 2, 1, 1; 2, 5, 3.
17. 2, 14, 4.   18. 4, 33, 8.   19. *Bibl.* cod. 121.
20. *Apol.*, 46.   21. *De Anima*, 1.   22. *Apol.*, 46.
23. *De Anima*, 3.   24. *Apol.*, 47.   25. *De Resurrect.*, 2–3.
26. *Herm.*, 28.   27. *De Carne Christi*, 11.
28. *Adv. Prax.*, 7.   29. *De Anima*, 7; cf. 8.   30. 48.
31. Cf. *De Anima*, 19.   32. *Adv. Prax.*, 12.
33. *Sermo, Ratio*.   34. *Apol.*, 21.   35. 2, 20 ff.   36. 19.
37. *Strom.*, 1, 5.   38. *Paedagogus*, 3, 11.
39. *De principiis*, 1, 1, 6.   40. 7, 38.
41. *Ibid.*, 1, 2, 10; 3, 4, 3.   42. *Ibid.*, 2, 1, 4.
43. *Ibid.*, 3, 5, 3; 2, 3, 4–5.   44. *In Joann.*, 2, 7.
45. *Contra Celsum*, 6, 64.   46. *De principiis*, 2, 6, 1.
47. *Ibid.*, 6, 1–3.   48. Cf. *ibid.*, 3, 6, 1 ff.; 1, 6, 3.
49. 11, 28.   50. 13, 13.   51. 10, 1; 10, 8; 10, 14.
52. 11, 8.   53. 11, 16; 11, 20.   54. 11, 23; 11, 29; 11, 31.
55. 11, 27.   56. 12, 27.   57. 13, 12; 12, 16.
58. 13, 19.   59. *De Vita Moysis*; P.G., 44, 336 DG, 360 BC.
60. Cf. *De anima et resurrectione*; P.G., 46, 49 C.
61. Cf. *Contra Eunom.*; P.G., 45, 341 B.
62. Cf. *Oratio Catechetica*; P.G., 45.   63. P.G., 44, 229 ff.

64. *De anima et res.*; P.G. 46, 29.   65. *Ibid.*, 44.
66. Ch. 24.   67. P.G., 94, 532 AB.

Chapter Three

1. *Conf.*, 1, 11, 17.
2. Manichaeanism, founded by Manes or Mani in the third century, originated in Persia and was a mixture of Persian and Christian elements.   3. *Conf.*, 8, 5, 10.   4. *Ibid.*, 8, 7, 16.
5. *Rom.*, 13, 13–4.   6. *Conf.*, 8, 8–12.   7. 9, 10, 23–6.
8. *Epist.*, 118.   9. *Vita S. Aug.*, 31.
10. *De vera relig.*, 24, 45.

Chapter Four

1. *De Intellectus Emendatione.*   2. 2, 10 and 14; 4, 27 ff.
3. *C. Acad.*, 3, 10, 23.   4. *Ibid.*, 3, 11, 26.
5. *De vera relig.*, 39, 73.   6. *De lib. arbit.*, 12, 34.
7. 2, 3, 7.   8. 2, 3, 7.   9. 15, 12, 21.
10. *Ibid.*   11. *De Civit. Dei*, 11, 26.
12. Cf. *De vera relig.*, 39, 72; *Serm.*, 330, 3; *Retract.*, 1, 8, 3; etc.
13. *De Trinit.*, 15, 12, 21.   14. *Conf.*, 6, 5, 7.
15. *De Trinit.*, 9, 6, 9.
16. Scotus repeated St. Augustine's suggestion that the status of sense-knowledge may be connected with original sin.
17. Cf. *De Musica*, 6–5, 9, 10; *De Trinit.*, 11, 2, 2–5.
18. 12, 2, 2.   19. *Ibid.*   20. *Ibid.*, 12, 14, 22.
21. *Ibid.*, 12, 13, 21.   22. *Conf.*, 13, 9, 10.
23. Cf. *De Trinit.*, 9, 6, 9–11.
24. Cf. *ibid.*, 12, 14, 22–3; 12, 15, 24; *De lib. arbit.*, 2, 13, 35; 2, 8, 20–4.   25. *De Ideis*, 2.   26. Cf. *Retract.*, 1, 3, 2.
27. *Conf.*, 10, 27, 38.   28. 35, 79.   29. *Solil.*, 1, 8, 15.
30. *Ibid.*, 1, 1, 3.   31. *Rep.*, 514–8.   32. 12, 15, 24.
33. *De Trinit.*, 9, 6, 9.   34. *De lib. arbit.*, 2, 13, 35.
35. *In. Ps.* 119; *Serm.*, 23, 1.   36. *In Ps.* 118; *Serm.*, 18, 4.
37. See, for example, the article on Augustine by Portalié in the *Dictionnaire de théologie catholique.*
38. 9, 3, 3.   39. *Ibid.*
40. *Solil.*, 1, 8, 15; *In Joann. Evang.*, 35, 8, 3; *De Trinit.*, 9, 15, 24; etc.

Chapter Five

1. *De lib. arbit.*, 2, 12, 33.   2. *Ibid.*   3. *Solil.*, 1, 1, 3.
4. 11, 4, 2.   5. *De Gen. ad litt.*, 4, 22, 22.
6. *In Joann. Evang.*, 106, 4.   7. *De doct. Christ.*, 1, 7, 7.

8. Ch. 2.
9. Cf. also G. Grunwald: *Geschichte der Gottesbeweise im Mittelalter*, in *Beiträge*, 6, 3, p. 6.
10. *Serm.*, 241, 2, 2 and 3, 3.
11. *Lehrbuch der Dogmengeschichte*, 3rd edit., t. 3, p. 119.
12. *De lib. arbit.*, 2, 17, 46.   13. *Ibid.*, 3, 23, 70.
14. *De Trinit.*, 11, 5, 8.   15. *De Civit. Dei*, 11, 28.
16. *De Trinit.*, 5, 2, 3; 5, 11, 12; 6, 4, 6; 6, 10, 11; 15, 43, 22; *In Joann. Evang.*, 99, 4; etc.   17. *De Gen. ad litt.*, 8, 26, 48.
18. Cf. *ibid.*, 5, 15, 33; *Ad Orosium*, 8, 9.
19. *De Trinit.*, 15, 7, 13.   20. *Ibid.*, 15, 13, 22.
21. 1, 6, 9.   22. 2.   23. *Ibid.*, 4, 1, 3.
24. Cf. e.g. *Summa Theol.*, Ia, 15, 2 and 3.

Chapter Six

1. *De lib. arbit.*, 3, 15, 42.   2. Cf. *De vera relig.*, 18, 35–6.
3. 12, 6, 6.   4. *Loc. cit.*   5. *De Gen. ad litt.*, 1, 15, 29.
6. *De Gen. contra Manich.*, 1, 17, 11.
7. *De Gen. ad litt.*, 6, 5, 8.   8. *De Trinit.*, 3, 8, 13.
9. 18, 1.   10. *De Gen. ad litt.*, 5, 4, 7–9.   11. Gen. 1. 11.
12. *De Gen. ad litt.*, 5, 4, 9.   13. *In Joann. Evang.*, 19, 5, 15.
14. *De quant. animae*, 13, 21.
15. *De moribus eccl.*, 1, 27, 52; *In Joann. Evang.*, 19, 5, 15.
16. *De Gen. ad litt.*, 7, 21, 28; *De Trinit.*, 10, 10, 14.
17. Cf. *Solil.*, 2, 19, 33; *Ep.*, 3, 4; *De Immortal. An.*, ch. 1–6.
18. 28, 54 ff.   19. *De anima et eius origine*, 1, 4, 4.
20. *Ep.*, 156.

Chapter Seven

1. *Serm.*, 150, 7, 8.   2. *Ep.*, 140, 23, 56.
3. *Serm.*, 150, 8, 9.   4. *De moribus eccl.*, 1, 11, 18.
5. *De lib. arbit.*, 2, 19, 52.   6. *De moribus eccl.*, 1, 25, 46.
7. 22. 37–9.   8. *Ep.*, 137, 5, 17.   9. *Conf.*, 13, 9, 10.
10. *Ep.*, 140, 21, 14.   11. *De lib. arbit.*, 2, 19, 35.
12. *De Trinit.*, 14, 15, 21.
13. *Expos. quarumdam prop. ex epist. ad Rom.*, 44.
14. *De spir. et litt.*, 19, 34.   15. *Ibid.*, 9, 15.
16. *Ep.*, 145, 3, 4.   17. *Enchirid.*, 23.
18. *De lib. arbit.*, 1, 16, 35.   19. *De moribus eccl.*, 2, 2, 2.
20. *In Ps.*, 64, 2.   21. *De Gen. ad litt.*, 11, 15, 20.
22. *In Ps.*, 136, 1.

Chapter Eight

1. *De Civit. Dei*, 4, 4.   2. *In Ps.*, 51, 6.
3. *De Civit. Dei*, 19, 24.   4. *Ep.*, 137, 5, 18.
5. Cf. *ibid.*, 105, 5, 6; 35, 3.
6. *A Monument to St. Augustine*, pp. 76–7.

Chapter Nine

1. *Exordium* to the *Divine Names*.   2. *Myst. Theol.*, 2.
3. *Ibid.*, 3.   4. *Div. Names*, 2, 1; St. Matt. 19. 17.
5. *Div. Names*, 4, 4.   6. 13, 1.   7. *Myst. Theol.*, 3.
8. *Ibid.*, 3.   9. *Ibid.*, 2.   10. *Ibid.*
11. The author of the mediaeval mystical treatise, *The Cloud of Unknowing*, doubtless wrote in immediate or mediate dependence on the writings of the Pseudo-Dionysius.
12. *Myst. Theol.*, 1.   13. *Div. Names*, 13, 3.
14. *Myst. Theol.*, 5.   15. *Div. Names*, 2, 5.   16. *Ibid.*, 2.
17. *Ibid.*, 3.   18. *Ibid.*, 4.   19. *Ibid.*, 5, 1.
20. *Ibid.*, 2, 11.   21. *Div. Names*, 5, 8.   22. *Ibid.*, 4, 4 ff.
23. *Ibid.*, 4, 35.   24. *Ibid.*, 5, 10.   25. *Ibid.*, 4, 18 ff.
26. *Ibid.*, 4, 20.   27. *Ibid.*, 23.   28. *Ibid.*, 24.
29. *Ibid.*, 26.   30. *Ibid.*, 27.   31. *Ibid.*, 28.
32. *Ibid.*, 30.   33. *Ibid.*, 4, 35.   34. *Ibid.*, 33.
35. In his *Christliche Lehre von der Dreieinigkeit und Menschwerdung Gottes*, Vol. 2, p. 42.

Chapter Ten

1. Vol. II, Pt. II, p. 208.   2. *Contra Eutychen*, 6.
3. *Ibid.*, 5.   4. 2.
5. Cf. the latter's *De Anima*, 17, 17, and his *De anima ibri mantissa*, 124, 7.   6. 4.   7. 3.   8. 12.   9. 2 ff.
10. 5, 3.   11. 5, 6.   12. 3, 9.
13. Cf. *Lib. de hebdom.*, 173.   14. *De Fide Catholica.*
15. *De Consol. Phil.*, 3, 12.
16. *Quomodo Substantiae.* I do not, of course, mean to imply that there is any doctrine of creation in Aristotle.
17. *De anima*, 12.   18. *Ibid.*, 4.

Chapter Eleven

1. If, however, Baugulf became abbot only in 788, the letter cannot be dated before that year.
2. *Ep.*, 4, 172.   3. *Ibid.*, 195.   4. *Ibid.*, 205.

Chapter Twelve

1. *De Div. Nat.*, 1, 64.   2. *Ibid.*, 1, 69.

Chapter Thirteen

1. Cf. 3, 1.   2. 1, 1.   3. 1, 11.   4. 1, 12.   5. *Ibid.*
6. 1, 13.   7. 1, 14.   8. *Ibid.*   9. 1, 14.   10. 1, 15.
11. 1, 70–2.   12. 1, 72.   13. 1, 69.   14. 1, 77.
15. 1, 75.   16. 2, 2.   17. *Ibid.*   18. *Ibid.*
19. 2, 20.   20. 2, 21.   21. 2, 27.   22. 2, 24, col. 580.
23. 2, 36.   24. Cf. 3, 1.   25. 3, 3.   26. *Ibid.*
27. 3, 4.   28. *Ibid.*   29. *Ibid.*   30. 3, 5.   31. 3, 4.
32. 3, 19.   33. See the long discussion in 3, 5 ff.   34. 3, 9.
35. 3, 17.   36. 3, 18.   37. 3, 19.   38. 3, 10.
39. 3, 23.   40. *Ibid.*   41. 3, 24 ff.   42. 4, 5.
43. 4, 7.   44. *Ibid.*   45. 4, 8.   46. 5, 3.   47. 1, 34.
48. 5, 25.   49. 5, 8.   50. 5, 20.   51. 5, 23.
52. 5, 25.   53. 5, 26–7.   54. 5, 27–8.   55. 5, 29–36.
56. 5, 36.   57. 3, 23.   58. 1 Cor., 15. 28.   59. 1, 69.
60. 1, 7.   61. 2, 16.   62. E.g. 3, 23.   63. 2, 2.

Chapter Fourteen

1. *P.L.*, 64, col. 82–6.   2. *De fide Trin.*, 2.   3. 10.
4. *De fide Trin.*, 2; *P.L.* 158, 265A.
5. *De fide Trin.*, 2; *P.L.*, 158, 265B.   6. *P.L.*, 178, 358B.
7. *Polycraticus*, 7, 12; *P.L.*, 199, 665A.
8. 2, 17; *P.L.*, 199, 874C.   9. *De div. omnip.*; *P.L.*, 145, 63.
10. *Hist. calam.*, 2; *P.L.*, 178, 119AB.
11. *Dialectica*, edit. Geyer, p. 10.
12. *De generibus et speciebus*; Cousin, *Ouvrages inédits d'Abélard*, p. 153.   13. *Hist. calam.*, 2; *P.L.*, 178, 119B.
14. Édit. Lefèvre, p. 24.   15. *Ingredientibus*, edit. Geyer, 16.
16. *In Boeth. de dual. nat.*; *P.L.*, 64, 1378.
17. *In Boeth. de Trinit.*; *P.L.*, 64, 1393. Cf. John of Salisbury, *Metalog.*, 2, 17; *P.L.*, 64, 875–6.   18. *P.L.*, 64, 1267.
19. *Ibid.*, 64, 1389.   20. *Ibid.*, 64, 875–6.
21. *Polycrat.*, 7, 12.   22. *Metal.*, 2, 20.   23. *Ibid.*
24. *Ibid.*, 3, 10.   25. *Ibid.*, 2, 20.   26. *Ibid.*, 3, 3.
27. *Didasc.*, 2, 18; *P.L.*, 176, 785.   28. *Contra Gent.*, 1, 65.
29. *S.T.*, Ia, 85, 1, ad 1; Ia, 85, 2, ad 2.   30. *Contra Gent.*, 3, 24.
31. *In Sent.*, 2; *Dist.* 3, 2 ad 1.
32. The distinction between *universale ante rem, in re* and *post rem* had been made by Avicenna.

Chapter Fifteen

1. *P.L.*, 158, 227.   2. *Ibid.*, 158, 362.
3. *De fide Trin.*, 4; *P.L.*, 158, 272.
4. *Cur Deus Homo*; *P.L.*, 158, 361.   5. *P.L.*, 158.
6. Ch. 15.   7. Ch. 16.   8. Ch. 17.   9. Ch. 20–4.
10. Ch. 24.   11. Ch. 26.
12. *Dialogus de Veritate*, 2; *P.L.*, 158.   13. *Dial.*, 4.
14. *Ibid.*, 7 ff.   15. *Ibid.*, 10.   16. *Ibid.*, 11.   17. Ch. 14.

Chapter Sixteen

1. *P.L.*, 176.   2. Cf. the Prologue.   3. 3, 24, 3.
4. *Metal.*, 1, 5.   5. *Metal.*, 4, 35.   6. Ed. W. Janssen, p. 42.
7. *Metal.*, 2, 17.   8. Ed. W. Janssen, pp. 44 and 63.
9. *P.L.*, 90, 1132.
10. Gilbert de la Porrée draws attention to the hylomorphic theory
    when commenting on Boethius's *Contra Eutychen* or *Liber de
    duabus Naturis et una Persona Christi*; *P.L.*, 64, 1367.
11. *De sex dierum operibus*, ed. W. Janssen, pp. 16, 21, 108, 109.
12. Ed. W. Janssen, p. 59.
13. *Liber ad Gebehardum*, 30 and 47.   14. *Ibid.*, 47.
15. *Polycrat.*, 4, 3.   16. *Ibid.*, 8, 10.

Chapter Seventeen

1. *P.L.*, 176, 800C.   2. See Vol. II, Pt. I, pp. 174–5.
3. *P.L.*, 176, 825A.   4. *Ibid.*, 176, 409.   5. *Ibid.*
6. *De Sacramentis*, 3, 7; *P.L.*, 176, 219.
7. *De Sacramentis*, 3, 10; *P.L.*, 176, 219, and *Sent.* 1, 3; *P.L.*, 176,
    45.   8. 1, 3; *P.G.*, 94, 796A.   9. *P.L.*, 176, 826.
10. Cf. *De Fide Orthodoxa*, 1, 3; *P.G.*, 94, 795B.
11. *De Sacramentis*, 1, 6, 37; *P.L.*, 176, 286.
12. *De Trinit.*, 1, 5; *P.L.*, 196, 893BC.   13. *P.L.*, 196, 892C.
14. *Ibid.*, 196, 72A.   15. *Ibid.*, 196, 894.
16. *Ibid.*, 196, 892.   17. *Ibid.*, 196, 893.
18. Cf. *ibid.*, 196, 893.   19. *De Trinit.*, 1, 11; *P.L.*, 196, 895–6.
20. *De Trinit.*, 1, 12; *P.L.*, 196, 896.
21. *De gratia contemplationis*, 1, 3, 7; *P.L.*, 196, 66CD, 72C.
22. *De gratia contemplationis*, 1, 3, 9; *P.L.*, 196, 110D.

Chapter Eighteen

1. The sources for our knowledge of the doctrine of the Albigensians
   are not rich, and the history of the movement is somewhat
   obscure.   2. *S.T.*, Ia, 3, 8, *in corpore*.

3. S.T., Ia, 4, 20, 2, *quaest. incidens.*   4. Ia, 3, 8, *in corpore.*
5. 2 *Sent.*, 17, 1, 1.
6. S. Alb. M., S.T., IIa, t. 12, q. 72, membr. 4, a. 2, n. 4.
7. *Ibid.*, Ia, t. 4, q. 20, membr. 2; *In Metaph.*, t. 4, c. 7.
8. S.T., Ia, 3, 8, ob. 3.

Chapter Nineteen

1. It is true, however, that some Islamic philosophers, like Avicenna, facilitated through their writings a Christian interpretation of Aristotle.
2. The name Avicenna, by which Ibn Sīnā was known to the mediaeval world, comes from the Hebrew version, Aven Sina.
3. *Šifā*, 1, 281 and 363.
4. It should be noted that it was the Averroistic doctrine of the unicity of the passive or possible intellect which *necessarily* involved the denial of personal immortality. The doctrine of the unicity of the active intellect does not necessarily involve such a denial, whether the active intellect is identified with a subordinate Intelligence or with God in His function as illuminator. As for Aristotle, he may not have believed in personal immortality himself, but the rejection of personal immortality does not *necessarily* follow from his doctrine of the active intellect, whereas it does follow from the doctrine of Averroes. On this point the positions of Avicenna and Averroes must be clearly distinguished.
5. On Avicenna's influence, cf. Roland-Gosselin, commentary on the *De ente et essentia*, pp. 59 and 150.
6. Cf. *De Pot.*, 5, 3; *Contra Gent.*, 2, 30.
7. More properly *Incoherentia philosophorum.*
8. *De Anima*, 3, 2.
9. For some further remarks on this subject see Vol. II, Pt. II, pp. 160-1.
10. *Intorno al tomismo di Dante e alla quistione di Sigieri* (*Giornale Dantesco*, XXII, 5).
11. *Islam and the Divine Comedy* (abridged Engl. Transl., London, 1926).

Chapter Twenty-one

1. St. Thomas's *Translatio Boethii.*
2. The *Timaeus* of Plato was known to the West, thanks to Cicero and Chalcidius, but it was not until the twelfth century that the *Meno* and *Phaedo* were translated (by Henricus Aristippus).
3. How far St. Thomas actually used William's translation has been much discussed.

Chapter Twenty-three

1. Cf. *De Universo*, 1, 3, 26; 2, 2, 8; *De Trinitate*, 1 and 2.
2. *De Universo*, 1, 1, 17.   3. *Ibid.*, 1, 1, 17.
4. *Ibid.*, 1, 1, 24 ff.   5. *Ibid.*, 1, 3, 2–3.   6. *Ibid.*, 1, 2, 8
7. *Ibid.*, 1, 2, 11.   8. *De Trinit.*, 7.   9. *Ibid.*, 6.
10. *Gesch. der Gottesbeweise im Mittelalter; Beiträge*, 6, 3, p. 92.
11. *De Universo*, 2, 2, 8.   12. *De Anima*, 1, 1.
13. *Ibid.*, 1, 3.   14. *Ibid.*, 1, 2.   15. *Ibid.*, 4, 1–3.
16. *Ibid.*, 5, 1 ff.   17. *Ibid.*, 6, 1.   18. *Ibid.*, 6, 7.
19. *Ibid.*, 6, 8.   20. *Ibid.*   21. *Ibid.*, 7, 3.
22. *Ibid.*, 5, 6.   23. 7, 6.
24. *La Philosophie au Moyen Age*, third edition, 1944, pp. 423–4

Chapter Twenty-four

1. *Compendium studii*, ed. Brewer, p. 469.   2. *Ibid.*, p. 472
3. *Opus Maius*, ed. Bridges, 1, 108.   4. Ed. Baur, p. 51.
5. P. 55.   6. P. 56.   7. *De colore*, p. 78.
8. *Physics*, 201 a 6; *Metaph.*, 1065 b 11.
9. *De motu corporali et luce*, p. 92.
10. *De unica forma omnium*, p. 109.
11. *De ordine emanandi causatorum a Deo*, p. 149.   12. P. 144
13. *De veritate*, pp. 134–5.   14. *Ibid.*, p. 135.
15. *Ibid.*, p. 137.   16. *Ibid.*, p. 138.
17. References below are to the *Summa theologica* in the Quaracch
    edition, according to volume and section.   18. 1, no. 10
19. 1, no. 15.   20. 1, no. 21.   21. 1, no. 15.
22. 1, no. 21.   23. 1, no. 25.   24. 1, no. 26.
25. S.T., p.l., tr. 4, q. 19.   26. Romans 1.
27. *De fide orthod.*, 1, cc. 1 and 3; P.G., 94, 790 and 794.
28. 1, no. 72.   29. 1, no. 73.   30. Cf. 1, nos. 123 ff.
31. 1, no. 276.   32. 2, no. 67.   33. 2, nos. 59–61.
34. 2, no. 321.
35. Cf. *De sp. et an.*, c. 42, (placed among works of Augustine; P. L
    40, 811) and St. Aug., *De Gen. ad litt.*, 7 cc. 1–3.
36. St. Aug., *De quant. an.*, c. 13, n. 22.
37. Cassiodorus, *De Anima*, c. 2.   38. 2, nos. 329 and 322.
39. 2, no. 322.   40. 2, no. 327.   41. 2, no. 347.
42. 2, no. 345.   43. 2, no. 351.   44. 2, no. 349.
45. 2, no. 372.   46. 2, no. 368.   47. 2, no. 372.
48. Cf. 2, nos. 393–6.   49. 2, no. 402.   50. Cf. 1, no. 2

Chapter Twenty-five

1. Alexander appears again as 'our father and master' in 2 *Sent.*, 23
   2, 3; II, p. 547.

2. Aug., *De utilitate credendi*, 11, 25; Bonav., *Breviloq.*, 1, 1, 4.
3. 1, 1.   4. 4.   5. 4, 2.   6. *In Hexaëm.*, 7, 3 ff.
7. *De Donis*, 3, 12.   8. *In Hexaëm.*, 6, 2.   9. *Ibid.*, 4.
10. *Ibid.*, 2–3.   11. *Ibid.*, 4.
12. *Aristote en Occident*, p. 147.

Chapter Twenty-six

1. *Itin.*, 3, 3.
2. 1, 3, 2: *Utrum., Deus sit cognoscibilis per creaturas.*
3. 1 *Sent.*, 3, 4.   4. 5, 29.   5. 1, 1, 10–20.
6. For example, in the *Itinerarium mentis in Deum*, c. 1.
7. *De Mysterio Trinitatis*, 1, 1, *conclusio.*   8. *Ibid.*, 12.
9. *Ibid.*, 1, 1, 7.   10. *Ibid.*, 10.
11. When speaking here of a 'natural' orientation of the will, I do not mean to use the term in a strictly theological sense, but rather in the sense that the will of man in the concrete is directed to the attainment of God, prescinding altogether from the question whether or not there is a *desiderium naturale videndi Deum.*
12. 1, 8, 1, 2.   13. 1, 1, 21–4.   14. *Ibid.*, *conclusio.*
15. *Ibid.*, 1, 1, 6.
16. Cf. E. Gilson's Commentary on the *Discours de la Méthode*, concerning the idea of the perfect.   17. 1 *Sent.*, 8, 1, 2, *conclusio.*
18. *Ibid.*, 5 and 7. Cf. *De Mysterio Trinitatis*, 1, 1, 26.
19. *De Mysterio Trinitatis*, 1, 1, 25.   20. 4, 1.   21. 3, 2 ff.

Chapter Twenty-seven

1. 1, 13.   2. *In Hexaëm.*, 1, 13.   3. *Ibid.*, 6, 2.
4. *Ibid.*   5. *Serm.*, 18.   6. *Ibid.*, 4, 19.
7. *Breviloq.*, 1, 3.   8. *Ibid.*   9. *In Hexaëm.*, 3, 4.
10. *Ibid.*   11. *Ibid.*, 1, 13.   12. 1 *Sent.*, 35, *art. unicus*, 4.
13. *Ibid.*, 5.   14. *Ibid.*, 2.   15. *Ibid.*, 6.   16. *Ibid.*, 3.
17. Cf. 1 *Sent.*, 39, 1, 2 and 3; *De Scientia Christi*, 1.
18. Cf. 1 *Sent.*, 39, 2, 3, *conclusio.*   19. *Ibid.*, 2, *conclusio.*
20. *In Hexaëm.*, 6, 4.   21. 2 *Sent.*, 1, 1, 1, 2, 1.
22. *Contra Gent.*, 2, 38.   23. 2 *Sent.*, 1, 1, 1, 2, 3.
24. *Contra Gent.*, 2, 38: *S.T.*, Ia, 46, 2, ad 6.
25. 2 *Sent.*, 1, 1, 1, 2, 5.   26. *Contra Gent.*, 2, 38.
27. 2 *Sent.*, 1, 1, 1, 2, 6.   28. *Ibid.*, *conclusio.*
29. *In Hexaëm.*, 6, 2.   30. *Ibid.*, 3.
31. Cf. 1 *Sent.*, 39, 1, 1, *conclusio.*   32. *In Hexaëm.*, 6, 3.
33. 1, 35, *art. un.*, 1, *conclusio.*
34. Cf. 1 *Sent.*, 3, 1, *art. un.*, 2, 3 and 1 *ibid.*, 48, 1, 1, *conclusio.*
35. 2 *Sent.*, 16, 1, 1, *conclusio.*   36. *In Hexaëm.*, 12, 15.
37. 1 *Sent.*, 44, 1, 1, *conclusio.*   38. *Ibid.*, ad 4.

Chapter Twenty-eight

1. 2 *Sent.*, 3, 1, 1, 2, *conclusio ad* 3.
2. 2 *Sent.*, 3, 1, 2, 3, *conclusio.*   3. 2 *Sent.*, 3, 1, 2, 2, *conclusio.*
4. *Ibid.*, 3, 1, 2, 1.   5. Cf. 2 *Sent.*, 13.   6. 4, 10.
7. 2 *Sent.*, 7, 2, 2, 1, *resp.*   8. 2 *Sent.*, 18, 1, 3, *resp.*
9. *Ibid.*, 2, 15, 1, 1, *resp.*   10. Cf. 2 *Sent.*, 7, 2, 2, 2, *resp.*

Chapter Twenty-nine

1. 2 *Sent.*, 18, 2, 3, *resp.*   2. Cf. 2 *Sent.*, 30, 3, 1 and 31, 1, 1.
3. *Ibid.*, 18, 2, 1, *contra* 1.   4. *Breviloq.*, 2, 9.
5. 1 *Sent.*, 8, 2, *art. un.*, 3, *resp.*   6. 2 *Sent.*, 17, 1, 2, *resp.*
7. *Ibid.*, *ad* 5.   8. *Ibid.*, 18, 2, 1, *ad* 1.
9. Cf., *ibid.*, 17, 1, 2, *ad* 6.   10. *Ibid.*, 18, 2, 1, *ad* 6.
11. *Ibid.*   12. *Ibid.*, 19, 1, 1, *resp.*   13. *Ibid.*
14. *Ibid.*, *sed contra* 3, 4.   15. *Ibid.*, 7 ff.; cf. *De Anima*, Bk. 3.
16. 2 *Sent.*, 11.   17. *Ibid.*, 18, 2, 1, *resp.*
18. *Ibid.*, 3, 2, 2, 1, *resp.* and *ad* 4.   19. *Ibid.*, 8, 1, 3, 2, *ad* 7.
20. *Ibid.*, 25, 2, *art. un.*, 6, *resp.*
21. *Ibid.*, 7, 2, 1, 2, *resp.*, where Bonaventure distinguishes memory as habit, *retentio speciei*, from the act of remembering or *recordatio.*
22. *Ibid.*, 24, 1, 2, 4.   23. *Ibid.*, *resp.*
24. *Ibid.*, 39, 1, 2, *resp.*   25. *Ibid.*, 39, 1, 2, *resp.*
26. *De Myst. Trinit.*, 1, 1, *resp.*   27. *Ibid.*, 1, 2, *ad* 14.
28. *De Scientia Christi*, 4, 23.   29. 1 *Sent.*, 17, 1, *art. un.*, 4, *resp.*
30. 2 *Sent.*, 39, 1, 2, *resp.*   31. *Ibid.*
32. 1 *Sent.*, *resp.*, *ad* 1, 2, 3; cf. *Breviloq.*, 6, 8.
33. *De Scientia Christi*, 4, *resp.*   34. *Ibid.*
35. *Ibid.*   36. *In Hexaëm.*, 12, 5.
37. *Itin. Mentis in Deum*, 2, 9.   38. 2, 4–6.
39. *In Hexaëm.*, 12, 5.   40. *Ibid.*, 12, 11.
41. *Itin. Mentis in Deum*, 1, 6.   42. 2 *Sent.*, 24, 1, 2, 2, *resp.*
43. *In Hexaëm.*, 1, 11.

OTHER IMAGE BOOKS

THE IMITATION OF CHRIST – Thomas à Kempis. Edited with an Introduction by Harold C. Gardiner, S.J. (D17) – $1.25

SAINT THOMAS AQUINAS – G. K. Chesterton (D36) – $1.45

ST. FRANCIS OF ASSISI – G. K. Chesterton (D50) – $1.25

VIPER'S TANGLE – François Mauriac. A novel of evil and redemption (D51) – 95¢

THE CITY OF GOD – St. Augustine. Edited by Vernon J. Bourke. Introduction by Étienne Gilson. Specially abridged (D59) – $2.45

RELIGION AND THE RISE OF WESTERN CULTURE – Christopher Dawson (D64) – $1.95

THE LITTLE FLOWERS OF ST. FRANCIS – Translated by Raphael Brown (D69) – $1.75

DARK NIGHT OF THE SOUL – St. John of the Cross. Edited and translated by E. Allison Peers (D78) – $1.25

THE CONFESSIONS OF ST. AUGUSTINE – Translated with an Introduction by John K. Ryan (D101) – $1.75

A HISTORY OF PHILOSOPHY: VOLUME 1 – GREECE AND ROME (2 Parts) – Frederick Copleston, S.J. (D134a, D134b) – $1.75 ea.

A HISTORY OF PHILOSOPHY: VOLUME 2 – MEDIAEVAL PHILOSOPHY (2 Parts) – Frederick Copleston, S.J. Part I – Augustine to Bonaventure. Part II – Albert the Great to Duns Scotus (D135a, D135b) – $1.75 ea.

A HISTORY OF PHILOSOPHY: VOLUME 3 – LATE MEDIAEVAL AND RENAISSANCE PHILOSOPHY (2 Parts) – Frederick Copleston, S.J. Part I – Ockham to the Speculative Mystics. Part II – The Revival of Platonism to Suárez (D136a, D136b) – $1.45 ea.

A HISTORY OF PHILOSOPHY: VOLUME 4 – MODERN PHILOSOPHY: Descartes to Leibniz – Frederick Copleston, S.J. (D137) – $1.75

A HISTORY OF PHILOSOPHY: VOLUME 5 – MODERN PHILOSOPHY: The British Philosophers, Hobbes to Hume (2 Parts) – Frederick Copleston, S.J. Part I – Hobbes to Paley (D138a) – $1.45. Part II – Berkeley to Hume (D138b) – $1.75

A HISTORY OF PHILOSOPHY: VOLUME 6 – MODERN PHILOSOPHY (2 Parts) – Frederick Copleston, S.J. Part I – The French Enlightenment to Kant (D139a) – $1.45; (D139b) – $1.75

A HISTORY OF PHILOSOPHY: VOLUME 7 – MODERN PHILOSOPHY (2 Parts) – Frederick Copleston, S.J. Part I – Fichte to Hegel. Part II – Schopenhauer to Nietzsche (D140a, D140b) – $1.75 ea.

These prices subject to change without notice

OTHER IMAGE BOOKS

OTHER IMAGE BOOKS

These prices subject to change without notice

OTHER IMAGE BOOKS

These prices subject to change without notice